# A VOYAGE TO SURAT

## IN THE YEAR 1689

# A VOYAGE TO SURAT

## IN THE YEAR 1689

J. OVINGTON

EDITED BY
H. G. RAWLINSON

GYAN

*Published by*

Gyan Publishing House
5, Ansari Road
Daryaganj, New Delhi-110002
Phone: 011-47034999, 9811692060
E-mail: books@gyanbooks.com

*Distribution Network*
gyanbooks.com
India, USA, Canada, UK, Australia, France



ISBN : 978-81-212-4558-6 (HB)
First Published, London, 1929

2nd Impression 2020

*Printed at:* Gyan Press, Delhi.

# A VOYAGE TO SURAT

## IN THE YEAR 1689

*By*

J. OVINGTON

*Edited by*

H. G. RAWLINSON, M.A.
*Indian Educational Service*

OXFORD UNIVERSITY PRESS
LONDON : HUMPHREY MILFORD
1929

SURAT: THE FORT FROM THE RIVER BRIDGE

# PREFACE

IT is astonishing that Ovington's racy account of Western India, as he saw it at the close of the seventeenth century, has never been reprinted. The present edition is a verbatim reproduction of the original (1696) issue, except that a number of obvious printer's errors have been corrected. To the 1696 edition was added an Appendix containing

A late Revolution in the Kingdom of *Golconda.*

A description of the Kingdoms of *Arracan* and *Pegu.*

An Account of the coins of the Kingdoms of *India, Persia, Golconda,* &c.

Observations concerning the *Silk Worms.*

This has been omitted in the present volume, as it contains nothing of value, and has no direct bearing on Ovington's narrative.

Nothing was known hitherto about John Ovington. For valuable assistance in collecting information from Parish and University Registers, which throw a flood of new light upon his birth and early career, I have to thank, among others, the Rev. J. V. Bullard, Vicar of Melsonby, the Rev. M. Collins, Vicar of Hutton Magna, the Rev. R. Williams, Curate of St. Margaret's, Lee, the Master and the Librarian, St. John's College, Cambridge, the Registrary, Cambridge University, and the Registrar, Trinity College, Dublin. Sir William Foster and Miss L. M. Anstey have both rendered me the generous assistance which they are always ready to extend to workers on the India Office Records, and the former has advised and helped me in the elucidation of many obscure references.

The maps of Bombay Harbour, from Strachey's *Keigwin's Rebellion,* and Surat, from Rawlinson's *British Beginnings in Western India,* 1579–1657, are reproduced by permission of the Clarendon Press, Oxford.

H. G. RAWLINSON.

POONA, INDIA, 1928.

# CONTENTS


| | *Page* |
|---|---|
| Preface | v |
| List of Illustrations | viii |
| Introduction | ix |
| Titles of Authorities | xix |
| Voyage to Surat | 1 |
| Appendix | 306 |
| Index-Glossary | 307 |

# LIST OF ILLUSTRATIONS


| | | |
|---|---|---|
| Surat: the Fort from the River Bridge | . | *Frontispiece* |
| Bombay Fort from the Harbour, *c.* 1720 | . | *facing p.* 90 |
| Bombay Fort from the Land . . . | . | „ „ 96 |
| The English Factory at Surat in 1638 | . | „ „ 226 |
| Map of Bombay Harbour . . . . | . | „ „ 80 |
| Sketch-map of Surat and neighbourhood | . | „ „ 192 |

# JOHN OVINGTON

LITTLE can be ascertained about the early life of the author of this diverting and important book of travel. John Ovington, son of James and Mary Ovington, was born at Melsonby, near Darlington in Yorkshire, early in 1653.[1] The Ovingtons were a respectable family of yeoman-farmers, many members of which lie buried in Melsonby Churchyard, and there is actually a hamlet of the same name a few miles distant. He was educated at the neighbouring Grammar School of Kirby Ravensworth. On 5 May 1671, at the age of fifteen, he was entered as a sizar at Trinity College, Dublin.[2] Ovington may have had relations in Dublin, and possibly went there for this reason. That there were Ovingtons in Ireland at the end of the sixteenth century is shown by the fact that a party of Anglo-Irish, led by two brothers of the name of Richard and Henry Ovington, was sent by Sir William Fitzwilliam to butcher some of the unfortunate Spaniards who had been wrecked on the Irish coast after the dispersion of the Armada, 14 September 1588.[3] The name is not uncommon in Northern Ireland to-day. He became a scholar in 1675, took his B.A. degree in the same year, and his M.A. three years later. On 12 May 1679 we find John Ovington, aet. 22, entering as a sizar at St. John's College, Cambridge.[4] He matriculated on 3 July following. It was a fairly common practice for graduates of the more important Universities to proceed to the sister institutions for periods of study, but this was usually for the

[1] Baptized 5 March 1653 (Melsonby Register).

[2] *Alumni Dublinienses*, 1593–1846, ed. Burtchaell and Sadleir. The discrepancy in dates is curious.

[3] MSS. Ireland, quoted in Froude, *History of England*, ed. 1870, vol. xii, p. 457.

[4] Information supplied by the Registrary, Cambridge University.

purpose of taking a degree *ad eundem*, and apparently John Ovington did not do this, for no further mention of his name can be traced in the University records. Nor has it been found possible to ascertain where or when he was ordained, though this must have been very soon after he left Cambridge. His life for the next ten years is a blank: on 11 April 1689 (the Coronation Day, as he takes care to remind his readers, of King William III), he set sail from Gravesend on the East India Company's vessel the *Benjamin*. He had been engaged as chaplain of the ship to fill a casual vacancy, and not as a regular servant of the Company. It was customary for almost every vessel, mercantile or naval, to carry a chaplain in those days; the only exceptions, Pyrard de Laval remarks, being the French, who being without the fear of God never cared to have Divine Service performed on board their vessels.[1] The *Benjamin* had an uneventful voyage from Gravesend to Madeira, except for a false alarm of the French fleet off Brest, which caused their cowardly escort to decamp in an ignominious fashion. At Madeira, of which Ovington gives a glowing account, the travellers were accorded a hospitable welcome by the English colony, and here a diverting incident occurred. A number of sailors deserted, and the Portuguese authorities refused to surrender them, whereupon the captain of the *Benjamin* kidnapped, by way of reprisals, 'a comely Abbot and a Vicar'. This, however, created such an uproar that the members of the English colony sued for their release. The captain agreed and weighed anchor—just in time, as it happened, for forty hours later two French men-of-war entered the harbour. The next halt was made at St. Iago, the largest of the Cape Verde Islands. The *Benjamin* now entered the region of the trade winds, and touched at the tiny island of Annobon,

[1] For a naval chaplain's life in the seventeenth century, compare the lively diary of the Rev. Henry Teonge, 1675–9: edited by G. E. Mainwaring, Routledge, 1927. Two points are interesting as a comment on Ovington—the incredible amount eaten and drunk, and the terrible mortality on board.

Malemba, on the African coast, near the mouth of the Congo River, and finally at St. Helena, where Ovington found the inhabitants a motley population descended from French Protestant refugees, English and Dutch deserters from ships, half-castes, and negro slaves, at a low ebb mentally and morally. After rounding the Cape in a terrible tempest and narrowly escaping shipwreck off the coast of Madagascar, the *Benjamin* at last found herself at Johanna, the largest of the Comoro Islands and once famous as a port of call. Ovington's experiences with the local potentate make amusing reading.

From Johanna the *Benjamin* made a straight run to Bombay, and reached the harbour on 29 May, just in time to avoid the burst of the south-west monsoon. Here, sorely against their wills, the crew were weather-bound for three and a half months. Ovington's account of Bombay in 1690 is of singular interest, though it must be remembered that he saw it during the most unhealthy period of the year, and this no doubt inclined him to take a somewhat pessimistic view. The town had recently passed through many vicissitudes. Ceded by the Portuguese to Charles II in 1661 and handed over to the Company six years later, it had been greatly developed by Gerald Aungier (1669–77). After his death much of his work had been allowed to lapse. The oppressive policy of Sir Josiah Child, the Governor of the Company, and his namesake and tool in Surat, Mr. John Child, brought about a revolt of the garrison under its commandant Captain Keigwin in 1683. Three years later a fresh series of blunders led to an invasion of the Island of Bombay by the Sidi, the Admiral of the Great Moghal, who landed with 25,000 men, cut down the coconut groves, and laid siege to the fort. After a prolonged blockade the garrison was forced to accept humiliating terms. Child was succeeded on his death by George Weldon, who married his predecessor's widow and was Governor when Ovington arrived.

Ovington's picture of Bombay as he saw it is a gloomy one. Aungier's schemes of colonization had not been successful.

The settlers were the dregs of humanity, discharged soldiers, 'debauched broken tradesmen and renegade seamen'. Drunkenness, largely due to the 'punch-houses', was fearfully rife. The young women, so entertainingly described by Ovington, who had been introduced by the Company in order to keep the English from alliances with Portuguese and natives, had proved so unsatisfactory that many of them had been deported. The result was that Bombay was a hotbed of vice. 'I cannot without horror mention,' says our pious author, 'to what a pitch all vicious enormities were grown in this place . . . Luxury, immodesty and a prostitute dissolution of manners found still new matter to work on.' Even the chaplains were little better than their flock.[1] The natural unhealthiness of the island, caused by the undrained swamps and the habit of manuring the coconut plantations with putrid fish, acting on constitutions undermined by drink and debauchery, made the place 'little better than a charnel house'. Children hardly ever survived, and it was commonly said that 'two mussouns are the age of a man'. In 1691 only eighty Englishmen were alive; five years later these had dwindled to twenty-seven. In the *Benjamin* herself during her short sojourn in the harbour twenty out of the twenty-four passengers and fifteen of the crew succumbed. No wonder, then, that Ovington prudentlydeclined the offer of a chaplaincy!

About the middle of September the *Benjamin* weighed anchor, not a day too early, from this pestiferous spot. Once at sea, the diseases of the crew disappeared like magic and in a short time the vessel reached Swally Hole, the roadstead for Surat. Here the *Benjamin*, after discharging her cargo, set off on a long coasting voyage to Achin and the Straits of Malacca, while Ovington stayed behind to officiate as chaplain of the English Factory until the return of the vessel in 1693. Ovington's description of the everyday life in the Factory is a valuable complement to the earlier narrative of

[1] e. g. 'That scandalous chaplain at Bombay', the Rev. Watson (1684). Anderson, *English in Western India*, p. 107.

Fryer. The president at the time of Ovington's visit was Bartholomew Harris. The factors lived in considerable pomp: they dined together in a common hall, attended daily service in the chapel, and when they went abroad it was in a stately procession. After death they were buried beneath those grandiose tombs which still survive and were looked upon at the time with considerable pride. Surat was still a rich and prosperous town, 'more populous than any part of London', when Ovington saw it, in spite of the Maratha raids of 1664 and 1670, since which time it had been furnished with a wall and a moat. In the centre stood the Castle in which resided the Moghal Governor. The factors were at the mercy of this officer, who imprisoned and otherwise maltreated them whenever he had any grounds of complaint: this, together with the Maratha menace and the distance of Surat from the sea, was steadily tending to transfer the balance of trade to Bombay, in spite of the unhealthiness of the latter.

During his two and a half years' residence at the Surat factory Ovington managed to collect a number of facts about the native inhabitants, Hindu, Mahommedan, and Parsi. He was a keen and diligent observer, and his picture of contemporary Indian life, customs, and religious observances is accurate as well as entertaining. Particularly valuable are his remarks about the Parsis, whom he describes as 'in their calling very industrious and diligent, and careful to train up their children to Arts and Labour'. Ovington's account of the Persian Gulf and Red Sea is of less importance, being based on hearsay and not on personal knowledge.

In February 169$\frac{2}{3}$ Ovington re-embarked on the *Benjamin* for the return voyage. He landed at the Cape, of which he gives us a full description. After touching at Ascension, he reached Kinsale on September 18th. Here the presence of French privateers imposed a long halt, and it was not until 5 December that the *Benjamin* once more cast anchor at Gravesend. The President had been highly pleased with

Ovington's work at Surat, and sent home the following recommendation to the Company by the *Benjamin*:

Mr John Ovington, Minister ever sence the first arrivall of the *Benjamin* (wee being destitute then of a minister) he[1] hath officiated here amongst us with much integrity and uprightness, his life and conversation being altogether conformable to his doctrines: a true pious good man. We promised him the settled salary of Your Honours to the ministers of Suratt of 50 *l.* per annum; and haveing served upwards of two years to all our contents and sattisfaction, wee most humbly recommend him to Your Honours for the gratuity you allways allow other good ministers as officiate here of 50 *l.* per annum more, and accordingly wee have made up his accompts and hath presumed to draw our bills for the same, and to recommend him and what wee have done to Your Honours favourable consideration.

The Court thereupon passed the following resolution:

This Court haveing received a testimoniall from the President and Councill of Suratt of the ministerial abilityes and good deportment of Mr John Ovington, for two years and upwards officiated as Chaplain amongst them, and took his passage for England on the ship *Benjamin*; and he being desirous to return back, it is ordered that he be entertained to serve the company as chaplain of their factory of Surat, at the salary of fifty pounds per annum and fifty pounds a year gratuity, as he shall be found to deserve.[3]

Ovington, however, appears to have changed his mind about returning to India. No mention is made of him in the letters or Court Minutes of 1694 or 1695, and a list of the Company's servants at Surat, May 1695 (O.C. 6037), does not contain his name. Probably he preferred to remain in England and write his *magnum opus*, *A Voyage to Suratt in the year* 1689, which came out in 1696. This work evidently met with the Company's approval, for in the Court Minutes of 16 April 1697 we find the following entry:

It is ordered that a warrant be made out for twenty five pounds to Mr John Ovington, late Chaplain at Surrat, being so much thought fit to be paid him for two wolf-dogs by him procured and sent from Ireland to Surrat at the desire of the late President, and

[1] *sic.*

[2] Surat to Company, 11 Feb. 1693 (O. C. 5862).

[3] *Court Minutes*, 15 Dec. 1693.

for a booke by him written and presented to the Company, called a Voyage to Surrat.

Ovington probably held a curacy in the London diocese at this time, but it is impossible to trace it. Evidently he was residing in or near London, for on 29 November 1698, the Directors of the newly established East India Company having resolved to ask the Archbishop of Canterbury to approve some prayers to be used at their establishments, on 16 December following:

> The titles were read of three prayers for this Company—one to be used at home, another to be used in their factories abroad, and a third to be used on board their ships—approved by His Grace the Archbishop of Canterbury and the Lord Bishop of London. Ordered that 1,000 of the said three prayers be printed and that Mr Ovington supervise the press.

In 1699 Ovington brought out a pamphlet entitled *An Essay upon the Nature and Qualities of Tea,*[1] no doubt inspired by a desire to popularize the use of this then novel beverage, whose acquaintance he had made in Surat, and so assist the Company's trade. It contained a woodcut of the tea-plant, and was fiercely assailed by one John Waldron in a coarse and scurrilous *Satyr against Tea, Or, Ovington's Essay upon the Nature and Qualities of Tea &c. Dissected and Burlesqu'd.*[2] The writer, having lavished upon Ovington the epithets 'female Ovington' and 'soft Hermaphrodite', concludes:

> Wise *Ovington* deserves green bays,
> For praising brightly foreign Teas;
> But, were we wise, *Ovington's* Tea
> Would be transported over Sea.

[1] 'An Essay upon the Nature and Qualities of Tea', by J. Ovington, M.A., Chaplain to His Majesty, London, printed by and for R. Roberts, 1699. Reprinted 1928 by Arthur Williams, F.G.I., with a preface by the Right Hon. Augustine Birrell, Institute of Certificated Grocers, London, E.C.3.

[2] Dublin, printed by Sylvanus Pepyat, Bookseller in Skinner Row, 1733. The publisher issued at the same time a reprint of the *Essay on Tea,* and the two are bound up together in the B.M. copy.

Almost as vicious is the attack on Ovington by Captain Alexander Hamilton, in the Introduction to his *New Account of the East Indies* (Edinburgh 1727).

'I know a reverend Gentleman,' he writes, 'in *anno* 1690, who came to *Bombay* in *India*, Chaplain of the ship *Benjamin*, the ship was sent on a Voyage to *Atcheen* and the streights of *Mallacca*, while the Chaplain stay'd at *Bombay* and *Surat*, employed in his ministerial Duties, and in making his ingenious Observations and Remarks, which he published when he returned to *England*, for which he received a great deal of Applause, and many encomiums from some of his Reverend Bretheren, and a particular Compliment from the Governors of the Church; yet I know, that his greatest Travels were in Maps, and the knowledge he had of the Countries any way remote from the aforementioned Places, was the Accounts he gathered from common Report; and perhaps these Reports came successively to him by Second or Third Hands; for, to my certain knowledge, there were none then at *Surat* or *Bombay* that could furnish him with any tolerable Accounts of some Countries that he describes, particularly the Growth and Nature of Tea, and shews its Bush very prettily among his Cuts; which Accounts are not easily procured, even in *China*, much less at *Bombay*.'

And no doubt the reference in his Dedication to 'scribblers who dedicate their works to Great Men who they hardly know any more than their illustrious names', is another sly hit at Ovington, who had dedicated his *Voyage to Suratt* to the Earl of Dorset, and the *Essay on Tea* to the Countess of Grantham. It must be remembered, however, that the old sea-captain was an Interloper, and the sworn enemy of the Company and its servants, at whom he never misses an opportunity to have a covert gibe.

In 1701, Ovington's labours found fitting recognition. He was already Chaplain to His Majesty. The University of Dublin gave him the Degree of Doctor of Divinity, and in the same year he was presented to the crown living of St. Margaret's, Lee, Kent (now the county of London), in the Rochester diocese. During his tenure of this benefice he acquired a considerable reputation as a sermon-writer; copies of two of these, *The Plausible Plea Silenced*, London,

1705, and *Christian Chastity*, London, 1712, lie in the Library of St. John's College, Cambridge.

Dr. Ovington remained rector of St. Margaret's until his death, which took place at the end of June 1731. He was buried on 2 July. By the terms of his will, which was dated 12 December 1729, he desired to be buried in the south-west corner of the churchyard. Doubtless the request was complied with, though the two tombstones standing in that spot are now illegible. He appears to have died unmarried;[1] no mention of wife or family occurs in his will, and the bulk of his estate was bequeathed to his nephews and nieces of the Warner family, Edward Warner being his sole executor. It is interesting to note that a Yorkshireman of the name of George Knight of Stockton and his sister figure among the beneficiaries.

Ovington was a shrewd and practical observer of men and manners, by no means devoid of a sense of humour, and his accounts of Bombay and Surat as he saw them at the end of the seventeenth century are of the greatest possible value to the historian of Western India, coming as they do midway between those of John Fryer and Alexander Hamilton.[2] The book is, indeed, one of the liveliest travel-books of the period, and the author is not altogether unworthy of Nahum Tate's encomium:

> You have so lively your Discoveries writ,
> We read and voyage with you as we sit,
> With you hoise sail and reach the *Indian* shore,
> The real scene cou'd scarce delight us more.

[1] See Waldron's coarse jibes, referred to above.

[2] The resemblances between many passages in Fryer and Ovington are very striking, and it is possible that Ovington owed something to his predecessor.

Dr. Fryer arrived in India in June 1673, went to Persia in 1677, and returned to Surat early in 1679, whence he sailed for England in 1681. But his *New Account of East India and Persia*, in 8 Letters; being 9 years Travels. Begun 1672. And Finished 1681, was not actually published until 1698. The early travellers borrow freely from one another, mostly without acknowledgement. Fitche's account of Burma, for instance, in Purchas (ed.

It is a curious fact that the *Voyage to Suratt*, though often quoted, has never been reprinted since its original publication by Jacob Tonson in 1696, and is now a rare work, whereas the *Essay on Tea* ran into three editions. The picture of Bombay Fort, dated 2 April 1668, seems to be an adaptation of one sent home in 1665, now on exhibition in the museum of the Public Record Office and reproduced in the 1665–7 volume of Sir William Foster's *English Factories in India*.

Early in the eighteenth century France was still dreaming of an empire in Southern India, and this no doubt led to the appearance of an anonymous French translation of Ovington's *Voyage to Suratt* in two volumes with the following title: VOYAGES / DE JEAN / OVINGTON / Faits à Surate, & en d'autres lieux de l'Asie & de l'Afrique. /*AVEC*/ L'Histoire de la Révolution du Royaume de Golconde: & des observations sur les Vers à Soye. / Traduit de l'Anglois. / A PARIS. / chez GUILLAUME CAVELIER Fils, Libraire, ruë S. Jacques, au Lys d'Or, près la Fontaine Saint Severin / M.DCC.XXV. / Avec Approbation & Privilege du Roi /.

The translator in his Preface praises Ovington's learning, inquisitiveness, patience, and circumspection, his 'yeux sçavans et capables de remarquer ce qu'il y avoit de curieux sur la route', but finds fault with his partisan spirit, his religious prejudices, the want of arrangement and order in his narrative, and the diffuseness of his style: this last defect he endeavours to remedy in his translation. Eighteenth-century French translations of English travel literature relating to India are not uncommon: another is a translation of Grose (Voyages aux Indes Orientales par Jean-Henri Grose, traduit de l'Anglois par M. Hernandez, l'un des Auteurs du Journal Étranger, M.DCC.LVIII. A Londres: et se trouve à Lille chez la veuve Pancoucke et à Paris).

MacLehose, vol. x) is largely a summary of Caesar Fredericke, the Venetian traveller.

# FULLER TITLES OF THE CHIEF AUTHORITIES QUOTED


ANDERSON, Rev. P. *The English in Western India.* London, 1854.

BRUCE, J. *Annals of the East India Coy.* London, 1810.

CAMPBELL, Sir J. M. *Gazetteer of the Bombay Presidency.*

*Cathay and the Way Thither.* By Col. Yule, 2nd edn. by H. Cordier. Hakluyt Society, 1913–16.

COBBE, Rev. R. *The Bombay Church.* London, 1766.

DA CUNHA, J. G. *The Origin of Bombay.* Bombay, 1900.

*Della Valle Pietro, Travels of.* Trans. and ed. Grey. Hakluyt Society, 1891.

DOWNING, Clement. *History of the Indian Wars.* Ed. W. Foster. London, 1924.

*Early Travellers in India.* Ed. W. Foster. London, 1921.

EDWARDES, S. M. *Gazetteer of Bombay City and Island.* Bombay, 1909–10. (*Bombay City Gazetteer.*)
*Rise of Bombay.* 1902.

*English Factories in India,* 1618–69. Ed. W. Foster. Oxford, v.d.

FREDERICI, Cesare. *Viaggio.* Venice, 1587.

FORREST, G. W. *Selections from the letters etc. in the Bombay Secretariat.* Bombay, 1885.

FRYER, J. *A New Account of East India and Persia.* Ed. W. Crooke. Hakluyt Society, 1912.

GROSE, J. H. *Voyage to the East Indies,* 1757.

HAKLUYT, R. *Principall Navigations, etc.* Ed. MacLehose. Glasgow, 1903.

HAMILTON, Capt. Alexander. *New Account of the East Indies.* London. 2nd edn., 1774.

*Hawkins Voyages, The.* Ed. Markham. Hakluyt Society, 1878.

*Hedges Diary.* Ed. Yule. Hakluyt Society.

HERBERT, Thomas. *Some Yeares Travels.* London, 1638.

*Hobson-Jobson.* By Yule and Burnell. 2nd edn. by W. Crooke. London, 1903.

HUNTER, Sir W. *Imperial Gazetteer of India.* London, v.d.
*History of British India.* London, 1900.

*Jourdain, John, the Journal of.* Ed. W. Foster. Hakluyt Society, 1905.

*Lancaster, Sir J., Voyages of.* Ed. Markham. Hakluyt Society, 1877.

*Linschoton, J. H. Van, the Voyage of.* Trans. and ed. Burnell and Trele. Hakluyt Society, 1884.

Malabari, P. B. M. *Bombay in the Making.* London, 1910.

*Materials Towards a Statistical Account of the Town and Island of Bombay.* 3 vols. (*Bombay Gazetteer*, vol. xxvi.) Ed. Sir J. M. Campbell. Bombay, 1893. (Referred to as *Gazetteer*, Bombay Town and Island.)

Müller, C. *Geographici Graeci Minores.* Paris, 1857.

*Munday, Peter, Travels of.* Ed. Temple. Hakluyt Society, 1884.

*Periplus Maris Erythraei.* Trans. and ed. Schoff. London, 1912.

*Purchas His Pilgrimes.* Ed. MacLehose. Glasgow, 1905–7.

*Pyrard de Laval, Voyages of.* Trans. and ed. Gray and Bell. Hakluyt Society, 1887–9.

Rawlinson, H. G. *British Beginnings in Western India.* Oxford, 1922.

*Roe, Sir Thomas, the Embassy of.* Ed. W. Foster. Hakluyt Society, 1922.

Ryley, J. Horton. *Ralph Fitch.* London, 1899.

Strachey, R. and O. *Keigwin's Rebellion.* Oxford, 1916.

Terry, Rev. E. *A Voyage to East India.* London, 1655.

Thévenot, J. De. *Voyages.* Amsterdam, 1727. Eng. Trans., London, 1686.

*Varthema, Ludovico di, Travels of.* Trans. and ed. Jones and Badger. Hakluyt Society, 1863.

# A VOYAGE TO *SURATT*,

## In the Year, 1689.

Giving a large Account of that City, and its Inhabitants, and of the *English* Factory there.

Likewise a Description of *Madeira*, St. *Jago*, *Annobon*, *Cabenda* and *Malemba* (upon the Coast of *Africa*) St. *Helena*, *Johanna*, *Bombay*, the City of *Muscatt*, and its Inhabitants in *Arabia Felix*, *Mocha*, and other Maritine Towns upon the *Red-Sea*, the *Cape of good Hope*, and the Island *Ascention*

To which is addded an *Appendix*, containing

I. The History of a late Revolution in the Kingdom of *Golconda*. II. A description of the Kingdoms of *Arracan* and *Pegu*. III. An Account of the Coins of the Kingdoms of *India*, *Persia*, *Golconda*, &c. IV. Observations concerning the *Silk worms*.

By *J. Ovington*, M. A. Chaplain to his Majesty.

*Qui mores Hominum multorum vidit & urbes.* Horat.
——*Orbesque novos trans æquora pandit.* Grot.

*LONDON*, Printed for *Jacob Tonson*, at the *Judges Head* in *Fleet-street*, near the *Inner-Temple-Gate*. 1696.

TO HIS EXCELLENCY

# CHARLES [1]

## Earl of Dorset and Middlesex:

*Lord Chamberlain of his Majesty's Household; Knight of the Most Noble Order of the Garter, &c. And one of the Lords Justices of England.*

May it please your Excellency,

AS the *Eastern* Princes, upon the News of any Foreigner's Arrival, are wont to expect some Curiosities of the Place from whence he came, to prepare the way for his Reception, and Introduce the Stranger into their Presence; so, in imitation of this respectful Custom, this Foreign Voyage hopes for admittance to your Favour and Acceptance, upon that Stock of Novelty which it presumes upon; and which it brings with it as well from *Africa*, as several remoter Parts and Kingdoms of the *East*: For in those Places, there are several Things here taken notice of, which have escap'd the Observations of other Travellers. I need not mention, my Lord, with what facility you can employ your Judgment, to penetrate into all that is any where useful, whilst your vigorous Fancy can as readily present to you all that is divertive in its Entertainment. And tho' I confess I have very great Reason to dread the strictnesss of your Censure, upon the strength of your admirable Endowments; yet methinks I find relief to this Fear, in that Native Candor, which so easily tempers the Accuracy of your Thoughts with favourable Constructions.

[1] Charles Sackville, 6th Earl of Dorset, 1637–1706, took a leading part in bringing William of Orange over to England. He was a generous patron of literature, and among his protégés were Prior, Dryden, Congreve, and Addison. Hamilton, in the Dedication to his *New Account*, spitefully insinuates that Ovington 'hardly knew more than his illustrious name'.

But I will not transgress those Measures of Civility, of which your *EXCELLENCY* is so absolute a Master, by being too tedious in this Address; nor thereby violate those Decencies and Respects, which your Practice recommends so fully to the World, and of which none have had more sensible Demonstration than my self: Especially considering how much is due to you from the Sacred Order, which you treat with that constant uncommon Civility, as if you design'd to ballance that Contempt, which is too apt to be cast upon it: Imitating, as in other Perfections, so in this too, the Ancient Poets, who instructed Men in Reverencing not only the Gods, but in a due Regard to such as were their immediate Servants; and in all things maintaining still that Greatness by your Munificence, which you freely part with in your Condescensions. I need not determine, with how much Reason the *Eastern* Subjects ascribe this Character to their Emperours, *That their Royal Condition is owing to their Merits, and that they as far transcend other Mortals in those, as they do in Power*; but I am satisfied, 'tis the unquestionable Loyalty, Prudence, Greatness of Mind, and other Virtues, which have justly rais'd you to that Sphere, wherein you move, kindly influencing the Affairs of this great Kingdom; and from whence you look down, like the Heavenly Bodies, from the highest Orb, with a kind and obliging Aspect. And that their other Opinion of their Princes, *That they are the Adopted Sons of Heaven,* may be your happy Portion too, is not more unfeignedly desir'd by any, than

*Your EXCELLENCY's*

*Most Obedient,*

*Most Obliged,*

*and Devoted Servant*

J. Ovington.

## TO Mr. J. OVINGTON, ON HIS VOYAGE TO SURATT.

*Hard is our Task to Read with fruitless Pain,*
*The Dreams of ev'ry Cloyster'd Writers Brain:*
*Who yet presume that Truth's firm Paths they tread,*
*When all the while through wild* Utopia's *led,*
*With Faiery-Feasts, instead of Science fed.*
*As dreaming Wizzards Midnight Journeys take,*
*And weary with imagin'd Labour wake,*
*So vain is* Speculation's *fancy'd Flight:*
*But search of Nature gives sincere Delight.*
*Through her vast Book the World, a curious Eye*
*May Wonders in each pregnant Page descry,*
*Make new Remarks, which Reason may reduce*
*To Humane Benefit, and Publick Use.*
*Then Happy they who quit their private Home,*
*And gen'rously through Foreign Climates roam;*
*Who, like* Ulysses, *can despise the Toil,*
*And make each Land they meet their Native Soil.*
*See Men and Manners scarce by Rumour known:*
*Visit all Countreys to improve their own.*
*But ah! how few, my Friend, with your Design,*
*On such Discov'ries bound, have cross'd the Line!*
*For sordid Gain, new Worlds they will descry,*
*Seize Nature's Wealth, but pass her Wonders by.*
*Their Fleet returns opprest with Trafficks Weight,*
*But Knowledge makes no part of all the Freight.*
*Yet this, of Old, was* Jason's *Noble Prize;*
*'Twas this that plac'd his* Argo *in the Skies:*
*Experience was the far-fetcht Golden Fleece,*
*The Prize so much admir'd by Ancient* Greece,

*From whence may be inferr'd what Thanks are due*
*From* Britain's *Sons, Industrious Friend, to you.*
*Fame shall in State, your useful Book Install*
*In* Bodley's *Pile, the Muses Capitol.*
*You have so lively your Discoveries Writ,*
*We Read and Voyage with you as we sit,*
*With you hoise Sail and reach the* Indian *shore;*
*The real Scene cou'd scarce delight us more.*
*As when some Prophet from a Trance awakes,*
*And to Attentive Crowds Description makes*
*Of Wonders, which he did in Rapture view,*
*The Listners think they see the Vision too.*
*Thus, Entertain'd with Nature and with Art,*
*We hear your Travels told, and well-pleas'd Guests depart.*

N. TATE[1]

[1] Nahum Tate, 1652–1715, was poet laureate and joint author, with Nicholas Brady, of the famous metrical paraphrase of the Psalms.

## THE CONTENTS

of the Principal Places and Things.


*The Island of* Madeira. . . . . . 10

*The Island of St.* Jago. . . . . . . 28

*The Island of* Annobon. . . . . . . 37

*The Coast of* Africa. . . . . . . 40

Malemba *on the Coast of* Africa. . . . . 48

*The Island of St.* Helena. . . . . . 57

*The Island of* Johanna. . . . . . . 67

*The Island of* Bombay. . . . . . . 79

*The Island of* Elephanta. . . . . . 97

*Of the* Great Mogul. . . . . . . 102

*The City of* Suratt. . . . . . . . 129

*The* Moor *Inhabitants of* Suratt. . . . 139

*The* Bannians *at* Suratt. . . . . . . 163

*The* Faquires *near* Suratt. . . . . . 210

*The* Persies *at* Suratt. . . . . . . 216

*The* Halalchors *at* Suratt. . . . . . 223

*The* English *Factory at* Suratt. . . . . . 225

*The Confinement of the* English *at* Suratt, *in the Years* 1691, 1692. . . . . . . 239

Muscatt *in* Arabia Felix. . . . . . 245

Mocha *and other Places on the* Red Sea. . . . 260

*The* Cape of Good Hope. . . . . . 279

*The Island of* Ascention. . . . . . . 297

TABLE OF COINS . . . . . . 303

APPENDIX . . . . . . . . 306

INDEX-GLOSSARY . . . . . . 307

# A VOYAGE TO SURATT, &c.

ON *April* the 11th, 1689 the Memorable Day, whereon their Majesties, King *William* and Queen *Mary* were Crown'd, did the *Ship Benjamin* break ground from *Gravesend*, towards her intended Voyage to *Suratt* in the *East Indies*. Whither she was sent as an Advice-Ship of that wonderful Revolution, whereby their Sacred Majesties were peaceably setled in the Throne, and had been receiv'd with the Universal Joy of all the Nation. In all places where we came, we were welcomed with loud and chearful Acclamations, and were entertain'd with unusual Congratulations and Respect, as happy Messengers of as grateful News, as ever arrived in those Parts. They were every where truly sensible of their unexpected Deliverance from that Misery and Thraldom which even there threatned them, and likewise of the invaluable Blessing of living under a Peaceable Government, free from their former Apprehensions, either of violence upon their Temporal Enjoyments, or disturbance to the Tranquility of their Minds.

*The Ships departure from* England.

We had not long left the Lands-End of *England*, before we espied a great Fleet of Ships, which appear'd to us at a distance like a floating Forest, and seiz'd us with no little Consternation. Their lying off not far from *Brest*, made us for some time conjecture them to be *French*, till we were happily undeceived by the approach of an *English* Frigot, which discover'd them to be Friends. However, one of our Company, who had faithfully ingaged to stand by us, and on whose Assistance we depended, without any Ceremony, being apprehensive of the danger, clapt upon a wind, and so left us.

After this, we kept on our course with a favourable Wind, till we arrived at *Madeira*, a small Island appertaining to the Crown of *Portugal*, situated about the Two and Thirtieth Degree of Latitude; it is in length, about Twenty Five Miles, about Eight or Ten broad, and Sixty in its Circumference.

# THE ISLAND OF MADEIRA[1]

*The Island of* Madeira.

THIS Island, as we are inform'd by good Historians, was first discover'd by *John Gonsalvo* and *Tristan*, under the Patronage of *Henry Infanto* of *Portugal.* But the present Inhabitants give us a different Account of its Discovery, *viz.* That in the Year 1344 an *English* Gentleman, having Married a Lady of a considerable Fortune, and setting out with her for *France* from the Port of *Bristol*, was by gusty weather, and opposite winds, driven into this Island: Where, upon his Landing, finding it a forlorn Place, both Uncultivated and Unpeopled, he fell into an extream fit of Melancholy, and yielding too much to that black Distemper, contributed by his own Death to make it still the more desolate. The Mariners however, who were not so readily dejected at this Misadventure, set Sail with their Vessel, and landed safely on the Coast of *Barbary*; where, after some Refreshment and Respite upon the place, they fortunately fell into the Company of some Ingenious *Portuguese*; to whom, after a little Conference, they Related the Hardships of the Voyage,

*The discovery of this Island by the* English.

[1] The Madeira Islands were apparently discovered by the Phoenicians, and are probably the Purple or Mauretanian Islands mentioned by Pliny. Portuguese vessels under Genoese captains touched there previous to 1351. The romantic story of the two lovers, Robert Machim or Macham, and Anna D'Arfet, who were driven there while eloping from England *circa* 1346, is given in Purchas, *Pilgrimes*, ed. Maclehose, ii. 12–14. 'This (Machico) was so named of an Englishman called Macham which had before arrived there by Tempest, and buried therein a Woman, whom he loved, with a memoriall thereof ingraven on the Stone of her Tombe.' They were rediscovered by two captains of Prince Henry the Navigator in 1419. The story of Machim and his bride was ultimately taken from the Portuguese account by F. Alcafarado, a translation of which, together with a reprint of this chapter of Ovington, will be found in an anonymous pamphlet in the B.M. entitled *A Historical Account of the Discovery of Madeira*, London, printed for J. Payne and J. Bonquet, in Paternoster Row, MDCCL.

the Situation and Native Pleasantness of the uninhabited, but most habitable Island they had left, and the just hopes and prospect they had of regaining a sight of it, were they but provided with Ships and Men. This excited the Attention of the *Portuguese*, and likewise, without much reluctancy, procur'd their Promise of endeavouring with their Prince to incline him to hearken to these Proposals, and likewise to equip them with Necessaries and Conveniences for a second Undertaking: And succeeding with him according to their wishes, they set forward, found the Island, landed their Men, and in a short time converted the Wilderness into a Garden of Pleasure.

*The discovery of this Island by the* Portuguese.

Some say *Madeira* was discover'd by the *Portuguese*, in *Anno* 1420, and deriv'd its Name from the abundance of Wood that grew there. It was overspread with Wildernesses and plenty of Trees, (which gave it this Name,) as with one intire Wood; the tedious thoughts of cutting down which, perswaded them to a more speedy Method of destroying it by fire. After it was kindled, the Flames grew to such a head, raged so violently, and by degrees became so furious, that the People were forc'd for their Ease and Preservation, to betake themselves to the water, to avoid the violence of the heat.

*The reason of the fruitfulness of the Island.*

The remaining Ashes contributed so much to the Fertility of the Ground, that it at first produced sixty for one, the fruitful Vines brought forth more Grapes than Leaves, Clusters of two or three spans length; and in all its Products, their Beauty and Fertility were so remarkable, that it gain'd the Title of the *Queen of Islands*.

*Its good Air.*

The Air here, to which the Pleasure as well as Health of Humane Life is so much owing, is generally very Temperate and undisturbed, and the Heavens smiling and serene. For those climates which are placed between the Thirtieth and Fortieth Degrees of Latitude, enjoy a Temperature, generally very equal and convenient, infested neither with the excess of Heat, nor rigid Coldness, but moderately participating of those troublesome Extreams. They seem indisputably to be most suited to the Pleasantness of Humane Life, and accommodated to our Constitutions, affording that delight to the Body, which Virtue imparts to the Mind, in avoiding all excesses, as dangerous and ungrateful, and opposite to the Ease, as well of the Sensitive, as Intellectual Part.

*The Metropolis.* The principal Town is *Tunchal* or *Tonzal*, some of them term it *Funchal*; from the abundance of Fennel which they say grew there. 'Tis the sole place of Trade, from whence they Export all their Wine and their Sugar, which is esteem'd superiour to any in the world.

The adjacent Rural Places are very Mountainous; but however, they Rival the Valleys in Fruitfulness and Delight; tho both are much fallen from their Primitive Fertility, and instead of sixty for one, which was the Original Increase, have gradually descended to twenty five. Seven or eight Rivers with variety of Rivulets refresh the place, which fall down from the Mountains, which, notwithstanding their heighth and steepness, are Planted and Improv'd, as well as the most Champaign ground in *England*. At the utmost top of the high Hills, the Corn thrives well, but the abundance of Clouds that breed there, are prejudicial to the Grapes.

*The present decay of the Island's Fertility.*

*Four sorts of Grapes that make the Wine.* The main product of the Island is Grapes, brought hither first from *Candy*, of which there are three or four kinds, whereof they make their Wine. One is coloured like Champaign, of little esteem; another is more strong and pale as White Wine; the third sort is rich and delicious, called Malmsey; the fourth is *Tento*, equalling Tent in colour, but far inferiour in Taste; it is never drunk unless in other Wines, with which it is mixt to give them a Tincture, and to preserve them. And for fermenting and feeding them, they bruise and bake a certain Stone, called Jess, of which nine or ten pounds are thrown into each Pipe. The *Madeira* Wine has in it this peculiar Excellence, of being meliorated by the heat of the Sun when it is prick'd, if the Bunghole being open'd 'tis expos'd to the Air.

*The singular Virtue of the Madeira Wine.*

The Product of the Vine is equally divided between the Proprietor and him that gathers and presses the Grapes; and yet for the most part the Merchant is Thriving and Rich, whilst the Grape-gatherer, imploy'd by him, is but Poor. Among the Merchants, the *Jesuits* are none of the meanest, who every where contend for precedence in Fortune, as well as in place; and have here secured the Monopoly of *Malmsey*, of which there is but one good Vineyard in the whole Island, which is entirely in their possession. Twenty Thousand Pipes of Wine, by a modest Computation, may be reckoned the Annual Increase of the Grapes, which number is thus exhausted and spent. Eight Thousand are thought to be drunk upon the Island, three or four are wasted in Leekage, and the remainder is Transported, most of it to the *West Indies*, especially to *Barbadoes*, where it is drunk more liberally than other *European* Wines.

*The Jesuits Monopoly of* Malmsey.

*The quantity of Wine which the Island produces.*

Plenty of Citrons grow here, of which the Natives make a delicate Sweetmeat, called *Sucket*[1]; and load with it yearly two or three small Ships for *France*. The Sugar which in candying them they make use of, and is often effectually prescrib'd against Consumptions, is but rarely transported, because of its scarcity, which hardly supplies the Necessities of the Island.

*Sucket a choice Sweetmeat.*

*The Excellence of the Sugar.*

They are some years under great want of Corn, because the Grain that grows here produces no great Plenty; so that sometimes they are threatned with Famine: For prevention of which, while I was there, they used their Authority in Pressing Ships which anchored in the Road, and commanded them, before they would allow them any Commerce, to the *Azores Islands*, to Import a quantity for their subsistence.

*The scarcity of Corn.*

This Island affords store of Peeches, Apricocks, Plumbs, Cherries, Figgs, and Walnuts; and the *English* Merchants, allowed to Reside and Traffick here, have transplanted from *England* Currans, Gooseberries, Philberts, *&c.* which are more kindly entertain'd in this Soil, than many of their Fruits are with ours, whose coldness and moisture are not so proper for the pregnancy of the Fruits of a hot Climate. The

*The Several Fruits.*

[1] Ital. *zuccata*. Candied fruit, 'a kind of meat made of pumpions or gourds'.

*Their fanciful Notion concerning the* Bonanoe.

*Bonanoe* is with them in singular esteem, and even veneration, affecting the Palat with that sensible sweetness, that it gains with them the credit of being the Forbidden Fruit. And for confirmation of this Surmise, they produce the extent of their Leaves, which being of a large size, they infer from thence, their fitness to make Aprons for *Adam* and *Eve*, to veil their Nakedness. 'Tis almost a Crime inexpiable to cut this Fruit with a Knife, which after dissection gives a faint similitude of our Saviour Crucified; and this they say is to wound his Sacred Image.[1] Oranges and Lemons abound here in that Plenty, that I have seen them drop into our Dishes, as we sat at Dinner under their delightful Boughs, and opportunely prevented the trouble of rising up to pluck them, by freely offering themselves to our wants. And these, tho they are in my Opinion as inviting as their Celebrated Fruit, and yield as useful and kind Refreshment to the Stomach, must yet not be suffer'd to vie in delicacie with their Venerable Admir'd *Bonanoe*, which by the awful Impressions of a powerful Priest upon the Thoughts of the Vulgar, commences Sacred, and must not be violated by the bold Attempt of any Weapon upon it.

*A description of a pleasant Entertainment.*

The *English* Merchants here, which are not reckoned above a dozen, imitate the *English* way of Living in their City and Country Houses; and, wearied with the Town, divert themselves in their Rural Plantations, to which they gave us *English* that were Strangers a Solemn Invitation; and placed us under the spreading boughs of Oranges and Lemons, with living Springs under their refreshing shade. Nature here displayed to us a Scene of Joy and Love, and waited on us in all her Pomp, in all the Delights and Beauties of the Field. The Hills were all cover'd with Vines, and the Valleys with

[1] The superstitions about bananas are very old. The following is a passage from John de Marignolli, *c.* 1350, quoted in Yule's *Cathay and the Way Thither*, p. 352. 'Istud vidimus oculis nostris, quod ubicunque inciditur per transversum, in utrâque parte incisurae videtur imago hominis transfixi. . . . et de istis foliis Adam et Eva fecerunt sibi perizomata.'

ripe Grapes, which yielded us a fragrant smell from the fruitful Vineyards. The Groves and Woods were all sprightly and gay, nothing seem'd to us drooping or languid, but all things smil'd round about the place of our Entertainment. The Air was clear, and made Melodious by the Voice of Birds. The Ships and Ocean were at a convenient distance, whereon we looked, and still new Charms sprung from that admirable variety of Objects, whither soever we turn'd our Eyes, and all things conspir'd to yield together a ravishing satisfaction to our Senses. Thus we spent the day in abundance of delight, happy and retir'd from Melancholy and all disturbance.

*The Food of the poor People.*

The ordinary Food of the poorer sort, is little else in the time of the Vintage, but Bread and ripe Grapes; which simple Nourishment affords sufficient pleasure and delight, when it meets with true Hunger, which never fails of Cooking the Meat with a gusto for the Palate. For Pulses and Leguminous Food, as it was a great part of the Diet of our Forefathers and Antediluvian Patriarchs, and very Congenial to the Nature of Man; so is this spare Food, with a very moderate mixture of Flesh, the frequent Repast even of those here of better Note, who find it easily elaborated and transmitted in such manner as is proper for Digestion; who thereby preserve their Bodies in Health and Strength, and keep the Crases[1] of the Parts pure, which are otherwise perverted by Intemperance. And were it not for this great abstinence in Eating, the danger of Fevers in the hot Season would be rarely avoided, and the Venereal Excesses to which they are strangely addicted, with the immoderate heat of the place, would be apt to put Nature under various disorders. Therefore Men of the greatest Consequence and Fortune, (whether it be that Sobriety might render them more Spruce and Amorous for the Exercise of Love, or that they are bred up in an Antipathy to that gross and scandalous Vice of Drunkenness,) seldom exceed the allowable bounds of Drinking, and accustom themselves to a very spare Diet. Nor are

*The Temperance of the People.*

[1] Κρᾶσις, 'a blending of the humours in the body, constituting a state of health or disease'.

they apt to impose their Wine upon others in their ordinary compotations; but the Servant attending holds the Bottle in his hand, and delivers the Glass to him that Drinks, to receive from the Servant's hand, who pours out leisurely what the Guest pleases, either a larger or a less quantity; by which means he that is intent upon Drinking, may take his Liberty, and he that is willing to refrain, is not forced. When the Company breaks up, the Porches and Entries of the Houses, and particularly the private place behind the door, are allowed for the convenience of Urine; because that action in the Streets is reputed Indecent, and liable to the Censure of Drunkenness.

*The odd conveniences for Urine.*

*Their Cloaths.*

The People very much affect a gravity in their Garb, and are cloathed all in Black, in complaisance (as I imagin) to the Sacerdotal Function, and the better to ingratiate with that Profession, which challengeth so much Authority among them. But they cannot live without the gallantry of wearing the Spado[1] and the Dagger; those inseparable Adjuncts, even of Servants attending their Masters at the Table, who proudly strut with the Dishes in their Hands, in that Solemn Garb, with a Basket Hilt to a Sword at least a yard long, even in the midst of Summer.

*Their Houses.*

Their Houses too, as well as Cloaths, are made without much Expence or Splendour; neither Curious by the Embellishments of Art without, nor Rich in Trappings and Furniture within; some of them shoot up a little in height, without any other Characters of greatness : The generality of them are flat-roofed, and all of them give admittance to the open Air thro the Windows, which, being without the use of Glass, are kept open all the day, and closed by Wooden shutters at night.

[1] Italian *spada*, a cut-and-thrust sword (σπάθη). Cf. the Ballade in Rostand, *Cyrano de Bergerac*, Act I:

Je jette avec grâce mon feutre,
Je fais lentement l'abandon
Du grand manteau qui me calfeutre,
Et je tire mon espadon. . . .

The Soil allows no venomous Inhabitant, nor Creature of Infcetious Malignity, which whether it is peculiar to the Earth or Air, or derivable from some other cause, I know not; who found nothing in this place different from the disposition of others of the same Climate. *No venomous Creature upon this Island.*

The Qualities of all Poisons are affirm'd by some to be either hot and inflaming, as *Euphorbium*; or cold, as *Opium*; or dry, as *Vitriol*; all which qualities may be found in the Elements here, as well as in other Regions, and therefore apt enough to supply Matter for all Venomous Animals, which for this reason might be presum'd to be found here; and much rather than in the Kingdom of *Ireland*, which is a Country of noted Humidity; and no Poisons, they say, are simply Humid, because Humidity is a quality purely passive, and of it self incapable of causing pain.

Lizards, of which they have here an infinite number, are very destructive to their Fruits and Grapes, and mighty devourers of whatever they light upon. But Snakes and Toads, of which in the *Indies* are such innumerable Multitudes, find here no Entertainment; there they haunt the Chambers and private Apartments of the Inhabitants, lurk frequently in the roofs of their Houses, as well as in the Grass; sometimes they espy them in their Chambers and about their Beds, in the Walls and Seelings of their Lodgings, and in the dark corners of their Vaults and Cellars. *A great number of Lizards.*

The Fertility of this Island is much abated from what it was in the time of its first Plantation, and the constant breaking up of the ground has made it in many places feeble in its Productions, so that it wholy discourages their Labours, till it has lain fallow for three or four years; after which time, if there springs up no Broom, as a token of its following Fruitfulness, they desist from all their hopes of its Fertility, and conclude it quite Barren. The present barrenness of much of their Land, reminds them of the growth of their Vices, to which they ingenuously ascribe it. Among which, their Effeminate Lewdness may very well stand in the front of their Accusations, which prevails not a little, even among *The present barrenness of the Island.* *The Ingenuous acknowledgment of their sins.*

those whose double Obligations, of Christians and Married Persons, should mightily deter them from that sin; especially considering how they may satisfie all their Desires at home, and double their Pleasure by their Innocence. But vagrant Lusts, like other Fires, when they once get head, are not easily tamed and stifled, till they consume those Materials that feed them. This Inconstancy in the Husband encourages (tho it cannot Legitimate,) the same Levity in the Wife, the weakness of whose Sex is not so much proof against the Charms of alluring Temptations. Therefore are the Women here as apt to defraud their Husbands, as the Husbands are to defraud their Wives, and both equally kind to Strangers, especially the Women, whose proneness that way, is more excited by their being cloister'd and kept in, and restrain'd from all Company. Their Appetites are augmented by difficulties, and increased by being oppos'd:

*Their Lewdness.*

*Quod licet, ingratum est, quod non licet acrius urit.*

This made *Lycurgus* Enact a Decree for keeping up Matrimonial Affection, 'That Married Persons should be as cautious as Celibates to enjoy one another, and never do it but by stealth.'

*No Interview before Marriage.*

Another reason that offers for their mutual Infidelity, is the Ignorance they have of each others personal Humours, and unacquaintance with their dispositions before Marriage, which sometimes is Celebrated before a mutual Interview has preceeded the Engagement. Whereas a competent time of Courtship and frequent Visits gives them some Inspection into each others Genius and Inclinations, engages their mutual Passions and good Liking, by their constant endearing Presents and Conversation, which by degrees unites their Hearts, and ripens their Affections for a happy Marriage. For which purpose it is practis'd in some parts of the World, in the very Minority of their Children, who are engaged by Contract at the years of five or six, as in the *Indies*.

During our stay upon the Island, a young Gentleman of an advanc'd Fortune, which was valued at 60000 Dollars, was ingaged in the Courtship of a Lady of 8000, and proceeded to Marriage, without the opportunity of one sight of her before the Solemnity, besides what was allow'd him the day before. He was then, as it happen'd, in the Company of her Brother, and espied thro' a Lattice two young Ladies, and imagining one of them to be his Mistress, was curious to enquire, whether of them it was? To which he receiv'd no more satisfaction, than, 'To morrow, Sir, is time enough for that.'

*No Marriages with* Jews *or* Moors.

In Treating about Marriage, their principal Enquiries are into the Family and Descent of the Courtier, for prevention of all occasions of the detestable Affinity with *Moors* and *Jews*, which among them are very numerous. To join in Matrimony with any of them, is esteemed a debasement of her Lineage and Extraction, especially in a Woman that pretends to Family and Education.

*The* English *Merchants esteemed by them.*

*A strange conception against Marriage.*

But the *English* Merchant is on the other side as Reputable, and stands as fair in their Accounts; his very Name makes way for his admittance, and Incorporating into the best Families, especially if any equality appears in his Fortune; for their subtle Casuists make sometimes an inequality of Fortune a just Plea for dissolving a Contract. But then, alas! the *English* Merchant, if he Marries, must first renounce his Religion, and abandon the care of his Soul, for the Enjoyment of her in whom he delights. But that which much surpriz'd me, was the prohibition of an Old Gentlewoman, to the Proceedings of a Young Pretender to her Daughter, upon this Account; because she was inform'd of the Health and Soundness of his Constitution, of the Moderation and Chastity of his Manners, so that he was never known to labour under any Venereal Disease; which she concluded to arise only from the weakness of his Constitution, for it seems she presumed there was no need of the restraints of Conscience for so Venial an Offence, the committing of which, in her Opinion, was Meritorious.

*Murther common and unpunish'd.*

The Execrable Sin of Murther has gain'd too not only an Impunity but Reputation among them, and it is made the Characteristick of any Gentleman of Rank or Fashion, to have dipt his Hands in Blood. To this they frequently are obnoxious, and readily incline, by reason of the easie recourse they have to their Churches, which shelter them from any Process, and are met with at every turn. For in the Metropolis, *Tunchal,* which exceeds not a good Country Town, are almost twenty Churches and Chappels, besides abundance in their Country Plantations. These Christians are as Licentious in commiting this Crime, as remiss in inflicting due Penalties for it, and indulge the guilt of it, even beyond what the Almighty did the *Jews,* tho' 'tis voluntary, by sparing the Criminal if he can lay hold on the Horns of the Altar; and make Banishment or Confinement his utmost Penalty, both which by a large Present are bought off.

*Many Clergie-men.*

The Numbers of their Clergy increase here, as well as in other Popish Countries, even to the oppression of the Laity, with whom they seem to vie for Multitude. 'Tis scarce imaginable, how so many Rich Ecclesiasticks can be supported by the Labours of so few People. But to abate this wonder, they tell us, that none of their Nation is admitted to the Priesthood, who is not possess'd of some Patrimony, to avoid a burthen to the Church. They are totally averse here from admitting any into Sacred Orders, whose Originals are either *Jews* or *Moors,* and yet this Caution is not observed by them at St. *Jaques,*[1] where Native *Africans* Officiate as Priests.

*No* Jews *or* Moors *Clergy-men.*

*The prevailing Authority of the* Jesuits.

The *Jesuits,* among all the rest of their Orders, are the only Men in Supream Repute, which they aspire to by the easie Absolutions of their Penitents, and pretentions to stricter Sanctity, and a more unblemisht Character, than the rest of the Orders. For this end, they closely conceal from publick notice all the Enormities and Irregularities of their Order, and all their Failures, but what are legible in their Ignorance, which was so remarkable, that scarce one in three of those I convers'd with understood Latin. If any Delinquent is expell'd the Convent, his Faults are stifled and kept as secret as Confession, lest the noise of them among vulgar Ears, should scandalously reflect upon their Society, and

*Their Ignorance.*

[1] St. Iago. See p. 28, note.

diminish that Veneration they so zealously affect. And the only Answer which is vouchsafed to any Querist, for the reason of their Expulsion, is, 'He was unworthy of our Society.' This is a Maxim worth the Wisdom of that Order, and the imitation of all others, and highly justifies the prudent concealment of such Men's Faults, whose Examples might eminently scandalize any kind of Profession.

*A prudent Maxim in use among them.*

The *Jesuits* Chappel is far the most splendid of all their Churches, which we chanced to view in the greatest Lustre, at St. *Ignatius*[1] his Eve, (as they are pleas'd to term him) a time observable for the Magnificence of the Ceremony and Pomp: Variety of the choicest Anthems were sung, with the sweetest Instrumental and Vocal Musick, sufficient, had their Doctrine been answerable to it, to have charm'd us into a Conversion. The Vigils of all their Saints, as well as that of St. *John Baptist*, are Celebrated with abundance of shining Lights, placed conspicuously upon the tops of their Steeples, after the Sun-set. But the bright Illuminations this Night about the Steeple of the *Jesuits* Oratory, far out-did the rest of the Apostles Eves, and dazled the Eyes of the Spectators at a distance. Some of the Chappels, as well as Houses, are built upon such steep declining Hills, that they seem to indanger the precipitation of such as come out of them; and questionless the protection of the Saint is extolled for the deliverance from those Perils.

*The Jesuits Chappel.*

Near the *Jesuits* Chappel is a certain Hospital, much frequented by the Natives, Erected for the Entertainment and Cure of such as have smarted for their Feminine Pleasures; whose miserable Spectacles are so ghastly and frightful, that were there nothing of future Punishment, that only might very well curb Men in their highest Career to those foul Sins. Among the rest of the Female Penitents, we espied one near the Altar, weeping bitterly, with a sorrowful dejected Countenance, and in deep anguish of Heart. This sight produc'd something of the same Melancholy Effects upon us, till I

*An Hospital for such as have been Lewd.*

[1] St. Ignatius Loyola's festival is on 31 July. This fixes the date of Ovington's visit.

recovered my self at the hopes I had of her happy Condition, which such floods of Tears seem'd to promise. Had all the rest evidenc'd the like Sorrow and Concern she did, this Infamous Society (for ought I know) had been the most Honourable upon the Island. But their Measures herein are very unequal, for a modest Salute is an Offence insufferable, whilst this abominable Vice many of them scarce stand to Parly with.

*Their burying places.*

Their Churches are most commonly made use of for Repositories of their Dead, in the Interment of whom they mix store of Lime with the Earth, to hasten the consumption of the Corps, by whose sudden mouldring away, upon this account, there is room made within a fortnight for a fresh Funeral. To signalize their Respect for the Deceased, the Corps is curiously trimm'd and adorn'd, as a faint Emblem of its glorious and triumphant Resurrection, in imitation of the Wise King, who buried with his Royal Father an invaluable Treasure.

*No burying place allowed to the* English.

But as their Church allows no Charitable Thoughts to the Souls of Hereticks, so does it forbid all kindness to their dead Bodies, and prosecutes the *English* that die there, with more inexorable hatred, than what they shew to the Carcasses of Beasts and Birds, which may find a resting place on shoar, and quietly remain upon common ground; both which are strictly forbid the *English*, who are cast into the Sea, and committed to the waves. And accordingly an English Merchant falling sick of a sudden Distemper at *Madeira*, was unfortunately carried off by it; which mov'd the rest of our Nation that were there, to contrive for his decent Interment. And therefore, lest a publick Burial might expose him to the Rage of the People, or the Clergy's Indignation, they concluded to deposit him among the Rocks, in order to his better concealment. But the Rocks were unable to shelter him from their Tyranny, which was exercis'd upon him in this barbarous manner, they dragg'd him from the place where he lay, up and down the Island, and expos'd him to the contempt of the Inhabitants, till they threw him into the Ocean.

This Inhumanity; which is carried even beyond the Grave, is propagated as far as their Plantations in the *East*; where if any Protestant chance to die among the Nation of the *Portuguese*, no place is allowed for his Reception, nor vile enough for his Sepulchre, but the very Corps of a rank Heretick annoys the Dominions of a Catholick Country, tho' it were buried under ground. And yet a powerful Summ of Mony, which is said to blind the world, prevail'd to open the Eyes of the Priests Intellectuals in this very case; for thus they stated the difficulty concerning an *English* Child, which had been clandestinely Interred there, that if it were immediately taken up, and then Baptized after their manner, and so made a Member of their Church, it might be admitted among their Dead. This Conclusion was approv'd of as Canonical, for the Child was Baptiz'd, Buried after their manner, and deposited where it was taken up.

*A dead Child Baptiz'd and Buried for a Summ of Mony.*

The Canons of the Cathedral Church, which stands about the midst of the City, are as exquisite in their contrivance for their Ease, as the others were for burying-mony. The Constitutions of their Church oblige their Attendance at Prayers by Four a Clock in the Morning. But because such early Rising is very troublesome, especially to Corpulent Men, therefore they agree, that the Clock shall never in the Morning strike Four, till it really be Five; and order its motions by this Method, always an Hour or so slower than the Sun, that they may punctually indulge their own Repose, by this mock obedience to the Orders of their Church.

*The laziness of some of the Clergie.*

Yet how negligent soever they may appear in this Instance, they all pretend a mighty Zeal for their Faith, especially in the Meritorious Conversion of any Stranger, upon which we suspected they had been too intent, by the loss we had of some few of our Men, whom no search could discover to us. The *Jesuits* we conjectur'd must be concern'd in it, because their Love for the Cause is generally more flaming than that of the other Orders among them; and therefore we resolved upon addressing to the Governour for demanding an enquiry after them in the College of the *Jesuits*; but we

*Some* English *Seamen kept on shoar.*

found his power could not reach it. The time grew on that we must depart, and were much concern'd to leave our Men, when we were engaged to set Sail, because the want of them on Board might be very prejudicial in a tedious Voyage. Our Commander therefore having got without Gun-shot of their Citadels, Mann'd out his Pinnace with twelve or fourteen Hands, well provided with Swords and Fire-Arms, and appointed them to Row along the Shoar, to apprehend, if possible, some few of their Fishers, to supply the places of our Sailers. As they cruised along, they met by chance with another Prize, *viz.* a Comely Abbot and a Vicar, coming up to *Tunchal* from the Country in a Boat. They were strangely surpriz'd, to find themselves unexpectedly taken, and Pirated by a Boat's Crew; but much more concern'd, when we told them they must bid farewel to all their Friends and Festivities at *Madeira,* and Imbarque with us in an *Indian* Voyage, or at least remain our Prisoners on Board, till the *Jesuits* restor'd our Men on Shoar. The thought of this amazed and struck them with confusion, and forc'd from their Breasts many a groan and sigh, for their Sorrow seem'd to surpass its expression by any Tears. And yet they were not so far lost in this Consternation of Mind, but that they kept within limits of Reflection, and recollecting a Method for their Release. Therefore they speeded an Express to the Governour, and passionately implored him for the sake of God, and the Virgin *Mary*, to bethink himself of some Project for their Liberty, for which their Prayers should continually ascend for his deliverance from such Disasters. And our Commander valuing his Sailers above the Priests, directed a Letter to the *English* Consul on Shoar, to this effect.

*An Abbot and a Vicar seiz'd in the room of our Seamen.*

*SIR,*

*The Captain's Letter to the Consul on shoar.*

*THE Honour and Duty we owe our King and Employers, obliged us to make this Restitution to our selves, since your Governour wou'd not. To deprive Princes of their Subjects, and Masters of their Servants, under a pretence of making them better Christians, is in my Opinion to make them worse. And if the Religion of your* Jesuits *admit of such Immoral Actions, neither our Laws nor Religion require our taking it at your Hands. If your Governour has little Command over them, he has less over us, and he therefore may take the keeping of some of your Subjects as patiently from us, as he does their detaining some of our Sailers (as we presume) from them. In the mean time, endeavour to see they be restored, or rest satisfied with the loss of those we here detain. If your Governour wou'd not give us satisfaction if he could, he cannot then excuse himself in this matter. If he wou'd, and cou'd not, we shall be so kind, as to do it for him, which may thereupon prove an Obligation, as well to him, as*

*Yours*, &c.

These Epistles were no sooner receiv'd and read, but the whole place was in an uproar about their Priests, either their Priests must be return'd, or all the *English* must suffer for it. This startled the *English* Merchants on shore, and awaken'd their Care of contriving some means for their Safety; for they perceiv'd the inraged Multitude, who stood upon the Strand, would not be pacify'd without them. And therefore lest our Commander should prove inexorable, and seriously resolv'd upon what he writ, the *English* Merchants brought along with them Money for a Voyage, after they had prevail'd to get on Board. For they durst not return without their Priests; and they knew not where the Voyage would end. After their difficult Passage on Board, they related the Confusion the Place was in, and how tumultuous the People had suddenly grown, upon the account of the Detention of their Priests; and how they were upon the Bank of the Sea, repeating their Exclamations, *Our Padres! Our Padres!* A sudden Joy sprung up in the Faces of the Priests upon the sight of our *English* Merchants, from whom they assured themselves of some Relief, and Release from the Confinement they were under; and with sorrowful Accents represented to them the unhappy Minute they set forward for *Tunchal*; but withal, the Hopes they had that their coming on Board would prove favourable to their Misfortune. The Commander, who heard all this, and reflecting upon the extreme Inconvenience attending the English upon this occasion, resolved to send them all on Shore, to remove that Disturbance which he saw was otherwise unavoidable; for he thought the Priests would be as useless to him at Sea, as they commonly are at Land, and a Burthen to either Element; and so dismiss'd them all to their great Satisfaction.

*The Priests dismiss'd.*

After this we stood off from Shore, fill'd our Sails, and without any Ceremonious Adieu, either to the Governour or to the Fort, we left the Island. For 'tis easier to depart, than to be admitted into the Harbour. Because when any Ship arrives there, two or three of the Inquisitors, who wear the Sacred Garb, are sent to examine it about any Sickness, or other Objection, which might hinder the Liberty of Traffick; and not suffering any Sailer's setting his Foot on Shore till they pronounce the Ship healthful.

*All Ships examin'd that come to the Harbour.*

By a kind Providence our speedy sailing that Day did occasion a greater Deliverance to us from the French, than what the Abbot and Vicar had from us. Within Forty Hours after our Departure, two *French* Men of War of good Force arrived in the same Port, who no sooner dropt their Anchor, but they weighed again in Chace of our Ship, and shaped their Course directly towards the *Canaries*, where some gave out we were design'd. But leaving the Island *Palmo* on the East, we steer'd directly to *St. Jago*, a Capital Island of *Cape Verde*, whereby we happily defeated their pursuit.

*Our escaping two French Men of War.*

*Our Departure from Madeira.*

So the *Cerne Atlantica*,[1] as the Ancients called it, being in a fortunate Minute left by us, we arrived with Safety at this Port. In our way we were entertain'd with an unusual prospect, which to fresh Navigators was very divertive, which was several winged Fish,[2] which took Flight in the Air, while

*Flying Fish.*

[1] Cerne is probably Cape Ghir, near Agadir on the coast of Morocco. See the learned note by Müller (*Geog. Graeci Min.* i. 9.), on Hanno's *Periplus*, § 8, where it is first mentioned.

[2] Flying fish are mentioned by nearly all the early travellers. See especially the lively account in Herbert, *Some Yeares Travels*,

their Finns were moist, but dropt into the Ocean as soon as they grew dry, and thereby unactive. Their Wings are always spread while they move in the Air, where they sometimes sustain themselves the space of a Furlong. When they drop into the Ocean, the watchful Dolphins are generally ready to devour them, whose Swiftness in the Water equals almost the Flight of the others in the Air. And as timorous Animals at Land seek for Shelter from Men, when they find themselves in apparent Danger from a merciless Persecutor; so the Flying Fish will betake themselves to our Ships, and fall upon our Decks and Shrouds, upon a hot pursuit of the destructive Dolphin. Here likewise we were affrighted with a Turnado,[1] which, without Care and speedy handing of our *A*
Sails, might have endanger'd our Ship. It came suddenly, *Turnado.*
without any previous signs of its approach, till a quarter of an hour before it came. 'Tis a violent surprizing Storm of Rain and Wind; and that which adds to render it more formidable, is its unexpected Rise, at such times as the Weather is sedate and temperate; but its precipitant Motion renders it less tedious, being as soon a dying, as it is short in it's Growth and Increase.

1638, p. 33; Fryer, *New Account,* ed. Crooke, i. 35; Pyrard de Laval, *Voyage to the East Indies*, ed. Gray, i. 9. There are actually two kinds of flying fish, one a Gurnard (*Dactylopterus*) and the other a Herring (*Exocoetus*). They do not really 'fly'; they leap out of the water, and the fins merely act as planes or 'gliders'.

[1] Turnado, a hurricane, tornado; Port. from *tornar*, to turn. These 'strange, self-opposing gusts, blowing from every point of the compass', are described in Terry, *Voyage to East India*, ed. 1777, pp. 5, 6.

# THE ISLAND OF ST. JAGO[1]

THE Islands of *Cape Verde* are distant from the Main of *Africa* 150 Leagues; they extend themselves in a Body from 13½, unto the 19th in Latitude. Ten of these Islands are considerable, tho' not inhabited, and are rang'd in Form of a Crescent; of which the Convex Part regards the Continent, and the Two points the Ocean.

*St.* Jago. The Night before we came to an Anchor we espied this Island of St. *Jago*, which is the greatest and principal of all the Isles of *Cape Verde*, and is dignify'd with a Bishop's Seat in a City of the same Name. They borrow their Appellation of *Cape Verde* from the Cape or Prominence of Land in *Africa*, which is the nearest Main Land to them, from whence several *Africans* come here to inhabit. These by the Ancients were call'd *Gorgades* and *Hesperides*, who feigned the Orchards with Golden Apples, which were kept by a Dragon, were placed here.

*Its Chief Port.* *The Danger which we escap'd.* In this Island are various Ports, the most noted of which we anchor'd in, named *Praya*, where, by the Blessing of Heaven, we escaped an eminent Danger, which arose from a violent Storm in the Night-time; and was so outragious, that the Ship dragg'd her Anchor; and our Ruine had been

[1] St. Jago is the English corruption of San Thiago, the chief of the Cape Verde Islands. These were discovered by one of Prince Henry of Portugal's many expeditions, in 1441 (Purchas, *op. cit.* ii. 15). They are inhabited mostly by uncultured half-caste descendants of slaves and convicts, and the climate is unhealthy. They are also described by Fryer, *New Account*, i. 44, 5. Praya, on San Thiago, is the capital of the 'Leeward' group; Hay is apparently the little island of Mayo. Gorgades or the islands of the Gorgon was the name given to these islands from the 'gorgons' (gorillas, no doubt) which inhabited them. Pliny (*N. H.* vi. 36) tells us that Hanno the Carthaginian brought back with him the hairy skins of two 'gorgons' from this spot. The islands are also described by Fryer, *op. cit.*, pp. 38–46.

inevitable, had it been much fiercer; because we rid so near St. *Jago*, which was on one side; and *Hay Island*, which lay on the other.

*Its Barrenness.*

The Island at our approaching it lookt very desolate and naked, without any apparent Verdure either of Grass or Leaves. And the reason for this, upon our Examination, was very plain, because in Three Years space before that Day we came thither, they had not been refreshed with one Shower of Rain, which occasion'd an extreme Drought and Sterility, and gave it the Face rather of the Desarts of *Arabia*, than of a plentiful Country.

*A Comparison of it with* Madeira.

The Air is neither so healthful, nor the Place so pleasant, as *Madeira*, which has so many Houses and delightful Inclosures, that it seems to be a Garden of Pleasure. Neither is it so mountainous as that Island, which makes it apt enough for Plantations; and yet here are but very few Vines, and those incompetent for affording any Wine; most of which that is drunk is imported to them from *Madeira*.

*Its Products.*

In the Valleys are Grains, Vines, Fruits, Sugar-Canes, Mellons, Bonanoes, better than those at *Madeira*, Dates, Coconuts. They abounded not with Cattle, but of Fowl they had plenty; for which, or for any other of their Commodities, we traded with them for old Cloaths, and cast Garments, a staple sort of Merchandise with these *Portuguese*, whose Humour, which generally is vain and haughty, will make them vaunt themselves like Fidalgoes,[1] when they are only thus apparell'd. But that which is meaner in them much, than strutting in the over-worn Garments of Sailers and other Men, they are strangely addicted to pilfering and stealth; and one or two of them will entertain you in Discourse, whilst the third takes off your Hat, or snatches away the Sword from your side. And if they meet any Stranger at a Distance from any Town, they seldom fail of stripping him naked.

*Many Natives poor and thievish.*

They are ignorant here in the Huswifery of making either Butter or Cheese, which are therefore valuable, because rare.

[1] Span. *filho de algo*, son of someone, a nobleman. Port. *hidalgo*.

*A Present to the Governour.* And accordingly, a couple of Cheese, twelve Stock-fish,[1] and two Dozen of Poor Jack were kindly received by the Governour of the Town, who was at this time unable to supply us with a Loaf of Bread; which made a Sea-Bisket as acceptable to them, as fresh Provisions, after a long Voyage, would be to us.

*The Governour of the Island.* A Romish Prelate govern'd the Island, and presided in their Civil as well as Ecclesiastical Affairs; and, without that Niceness which is practic'd at *Madeira*, admitted the Native *Africans* to officiate in their Oratories and Convents.

*The Inhabitants.* Most of the People are Negroes, transported from *Africa* to settle here, converted to the *Roman* Faith. Their Cloathing is a kind of Indian-like Stuff, turn'd about their middle carelessly; the rest of the Body is all bare, save their Breasts and Shoulders, which are covered with some thin Stuff.

Notwithstanding the Penance they were under by the Scarcity of Bread and Wine, the Women were very loose in their Behaviour, and easily led away by the Sailers, whose Immoral Extravagancies have occasion'd this Proverbial Speech in *India*, That *in Sailing from hence thither, they leave their Consciences on this side of the* Cape; *and in returning from thence to* Europe, *they leave their Consciences on the other side the* Cape. So that except it be in doubling the *Cape*, they will scarce allow an *East-India*-man any Conscience at all.

*An English Proverb in* India.

*The Island* Fogo. Near this Island is another called *Fogo*,[2] remarkable for its Sulphureous Vapours, which like *Ætna* and *Vesuvius*, it continually emits; which sally forth in such Eruptions, that it annoys all the adjacent parts, by continual vomiting of Flames and Smoak; from this burning Mountain such quantities of Pumice-stones are ejected, that they swim upon the Main Ocean, and are variously dispers'd by the Currents of the Water to distant places; some floated as far as St. *Jago*, and spread themselves by our Ship's side. The Height of this *Volcano* is considerable, and its aspiring Top is raised above

*Pumice-stones.*

*The height of the Island* Fogo.

[1] Stock fish are salted cod and hake: 'poor Jack' is another name for the same article.

[2] A volcanic island thirty miles from San Thiago.

two Stories in the Clouds, which are rang'd each below the other upon its declining sides. The Head of the Mountain advanced in height in a double Proportion to the highest of the Clouds; which were not very long in ripening, but presently put on their Aery Body. The same thing I observed upon the Table-Land of the *Cape of Good Hope*, where the Vapours fashion'd themselves into Clouds immediately upon their Exhalation from the Mountains, and ranged themselves, as they rise, in due Order and Progress through the Air.

*Trade-Winds.*

Before we had sailed many Leagues from this Shore, we were under the Influence of the Trade-Winds,[1] which blow on both sides of the Lines to many Degrees distance; and with such constant gentle Gales, that except it be upon occasion of a sudden, violent, and stormy Gust of Weather, the Sailers make all that passage Holiday, and are not forced to hand a Sail in the space of many Days. The Days here are regular, and almost of an equal length, not apt to be infested with Storms, or darkned with Clouds, or overcast with Showers, except it be upon the nearer Approaches of the Sun, who usually skreens his direct scorching Beams by the Interposition of watry Vapours; and now neither boisterous Winds nor swelling Seas do raise any Fear or Disturbance in the Mariners Breast. 'Tis this kind indulgent Weather that mainly animates Men to the undertaking of this tedious Voyage. For otherwise the length of it would be insupportable, were it all along incommoded by the Storms and Dangers of our Northern Seas; the Thoughts of which wear off by degrees, as we recede from them, and fall insensibly into milder Climates; where the calm Face of the Heavens smooths the rugged Aspect of the Men, makes them forget their former rough and troublesom Weather, and solace and enjoy themselves in this sweet welcom change of Air.

*Pleasant sailing between the Tropicks.*

Great store of Sharks swum now about our Ship, with their

[1] These winds blow continuously in the Atlantic in the vicinity of the Equator, the NE. trade wind between 7° and 30° N. and the SE. trade wind between 3° N. and 25° S. Midway between the two systems lies the region of calms.

*The Shark, Pilot-fish, and Sucking-fish.* Attendants and Adherents the Pilot-fish[1] and the Sucking-fish, which are about four or five Inches long. The Pilot-fish are the same to the Shark, as the Jackalls are to the Lion, direct him in his Course, and find out his Prey, and give him notice of any Danger. The Sucking-fish stick close to the Shark, as some small Fish do upon Lobsters, and suck their Nourishment out of him. This Fish forsakes not the Shark in the greatest Dangers, is his faithful Adherent in his utmost Extremities; he cleaves to him even when he is forc'd out of his Element, and brought on Board the Ship, attends him to his Funeral, and dies with him. The Under Jaw of the Shark is so much lower than the Upper, that he cannot take his Bait, but by turning upon his Back to receive it with more Facility. They are eagerly voracious, and are furnish'd with Instruments accordingly; with a Sett of Teeth as keen as their Stomachs, which easily lop off the Leg or Arm of a Man, and afford no more than one Morsel to that ravenous Animal. Yet are they peculiarly tender and indulgent to their Spawn,[2] and shelter them in the place that gave them Birth: For when ever the Young Ones are in Danger, they immediately hasten to the Mouth of the Old One, and retire to its inward Parts for Safety. By this I was apt to think, that they spawned their Young Ones at their Mouth, because we have seen them come out and go in at the Sharks Mouth, and found one Six Foot long in a Sharks Belly.

*A Conjecture how the Sharks spawn their young ones.*

*Dolphins describ'd.* Several Dolphins followed our Ship, which surpass all the Creatures of the Watry Element in Beauty and a quick Finn, and is therefore called the Arrow of the Sea. They shine the brightest, and swim the swiftest, of any Fish in the Ocean; and their lively Colours represent in the Water the shining Wings of some

[1] The story of the pilot-fish (a Horse Mackerel, *Naucrates Ductor*) is a traveller's tale. Both it and the sucking-fish, *Echeneis*, are 'commensal' parasites of the shark, following him just as he follows the ships, and picking up such scraps of offal and refuse as their host leaves unnoticed. The same holds true of the jackals and the lion. Cf. Terry's remarks, *Voyage*, pp. 7–9.

[2] Ovington's remarks about the spawning, &c., of sharks are uncorroborated.

bright Flies. But as they leave their Element, their Beauty fades; and as their Life, so does their Splendour decay; the lightsom Colours begin to fade and mourn at Death's Approaches, and turn quite dark and dusky at their Expiration. It is neither the Number, nor the Largeness of the Finns, that contribute towards their extraordinary Swiftness; for they are but few, and very small; two only near the Jowl, and two small ones under the Belly, and a narrow long one upon the Back. The Head is fashion'd sharp above, and downwards descends broader, almost like the Head of a Hatchet with the Edge upwards. Upon the top of his Tongue he has many little Teeth. It is a lovely, neat, and clean Fish, and as like to the Dolphin on the Sign-Posts as a Mackrel is to a Flounder. The Flesh of it is white and delicate, which when larded and roasted fresh, no Roman Dainties or Eastern Luxury can out-vie the grateful Food.

*Abundance of Porpoises.*

After these an infinite number of Porpoises[1] plaid about our Vessel, and spread themselves near half a League round our Ship. One of them was caught by the Tail with a running Knot made by the Sailers, whose Liver and Entrails nearly resembled those of an Hog; and the Blood that issu'd from it was thick and red, like that of a Bullock: It strangely detain'd its Blood, after a deep Wound in the Throat, and stopt the Effusion of it for a very considerable time, before it gave it any vent.

*Albicores and Bonettoes.*

We met likewise with Shoals of Albicores (so call'd from a piece of white Flesh that sticks to their Heart) and with multitudes of Bonettoes,[2] which are named from their Goodness and Excellence for eating; so that sometimes for more than twenty Days the whole Ship's Company have feasted

[1] The Porpoise, gen. *Phocaena*, is, of course, a mammal, not a fish.

[2] Cf. Terry, *op. cit.*, p. 10: 'Bonitoes and albicores are in colour, shape and taste much like unto mackarel, and as good fish as they; but they grow to be very large.' They belong to the genus *thynnus* or tunny. 'Bonito' is Port. 'fine'. 'Albicore' has nothing to do with 'albus'. It is probably a Spanish corruption of an Arabic term. Hobson-Jobson, *s.v.* The bonito is also known as 'Cobily mash', i.e. *kālu-bili-mās*, 'black bonitō fish', by early travellers.

*Sailers Lives preserv'd by Sea-fish.* on these curious Fish. Several Vessels in tedious Voyages, which by contrary Winds have been retarded in their Sailing, have owned the Preservation of their Lives to this kind Providence, which has often supplied them with this sort of Food in the time of their Extremity.

*Whether Fish sleep?* As we sailed along there happen'd an Accident, which made me conclude, that either the Fish do not sleep, or that they subsist much longer without it than other Animals. We struck an Albicore upon the Tail with a Fish-spear, which afterwards made its Escape by dropping off the Hook. This very Fish, as we all observ'd, follow'd our Ship daily above a Week, when we sailed at least two Degrees, that is, an Hundred and Twenty Miles a Day, and never left us all the while. We saw it early in the Mornings, by that time we were able to discern any such things at that Distance; and till the Darkness of the Evening intercepted our Sight, we never missed it. The peculiar Mark we distinguisht it by, was the large Wound in the Tail, which was lacerated by the Fish-spear, when it fell off, and in constant swimming near our Vessel discover'd it very plainly to us; all which time it kept Pace with us, and rested no more than we.

*An Account of the Cramp-fish.* We had not the luck of seeing a Cramp-fish,[1] for an Experiment, all the Voyage; but Dr. *Kempfer*,[2] in his Passage through the *Persian Gulph*, relates how he caught one, and

[1] The Cramp-fish referred to may have been an Electric Ray or Torpedo, an electric sheath-fish (*Malapterurus*), or an electric eel (*Gymnotus*). The story that the shock may be neutralized by holding the breath is purely imaginary. A very dry hand, or the use of a covering or glove of non-conducting material, is the only feasible explanation.

[2] Dr. Englebrecht Kaemfer, 1651–1715, a very celebrated German naturalist, visited the Persian Gulf, Java, Sumatra, Siam, and Japan in his capacity as chief surgeon of the Dutch East India Company. Evidently he had met Ovington, *infra*, p. 150. His collected papers, *Amoenitatum Exoticarum Fasc. V.*, were published in 1712. Other MSS. were purchased by Sir Hans Sloane, among them being his *History of Japan* (London, 1728), recently reprinted in Blackwood's *Universal Library of Standard Authors*. See the *Edinburgh Review*, July 1924, p. 80.

that it struck the Person with a frightful Tremor, whoever touch'd it with Hand or Foot; but the benumming Quality would not reach to the length of a Line or a Pole, according to the vulgar Opinion, and operated only when it was sensibly struck or handled. But the way of preventing this Trembling and Stupidity of him that felt it, was most worthy Observation, because unknown, and scarce mentioned by any Writer. For a certain Person on Board, to the Amazement of all that saw him, could touch the Torpedo as oft as any, and was never affected by any Insensibility upon it. He was shy of divulging his Receipt, but by Importunities was at length won to declare the Secret, which consisted only in holding in his Breath very hard when he touched it. The rest upon Trial found it true. And the Reason for this (as 'tis supposed) is, that stifling the Breath, and detaining the Spirits, repels the Force of that Narcotick or stupifying Quality which issues from the Body of the Cramp-fish.

*The way of trying the Current of the Water at Sea.*

At our approaching the *Æquator* the Winds grew calm, the Sails flapt to the Mast, and the Face of the Ocean was as smooth as that of a Crystal Mirrour. This gave an Opportunity to our Commander of sending out his Boat to try the Current of the Water. For even in the Main Sea are sometimes such Streams and strong Tides, and imperceptible Currents, as carry a Ship many Degrees in Longitude beyond the Observation of the expertest Navigator, before ever he knows where he is, if he be not help'd by his Azimuth Compass. An Instance of this Nature happen'd while I was in *India*. An *East-India* Ship bound for *Bombay*, was suppos'd by the Master of her to be near that Haven, upon his first sight of Land; but making better Observation, he found himselfe driven many Degrees to the Westward, very near *Muscat*[1] in *Arabia Fœlix*, which lies upon the *Persian* Gulph. For this no Reason can be alledged, besides the undiscernible Currents of the Water, which carry the Ships so wide from that place, which by their Course they steered towards: For in one Hours time the Water runs above a League, some-

[1] Muscat, *vide infra*, p. 245 ff.

times in the very midst of the Ocean. And another Ship bound for the same Port, was upon the first Discovery of Land very near the Coast of *Persia*. Therefore the wary Pilots, when the Winds are silent, and the Sea calm, use this Expedient for trying the Motion of the Water, which way, and how fast the Currents set. At Seven Minutes Distance from the Line, our Commander mann'd out the Boat, with the chief Mate in it, and ordered it to be rowed about half a League from the Ship. They took with them in the Boat a Basket, into which they put Forty or Fifty Pound Weight of Iron or Lead, which tied to a Line of eighty, or an hundred Fathom length, they dropt into the Sea; by whose Weight the Boat was fixt as immovably and steddy, as if it were at an Anchor. After this they cast out the Log-board, which discovers the Tide-way of the Water, and by the Half-Minute Glass which they set a running, they know how fast the Stream runs. For at certain Distances of the Line, to which the Log-board is fastned, are certain Knots, for every one of which that the Board drew off, while the Glass runs, they reckon a Mile. The Tide set here Northward, but not very fast. This Experiment of finding out the Swiftness of the Current, and to what Points it runs, is never attempted but in a perfect Calm, when both the Winds and the Sea are peaceable and still; which is the reason that Mariners, by not meeting with such an opportunity, are sometimes driven very distant from their designed Port.

*The Experiment of an empty Bottle let down into the Ocean.*

The Sailers at this time let down an empty Bottle into the Water tied to the Basket, with a Cork in the Mouth of it, so very large, that a Mallet could not drive it in further; and yet the Cork was forc'd into the Bottle in its Descent, and the Bottle was drawn up full of Salt Water.

*Two remarkable effects of the Heat under the Line.*

Under the Line there is such a constant brooding Heat, that the Rain Water which has been receiv'd in Casks, has been full of small Worms in less than four Hours time. Nor can any Care prevent the rusting of the best polish'd Steel or Iron, nor hinder the best temper'd Blade in *England* from being apt to stand bent, by reason of the warm insinuating *Æther*, which softens its Spring and Elastick Spirit.

# THE ISLAND OF ANNOBON[1]

THE first Land we made after our crossing the Æquinoctial, was *Annobon*, which lies in the Latitude of one and a half, and is reckon'd about Ten Leagues in its Circumference. We were driven unhappily to the Leeward of it, and luffed up to it for the space of two days, but were hindred from fetching it, by its lying directly in the Eye of the Wind. It had the name of *Annobon* given it, because it was first discovered upon the first Day of the Year. Annobon *describ'd.*

The scarcity of our fresh Provisions, which by this time were almost spent, made us beat up to Windward more vigorously, especially when we heard that they were to be purchased at such easie rates, that a roasting Pig might be bought for a Sheet of Paper. *Its great Plenty.*

But tho' we judg'd our selves unfortunate in not being able to reach this plentiful Island, yet we were pleas'd with the Prospect which we had of it, because we had been long Strangers to such a Sight. And it gratified us with the fragrant Smells which were wafted from the Shoar,[2] from whence

[1] Annobon is a tiny island off Cape Lopez, with a fertile soil, and densely-wooded mountains rising to a height of 3,000 feet. It was frequently a port of call in the old days. The inhabitants are illiterate half-castes. It was so called because the Portuguese discovered it on the 'Dia de Anno Bom', New Year's Day, 1473.

[2] Cf.

As when to them who sail
Beyond the Cape of Hope, and now are past
Mozambic, off at sea north-east winds blow
Sabean odours from the spicy shore
Of Araby the Blest, with such delay
Well pleased they slack their course, and many a league
Cheered with the grateful smell old Ocean smiles.

*P. L.* iv. 159 ff.

and also Bishop Heber's

Spicy breezes
Blow soft o'er Ceylon's isle.

*Land smell'd by the Sailers at a great distance.* at three Leagues distance we scented the Odours of Flowers and fresh Herbs. And what is very observable, when after a tedious Stretch at Sea, we have deem'd our selves to be near Land by our Observation and Course, our Smell in dark and misty Weather has outdone the Acuteness of our Sight; and we have discover'd Land by the fresh Smells, before we discern'd it with our Eyes.

The Inhabitants observing our Toil and Industry to stretch into the Harbour, made Fires on Shoar to give us Light in the Night time, and sent off to us with some Oranges and Fowls a Canoo or two, that is, a long sharp Boat fashion'd out of one piece of Timber, which was rowed with Six Oars. The Islanders that came in it were formerly known to some on Board us, whom we conferred with concerning their Belief, and the Religion which they professed. They confess'd themselves of the *Roman* Faith, and were eminent Believers *The Ignorance of the People.* of that Church by the profound Ignorance which they profess'd, in scarce knowing what Mass meant, or the Pope from the great Mogul. They were born in *Africa*, and, bating the Name of Catholicks, were as Heathenish, as if they had never come from thence, which they ascrib'd to their want of Priests among them. No Priests! This amaz'd me, and put me to a stand, to consider how those who travel Sea and Land to make Proselytes, to whom neither *Siam*, *China*, nor *Japan* are esteemed too remote a Pilgrimage for making Converts, should yet neglect a place so nigh as *Annobon*, overlook a Care so much nearer. Surely some fatal Disease, some Infectious Air must ravage and lay waste the place, that affrighted those zealous Fathers from inhabiting among them. No, the Air was healthful and serene, the Island fruitful, but very poor; they know of no reigning Distempers among them, unless we would account Poverty one. They were stor'd with plenty of Provisions, and indigent in nothing but Gold and Silver, of which they had none. Or if they were Masters of a little of that at some chance time, the first Priest that happen'd to come upon the Island, was certain of draining it by Confessions, whose stay was never longer among them, than the Money lasted, but his Minutes were always spent as soon as their Mites. Now I imagin'd that a place, where was such scarcity of Wealth, should have best suited with those whose Profession is Poverty; because they seem then to be in their proper Element, and freed from the Temptations of Riches, which they voluntarily renounce. And that the Eastern Nations, which abound in Wealth and Luxury, should be less frequented by Men that pretend to be dead to the World.

*The great Convenience of some Harbours.*

Upon this Island, as well as upon many others, the Road for Ships lieth conveniently on the Leeside, as at St. *Thomas*, which is under the Line, *Ascension, St. Helena, St. Jago, Mauritius*, and many more, as well in the *East* as *West Indies*, which are by an All-wise Providence made this way serviceable for avoiding the danger of Shipwrack, which would be inevitable on the Weather-side, when the Winds blew fresh, and the Seas were high. For in these places the Winds generally hang towards one Quarter, which renders the opposite part of the Island calm and safe. And though some few Islands are observ'd destitute of this Convenience in their Harbours, and are not so well accommodated with Ports for the securing of Ships, yet are these very rare, and for the most part not very necessary for Navigators to come near them. With such an Infinite Wisdom are all things contriv'd for the peculiar Ends and Designs to which they serve!

# THE COAST OF AFRICA[1]

*Part of* Africa.

NOT long after this we espy'd the Coast of *Africa*, a Degree Northward of the River *Congo*, and coming near the Shoar were becalm'd and driven backward in one Night's time five Leagues towards the North. But that Misfortune was drown'd by the Pleasure we receiv'd in the refreshment of abundance of Rain which fell that Night, a Drop of which we had not seen for at least two Months before. The richest Wine could not please our Palates with half that Delight, as this Blessing which descended from Heaven in Showers upon us. For being all this while under the hot Influence of the Sun-Beams confin'd to the Torrid Region, the Provisions, being salt Beef, and the Water in the Cask so unsavoury and corrupt, that to quench our Thirst we must stifle our smelling, and shut our Nostrils when we open'd our Mouths; and of this poor stinking Liquor, in all this Feverish Weather, the Allowance being only a Quart a Day, this made a Glass of this fresh Liquor drink most pleasant, and cheer'd our Hearts, as if they had been refresh'd with the noblest Wine. For impatient of letting it fall into the Tubs, which were placed upon the Decks on purpose to receive the falling Water, no Wine was more greedily catcht at by the Vulgar out of publick Conduits on a solemn Day, that the Rain was by the Sailers in their Bowls and Hats. Such a Relish does a

*Scarcity of Water on Board.*

[1] Ovington landed in the country of Malemba or Molamba, now Portuguese territory, slightly north of the mouth of the Congo river. Malemba, with the adjacent lands of Loango and Kabinda, is highly praised by travellers, and fully justifies Ovington's enthusiastic remarks. The seaport of Kabinda (which may be the actual spot where the *Benjamin* dropped anchor), 'from the beauty of its situation, and the fertility of the adjacent country, has been called the paradise of the coast'. The inhabitants are Bantu negroes, and are energetic and enterprising. Possibly Ovington had read Pigafetta's *Report of the Kingdome of Congo* (1597). See *Enc. Brit.*[11], and Proyart's *Loango*, in Pinkerton's *Voyages*, xvi. 551.

starved Appetite find even in course Fare! To such Inconveniences are Men sometimes driven by tedious Voyages!

Stretching along this Shoar, a Strand extended in the Semicircle of more than twenty Leagues, presented us with a most delightful Prospect, which received in its Bosom *Neptune*'s rowling Waves upon an even and plain Surface. Above this extended Plain were several gently rising Hills, cloathed with Grass and variety of Trees, all in their Summer Livery. This unexpected Verdure of the Fields tempted us to fancy our selves rather in *Europe* again, than upon the Confines of scorcht *Africk*. Such was the Beauty of the pleasant Fields and fruitful Valleys, the Gayety of the Woods, and diversity of Inclosures, cut out by Nature, rather than cultivated by Art, that it would almost foil the Pencil of a Painter to outdo the Original, but surely it would afford him Ground for an admirable Landskip. The Fertility of this populous Climate, which lies within the Torrid Zone, has quite confuted the Opinion of blind Antiquity, which could not discern the Life of either Man, or Vegitable there. I could not behold any great Plenty of Corn or Grain; but this proceeded rather from the Native Laziness, than from the Penury of the Soil, whose Native Turf seem'd well prepar'd for Fertility and Production; but it abounds with store of Fruits, particularly Coco-Nuts, and the most fragrant Pine-Apple, which carries the Precedence from all the rest, whose Excellencies are center'd there, and exert themselves in its incomparable Taste and Smell. Abundance of well-grown Deer are ranging in the Fields and Pastures, whose Fatness is very apt to make them almost a Prey to a nimble Footman, without the Assistance of any Hound. But Horses and black Cattle are not many.

*The pleasant Shoar.*

*The fruitfulness of the place.*

We were not yet come to an Anchor, which continued the scarcity of our Water, notwithstanding the former shower; and made us prize it almost equal with our Wine, with which we were well stockt from the fruitful Island of *Madeira*; but on a sudden we were more concern'd and affrighted at the sight we had of that Element, than we were refresh'd by it. For we espy'd very near us a mighty Mass of Water drawn up

*A Spout at Sea.*

into the Air from the Surface of the Ocean, in fashion of a large round Pipe, incircled with a hoary Mist, or grey Cloud; it rose gradually, and for some time hover'd there, till at length it fell in such a Cataract, such a Torrent and mighty Flood, that no Ship was able to sustain its fall, but would sink and founder by its Weight. This Spout, which is a kind of Aqueduct between the Clouds and the Ocean, put us in a great Fear of its ruinous Descent upon us, had we not industriously steered from it, and kept to Windward. But if there is no avoiding the likelihood of being driven under it, there are two ways prescrib'd for breaking its pendulous resting in the Air before a Ship comes too near it. The first, which is seldom used by any Protestant, prevents its Danger by a kind of Charm. When they espy a Spout at Sea at some distance from them, the Master of the Ship, or any one else a-board, kneels down by the Mast with a Knife in his Hand, which has a black Handle; and reading in St. *John*[1] the Verse of our Saviours Incarnation, *Et verbum Caro facta est, & habitavit in nobis,* he turns towards the Spout, and with the Inchanted Knife makes a Motion in the Air, as if he would cut it in two, which, he says, breaks in the middle, and lets the inclosed Water fall with a Noise into the Sea. Another Method for preventing all Peril that might arise from this Mass of Water suckt up from the Ocean, is to fire a Cannon or two, when they are near it, which immediately shakes and dissolves its threatning Suspension aloft, and this softer Thunder and Lightning scatters and dissolves it from its unnatural Position. What the Quality of this Water is, which is thus powerfully exhaled, whether fresh, or mixt with Saline Particles, those that had the Fate to try, had scarce the Happiness to discover; but sure the Phænomenon is very stupendous and unaccountable, that such a vast Body of Water

*The way of breaking a Spout.*

[1] The Last Gospel, i.e. St. John i. 1–14, vulgarly known as the *In Principio*, was looked upon as a powerful charm and exorcism in the Middle Ages. Cf. Tyndale, iii. 61: 'Such is the *limiter's* saying of *In Principio erat Verbum* from house to house'; and Chaucer, *Prologue*, 254.

should by a forcible extraction out of the Sea bubble and mount upwards, like a small Rivulet springing up into the Air. And indeed, the Works of the Almighty are inscrutable, and these may be some of *his Wonders in the Deep*, which the Royal Prophet extolled and was amazed at.

Having arrived within four Leagues of the Shoar, Eight *Negroes* came towards us in a *Canoo*, who stood upright as they rowed, and looked forward, contrary to our Proverbial Observation. The Shaft of their Oars was framed out of a long piece of Timber, and a thin broad square board resembling a wooden Trencher, serve for the Blade. They had caught in their Boat a Shark, of a different shape from the common Fish of that Name, and of a different appellation; for on each side of his Mouth grew a large piece of Flesh, six Inches broad, in form of a Shovel, which gave it the Name of Shovel-mouth; and at the extremity of those parts were the Eyes placed, as Centinels at the Out-Guards to preserve the Body.[1] With these came two of the Principal Men of the place, one of them appertaining to the King, the other a Retainer to the *Mafoucko* or General. Upon their Heads they wore Caps very Curious and Costly, the Work of the Natives, wrought with so much Ingenuity and Art of the Needle, that they are not only valued there, but admired in all the parts whither the *Europeans* carry them. Their Expence in Cloathing is otherwise small, as the Garb is that they put on, which only consists in a Clout about the middle, to hide their Nakedness; and the Furs of an Hare or some such Animal, which hangs down before them between their Leggs, which they value as the richest Ermin or Sables. Their frizled Hair was tyed up in a Bunch upon the Crown of the Heads of some of them, others wore it neatly braided behind. Some cut their Hair in the figure of a Cross, others were shaved all bare, excepting a small Tuft above, like a *Mahometan* Lock, as each Man's Humour or Fancy led him.

*Hammer Fish.*

*A Shark called a Shovel-Mouth.*

*Curious Caps made in* Africa.

*The Cloaths of the Natives.*

[1] The reference seems to be to the Hammer-headed Shark (*Zygaena*), in which the anterior portion of the head is produced into a lobe on each side, the extremity of which is occupied by the eye.

*Their Ornaments.* On each side of their Temples, and on their Fore-heads, the Skin was raised, as if it were with the pricking of a Pin, in Figures of a Diamond cut; which with them is not only a Badge of Honour and Character of Greatness, but is esteem'd a sort of Cosmetick to the Face, and admired as Fucus[1] and Black Patches are with us.

Coral Beads, Coories, or Indian-shels, and Black Jet Beads are wore as Ornaments about their Necks; and about their Wrists, ten or twelve Wreaths of Brass, Iron, or Copper.

*Ill Language not allowed of.* These *Africans* are by Nature apprehensive of the least Affront, tho' it proceeds no farther than Ignominious Expressions. Scurrility and reproachful Words are so detestable, that a Penalty is imposed on all foul and abusive Language, according to the quality of the Offender, and the Person abused. The *Scandalum Magnatum*[2] is in force among these Heathens. For since Urbanity and good Words are things so pleasant in themselves, and so easily attainable, and a pleasant Look and Expression may as soon be given, as what are Sowre and Offensive, they pity no Man that either loses his Friend, or Fortune by course Behaviour and rude Expressions; since Courtesie and a debonaire Air are like Letters Commendatory, which a person may at all times carry about him, to render him grateful unto others, and others acceptable unto him.

*The Fateish its Virtue.* They Travel no where without their *Fateish*[3] about them, one of which looked like the small end of a Stag's Horn, with a Bell tied to it, about the bigness of a Man's Thumb. But each of them has his own made of such Materials, as the Priests, or *Mafouko* think fit to bestow upon them. To these *Fateishes* they ascribe their Security from Peril and Mischief,

[1] Cosmetic, rouge.

[2] Defamation of persons in high office, 'speaking evil of dignities'.

[3] 'In the craft of the West African sorcerer (*mganga*) a principal part is played by what the English in Africa (using the Portuguese *feitiço*, charm or amulet) call "fetiches", which are claws, fangs, roots, stones, and any other odds and ends fancied to be inhabited by spirits or invested with superhuman power.' *Encyc. Brit.*[9] xv. 200. See also Hobson-Jobson, *s.v.* Fetish.

and believe themselves safe from danger, while they carry them about them. They appear to be to them instead of *Talismans*, whose Figures are supposed to act upon Natural Things, so as to drive away from any place, Rain, Hail, or Wild and Venomous Beasts, by occult and Sympathetick [1] Virtues, which the Ignorant People incongruously ascribe to Magick, or Sorcilege; such were *Virgil's* Brazen Fly, and Golden Horseleach, with which he hindred Flies from entring *Naples*, and killed all the Horse-Leaches in a Ditch: [2] And the Figure of a Stork placed by *Apollonius* at *Constantinople*, to drive those Birds thence, in the Year 1660. And that at *Florence* made against the Gout by a Carmelite, named, *Julianus Ristonius a Prato*. Unless you will rather imagin that the Ignorance of these People in these great Secrets of Nature, and their too great Familiarity with the Devil, may make us think their Characters Magical and Diabolical; whose Virtues for the most part depend rather upon a tacit, or express Compact with the Evil Spirit. For I believe in this, as well as other Nations, there are some who have entred into Leagues and Diabolical Associations with Infernal Spirits, by whom they have been inabled to effect things above the common reach of Human Nature. Upon several occasions the Natives make use of these Inchantments or Images, but particularly in the preservation of their Trees laden with Fruit, upon which while they fix one of these Figures, no Native dare approach to take it. The ancient *Romans* were much addicted to these superstitious

[1] Sir J. G. Frazer points out that all magic is sympathetic, i.e. the belief that things act on one another by a secret link due to similarity. *Similia similibus curantur. Encyc. Brit.*[11] xvii. 305, and Hastings, *Encyc. Rel. and Ethics, s.v.* Magic.

[2] The extraordinary mass of medieval legends by which the poet Virgil was transformed from a poet to a necromancer will be found summed up in *Encyc. Brit.*[11] xxviii. 116, *The Virgil Legend.* The story of the Brazen Fly is first found in John of Salisbury (1115–1180). They were collected in French under the title of *Les Faitz Merveilleux de Virgille, c.* 1499.

Vanities, and ascrib'd the safety of their City and Empire to the *Palladium* which fell down from *Jupiter*.

*A Floating Island.* A floating Island washed from the Shoar, sailed by our Ship, extended about an hundred Foot in length and breadth, overspread with Grass of three Foot height, tho' it grew so near the Line. We judged it was bore down by the River *Zaire* into the Sea; for this River has 400 Leagues course, and is very rapid, by reason of the many Cataracts, or great Falls which it has from the Mountains. At its entrance into the Estates of *Congo* (upon which account it sometimes borrows this Name) it inlarges it self much, embraces quantity of Islands, and at its Mouth expatiates into Eight or Ten Leagues in breadth; yet throweth its Water near thirty Leagues farther into the Sea, with so great a violence, that it retains its natural Colour, (if not Sweetness) as we observed, without being any more than dasht with the Salt Waters of the Sea. But it forceth its Waters along the Shoar with more ease, and therefore presseth them much farther, as far almost as *Cape Lopus*,[1] which is about Two Degrees Southward from the *Æquinoctial*. But the Saltness of the Springs on Shoar is not less remarkable, than the freshness of the River in the Ocean, and carrying its Waters uncorrupted at that distance into the Sea; for when in the Sea it is Tide of Ebb, there is a sensible Saltness in the fresh Springs that are near it, but according as the Waters of the Ocean rise and swell in the Tide of Flood, the sweetness and freshness of the Springs increase and return again.

*The River* Zaire *[Congo].*

*Its not mixing with salt Water.*

*The Saltness of some fresh springs near the Sea.*

*The Fruits and Commodities.* The places situate near this River, such as *Loango* and *Cabenda*, are indifferent Fertile in Grains, afford excellent Fruits, Wine of Palms; breed many Cattle, and all things necessary for Life are found here: They are well stored with Elephants, in which they abound more than any adjacent Countries, by which they have quantities of Ivory, but nothing of Gold or Silver. Those Metals are of no esteem with them. They value all Metals according to their Bulk; for a Pewter Bason is preferred with them to one of Silver of less

*Their contempt of our Mony.*

[1] Cape Lopez.

quantity and size, and a large Brass Ring to a small one of Gold. We offered them a Dollar for a Dung-hill Fowl, which they rejected, and exchanged at the same time for half a dozen Needles. For these they thought they might have use for, but our Money was an useless, dead Commodity. The Money current among themselves, is small Matts of Grass, very thin, about sixteen Inches square; for one of which they buy three *Kankies*,[1] or small farthing Cakes, when Corn is dear, and five when it is cheap. They use these Matts in adorning their Bodies, and covering their Private Parts.

*Their Mony current among them.*

The Air is very hot and sulphurous, as must be expected from a place in this Climate, but the Natives endure it with ease, are healthful and vigǒrous, are as well proportion'd, and in their shapes of as exact Symetry, as any in the World; and the Inhabitants are numerous.

*The nature of the Climate.*

Instead of that soft Wool which Cloatheth Sheep, a harsh kind of hair, not unlike that which grows upon Dogs, is the usual excressence; the supple Oily Particles are wasted and dried up by the intense Heat of the Weather, which gives it that roughness and stubborn quality. The like I observ'd in the Sheep that are in the *Indies*.

*Hard Wool upon their Sheep.*

[1] Kankies are small cakes of maize-flour.

## MALEMBA

*The Present to the* Mafouko.

AT *Malemba* our Commander sent to the *Mafouko*, as a Present, a large Cheese with two Bottles of Brandy; which he return'd with a Kidd, a small Calebash of Palm Wine, a Cock, and a little Vessel of Lime-juice; deliver'd to us by those who brought them, in the English Dialect, a Language to which many of them have in some manner attain'd, by the frequent Traffick and stay of the English in those parts. Among those who were pleased to give us a Visit on board, was the little *Mafouko*, or Deputy General, who while he diverted himself with us, espyed among the Negroes, a Native of that Country, who was formerly sold from thence, and falling into the Hands of our Commander, was brought thither again to attend him in the Voyage. The Deputy General disguised his knowledge of him a while, and cast only a negligent Eye towards him, 'till the Negro observing it, approached him with Ceremony, and gave him the Regards of the Country.

*Their mutual Salutation.*

Their mutual Salutations were after this manner, the *Cafree*[1] at some distance bowed his Head, and fell upon his Knees, and rising up a little after, clapt his Hands together four or five times, the *Mafouko* then clapt his Hands together likewise four or five times; upon this the Black addressed nearer him, so that they mutually joined their Palms together first, and then joined their own Hands four or five times; this ended the particular Ceremony with the *Mafouko*; which was repeated by the Negro to every principal Man on board; and then in conclusion, as a token of publick Mirth and universal Joy for the happy meeting, they loudly clapt all of them their Hands together, and the Salutation ended.

*Their Civility and Condescension.*

The inequality of their Condition made them not forget the Complement of a condescending carriage to this Inferiour Slave, who were no way Barbarous in their Behaviour, whatever they were in their Opinions, but as the access to their Per-

[1] Cafree, Kaffir, a native of Africa, from Ar. *kāfir*, infidel.

sons was very easie, so was their Humour smoothed with a complaisance, void of all supercilious stiffness and Morosity.

*The Respect given to great men.* Not only the Prince, but all others of the highest Figure and Quality are served upon the Knee, by the Attendants that Minister to them. This is the usual manner too of supplicating an Alms, or asking any considerable Favour; and in this posture one of those on board requested a Bottle of Brandy, a Liquor highly esteem'd by the Noblest among them.

*Aparrel or Garb.* The more Eminent and Noted wore a sort of Nightrale of Net-work about their Shoulders, very close wrought, either White or Black, made of one entire piece, with a Hole in the middle, of that convenient size that they thrust their Heads thro' it, when they put it on; but some of them delight themselves with an *English* Dress, if they can purchase it from any of our Nation, but then 'tis never wore but at great Solemnities, and on stated Days. I wish they had used our Language as innocently, as they did our Garments, and that they had been less accustomed to the execrable sin of Swearing by the Name of God, and the habitual venting of horrid Oaths.[1] This custom they impiously Imbibed by their Conversation with our Sailors, whose frequent Oaths made them believe them an Elegance of our Speech, and the most laudable Expressions they could use; and this deadly sin they now digest with as much ease, as the young Maid, whom *Albertus*[2] reports, brought her Stomach to live upon Spiders.

*Swearing used among them.*

*Their Faces painted.* The second Person of Eminence who came to visit us, had all his Face besmear'd with Red Paint, a thing customary among the Nobler Rank; as in *India* this Colour is put upon their Cattle, especially their Horses, and is the usual Paint of their Fruit Trees. This *Epiphanius*[3] reports of the *Egyptians*; that tho' they had forgotten the History of the Work

[1] Compare a similar statement of Clement Downing, *History of the Indian Wars*, ed. Foster, p. 77.

[2] The celebrated scholastic philosopher, *c.* A.D. 1200.

[3] A father of the Church, *c.* A.D. 400, an opponent of Origen and a rival of St. Chrysostom.

of God, yet they rubbed over their Cattle with a Red sort of Keil,[1] to save them that no Evil should befall them that Year; ignorantly Counterfeiting that Blood Sprinkled upon the Lintels of their Doors, which saved the *Israelites* once in *Ægypt*. But how this Custom should be derived to these Nations from the *Israelites* and *Ægyptians*, or whether they practise it upon that Superstitious account which the *Egiptians* did, to secure them from Misfortune, I could not learn, I rather believe that they use it as an Ornament, because it looks lively and Gay.

*The ordinary Food of the Poor People.* The Diet of the common People is very ordinary, and seldom reacheth the Flesh of any Animal, which is not prohibited them by any Law, but their Inability to purchase it. Corn, and Herbs, and Spring Water are their common Food. Sometimes they Feast with a little Fish, and that with a few Pindars[2] is esteemed a splendid Banquet. These Pindars are sown under ground, and grow there without sprouting above the surface, the Cod in which they are Inclosed is an Inch long, like that of our Pease and Beans, and they are eat with Beef or Pork instead of our Beans or Pease. Some of these I brought for *England*, which were sown in the Bishop of *London*'s Garden, but whether they will thrive in this Climate is yet uncertain. The Flesh which they eat, they never account Palatable, till it grows unsavory; they expose it upon the Roofs of their Houses till the moisture is exhausted, and it looks like dryed Fish; and sometimes bury it under ground, till it proves tender by being tainted. *Their Temperance.* They Indulge not their Appetites with Excesses, nor force upon themselves Diseases by over-loading of their Stomachs, but Eat according to the Rules of Nature, for Health, and not for Luxury, and live according to Nature's Periods, to Seventy, or Eighty Years of Age, Healthful and Sound. They are wiser than to cut short the thread of Life, by that Meat which should prolong it.

The extent of Dominions, and Love of Wealth, are as

[1] A kind of red ochre or ruddle, used for marking sheep, &c.

[2] Pindar or Pinda (Port.) is the ground-nut, *Arachis hypogaea*.

prevalent with those that are placed in the highest Orbs of Fortune here, as they are with other Monarchs of the Earth. A Native Ambition renders those that are Powerful, as well as men of lower Stations, restless and troublesome, and sets them upon soaring higher and higher, insomuch that a hot War is now on foot between the two Kings of *Malemba* and *Cabinde*, commenced upon the departure of a Beautiful Woman from the Country of *Malemba* to the King of *Cabinde*. But the truer Original of this War, is the desire of Conquest for the sake of Subjects, who as soon as they are Captives are made Slaves, and in the multitude of them the Strength and Wealth of their Kingdoms consist. Arms and Ammunition are the undeniable Commodities, for which they exchange their Slaves, and in the use of which they grow expert; but Bows and Arrows are their own proper Instruments of War, and the Weapons commonly, and very dexterously used: Their Bowstrings are made of the Rhine or outside of a Cane.

*The occasion of a War.*

*Their Arms.*

To preserve the Line of their Kings untainted, they make choice of the King's Sister's Son,[1] to be always Hereditary in the Soveraignty, imagining that the Female Off-Spring secures the Succession more than the Male, and in this she is under no Confinement to any single Person, but is allowed her Choice out of the whole Kingdom, to satisfie her Desires, and gratifie her Fancy with whom she thinks fit; and thus without any Censure or Blemish to her Character, she takes her liberty with Subject or Foreigner, *African* or *European* at her will; imitating in this the *Lacedemonians*, a *Wise and Grave People*, who permitted their Wives, for the Procreation of a generous Progeny, to be familiar with any Stranger, whose company they hop'd might Improve the Off-Spring. And thus likewise upon the *Malabar* Coast,[2] the first Nights lodging is allowed the *Bramin*, when the King Marries any

*The Succession of the Crown.*

*The liberty given the Queen.*

[1] This system of matriarchy is still common among the Nairs and other S. Indian tribes. See the list of authorities quoted in Crooke's note on Fryer i. 133, note 3.

[2] For the *Jus primae Noctis* in Malabar, see Hamilton, *New Account* (ed. 1727), i. 308–9.

person; and therefore the Sister's Sons, as in *Africa*, and not the King's, are Heirs to the Crown, because the Blood Royal runs certainly in their Veins. And the King's Sisters are also indulged here the freedom of bestowing their Virginity on whom they please.

*Circumcision used here.* The Natives of *Malemba* retain among them the use of Circumcision, and of admitting Children into their Religion by that Ceremony, which one among them, dedicated to that Office, performs upon them. Neither are they unmindful of a due Veneration to the great Creator of all Things, nor so far lost to all Sacred Thoughts, as to neglect a constant Homage to him, and a stated Exercise of solemn Worship; and in this they exceed what Christianity prescribes, and for our Seventh, appoint every Fifth Day Sacred for Religious Duties; *Every fifth Day appointed to be kept holy.* on which Day they convene their People, who unanimously assemble in a Publick Congregation. On this Day some Person of Years and Discretion, of Repute for Sobriety and Civil Converse, entertain the Youth and those of greener Years with strong Disswasives from the customary Vices of Stealth, Impurity, Adultery, and Murther; and with all the Rhetorick which Nature taught him, and Zeal inspires him with, disclaims against those Criminal Practices, and raises his Invectives against Vice and Folly, and whatever is odious and prohibited among them. For all the hainous Vices are under a Proscription with them, as well as us, and are only committed by daring Profligates. The Terror of immediate Punishment is not the only Restraint from these Commissions, but the sage Admonisher affrights their Consciences with a future miserable state, in the dreadful Society of *Benimbe*, that is, the Devil, if they obstinately persist in Wickedness; and encourages them with the Promise of being hereafter happy with *Zammampoango*, which signifies God, if they carefully advert to, and practise his Instructions. *Their Notion of God, and the Souls Immortality.* These Ignorant Heathens have not yet lost the Notices of the Soul's Immortality, and the Impressions of future Rewards and Punishments are fresh and undefaced among them. I enquired of them what their Sentiments and Notions were of their *Zammampoango?* They told me that he inhabited above. Then I further asked, whether they meant by that, the glorious Lights above, the Sun, the Moon, or the Heavens? They answered, No, but he who had Dominion over them, who made them by his Power, and this visible World we stand upon.

*The Devil's Cruelty to some of the People.*

They generally affirm'd that *Benimbe* is frequently in the Fields cover'd with Mists and thick Darkness, where he sometimes exercises his Infernal Authority over infamous and lewd Persons, in the milder Chastisements of some, and severer Treatment, even as far as the loss of Life, of others. Therefore they are terrified from walking abroad in dark and gloomy Weather, because they expect nothing but Horror and Misery from that Spirit of Darkness. This Infernal Spirit in all his wild Insults and Frolicks over them, is careful to preserve his Appearance as dark as the place he chuses to revel in, scarce assumes any lasting Form, and is known by nothing so much as the plentiful effects of his Stripes and severer Strokes upon their Bodies. He conceals the Deformity which he usually makes of his Figure, whilst he exercises the Malignity of his Temper. Some die of the Bruises they have received from him, and others have been confin'd to their Beds, as they assured me several times, and therefore they avoid the Fields in rainy dull Weather, that they may escape the force of his Malice, who is ashamed to appear abroad by Light, but chuses these melancholy Seasons for inflicting his Vengeance, to which he seems to have most right, as he is a Spirit of Darkness.

*A Negroe impal'd for committing several murthers.*

Walking along the Shoar, we were arrested by a very deplorable Spectacle, a lusty Negro stretched Dead upon the Sand, who, after the manner of Impaling, had a long Stake thrust up his Fundament, which by a sharp Passage through his Bowels forced its way upwards towards his Head. The dreadful sight at first moved us to condole the sad Object, till we were inform'd of the execrable Villanies which brought him to this lamentable and painful end, and made us applaud the Justice of those who were the Executioners of this

Vengeance upon him. For no Severity was able to match those Crimes wherein he had been a long and skilful Practitioner; even this Destiny, tho' so horrid and severe, will yet be thought Indulgence, and an Act of Clemency. This Miscreant being possess'd with a Spirit of Cruelty, and actuated by Malice, had successfully contriv'd the Death of near twenty Persons about this place, by mixing a deadly Poison with the Palm Wine, which he seasonably offer'd for the refreshment of their parched Palates. This deadly Liquor was not subject to any suspicion of being mortal, because the Juice of the Palm, with which it was intermixt, was a Liquor so common and inoffensive, and their best and most pleasing Drink. The King therefore, upon the Information of this Fellow's treacherous dispatching of his Subjects by such poysonous Draughts, immediately decreed a Punishment, and sentenc'd the Criminal to this torturing Death, peculiar only to such barbarous Villans. The News of which made him seek a Refuge among the Desarts and the most inhabitable parts of the Country; but the pursuit after him was so vigorous, that no Thickets could shelter or secure him, the whole Country hotly pursued him, and chased him as a common Enemy, till at length he fell a Victim to their just Rage upon this Shore; where his noisom Carcase, being under an Interdict of being Interr'd (the ordinary manner of burying among them) became as loathsom and offensive as his Life had been, and was left a Prey to the Savages of the Wilderness, and the wild Beasts of the Field. The unusual manner of tormenting this Malefactor, by exposing his Body to the Inclemency of the Weather, and the Beasts of Prey, was wisely design'd by the King as a Terror to such abominable flagitious Practices, and to retain the People in their Duty.

*The* Africans *given to Poisoning.*

The Art of Poysoning is what these *Africans* do very commonly exceed in, and to which they are generally propense upon any occasional Quarrel or Abuse. They seldom discover a generous Resentment by an open Challenge, or disputing it in the Field by the Dint of the Sword, or the force of a Bullet; their dark Complexion inclines them rather to vent their Anger by clandestine Courses, to destroy by the swift effects of Poyson, and mortal Infusions of the Juices of Herbs, in which they industriously acquire a Skill, that in their Designs against a Man's Life, they may be ready and prepared to put their Revenge in Execution that way. Their sly and crafty Natures keep them from endeavouring to right themselves at the hazard of a publick Vindication; but that inhumane Rage and Animosity which is excited in them by a preceding Provocation, being commonly accompanied with Cowardise and sordid Fear, puts them upon avoiding all Dangers incident to themselves, and contriving the Ruin of those they hate, by some covert Method, and after an obscure way. Doing herein what *Asinius Pollio* did to *Plancus*, against whom he writ a Libel, but deferred to publish it, till after his Death, because he was then secure from all sharp Replies.

They practise this Diabolical Art with as much Secresie as Skill; so that it is neither easily discern'd when they are about it, nor is it always discover'd by any visible immediate Effects. They qualifie the violent poysonous Qualities with some mitigating Ingredients, and the lurking Operation will by that means sometimes not discover it self in a Month's or a Year's space, as some of our English have affirm'd. Which cautions the more wary *Europeans*, who traffick with these People, from treating them with any Indecency of Offence, and keeps them always very circumspect and abstemious in eating and drinking with them, lest some unknown Miscarriage might expose their Lives to their Hatred and Discontents. For they know that all Degrees of Anger are least dangerous, when most seen, and then most pernicious when they lurk under a Disguise and dissembled Temper.

This inhuman Practice is not less customary among the *Indians*, who by this detestable Vice have been very fatal to the free Conversation of *Christians* among them. For in *India*, where Punch of *Arak*[1] is the ordinary chearful Enter-

[1] Punch is from Hind. *Pānch*, 'five', alluding to the five ingredients, viz. arak (the juice of the toddy palm), sugar, lime-juice, spice, and water.

*How the Indian Women poison some, and save others that drink together.*

tainment, it too often happens, that the Black Wench, whose constant Employment is making this Beloved Mixture, will, upon a Disgust, or slight Affront, contrive the Bowl fatal to him that abus'd her, with Safety to all the rest of his Companions. For having infus'd the Poison into the Bowl prepared for the Person that offended her, after presenting it to him, she has been often known, when the next was taking it, to dash it all upon the Ground, by a designed, but pretended Inadvertance. And it rarely fails, but that all that taste it for ever quench their Thirst, and seldom long survive the mortal Draught. This is frequently the effect of the rudeness of unpolish'd Sailers, who shewing a Freedom peculiar to our Northern Nations, but unagreeable to the Niceness of those Eastern Dames, have lavisht away their Lives by a frank innocent Kiss, or railing Expression, and inevitably perisht before they were aware.

# THE ISLAND OF ST. HELENA[1]

WITHIN less than a Month after that we loosed from the Coast of *Africa*, we with much Difficulty weather'd the Island of St. *Helena*; which was taken formerly from the *Dutch*, belonging to the *East-India* Company, by a Grant from the Crown of *England*, situate in about the Sixteenth South Parallel, and as distant from any main Land, as any Island in the World. Hither we brought with us several Refugees from the Tyranny and Persecutions of *France*, who found a competent Subsistence and Relief from the Bounty of the Company upon this Island; some of whom were placed in the more eminent Stations, and advanced to Posts of Dignity and Trust.

*St.*Helena *describ'd.*

*Several French Protestants entertained kindly here.*

They were highly sensible of the comfortable abode they enjoy'd in this distant Region, which was made their Sanctuary in their Miseries; and how much the Misfortunes of their Lives were sweetned by the Kindness they receiv'd from their new Masters. But could not without melancholy Resentments, and hearty Sorrow, recount the various Hardships and Difficulties they strugled with, in making their Escapes from the Rage of their Natural Prince, by whose Commands so many Massacres and Butcheries were acted upon their Fellow Christians, and such frequent bloody Tragedies were lately visible in *France*, fomented by those whose Sanguinary Principles ventilated all those publick

[1] St. Helena, the 'Sea Inn' of the East India Company, was discovered by the Portuguese navigator, João da Nova, on 21 May 1501. Twelve years later it received its first inhabitant, one Fernandez Lopez, who was marooned there. It was visited by Cavendish (1588) and Lancaster (1593). In 1657 it was taken over by the Company; Captain Stringer was appointed Governor, and attempts were made to induce English colonists to settle there. In 1665 and again in 1673 it was seized by the Dutch, but retaken and restored to the Company. The tyranny of the Governor led to a rebellion on the part of the colonists, which was cruelly suppressed; *vide* Hunter, *History of British India*, ii. 200–12.

Calamities; and who stimulated their Prinee by suspicious Chimera's of a possible Conspiraey, to punish his Innoeent Subjeets by Antieipation, for Crimes of whieh perhaps they never might be guilty. By whieh State-Artifiees they pursu'd a Self-interested Revenge, under the barbarous Disguise of euring untimely Jealousies, and preventing unthought of Insurreetions, from which the Protestant Subjeets were as free in their Principles, as they had evideneed themselves to be in their Praetiees; and hoped in God that these unnatural Misehiefs may at length be eurbed, these severe Cruelties, whieh have kept no stand, be at length restrain'd, to their Comfort.[1]

Among those who fled to this Island from the outragious Insults of their Superiours, was one Captain *Porier*, stript of all but the Freedom of his Thoughts and the Serenity of his Mind; who by the Favor of his Patrons was seated in the riehest part of the Island, and allowed there a Maintenanee for Three Sons and Five Daughters whieh eseaped the Perseeution.

*The height of the Island.*

The Land here is very mountainous, and raised to that Height above the Valleys, that we had a sight of it at 25 Leagues distanee at Sea. I question whether *Tenerif* will afford a more distant Prospeet.

*The nature of the Climate.*

It enjoys an Air temperate and serene, to that degree, that the Sky is seldom elouded or overcast, whieh produces a general Clearness in the Natives. And tho it lies so near the *Æquinoctial*, and the Sun was then in the *Zenith*, yet was the Heat so temper'd and allay'd by the gentle Winds that flew along the Land, that the Northermost parts of the Island, espeeially after the Sun's Deseent, made an artifieial Warmth very eonvenient, when the natural was withdrawn. Whereas both *Moscat* in *Arabia*, and *Gombroon* in *Persia*, whieh are at a mueh remoter Distance from the *Æquator*, are at some Seasons of the Year so intensely hot, that the Lungs being destitute of that due Frigidity whieh is necessary for Respiration, are suffocated by the excessive Ferment of the Air,

[1] Revocation of the Edict of Nantes, 1685.

by which both Man and Beast expire. Mr. *Cook* has often reported, that in the time of his abode in *Persia*, a certain Person approaching his Apartment, met with such a hot Breath of Wind at the entrance into his Chamber, that he stagger'd upon the Floor, and fell down upon it just expiring.[1]

*The Healthfulness of the Inhabitants.*

But the Inhabitants of St. *Helena* are not liable to such Casualties, the Clemency of the Weather they are under subjects them not to the most common Diseases, even that of the Small-Pox, but gives them a Complexion fresh and beautiful, equal to that of celebrated *England*. The Poverty of the Place may be likewise thought another Ingredient of its Health; since Physicians tell us, that most Diseases arise rather from Repletion than Emptiness; from too Luxuriant, than too spare a Diet. And here they are not too much cloy'd with Varieties. For were the Plenty of the Island equal to its Health, did the other Conveniences of Life match the Pleasantness of the Air, it might fairly invite the Wealthiest, as well as the most Indigent, to inhabit it. But the People are confin'd to Poverty by a solemn Restraint they are under to the Traffick of all Foreign Countries, by being permitted no single Vessel of Burthen, or what's fit for Trade; and are destitute of all Cloaths, but what are transported from *Europe*, or brought by accident; which makes the Island (to speak the Truth) abate much of the Pleasure of its Habitation, and much more to those who want Opportunities of leaving it when they please.

*The Poverty of the place.*

*A plesant Account how the Island was peopled.*

Yet at our Arrival it was well stockt with Inhabitants of both Sexes, whose numerous Progeny shew'd little of Sterility among them, how barren soever the Island was otherwise. This put me upon the Curiosity of enquiring from the Women, how such Plenty of them came there? The Decoy, they told me, was worth my Attendance to hearken to it; and it would not appear strange to see such a number of them there, when they discover'd the Means that brought them thither. For at their first setting out from *England*, a Colony for this Island, the current Report that then prevail'd was,

[1] For Mr. Cook, *vide* p. 86, *infra*, Note.

that all the single Persons upon the Island were either Commanders, or Lords Sons, of whom they might have Choice upon their Arrival. This made them eager for imbarking for the Voyage, and was Charm enough to make them set forward with full Sail for the remote Island, tho' the Distance had been farther. No Curse was like a contrary Wind, to check the speedy sight of those gallant Gentlemen that awaited their coming; the ravishing Thoughts of whose Embraces kept them in Life and Alacrity all the way, and inriched their Fancies with the Hopes of being immediate Mistresses of great Fortunes, and rais'd so far above their Native Birth, that nothing now but Pleasures and Respect should succeed in the room of their former servile state. The long'd-for Island was at length espied, and now fresh Springs of Love and Delight appear in every Eye and Countenance. The joyful Maids begin to ransack all their Stores for an Ornamental Dress, in which though they cannot much exceed, however they fancied themselves Trim and Gay; and she that could not outvie the other in point of Attire, endeavours to outdo her in Nature's Ornaments, in Chearfulness and Mirth, in a Nuptial Look and taking Air. Thus they stept on Shore, full of the Thoughts of a stately Reception, and of the sight of those Gentlemen they had heard so much of. When, alas! all these Blandishments of Fancy, which were so sweet in the Voyage, carried a Sting in the end of them, which imbitter'd all their Joys. For instead of that Heroick Address which they expected from Men of Wealth and Honour, they were saluted only in the plain Courtship of Men employ'd in Agriculture, and ordinary Mechanick Arts. However, the pleasing Expectation they had, gave them this Advantage over the tedious Passage, that whereas the boisterous Waves and impetuous Winds, the Fury of the Sea, and the Dangers of Rocks and Sands, are apt to render so long a Voyage very dreadful, their aiery Hopes made them take Courage, and defie the Power of Storms, and gladly encounter all the Perils that attend such a forlorn Passage.

The fruitful Soil is capable of producing the Increase of

many Hundreds for one Grain of *Indian* Corn injected in the Ground, but then it requires several Inches of Ground for its Growth. Yet were it never so prolifick, the Rats and Vermin so infest the Land, that all their Hopes are quite devoured by them before they arrive to any maturity; which reduces them to their last Refuge, to Yams and Potatoes, the only staple Increase for Meat and Drink which the Island produces. *The Land infested with Vermin.*

The *East India* Company are upon a Project for Planting Vines, and thereby rendring the Product of them serviceable, both to the refreshment of the Sailers, and of the Inhabitants; and will be a very seasonable relief to the abject Condition of such as are willing to forget their Poverty, and remember their Miseries no more. The Soil is qualified for their Expectation, could they guard it from the destructive Vermin, which do every where make great waste of all things tender and delicate; and is therefore made fitter for nourishing Fruit Trees, whose stubborn and well fortified Bulk defies the onset of those small rapacious Animals, and is not a proper Food for them. I have observ'd among some of those Trees that bear Fruit, especially upon an *English* Apple-tree, transplanted thither from hence, at the same time Apples that were Ripe, others Green, and others in the Blossom. For the genial Heat of the Sun-Beams, to which the Island is happily expos'd, hastens the maturity of the Fruit, by a constant quick attraction of the seminal Juyces from the Root to the upper Branches continually. *A Project for Planting Vines.* *The Richness of the Soil.*

Instead of the common Grass of the Fields, those here are covered with Mint and Purslain, and are the ordinary Food of the Beasts of the Field, whereon they Feed deliciously themselves, and are made themselves more Luxurious morsels to such as eat them. The whole Island is in this respect, as it were a spacious Garden of Herbs. *Mint and Purslin grow wild in the Fields.*

The management of Affairs is in the Hands of a Governour, a Deputy Governour, and Store-house-keeper, all maintain'd by competent standing Salaries from the Company; besides the allowance of a publick Table, spread with plenty of Provisions, to which all Commanders, and Mates *The Government of the Island.*

of Ships, and Passengers of note are freely receiv'd. These Govern the Concerns of the Island, and are steer'd in their Councils by the directions they receive from their Masters in *England*. The Results of their Consultations are sometimes called Impositions by the Natives, and their Determinations are branded with infamous Characters of severity, especially when they appear less favourable to the Ease and Interest of the Publick; and from which, if there be any Relief from the Company, yet the unavoidable delays in returning a Redress to that distance, puts sometimes a tedious hardship upon the Addressors. And I believe were not the convenience of its Situation so very serviceable to the furtherance of the *East-India* Voyages, particularly to the Ships homeward bound, the constant trouble and Expence which do seem to ballance all the Advantages, would tempt the Company to quit all Claim and Propriety in the place, and abandon it to the Power of the first Designer. For tho' 'tis furnisht with conveniences for Life, yet with no Commodities as yet proper for the profitable Negotiations of a Merchant. And therefore as the Kings of *Portugàl* did formerly Enact, that none should remain to Inhabit the Place, except some sick persons for the restauration of their Health, that the Fleets might be plentifully furnisht with great variety of Grains, of fresh Victuals, Fowls and Water; so would the Company, I imagine, be willing to remit their Right to those Original Proprietors, did not they rather consult the Convenience of their Ships, than any other private Interest in keeping it.

*The Island not very Profitable to the* East-India *Company.*

*The first discovery of the Island.*

The first Discoverer of this Island, was *Juan da Nova*, a *Portuguese*, on St. *Helen's* Day, being the 21*st* of *May*, *An.* 1502,[1] whose Country-Men in a short time stockt it plentifully with Hogs, a thriving Cattle at Land, and the most hardy for enduring a long Voyage at Sea; and likewise brought hither Geese, and Hens, Partridges, Feasants and Guiney Cocks from *Europe*; and of late, the Increase of Turkies has been so numerous, that the smallness of their Rates will scarce encourage their Care to look after them.

[1] Actually 1501. Ovington's dates are often inaccurate.

In the Woods grew formerly Ebony and Cedar, and infinite store of Oranges, Lemons, Limes, and other sorts of Fruit; and now in the Governour's Garden, and some others of the Island are quantities of Plantins, Bonanoes, and other delightful Fruits brought from the *East*. *Its former fruitfulness.*

The Soil is of a Red Colour, and in some places is friable, and resembles Ashes, and in very many places lies uncultivated and bare. *The nature of the Soil.*

And the minds of the Inhabitants are generally as Uncultivated as the neglected Soil, their Intellects as ordinary as their Qualities, but what is infinitely worse, the pravity of their Manners compares them with the rankest Soil, productive of nothing but noxious Herbs, untractable to all the Arts of Husbandry or Improvement. For tho' the Company have not spared the Encouragement of a Minister, by the stated Sallary of an Annual Allowance of an Hundred Pounds, besides Gratuities from the Inhabitants; yet are the Sacred Administrations but ineffectually, for the most part, used towards the reclaiming their Enormities, and reduceing the Lives of the Inhabitants to Sobriety and a Religious Behaviour. The looseness of which may in a great measure be deriv'd from the Poverty of the place, which affords but slender Encouragements to live there. And where there are no Rewards for Piety, but present inward Tranquility, and the lively Hopes of a Happy Futurity, where nothing is visibly attainable but barely Peace of Conscience, attended with the expectation of a better State hereafter; these to a Man, the dependance of whose Life is upon his daily Pains, and who is continually sollicited with anxious Thoughts for his secular Concerns, appear too thin and airy Diet to his gross Mind, which is unaccustom'd and unprepar'd, and not at leisure to relish it. For sensible Allurements do soonest gain upon Vulgar Spirits, and Temporal Motives do most easily strike the Fancy of less Spiritual and refin'd Minds, therefore has the Wisdom of Providence designedly annext the Promise of many Worldly Felicities to our Duty, and made our present Enjoyments a powerful Bait to entice us to the security of *The lewd lives of the Inhabitants.* *A Reason of their Immorality.*

the Future. And for this cause Modesty and Temperance are as much Strangers here, as Wealth and Honour.

*An Account of three Pyrates.* While we Anchor'd here, there came into Harbour, a Ship Laden with Negroes from *Madagascar*, belonging to *New York*: who acquainted us with three Pirates which she left Rendezvouzing in St. *Augustin's Bay*, a Port belonging to that Island. Two of the Ships were *English*, and the other *Dutch*, and were all richly Laden with store of Silks, which they had taken in the *Red Sea*, from the *Asian* Merchants that traded from *Mecha* to *Suratt*, and other Coasts of *Indostan*. Their Rigging was much worn and Weather-beaten, and for want of a New suit of Sails, they were forced to employ double Silk instead of Canvas, and proffer'd that Exchange to this Commander. They had spent so much time in the Naval surprizes of the *Moors*, and loading themselves with the Rich Booties which were easily taken in the *Red Sea*, that their Ships became almost useless and unfit for Navigation, which brought them thither for Recruits. They were Prodigal in the Expences of their unjust Gain, and quencht their Thirst with *Europe* Liquor at any rate this Commander would put upon it; and were so frank both in distributing their Goods, and guzling down the noble Wine, as if they were both wearied with the possession of their Rapine, and willing to stifle all the Melancholy Reflections concerning it.

*St.* Augustine'*s Bay.* This St. *Augustin's Bay* is the Harbour generally frequented by the *European* Pirates, when the approach of the *Mussouns* threatens their Navigations any longer in the *Eastern* Seas, where Fifteen or Twenty *English* or *Dutch* will, without peril of either Ship, or Men, attack and board the largest *Moor* Ships that commonly Sail in those Seas. Madagascar. *Madagascar* is a very large Island, and affords plenty of Provisions for the Ships that put in there. It is govern'd by several Kings, Independant, and Hostile to one another, designing continually upon each others Territories, being possessed with that restless Spirit of Ambition, which allows as little Ease to a Man's self, as it does security to his Innocent Neighbour. And here too, as well as in *Africa*, where we landed; they compute their Wealth by the Numbers of their Slaves, and wage their Wars upon their accounts. The value of Gold is yet unknown to them, that Sun of the Earth, as an Ancient called it, amazes them not with its Lustre, nor fires their Hearts with an ardent desire of it; Steel and Iron are their darling Metals, whereby they perform their generous Exploits by open Violence, and not by the treacherous Persuasions of Gold. Therefore this Commander purchased here a Ball of Gold of 80 Ounces weight for a Trifle of no value, only it pleased the Spectators Eyes.

*Gold not valued upon* Madagascar.

And because these Pirates have been a publick Scandal, as well as Damage to our Nation, and both the *English*, *French* and *Dutch* at *Suratt*, have suffer'd in their Fortunes as well as Reputation from the *Moors* by the Violence and Rapine of these Men; therefore I might here insert a Relation of their Sufferings, did it not fall in more properly with the succeeding Account of the *English* Factory at *Suratt*, and of the hardships the *English* underwent there.[1]

Within three Weeks after we loosed from St. *Helena*, we reached *Cape bone Esperanse*,[2] in the doubling of which it blew so violent a Fret of Wind, and the high-wrought Seas were so tempestuous, that unless that extraordinary Providence which sets Bounds to its proud Waves, had not likewise restrain'd their outragious Swellings, we had all perisht in the merciless Surges. The Commander who was a stout and

*A mighty Storm at our doubling the* Cape.

[1] The pirates of the west coast of India date from Roman times. See the *Periplus*, § 53. They were equally formidable in the Middle Ages, *Marco Polo*, III. xxiv. In the days of the East India Company, much trouble was given by the Sanganians of Kathiawar, for whom *vide infra*, p. 162, note. Hardly less troublesome were the swarms of European pirates, unlicensed traders, and interlopers who hung about the Indian Ocean, plundering Indian and English vessels alike, and by their conduct causing the English factors at Surat to be imprisoned many times by way of retaliation on the part of the Moghul officials, *infra*, pp. 239 ff.

[2] The Cape of Good Hope was discovered by Bartholomew Diaz in 1486. He called it the Cabo Tormentoso (Cape of Storms), but the King of Portugal altered the name to a more auspicious one. Cf. p. 281.

expert Mariner, and who had past nine times to the *Indies*, confest a severity in this Tempest beyond whatever he was ingag'd in before. The Fiery Meteors which arise from the impetuous clashing of the Elements, fixt themselves upon our Masts and Shrouds, and with ominous appearance shew'd us the eminence of our Danger; and though they gave us Light, 'twas less desirable than the thickest Darkness; and the Thunder and Lightning which were very frightful and amazing, added yet a deeper Accent to the common Calamity. But what was most lamentable, the immediate Hazard of their Lives made little Impression upon the Sailers, nor did the apparent Apprehensions of Death, and of another World, make them either bewail their unhappy Fate, or summon them to a review of their past Actions; but as if they seemed to vie with the Noise of the Waves, the more boisterous they grew, the lowder were their Oaths and Execrations. Till the miraculous Divine Goodness, uncall'd upon, and thus provok'd, freed them by a wonderful Deliverance from the imminent Danger.

*A narrow escape from Shipwrack.* We were just recover'd from the Thoughts of this, when there arose another as inevitable a Danger, by which we had suffer'd an inavoidable dismal Fate, had it escap'd our Notice a little longer. For sailing between the Main of *Africa* and *St. Lawrence,*[1] we were carried unexpectedly by a Current nearer this Coast, than consisted either with our Designs or Safety, and had thereby been driven directly upon a Shelf of Rocks that lay off from the Shoar, had not the watchful Sailers upon the Decks espied Breakers, and all amazed cried out at the immediate Hazard of our Lives that we all were in. It was about Four in the Morning, and the faint Glimmerings of the Moon shed an imperfect Light, just enough to give us a sight of our Danger, and of avoiding it before we were upon it. We lost no time in turning about our Ship, and steering off some other way, and within a few days gain'd the sight of that Land we look'd for, the Island of *Johanna*.

[1] The Portuguese name for Madagascar, discovered by Fernando Soares, 1 February 1506.

## THE ISLAND OF JOHANNA[1]

THE Island of *Johanna* is one of the Four Isles of *Comora*, their Names are *Comora*, *Monilla*, *Johanna*, and *Mayotta*. *Johanna* lies near the Foot of St. *Lawrence*, between that and the Main Land of *Africa*, in about 12½ of South Latitude, by our Observations we made no more than 12 and 6 Minutes. 'Tis guessed to be stretch'd in Length about Thirty Miles, and in Latitude half the number. Its Fertility invites all the *Europe* Ships tending towards *Suratt*, and the Northern parts of *India*, to refresh themselves there. Here are Plenty of Black Cattle at very low Rates, and Goats so well flesht, and of so large a Size, that they are valued one third above the others. A Bullock may be bought for two Dollars, when three are expected for a well-fed Goat.

Johanna describ'd.

*Its fruitfulness.*

The Island abounds with Fowls and Rice, with Pepper, Yams, Plantins, Bonanoes, Potatoes, Oranges, Lemons, Limes, Pine-apples, *&c.* most of which sort of Fruits grow wild, and are allowed any Sailer to gather Gratis at his pleasure. They have store likewise of Honey and Sugar-Canes; and the Climate and Soil are well prepar'd for other Productions, as Grapes, Tobacco, Cotton. The Island is free for any Native to make his Election of any Plantation, he likes best,

[1] Johanna is the chief of the Comoro Islands, lying between Madagascar and the mainland, in the Mozambique Channel. Johanna is in lat. 12° 14′ 17″ S., and long. 44° 27′ 34″ E. It ' rises in a succession of richly-wooded heights till it culminates in a central peak upwards of 5,000 feet above the sea '. The capital, Moussamondon, on the north side of the island, is the seat of the Sultan. The natives, who are Arabs with a mixture of Malagasy blood, are hospitable to strangers; the islands are very fertile, producing nearly every kind of tropical fruit and vegetable, and also cattle, sheep, and turtles. Johanna was well known in the days of the Company and is described by a number of travellers, including Fryer (ed. Crooke, i. 57–70), who gives a long account; Herbert, p. 25; Terry, p. 50; Sir T. Roe, i. 18; Grose, p. 19, &c. The remaining islands of the group are Great Comoro, Mohilla, and Mayotta.

*Many Fruits here common.* and all the Fruit is common, except that of the Coconut-Trees, in which they chalenge particular Properties, and debar the common Liberty of plucking them at Pleasure.

*The Servility of Women in the East.* The Women are in some measure servile, and chiefly employ'd in laborious toiling, and in planting the Ground, whilst the Men indulge their Ease, and enjoy the Fruits of it. For the Orientals generally keep their Women under a severe Discipline, and bind them more absolutely to the Laws of Obedience and Subjection, than is practis'd among those of *Europe*. They require an Attendance from them, and expect the Preparation of the Victuals they eat from their Hands, and forbidding them the Privilege of their Company at Table, think it sufficient for the Wife to begin her Entertainment when the Husband leaves off. Which Servility comports very ill with that Tenderness and Regard, which Marriage should be presum'd to create in their joint Interests and Affections.

The Native Turf here is rich, and the Productions so very numerous, that the Island affords a most pleasant and plentiful Habitation to the Natives. *The Island offer'd to the English.* Yet have they formerly tender'd it to the *English* to build upon it, to Plant, and to accept of as a place of their uninterrupted Abode and fixed Residence; where some, I am sure, may enjoy more Ease and Plenty than they do at home.

*The Succession of the Government.* At our Landing we met with the late King's Brother of the Island, who after his Decease acts in some measure with Royal Authority, though the Supreme Power is really lodged in the Queen Dowager, upon whom the Soveraignty devolves after her Husband's Death. *The King's Brother's mean Appearance.* He was seated upon the Ground under the shady Boughs of a large Tree, near a small Rivolet, attended by half a Dozen of his Nobles, all round him in that familiar humble Posture. We were told of his Knowledge in the *English* Tongue, which invited us to address to him in our own Dialect, in which likewise he replied and entertained us. His Equipage was very slender, and unsuitable to the Greatness of his Person; for here were no Arms to defend him, his Innocence was his only Guard, and a Tuft of

Grass his Chair of State. The Leaves of the Trees were his only Canopy, and the Herbage of the Field was all the Carpet that was spread under him. We had a very free Access to his Presence, without the usual Formalities of Address, or Punctilio's of approaching, which prevented all need of a Master of Ceremonies to introduce us. And he was as frank and open in his Kindness, as he was easie of Access, allowing us the same Liberty which he took himself, by inviting us to sit down near him. Now tho' the Accommodation was not extraordinary, 'twas recompens'd however by the Favour of a Royal Invitation. The Freedom he had taken with himself, and given to us, made us at first amazed, not expecting to meet with a Person of that Eminence and high Character, much less with such Civilities from him; but they embolden'd and led us on to a little more Assurance, than we could have otherwise taken in a Prince's Presence. We were doubtful of finding any fit Food, or ready Accommodations for Strangers among the Natives, and therefore brought with us a little homely Diet of Bread and Cheese, which we humbly offer'd to his Princely Condescentions to taste, and partake of: For we found that Ceremonies were not much in Fashion, by his plain and unaffected Appearance, by his familiar Admission of us to seat our selves near him upon the Ground, which we thought encouragement enough for our offering this ordinary Refection. The making Cheese or Butter is an Art, which his People have not yet attain'd to, which made the Novelty by good luck recommend it self more gratefully to their Palates; and both the Prince and his Court thought themselves highly regaled by that, which an *English* Peasant so little esteems of.

*His Entertainment of us.*

*Our Entertainment of him.*

*Little Houswifery in this place.*

While we were thus banquetting our selves upon this course Fare, the Prince was pleas'd to enquire kindly of our Affairs at home, and of the Welfare of his Brother the King of *England?* Under whose auspicious Government, I told him, we were not only entitled to a Blessing, but he was visibly such to the Nations that were round about him. That he was raised up by the Arm of the Almighty, as a publick

*The Prince enquires of our Affairs.*

*An Account of the K. of* England.

Defence of his own Territories, and to put a stop to the Tyrannical Incroachments upon the Dominions of the Neighbouring States; and was caressed by his loving Subjects as their true Patriot, whom he protected not only by a mild and peaceable Government at Home, but by a frequent exposing his Royal Person to the utmost Perils for their Safety abroad, so that his Brave and Generous Mind shunned no Dangers to preserve them; as if he thought it a glorious Martyrdom to die in the Defence of his Kingdoms. But we hoped the Almighty, who had all along protected his Sacred Person, would favour him with a long Life and Series of Years, blest with continual Health and Victory over all his Enemies. This Relation he hearkned to with Attention and Delight, which I endeavour'd to heighten by a grateful Present, very suitable to the Discourse, which was, the Picture of our Gracious Soveraign K. *William*. He received it with a Smile, and a Countenance full of Satisfaction, and was resolved to lay it by in Safety in remembrance of its great Original.

*The Satisfaction which the Prince received at this Relation.*

*The Prince his Enemy.*

*Stones their only Weapons.*

*The Prince his Armory.*

When he had a while consider'd the Strength and Power of the English Arms, and the Native Valour of our Puissant Prince, he heartily wished he had been happy in a nearer Neighbourhood to his Dominions, that by securing an Alliance with him, he might engage his Arms in crushing a troublesom offensive Enemy, who had sometimes made Incursions upon his Island, and slaughter'd some few numbers of his Subjects, that is, the King of the adjacent Island, *Moheila*. Multitudes indeed could not well be mowed down by their Martial Weapons, which were neither Sword nor Spear, only Hand-stones taken up in the Streets, and thrown at their Enemies, as they had skill to aim them. Iron, and such like hostile Instruments of Terror they were unacquainted with. The King's Armory was furnisht with another kind of Weapon much as harmless as these, *viz.* Two Guns with broken Locks, and one Pistol, whose Touch-hole was near half as large as its Bore. These in skilful Hands might have done some Execution by the force of their Barrels.

The peaceable Inhostile Temper of this Prince, and the quiet submission of his Subjects, who pay him a profound Veneration, makes his Happiness equal to that of the greatest Monarchs, and infinitely superiour to those, whose Foreign or Domestick Enemies create perpetual Feuds and Tumults. Were no more Arms necessary for the Defence of Princes, than what he possesses, we might enjoy a Golden Age again, and triumph more in the Blessings of an Universal Peace, than in all the Laurels and Acclamations that wait upon victorious War. And as the Resignation of the Dominions of *Charles* V. shewed a greatness of Mind much superiour to all his other Conquests, that sought for Quiet in a private Cell, which it had long in vain searched after in Palaces and Camps; so the contented Obscurity of this Prince raises his Felicity to the rivalling that glorious Heroe in the nobler Instances of his Life, by affording his Mind as ample a Satisfaction in his narrow Territories, as that potent Prince enjoy'd either in his exalted or inferiour State.

*The peaceable manner of Life which the Prince enjoys.*

The Queen here, as the Queen at *Achen*,[1] is never exposed to the view of Strangers, but is kept from their Sight by a thin piece of Silk, when she condescends to speak with them; and very rarely vouchsafes to put forth her Head. When she is Chamber-sick, or by urgent occasions invited abroad, she is then kept private and unseen by a Sett of Curtains hung about her.

*The Queen seldom seen.*

This present Prince is blest with several Daughters, one of which was match'd to an *Arabian* Master of a Junk, and was Portion'd with Five Hundred Dollars by her Father, which was thought the third part of the Money he was computed to be worth; to this was made some Addition of Slaves and Cattel to increase the Dowry; and in these the greatest part

*The Portion of the Prince's Daughter.*

[1] Achen, or more correctly Āchīn, a state in north-western Sumatra, was once of enormous importance in the spice trade, and was thronged with English, Dutch, and Portuguese merchants. The first English commercial expedition to the East, under Lancaster (1602), had Āchīn as its objective. Purchas, *Pilgrimes*, ed. Maclehose, ii, chapter iii (pp. 392–438).

of their Wealth did consist, before the *Europeans* brought in of late the use of Dollars among them. They maintain a small Commerce from hence to *Patta*,[1] whither they export Rice in a sort of Vessels call'd Junks, which are framed all of Wood, without one Ounce of Iron in them.

*Vessels made without Iron.*

*Sleeping upon the Grass fatal for* Europeans.

The first coming hither has been very fatal to such as sleep upon the Ground,[2] and carelessly expose their Bodies to the cool nocturnal Mists, which by Damps that arise from the Earth, and a disuse to those moist Vapours, are frequently as pernicious to their Health, as lying abroad in the Fields in the Northern Climates would be. But those *English* who had fortunately made their Escape hither after a Shipwrack, were by a due Care and Regimen vigorous in their Constitutions. The Natives, after the loss of their Ship at Sea, received them all very kindly, condoled their Misfortune, and supplied their Exigencies with a Generosity extraordinary. One of the *English* was honoured with a piece of Silk from the Bounty of the Queen, and was offer'd by her Directions Diet and Lodging while he pleased. Their Cordial Affection to the *English* readily kindled their Liberality, that was expressed without Reluctance, or any signs of a repining Humour, and is increased into so dear and intimate a Kindness, that 'tis a common Proverb now among them, *Johanna-man, English-man, all one.*

*A Proverb at* Johanna.

*The* English *kindly entertain'd here.*

Neither the *French*, nor other Nations, meet with half that Welcom from them which the *English* receive; because of the exact Justice that we maintain with them in our Traffick, which very much surpasseth the Equity of the Commerce in others; and all Men, even such as rudely treat others, desire their Society most of all who are kindest and most just to their Affairs. But above all Nations they have the least

[1] Patta is a small island on the coast of British East Africa, *vide infra*, p. 158. Junk, Malay *jonga*, a large vessel, seems to occur first in Friar Odoric, 1331.

[2] Sleeping on the ground, or exposure to the 'land wind', the dry, cold NE. monsoon breezes, was said to cause a kind of palsy or dropsy known as 'barbiers' (perhaps beri-beri). *Vide infra*, p. 205.

Friendship for the *Danes*: For a large *Danish* Ship touching here at such a time, as they were sore infested by a War with their Neighbouring Island *Moheila*, was hired in their Defence, and prevailed with to take on Board several of their Men to assist in the Conquest of their Enemies; and some hundreds of Dollars were rais'd by a Contribution, and given as an Encouragement and Reward to the Undertaking. But the *Danes* vanquisht their Expectations, instead of conquering their Enemies; and instead of putting them to flight, fled themselves with both their Men and Money, so that to this Day they were never heard of. These Cheats and gross Impostures fix that Infamy upon Christianity, which it rigidly disclaims, and make it look like a very formidable Profession to the Native Simplicity of these People, whose pliable Tempers would readily prompt them to its Entertainment, were they not debarred by an Invincible Antipathy to such Injurious Transactions.

*An instance of Villany in the* Danes.

*A Reason why Christianity prevails not.*

The Buildings of their Country Villages are slight and without Ornament, but *Kings Town* and *Queens Town*, which are the Capital upon the Island, have some Structures more polisht, and made strong by Stone-Walls and Timber Roofs. The former is the usual Residence of their Kings, where they keep their Court, at 25 Miles distance from the Harbour. The Inhabitants of this place enjoy some peculiar Privileges above the rest of the Natives of the Island, because of their being seated so near the Royal Palace, which defends them from those Injuries to which those that dwell at a Distance are sometimes exposed.

*The Towns and Buildings.*

They are all of them industrious in concealing their Wealth from the notice of their Prince, whose Avarice and Injustice cause all their Goods and Estates to be seised to his own proper Use, when they die; whereby many times the Widow and Children are reduced to the lowest state of Misery, when once the Natural Death of the Husband has made the King Heir to his Wealth and Fortune. Which is an Oppression very unjustifiable even among the Mahometan Princes, and those Arbitrary Governours of the East; but

*The King Arbitrary.*

could never be bore with any Patience, by a People secur'd in their Estates by the same Laws with those which confirm that of their Prince, and who like us are freed from all Royal Violences, by a tame Resignation of our Possessions.

In *Queens Town*, which is a Maritime Village, many of their finest Houses stand uninhabited, almost half of them, because some of the People were formerly killed in them by the Islanders of *Moheila*, and their Bloodshed polluted the Habitation. The Death of the Master and Mistress, and one or two more of the Family, does the same; as if they mistrusted, that upon the Destruction of the Root, the Natural Branches would, without a Transplantation, wither and decay. And the Death of any Person whatsoever so far defiles the Purity of the Dwelling, that it hinders the Dressing of any Meat there for the next Month or two succeeding.

*The Causes that many Houses stand uninhabited.*

*The great usefulness of the Coco-Tree.*

The Coco-nut, upon which the generality feed, supplies them not only with Meat, but Drink, and serves instead of a Cup to drink out of; and, with the Tree upon which it grows, is so variously serviceable to Navigation, that a Ship may both be built, and rigg'd, and victuall'd, and freighted by them. A little Rice and this Nut together, without any other Food, do gen'rally allay the Hunger of the Common People.

*Large Entertainments.*

The Entertainments prepar'd by the King, and those of the best Note, are very large and hospitable, at which a whole Town will be at one time treated, and all the Inhabitants as Guests. At these Feasts the Increase of the Island is serv'd up in Plenty, but eat with Moderation, and without much studied Niceness in the Preparation; boil'd Meat and Rice do generally cover all their Tables.

*Strong Drink forbidden.*

Strong Drink is not so much their Aversion, as Restraint, being kept from it by their Obedience to the Mahometan Law, contrary to their eager Desires. Yet here, as in places more Oriental, they warm their Spirits by the smoaking of Tobacco; and Beetle-nut and Chinam are very rarely out of their Mouths. Beetle-nut fortifies the Stomach, and comforts the Brain; it preserves the Teeth, and cures or prevents a tainted Breath.[1] The Beetle-nut resembles a Nutmeg, and is shaved into thin pieces. Chinam is Lime made of Cockle-shells, or Lime-stone; and Pawn is the Leaf of a Tree, wherein the other two are wrapped up. These they take and chaw betwen their Teeth, till they squeeze out their Moisture, which is spit upon the Ground. Upon this two effects follow. First, It leaveth a red Tincture upon the Teeth and Lips, which is esteem'd with them very Ornamental; and then it chears and heats their Spirits, even almost to the Intoxication of such as are unaccustom'd to it. Thus they commute for the use of our prohibited Wines. The Rheum which is hereby raised in the Mouth, is spit generally into a Hole in the Room, design'd for that purpose, which serves instead of a Pigdan,[2] or Spitting-pot. The Floor where the Prince entertain'd us was so uneven and full of these Holes, as if the whole Room had been contriv'd for that purpose.

*Beetle-nut.* *Chinam.* *Pawn.*

In the middle of *Queens-Town* is a Mosque daily frequented by the People, into which we were admitted with this necessary Respect of putting off our Shoes upon the entrance into it.

*The Mosque.*

But this was an Instance of Civility rarely allowed us Infidels by the Mahometans. Near the Porch of the Mosque is a Draw-well for the washing the Hands, Face, and Feet, of all that enter, or come out of it. They take Care to preserve it neat and clean, with Mats spread upon the Floor for the Convenience of such Men as pray, for the Women are not much concern'd to frequent it. In repeating their private Prayers they make use of Beads, as the Romanists do, and commonly with the same neglect, intermixing their Secular Conference with the handling of them.

[1] Beetle-nut and Chinam are betel, the leaf of the *Piper betel*, and chunam or lime. These, together with *supāri*, the areca-nut, form *pān supāri* (Hind. *pān*, a leaf), which is handed to guests on ceremonial occasions, and is used for chewing all over the East. Ovington makes the common blunder of confusing the betel, which is the leaf or *pān*, with the areca-nut.

[2] Hind. *pīk* (spittle) + *dān* (a receptacle).

*The Women married young.* The Women are Courted sometimes at Seven or Eight Years old, and married when they come to Maturity, which is about Eleven or Twelve in these warmer Countreys; at which time they prepare a publick Feast for the space of Seven Days, as they do at their Funerals, and entertain all that are pleas'd to come.

*The Condition of married Women.* The Woman contributes to the Maintenance and Support of her Husband, and upon some Occasions can leave him. They are kept secluded from the Society of Strangers, and that freedom of gadding abroad; which they so eagerly desire, which they sometimes unlawfully venture upon, to the hazard of their Lives upon Discovery. The Orientals are all of them generally jealous, and very circumspect about their Wives; and seldom fail of punishing their Infidelity, if it come to light. *A severe Law against Adulteresses at* Tunquin, *and at* Japan. And particularly, the Laws of *Tunquin*[1] are very severe against Adulteresses, who upon Conviction are cast to an Elephant bred up for that purpose, who tosseth them in the Air with his Trunk as long as he finds any Life in them. And thus in *Japan* Adultery is punished in the Women only; tho' Deflowring of Virgins, Coinage of false Money, and some other Vices, are punished as well in their Relations, as in the Persons of the Criminals.

*The Burial and mourning Apparel.* They make great Lamentations at the Death of their Friends, for whose Sepulture they have no particular places set apart, but lay them often any where in the Fields. Their Mourning Apparel is plain and simple, and of inconsiderable Expence, made up of a few Leaves of Trees, tied about the middle, in fashion of a Hanging Fringe. Which is as strange in its kind, as the Colour is to us at *Tunquin*, where the new King and all the Princes of the Blood mourn in Robes of White Sattin, instead of the Dark Colours used in *Europe*.

*The time of naming their Children.* Seven Months after the Birth they name their Children, at which time is a publick Feast celebrated for their Friends.

[1] Tonquin is in the modern French Indo-China. The East India Company founded a factory there in 1672. Bruce, *Annals*, ii. 322 ff.

If the Child chance to die before that time, they are perswaded of the Efficacy of their Prayers in contributing to its future Felicity.

*The Devil's frequent appearing.*

Their Idea's of Religion are very dark and superstitious, increas'd in them by the constant Apprehensions of the Devil's frequent appearance among them. They give him here the Name of *Gregory*, and affirm, that they often meet him in the High-ways, and in the Streets, and in the Evenings especially, by the Water-side. The Dread of him confines them to their Houses when it thunders, for then they say *Gregory* is abroad, and no Mortal dare stir out of his Dwelling. As the City of *London* had a Custom of burning the Pope every Year, so here they commonly burn the Devil. At an appointed time of the Year all the Dirt of the Country thereabouts is laid in an Heap upon a Black Rock, lying between *Queens-Town* and the Harbour, which by the Neighbourhood is put into a Flame till all be consumed. But the malicious Spirit returns this Affront in a very spightful manner; and for the imaginary Injury done to him, inflicts a real and grievous Punishment on them, by the private Stealth of one of their Children every Year, which is yearly wanting upon the Island, against all their Vigilance and Care, which with melancholy Countenances they often confirmed to us.

*The burning of the Devil.*

*A particular Act of Malice in the Devil.*

*Negromancy practised.*

Many of the Natives affect a Familiarity with this Evil Spirit, are addicted to the Invocation of him, by their Skill in Negromancy;[1] and have often recourse to him upon any Emergencies of Consequence; the obsequious Devil never failing of being their Oracle, when once the Ceremony of Invocation is over. By Advice from him they assur'd us of some *English* and *French* Ships which would soon be in the Harbour, and accordingly happen'd. For the *Herbert*, an English Merchant-man belonging to the *East-India* Company, was in a short time after our Departure set upon in this Road by three or four *French* Ships, and after a vigorous

[1] A corruption of Necromancy, no doubt arising from false analogy with *niger*—the Black Art.

Resistance of their united Force, was unfortunately blown up, when she was almost ready to give them Chace. However we, by a careful Providence that preserv'd us, left this Island before this Danger, and on *May* the 29th, 1690, fortunately arriv'd at the Island of *Bombay*, which is unquestionably one of the most convenient Harbours in the *Indies*.

# THE ISLAND OF BOMBAY[1]

THIS Island has its Denomination from the Harbour, which allows the safest Rideing for Ships of any in these parts, and was originally called *Boon Bay, i. e.* in the *Portuguese* Language, a Good Bay or Harbour. By *Ptolomy* it was describ'd under the Name of *Milizigeris.*[2] And before it fell into the Hands of the *English*, was under the Dominion of *Portugal*, from whence it was translated to the Crown of *England*, upon the Marriage of the *Infanta* of *Portugal* to King *Charles* the Second, *Ann.* 1662. And is now put into the Possession of the *East-India* Company, for the convenience of their Ships and Traffick.[3]

*The occasion of the Name of this Island.*

*It belongs to the Crown of* England; *and is now possess'd by the* East-India *Company.*

Before we espyed the Main of *India*, several Snakes[4] of different sizes came swimming round our Ship near the surface of the Water, by which we knew we were not far from Land, because they are never seen at any great distance from the shore; they were washed from it, I presume, by the violence of the Rains in the times of the *Mussouns*, which I shall afterwards describe. This was seconded by another sign of our approaching the Land, *viz.* by a multitude of

*Snakes seen at Sea, a token of the nearness of Land.*

[1] The derivation of Bombay from Port. *Bom-bahia*, 'Good Bay', is an excellent example of the 'Hobson-Jobsons' which have nowhere played such havoc as among place-names of this locality. The mistake also occurs in Fryer, i. 160. The true derivation is no doubt from Mumba Devi or Mumba Bai, the goddess whose temple used to stand in the present Esplanade, and is now removed to Pydhoni.

[2] Melizigiris is probably Jaigarh or Rājāpur, much further south. There is no reason to identify it with Bombay. It occurs in *Periplus Maris Erythraei*, § 53.

[3] Bombay was handed over to the East India Company by the Crown in 1668.

[4] Water-snakes (*Hydrophidæ*) are common on the Indian coast. They are constantly mentioned in old travel-books; see Crooke's interesting note *apud* Fryer, i. 127. It is curious that ever since the days of the *Periplus* (§ 55) snakes in the water were a recognized indication of land ahead.

*Locusts lighting upon our Ship at Sea.* Locusts, which came flying upon our Masts and Yards, when we were distant from it Thirty Leagues, as we found by our Computation afterwards. They were above two Inches in length, and their reaching us at that distance from the Shore, argued their great strength of Wing to flie to us so very far; by which they mounted aloft, after they had rested themselves a while, and took their Flight directly upwards. While I was at *Suratt*, the President and some more of us observ'd for several succeeding Nights, an Infinite number of these Creatures Flying over our Heads for several hours together, in such numerous Armies and vast Bodies, that they cast a Cloud over the Moon, tho' it then was at the Full. They directed their Course towards the *South*, but some of them called by the way, and lighted upon a Field of Corn near the City of *Suratt*, and in one Nights time devour'd it all. The Poor Husbandman bewailed his Loss to the Governour of the City, who was invited forth as a Spectator of the sudden devastation, that he might be more sensibly moved to repair the Damage, and relieve the Man.

*A Field of Corn devoured by a multitude of Locusts.*

It was just the Season of the *Mussouns*[1] when we fell upon the Coast of *India*, which generally is extreme dangerous, because they break out for the most part in such Thunder and Rains, and impetuous Winds, that if the Ships are not laid up and in Harbour before that time, they incur the hazard of being lost. This made our Commander wish himself an hundred Leagues from Land, tho' we were then in sight of it; because that all his Care and Skill had scarce secur'd him from being driven by the Violence of the Storm upon a Lee-Shoar, by which he saw he must inevitably perish. But in 24 Hours space the Danger was well spent, and the joy of our Safety commenc'd about the same time that the fear of our Ship

*The Ship indanger'd by the* Mussouns.

[1] Mussoun, monsoon, from Arab. *mausim*, 'season', Port. *monçao*, French *mousson*, Ital. *monsone* (this was no doubt the origin of our modern word). This is the periodical wind of the Indian coasts. In western India, the south-west monsoon sets in at the beginning of June, with violent storms and heavy rain, lasting until the end of September.

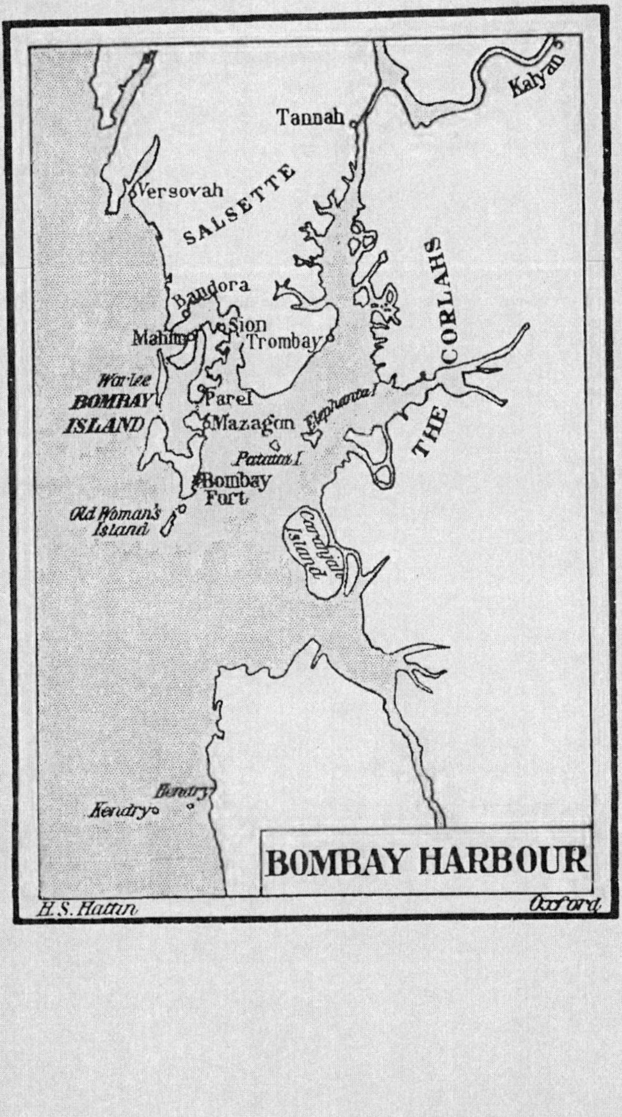

Tannah
Kalyan
Versovah
SALSETTE
THE CORLAHS
Bandora
Sion
Mahim
Trombay
War-lee
BOMBAY ISLAND
Parel
Mazagon
Elephanta I.
Patata I.
Bombay Fort
Old Woman's Island
Caranjah Island
Kendry
Kendry
BOMBAY HARBOUR
H.S. Hattin
Oxford

wrack did begin, according to the Maxim and Observation among Mariners, *That a Tempest ceases about the same time generally that it does arise.* And because I am fallen upon this Subject, I shall, before I enter any farther upon *Bombay*, give a brief Account of the Nature of these *Mussouns* in *India*.

*An Observation of Seamen.*

This is the only proper Season of the Year for Rain, which falls here with such violence, and on all the Coasts of *Malabar*, that it hinders all Navigation, and puts a general stop to all Journeys by Land: For during this time, all the Land Carriages cease, and all the Ships both *European* and *Indian* are laid up in Harbour: It continues in these parts for the space of three or four Months, from the latter end of *May*, 'till the middle of *September*; but in *June* and *July* do fall the most plentiful Showers, and that sometimes without intermission, for ten or fifteen days together, intercepting the appearance of either Sun or Star all that while. The whole Hemisphere then is most sullenly Dark, and the Sky overcast with the thickest weighty Clouds, so that the Earth seems rather inclosed within a huge Ocean of Water, than only a few watry Clouds, whose black and lowring Aspect is so very melancholy, that it gives the fairest representation imaginable of the terrours of a second universal Deluge. Sometimes in Three or Four Hours time, such Showers fall from these full Clouds, that the Currents run along the Streets, swelled to that height, that they are scarce fordable on Horse-back. After this Excess in *July* the Showers gradually decrease, the Horizon clears up like the first dawning of the Day, 'till at length the Heavens are all over Bright, and the benighted Sun displays his vigour and banish'd Rays again. Then do the *Bannians* endeavour to appease the incensed Ocean by Offerings to its inraged Waves, and in great plenty throw their gilded Coco-nuts into the Sea to pacifie its storms and Fury, and render it peaceable and calm.[1] And after these Ceremonious Oblations are past, the

*A Description of the* Mussouns.

*The time of its Continuance.*

*Its Violence.*

*The* Bannians *Offerings to the Ocean to appease it.*

[1] The great Hindu festival of *Nārali Purnima* or Coconut Day is held on the full-moon of the month Srāvan (July–August). Fairs are held all along the Western Coast, Ocean is worshipped, and

Oraculous *Bramins* declare safety to the Ships that will venture upon the Ocean, before which not one of them will offer to weigh an Anchor. The Young Boys are much delighted with this Custom, for whatever Coco-nuts are thrown into the Water, they immediately swim in and fetch them out.

*Rains fall only at these times.*

The *Mussouns* are the only Season for watering of their Fields, their Meadows, and Arable Land. And for the preservation of this Element, wherever they sow their Rice, they endeavour to reduce the Ground to a Level, that nothing of this Heavenly Moisture may be lost.

*The foulest Weather when the Sun is nearest.*

The Sun's approach to the Natives of *Europe* promiseth them the fairest Weather, and here the fowlest. The reason of which is his Vertical Exaltation, which with great violence Exhales the Vapours of the Earth, and returns them as plentifully again. Therefore both under the *Æquator* and the *Tropick*, when the Sun has been in the *Zenith*, I have perceiv'd the Air has been more temperate, and the Weather cooler, than at ten or twelve Degrees distance from it: And that abundant moisture which is always powerfully drawn up, near the *Æquator*, from which the Sun is never very far distant, abates that scorching Heat of his Influence, which otherwise would be scarce tolerable to either Animal or Plant. And therefore in the Middle of *May*, before the *Southerly* Winds set in, which bring the Rains along with

*Ink dried up in the Pen by the Heat.*

them, the Air at *Surat* is so very dry, that it licks up the Moisture in the Pen, before we are able to write it out; and so intensly Hot, especially about 3 in the Afternoon, that we cannot well endure the standing for any long time upon the

*The Floors commonly sprinkled with Water.*

Grass, where the Sun's Beams have their full force. This causes our sprinkling the Floors of our Chambers frequently with Water, to create a kind of *Fresco* in them, during this Season, and makes us Employ our Peons in Fanning of us

*Murchals.*

with Murchals[1] made of Peacocks Feathers, four or five Foot

gilded coconuts are thrown into it as offerings. After this propitiation, the monsoon is supposed to subside. In 1928 this festival falls on 30 August.

[1] *Morch'hal* (Hind.) peacock-feather fan.

long, in the time of our Entertainments, and when we take our Repose.

Now, as in other Countries, the periods of the variety of Weather are uncertain, the Fair and Foul succeeding one another with great variety and alteration; and as in *India* they have stated and fixt times without any doubtful vicissitudes; so likewise even there they do not observe throughout all places the same Months. For upon the *East* side of Cape *Comorin*, on the Coast of *Coromondel*, from *April* to *September* the Weather is Fair, and in the other Months is the Winter-like Weather; whereas on the Coast of *Malabar*, which lies to the *West*, the Fair Weather begins in *September* and ends in *May*.[1] So that in passing over-land from one Coast to the other, the Travellers, who are unacquainted with it, are at a stand to find two different Seasons of Winter and Summer in 20 or 30 Leagues distance. The Rains likewise come from different Quarters in these different Regions; some from the *South*, some from the *West*, and some from the *East*. And at the *Maldive* Islands, which are reckoned 12 Thousand, the Rains follow the Course of the Waters from the *West*, which are carried by an impetuous Current for six Months together towards the *East*, that is, from *April* to *September*; the other six Months are Hot and Calm, with the Winds settled from the *East*.

*The time of the* Mussouns *different in some places.*

*The* Mussouns *arise from several quarters.*

The *Mussouns* are rude and Boisterous in their departure, as well as at their coming in, which two Seasons are call'd the *Elephant*[2] in *India*, and just before their breaking up, take their farewell for the most part in very ruggid huffing weather. As if they were constrain'd to force their Entrance, and Combat the fair Seasons, before they could make way for their

*The Stormy Seasons of the* Mussouns.

[1] The east coast of India catches the north-east monsoon, and the rainy season is just the opposite to that in western India. The word 'winter' in the older travellers was applied invariably to the monsoon season, and not to the cold weather.

[2] The Elephant is the Hindu constellation *Hasti* (really *hasta*, hand, the 13th Lunar Mansion), the rising of which coincides with the end of the south-west monsoon. This period is often marked by violent thunder-showers. Cf. Fryer, i. 126–7.

admittance; and were likewise resolv'd to try their utmost effort, sooner than tamely resign their Empire, and quit the Coast. For Nature must needs be under great Conflicts and disorder, by such a suddain Change from an uninterrupted Sun-shine to such constant Rains.

India *wants Rain for 8 or 9 Months.* When once the *Mussouns* are past, the other Months are under the serenest influence of the Heavens, without one Fertile Cloud for several succeeding Months visible in the whole Firmament, but the chearful Sun, from six to six, is never veil'd with gloomy Meteors, or Eclipsed with dark and Melancholy Exhalations from the Earth: But all the Animal Generations bask themselves in his warm Rays, without any fear of Rain, or Tempests, or chilly nipping Weather. And now the Vegetable Race below, Trees and Corn, Flowers and Herbs grace the World with infinite variety of delightful Forms, and pleasant Colours, being refresh'd by Nature's Seminal Juice, the plentiful Showers that descended in the time of the *Mussouns*: Wherein several Trees, by quenching their Thirst with such a large Draught at that Season, maintain a flourishing Verdure all the Year round. And what is more remarkable, some of those Trees will yield each Night a Quart of *Tary* or *Toddy*,[1] tho it be at eight Months distance from the falling of the Rains; the greedy Soil imbibed at that time such a quantity of this pure Liquor when it fell upon the Earth. This gives *India* the lovely Aspect of those Blessed Seats, which are sweetly described by the Poet,

*Green Trees all the Year round, and full of Moisture.*

*Quas neque concutiunt venti, neque nubila nimbis*
*Aspergunt, neque nix acri concreta Pruina*
*Cana cadens violat, semper que innubilus Æther*
*Contegit, & late diffuso lumine ridet.*[2]

[1] Tary, Toddy, Hind. *Tāḍi*, is the fermented juice of the palmyra and other palms, 'palm-wine'. It was one of the chief products of Bombay at the time of Ovington's visit. The trees were tapped by the Bhandāris. Cf. Fryer, i. 195.

[2] Lucret. iii. 21.
Where falls not hail, nor rain, nor any snow,
Nor ever wind blows loudly.

But at *Bombay*, *September* and *October*, those two Months which immediately follow the Rains, are very pernicious to the Health of the *Europeans*; in which two Moons more of them die, than generally in all the Year besides. For the excess of earthy Vapours after the Rains ferment the Air, and raise therein such a sultry Heat, that scarce any is able to withstand that Feverish Effect it has upon their Spirits, nor recover themselves from those Fevers and Fluxes into which it casts them. And this the *Indians* remark concerning the excessive Heats at this time, that they say, *'Tis* September's *Sun which causeth the black List upon the* Antilope's *Back*.

September *and* October *unhealthful Months at* Bombay.

*An Observation of the* Indians.

Thus I leave this Description of the Season and Nature of the *Mussouns*, and return to *Bombay*, which is only a small Island, situate in about Nineteen Degrees of North Latitude, not eminent for any thing so much as its Fort and Harbour.

They have here abundance of Coco-nuts, which bring some Advantage to the Owners, but very little either of Corn or Cattle, but what is imported from the adjacent Country; and these not in great Plenty, nor of very good Growth. A Sheep or two from *Suratt* is an acceptable Present to the best Man upon the Island. And the Unhealthfulness of the Water bears a just Proportion to the Scarcity and Meanness of the Diet, and both of them together with a bad Air, make a sudden end of many a poor Sailer and Souldier, who pay their Lives for hopes of a Livelihood.[1] Indeed, whether it be that the Air stagnates, for the Land towards the Fort lies very low, or the stinking of the Fish which was used to be applied to the Roots of the Trees, instead of Dung; or what-

*Plenty of Coco-nuts, but not of Cattle.*

*An unhealthful Air.*

[1] The unhealthiness of Bombay was proverbial. A list of the chief diseases, fevers, cholera, and the barbiers, a kind of beri-beri, is given *infra*, pp. 204 ff. It was due partly to the intemperance of the Europeans themselves, and partly to the habit of manuring the coconut gardens with putrid fish known as 'Buckshaw'. The 'drowned lands' or swamps left by the sea at low tide were another contributing cause. Fryer calls it a charnel-house. See his *New Account*, i, pp. 178–181, and compare Anderson, *English in Western India*, p. 274; Forrest, *Selections, Home Series*, i, pp. 66, 74, 148; *Bombay City Gazetteer*, vol. ii, pp. 71 ff.; and Edwardes, *Rise of Bombay*, pp. 120 ff.

ever other Cause it is which renders it so very unhealthful, 'tis certainly a mortal Enemy to the Lives of the *Europeans*. And as the Ancients gave the Epithet of *Fortunate* to some Islands in the West, because of their Delightfulness and Health; so the Modern may, in opposition to them, denominate this the *Unfortunate* one in the East, because of the Antipathy it bears to those two Qualities.

*Above 35 buried out of the Ship in less than 4 months.* We arrived here (as I hinted before) at the beginning of the Rains, and buried of the Twenty Four Passengers which we brought with us, above Twenty, before they were ended; and of our own Ship's Company above Fifteen: And had we stay'd till the end of the next Month, *October*, the rest would have undergone a very hazardous Fate, which by a kind Providence ordering our Ship for *Suratt*'s River-mouth, was comfortably avoided. A fortunate Escape indeed! because neither the Commander, nor my self, were in any Hopes of surviving many Days: neither Temperance, the most Sovereign Medicine, nor the safest Prescriptions in the Physical Art, could restore the Weakness of our languishing decay'd Natures. And that which thoroughly confirm'd to us the unhealthfulness of the place we had lately loosed from, was the *The healthfulness of a good Air.* sudden Desertion of our Diseases, and return of Health, before half the Voyage to *Suratt* was finisht: In the middle of which Passage we manifestly perceiv'd in our Bodies as evident an alteration and change of Air for the best, as our Palates could distinguish betwixt the Taste of Wine, and that of Water.

*An Invitation for the Author to stay here.* The Deputy-Governour, Mr. *George Cook*,[1] a pleasant and obliging Gentleman, sollicited me upon the account of my Function to reside with him upon *Bombay*, and invited me with all the Proposals of a frank and generous Civility, to wave my Voyage, and continue with him there, because they were then destitute of a Minister. And indeed the Deference I bore to such kind Expressions, and to the Duty of my Calling, were invincible Arguments for my Stay, had I not been

[1] In 1690–1, on the death of Sir John Child, Mr. Harris was proclaimed Governor of Bombay, and Mr. Cook (and shortly after him Mr. Weldon) Deputy Governor. Cf. p. 92, note 2.

satisfied of the immediate infallible sad Fate I was under, like that of my Predecessors; one of whom was interred a Fortnight before this time, and three or four more had been buried the preceding Years: Which common Fatality has created a Proverb among the *English* there, that *Two Mussouns are the Age of a Man*. This is much lamented by the *East-India* Company, and puts them upon great Expences for supplying the Island with fresh Men, in the room of those that are taken away, and providing able Surgeons, furnish'd with Drugs and Chests from *Europe*, to take care of the Infirmaries, and all that are sick.

*An English Proverb at* Bombay.

But there seldom happens any great Defect in the Natural World, without some preceding in the Moral; and the Springs of our Miseries and Misfortunes rise higher than meerly from Second Causes. For I cannot without Horror mention to what a Pitch all vicious Enormities were grown in this place, when the Infection was most outragious; nor can I but think that the Divine Justice interposed, and forwarded these fatal Infelicities, which are not wholly imputable to an impure Contagion of the Air, or the gross Infection of the Elements. These were made use of as Fatal Instruments of the direful Excision, but the true Cause of the Malady lay deeper. Their Principles of Action, and the consequent evil Practices of the *English* forwarded their Miseries, and contributed to fill the Air with those pestilential Vapours that seized their Vitals, and speeded their hasty passage to the other World. Luxury, Immodesty, and a prostitute Dissolution of Manners, found still new Matter to work upon. Wickedness was still upon the Improvement, and grew to such a Perfection, that no Vice was so detestable as not to be extremely vicious;[1] whereby Satan obtain'd a more Despotick Authority in the Hearts of the Christians, than he did among the Gentiles in the Pageantry of Heathen Worship. And when the Seeds of Avarice and Prophaneness, of Envy and Injustice, and a thousand other black Infernal Vices grew up and flourish'd, and were made the Ambition of every Individual; we need

*The great wickedness that reigned upon the Island.*

[1] So in the 1696 edn. Perhaps a misprint for 'common'.

not then admire, if the pure Luminaries of Heaven should set themselves against their Impieties, and dart their mortal Poysons on the Earth; if the Planets should wisely shed their venomous Aspects upon profligate Men, and thereby in Vengeance produce the mortal Fruits of Death.

*Vermin and Venomous Creatures very large.* The prodigious growth of Vermin, and of venomous Creatures, at the time of the *Mussouns*, do abundantly likewise demonstrate the malignant Corruption of the Air, and the natural Cause of its direful Effects upon the *Europeans*. For Spiders here increase their Bulk to the largeness of a Man's Thumb, and Toads are not of a much less size than a small Duck; whereby 'tis easily seen by these venomous Creatures, what encouragement these infectious and pestilential Qualities meet with in this place, and under what a contagious Influence all the Inhabitants must consequently be seated. This induc'd a Gentleman one time in the Governours and my Company, and some other Persons of Note, to affirm, that he believ d it rain'd Frogs; because he espied upon his Hat small Frogs, about the bigness of the end of one's Finger, when he was at a great distance from any House or Covering, from whence they might drop.

*Wounds hardly cured.* All Wounds and Contusions in the Flesh are likewise very rarely healed here; and if they are, 'tis with Difficulty and extraordinary Care; they happen generally to be very dangerous, and the Cure admits of more Delays and Hazards in the healing, than what is usual in other parts. But the Corruption of the Air has a more visible and immediate Effect upon young *English* Infants, whose tender Spirits are less able to resist its Impressions; so that not one of twenty of them live to any Maturity, or even beyond their Infant days. Were it otherwise, the Island might in time be peopled with the *Europeans* transmitted thither, as the Western Islands are, which belong to the Crown of *England:* For the Company allow Marriage to their Factors, and Liberty to young Women to pass thither to gain Husbands, and raise their Fortunes. But so very few of their Children live, and of those that do, so many of them are sent for *England*, that fresh

*Infants seldom live here.*

*The Factors in* In*dia are permitted to marry English*

Colonies from thence are very necessary for supporting the Government and Affairs of the Island.[1] A Modish Garb and Mien is all that is expected from any Women that pass thither, who are many times match'd to the chief Merchants upon the place, and advance thereby their Conditions to a very happy pitch. And considering what trouble attends the Passage, especially of Women, considering the Hazard, as well as length of the Voyage, with some other Casualties that sometimes happen on Board, a modest Woman may very well expect, without any great Stock of Honour or Wealth, a Husband of Repute and Riches there, after she has run all this Danger and Trouble for him. And indeed the fond Indulgence of the Husbands, as well as their Wealth, is another valuable Recompense to Women for the Toil and Trouble of the Voyage.

*Women sent thither.*

*The English Husbands in* India *very kind.*

The Island lies in about Nineteen Degrees North, in which is a Fort,[2] which is the Defence of it, flanked and Lined

*The Fort.*

[1] Gerald Aungier tried the experiment of bringing out English girls to Bombay as wives for the settlers, chiefly in order to prevent them from forming alliances with Portuguese and half-caste women, and becoming converts to Catholicism (Forrest, *Selections*, i. 55). This was not altogether a success, and contemporary records constantly refer to the trouble these women gave. The Surat factory was organized 'more like unto a College, Monastery, or a house under Religious orders', and the factors had at first to be bachelors. Gradually, however, the rule was relaxed, probably in imitation of the Dutch. *Infra*, p. 232, Ovington speaks of the members of Council as having their wives with them. See Fryer, i. 179; Anderson, pp. 102, 215; *Gazetteer*, Bombay Town and Island, i. 79; Rawlinson, *British Beginnings in Western India*, pp. 130–1.

[2] Bombay Fort. It will be noticed that the engravings reproduced by Ovington are dated 1668, and not 1692, when Ovington landed there. They therefore represent the original fort and citadel, begun by Sir George Oxinden immediately after the acquisition of the island by the Company. These were carried out by two local officers, Captains Smith and Toldery, trained engineers being considered too expensive. The results of the efforts of these amateurs are derided by Hamilton, *New Account*, i. 184, who says that the fort was wrongly sited, and this led to the humiliating surrender to the Sidi's forces in 1689. However, it was sufficiently strong to enable Gerald Aungier to present a bold front to the

according to the Rules of Art, and secured with many Pieces of Ordinance, which command the Harbour and the parts adjoining. In this one of the Companies Factors always resides, who is appointed Governour to inspect and manage the Affairs of the Island;[1] and who is vested with an Authority in Civil as well as Military Matters, to see that the several Companies of Soldiers which are here, as well as Factors and Merchants, attend their various Stations, and their respective Charge.

*The Governour.*

The Island is likewise beautified with several elegant Dwellings of the *English*, and neat Apartments of the *Portuguese*, to whom is permitted the free Exercise of their Religion, and the Liberty of erecting publick Chappels of Devotion; which as yet the *English* have not attain'd to, because the War with the *Mogul* interrupts the finishing of a stately Structure which was going on for their publick Church.[2] For want of this a particular Room is set apart in

*Liberty of Religion.*

threatened Dutch attack of 1673 (Fryer, i. 170–1). Fryer gives picturesque details of the building of the Fort on the site of the old Portuguese Manor House (i. 165, and see Crooke's learned note, with the list of authorities there quoted). He tells us that the fortifications were mainly due to the exertions of Philip Gyfford, Aungier's Deputy Governor (1670–2). An excellent contemporary view of the Fort from the sea is given in the *Bombay City Gazetteer*, vol. ii, p. 275. Official documents of the Bombay Government are still issued from 'Bombay Castle'.

[1] Up to 1687, Bombay was subordinate to Surat and was administered by a Deputy Governor appointed by the President. In that year Sir John Child transferred the seat of government to Bombay, and Surat gradually declined in importance, though down to 1800 we find the double title of President of Surat and Governor (or General) of Bombay still in use.

[2] Hamilton's malicious statement that the Bombay church (now St. Thomas's Cathedral) was started by Sir George Oxinden, but was after his death not proceeded with, partly because 'Piety grew sick, and the building of churches was unfashionable', and partly because Sir John Child converted to his own use the £5,000 collected for building it (*New Account*, i. 185), has been accepted and handed down without verification by Anderson (p. 66) and later writers. It has now been entirely disproved by the Stracheys (*Keigwin's Rebellion*, Appendix D, p. 168). The church was

BOMBAY FORT FROM THE HARBOUR, *c.* 1720

*Publick Prayers twice a day.*

the Fort for Publick Service twice a day, at which all are enjoyn'd to be present; and for performance of which, and other Sacred Offices, a Salary of an 100 *l.* annually, besides the convenience of Diet and Lodging, is allowed to the Minister by the Company.

*A small Pagode.*

The Gentiles too, as well as Christians, are permitted the Freedom of their Religion, and conniv'd at in their Heathen Worship. I accidentally once entred into one of the Gentiles Chappels, but durst not stay for fear of disturbing the *Bramin* with the Visit. The smallness of it would scarce admit of above Nine or Ten to enter into it. At the remotest part of it was placed the Pagod[1] upon the ground, which was only a Face form'd of Tin, with a broad flat Nose, and Eyes larger than a Crown Piece. On the right side of this Image hung a small Purse for the Peoples Oblations; on the left, very near it, lay some burnt Rice, which the Bramin had sacrificed; and at the entrance of the Door stood a Trumpet, which sounded all the while he was a sacrificing.

*The War with the Mogul.*

The Island by the War with the *Mogul*[2] was much

started by Aungier, who left it a legacy of 5,000 rupees. The delay was caused by Aungier's executors and Keigwin's rebellion, and not by Child. In 1686 two rooms in the Fort were made into a temporary church by Sir John Wyborne, and an organist was engaged. The building was finished by the exertions of the chaplain, the Rev. Richard Cobbe, and opened by Charles Boone in 1718. It was built at a central spot, in order that the native population might be duly impressed 'by the purity and gravity of our devotions' (Cobbe's *Bombay Church*, 1766).

[1] Here used not of the temple but the idol. Ovington derives it from *but kadah*, 'idol house', *infra*, p. 97. But see Hobson-Jobson, pp. 652 ff.

[2] Ever since 1672 Bombay had been troubled by the Sidi, the admiral of the Moghul fleet, who wished to use the harbour as a base for operations against the Marathas along the coast. In February 1689 Sidi Yakut landed on the island with 20,000 men and closely invested the fort. He raised batteries on Dongri Hill which harassed the besieged, and by the following December Sir John Child had to submit to an ignominious peace. Alexander Hamilton went through the siege, and gives a highly entertaining if biased account of it (i, chapters xviii, xix). Low, *History of the Indian Navy* (1877), i. 75 ff.; and Bruce, *Annals*, ii. 601–41.

Depopulated and Impoverished, both by destroying the *English* Inhabitants, and wasting the Fruit of the ground, especially of the Coco-Trees, whose Nuts are the staple Income upon it. And whatever the Original of this unhappy War was in other places, or upon what other Grounds soever it was commenced here, the *English* had some just Cause of murmuring and Complaint, from the Treatment they had from the *Mogul's* Officers at *Suratt*, very different from what they might in Reason and Equity expect. For at the first settling a Factory there, it was agreed upon between the great *Mogul* and our President, to have a permission of free Trade for Two and an half *per Cent* [1] for all Goods Imported or Exported; which were without any Reason arbitrarily advanced to Four *per Cent* beyond the Bounds of the first Agreement. And upon this very occasion the late Honourable President *Bartholomew Harris* [2] has urged to me often this Case, that he thought it no Injustice to evade the payment of as much Customs for the *English* Goods, as they were injur'd in them above two and an half *per Cent* by the *Mogul*. But this was not the only Severity the *English* were, and still are treated with; but before the Eruption of this last War, the very Plate Gold Buttons which the chief Factors wore upon their Cloaths, were demanded to be paid Custom for, as often as they cross'd the River of *Suratt*. This, to the Purser Marine particularly, was insufferable, whose Employment engages him frequently at *Sualy*, to which he must always pass the River; inasmuch as in a short time the very Intrinsick Value of his Gold Buttons would be spent in

*The Severity of the* Mogul's *Officers to the* English *at* Suratt.

*Another instance of their Severity.*

[1] In 1680 Aurangzeb reimposed the Jizia or tax on all infidels. The East India Company refused to pay, whereupon he raised the duty on European goods from the 2 per cent of the original charter granted to them by the Court of Delhi to 3½ per cent. and afterwards 4 per cent; ½ per cent. was remitted for a short time as a reward to Oxenden for his defence of Surat against Sivaji in 1664.

[2] Harris succeeded Sir John Child as President of Surat and Governor of Bombay on the latter's death in 1690. He was at the time in prison, in retaliation for Child's seizure of the Moghal ships. *Vide infra*, p. 240.

Custom. And we are all sensible how hard these violent Despotick Proceedings bear upon *English* Spirits, totally unaccustom'd to such Servility, and bless'd with such Paternal Constitutions, as appoint the meanest Subject Absolute Monarch of his petty Free-hold, exempt from all Impositions, but what are voted by the Assembly of the whole Kingdom, in its Representatives.

*The* Siddy *landing upon* Bombay.

These, with other things, made a Rupture; and after some small Disputes at Sea, at which the *Indians* are never vigorous, the *Mogul* attempts the sending a Land-Army upon *Bombay*, whose *Siddy* or General having receiv'd Intelligence of Sir *John Wyburn's* Death, who was Governour of *Bombay*, and a Man bred to War, immediately prepares to land his Men upon the Island, and storm the Fort, and totally rout the *English* upon it. For now the *Siddy* expected great Success in his Attempts, because he challeng'd our General at that Weapon, in which he knew he was not skilled. Sir *John Child*,[1] who was bred a Merchant, and created Baronet by the King, and appointed General of the *English* Forces in *India* by the Company, was, he knew, a General but no Souldier; and better skilled at his Pen, than his Sword; and more expert at casting an Account, than in martialling and conducting an Army. And accordingly, his neglect of fortifying the Island till the *Siddy* was upon it, tho the Company had frequently requir'd it from him, and his vain Expressions, *That he would bring the* Mogul *to consent to his Proposals of*

*Sir* John Child *unfit for a General.*

*His neglecting to fortifie the Island.*

[1] Sir John Child was appointed President or General of Surat in 1682, and Governor-General of all their possessions in the East four years later. He transferred the seat of government from Surat to Bombay and started upon a vigorous policy of suppression of various abuses, private trade, interlopers, &c., which made him cordially detested. He first conceived the idea, developed by Clive, of making the English a territorial power in India. His challenge to Aurangzeb, however, led to disastrous results and he was forced to sue ignominiously for peace. Hamilton (*New Account*, xvii-xix.) gives an amusing but biased account of Child's blustering, cowardice, and incompetence. He died in 1690. His namesake and patron Sir Josiah was actually no relation of his (R. and O. Strachey, *Keigwin's Rebellion*, p. 162).

*Peace, and blow the* Siddy *off the Island, if he ever came upon it*; were all inconsistent Frailties with his station, whose Province and Employment would have looked with a better Character, had he foreseen the Danger to which the Island was exposed, and timely applied his Prevention. But the Merchant was unfit for that great Post, and grew unwieldy with too much Honour.

*The* Siddy *was Ten to One.*

The *Siddy* therefore in the Year 1688 [1] landed with an Army of Twenty Five Thousand Men, to encounter which the General commanded only Twenty Five Hundred; so that the Enemy was just Ten to One.

*The English Valour.*

Notwithstanding which Odds the *English* kept them warmly in Play, and for all that Disadvantage, repuls'd them with such Vigour, that for some Months they were unable to approach the Fort, though they landed not very far from it. The *English* were bouyed up with a strong Opinion of their own Valour, and of the *Indians* Pusillanimity, which carried them on to such bold Adventures, that they promised themselves Victory in the most dubious Engagements; and had they not been betray'd by Renegades, who discover'd their Weakness, and smallness of their Numbers, might have hoped to have repelled that numerous Host, with that weak Force they had to resist them. But the Enemy being taught the Art of mineing, and sheltering themselves in their Trenches and Basket-works, (which they learnt from the Deserters) came at length so near, that they Bombarded our

*Large stones instead of Bullets.*

Fort with massie Stones instead of Iron Bullets, whilst our Shot from thence was scarce able to annoy them, they were so defended by the Moulds they had cast up. Our Fort was well flanked with Bastions, having the Sea on one side, and encompassed on the other with a broad and deep Ditch, and had mounted on all sides very large Guns: But the Decay of Powder and Ammunition, which the constant Firing had produced, and the *Mogul*'s Army close investing of the Fort, made it advisable in our General to think on a Peace, which

*A Peace concluded.*

was in a little time concluded upon; upon which the *Siddy* left the Island.

[1] February 1689.

The General, before the Terms of Accommodation were agreed upon, dies; by a too deep Concern, as its presum'd, for suffering the *Siddy* to invade the Island; and for fear that such Proposals in a Firmaun as might suit with the Honour of his Masters the *East India* Company, might not be hearkned to by the *Mogul*. He was a quick and expert Merchant, and totally devoted to his Masters Service : Tho' the Factors in *India* charge him with Partiality to his Relations, in advancing them to Stations above their standing, to the Prejudice of those who were their Seniors, and better qualified for such Promotions. They accuse him likewise of a penurious Temper, and injuriously depriving them of the Comfort of *Europe* Liquors, which the Company's Bounty yearly bestowed, that he might the better ingratiate with his Masters for sparing their Expences, though it were a Diminution both to their Credit and their Factors Health.

*The General's Death.*

*His Skill in Merchandize.*

*Exclaim'd against by the Factors.*

He amassed abundance of Wealth during his stay, which was more than Twenty Years in *India*; the least Conjecture which is made of it is 100000*l*. His Lady, whom he left behind him, who is fam'd for Piety, Charity, and an agreeable Behaviour, is since married to Mr. *George Weldon*, fit to succeed him in his Fortune and his Bed. He is a Gentleman well descended, of easie and obliging Converse, extreme temperate and circumspect, and manages the Affairs of the Island, wherein he now as Deputy-Governour presides, with the universal Esteem and Approbation of all upon it. The Wealth which the General's Lady and Children do possess, demonstrates to what height of Fortune the Companies Servants may advance, when their Diligence and Fidelity engage the Bounty and Countenance of their Masters to encourage them.

*The General's Wealth.*

*The General's Lady married to Mr.* Weldon.

I shall remark but one thing to entertain the Reader, and conclude this part of my Discourse. As he whose Title is *most Christian*, encouraged him who is its principal Adversary to invade the Rights of Christendom, so did Senior Padre *de Pandara*, the principal Jesuite in an adjacent Island to *Bombay*, invite the *Siddy* to exterminate all the Protestants there..

*The treacherous dealings of a*

*Jesuite with the* English.

To facilitate which pious Design, he allowed the *Siddy*'s Army all the Revenues belonging to himself to aid and support the Work that was to be carried on. But with this Proviso, that when the *English* were beaten off, their Possessions, and of all the Churches belonging to the *Portuguese*, should be restor'd to him, for his own Benefit and Use. This *Padre* likewise, when the *Siddy* had invaded the Island, plentifully supplied his want of Provisions, and with great Liberality took Care to have them seasonably convey'd to him and his Army. But the *Siddy* being beaten off, these and such other perfidious Actions have forfeited all the Right of the *Portuguese* to those Lands and Estates, which the Favour and Civility of the *English* allowed them to enjoy upon the Island; and therefore this *Padre* and his Associates are more likely to suffer a disseizing of what they had, than the *English*, as they design'd. This breeds no small Heat and Fury in the Breasts of the turbulent Jesuites, who upon this have rais'd some strong Commotions; it has excited their Revenge, and makes them sometimes threaten in a passionate Rage the retaking of their Lands by Force. Few Men can enjoy very peaceable Lives, who have any fair Possessions near the Convents of these men: For even in the *Indies* they have gain'd that Ascendant over the Tempers and Estates of the People, that a pleasant Seat, and a fruitful Plantation, can hardly escape their gaining: Which renders that Society a Burden insupportable to all the rest of that Religion, who are seated there. The Incomes of that Church, whereof this *Padre* is chief, shews in some measure their growing Wealth; for they are said to amount to the value of a Pound of Gold a Day.[1]

*The Jesuites growing Power in* India.

[1] The Jesuits had bitterly opposed the transfer of Bombay to the British. Their great stronghold was the Bandra College, for which see Fryer's account, i. 182 ff. They helped Humphrey Cooke in his attempt to seize the island of Bombay in 1667. They had extensive lands in the north of the island, which were confiscated because they helped the Sidi in 1691. Their church at Parel was confiscated for a similar reason in 1719, and became successively a Government House and a Bacteriological Laboratory.

BOMBAY FORT FROM THE LAND

# THE ISLAND OF ELEPHANTA[1]

AT three Leagues distance from *Bombay* is a small Island called *Elephanta*, from the Statue of an *Elephant* cut in Stone, in equal proportions to one of those Creatures in his full Growth. This Figure is placed in the middle of a Field, conspicuous to any Passenger that enters upon that part of the Island. Here likewise are the just dimensions of an Horse Carved in Stone, so lively, with such a Colour and Carriage, and the ſhape finisht with that Exactness, that many have rather Fancyed it, at a distance, a living Animal, than only a bare Representation. These Figures have been Erected not barely for displaying the Statuary's Skill, or gratifying the Curiosity of the Sight, but by their admirable Workmanship were more likely design'd to win upon the Admiration, and thereby gain a kind of Religious Respect from such Heathens as came near them.

*The reason of the Name.*

*An Elephant and Horse well Cut here.*

*The Design of the Figures.*

But that which adds the most Remarkable Character to this Island, is the fam'd *Pagode* at the top of it; so much spoke of by the *Portuguese*, and at present admir'd by the present Queen Dowager, that she cannot think any one has seen this part of *India*, who comes not Freighted home with some Account of it. A *Pagode* is the Heathens Temple, or a place Dedicated to the Worship of their False Gods, and borrows its Name from the *Persian* Word *Pout*,[2] which

*A Famous* Pagode *described.*

*The Derivation of* Pagode.

[1] Elephanta is the Portuguese name for the island of Ghārpuri or Puri in Bombay Harbour, containing a wonderful Hindu cave temple, belonging to about the eighth century A.D. The life-size stone elephant which gave the island its name was removed to Victoria Gardens in 1864. The horse had disappeared before 1764. Compare Fryer's account of his visit (i. 194). Nearly all the travellers, from De Castro (1541) onwards, expatiate on them. The best descriptions are in Burgess, *Rock-cut Temples of Elephanta or Gharapuri* (Bombay, 1871), and the *Gazetteer*, Bombay Presidency, xiv. 59 ff.

[2] Persian *but kadah*, 'idol house'. *Vide supra*, p. 91, note.

signifies Idol; thence *Pout Gheda*, a Temple of False Gods, and from thence, *Pagode*.

At the Ascent of an High Hill upon this Island *Elephanta*, is therefore a very large *Indian Pagode*, cut out of the very Heart of a hard Rock, whose Dimensions are about an Hundred and Twenty Foot Square, and in Height about eighteen; besides several Out-Rooms appertaining and adjoining to it. At sixteen Foot distance from one another are sixteen Pillars of Stone, Cut out with much Art and Ingenuity, whose Diameters are three Foot and an half, design'd as it were for the Support of this weighty Building, whose Roof is a lofty Broad Rock. Out of the sides of this *Pagode*, thus Beautified with these lovely Columns and curious Arches, are Figures of Forty or Fifty Men, each of them Twelve or Fifteen Foot High, in just and exact Symetry, according to the Dimensions of their various Statures. Of these Gigantick Figures, some had six Arms, and others three Heads, and others of such vast Monstrosity, that their very Fingers were larger than an ordinary Man's Leg. Upon some of their Heads were Ornamental Crowns, neat and Artificially wrought, whilst others near them held Scepters in their Hands, and above the Heads of others are multitudes of little People represented in a posture of Devotion; some I observ'd leaning upon Women, and others upon the Head of a Cow, an Animal most venerable in *India*. Here are some taking an Amiable Charming Lady by the Chin, and there the horrid Prospect of others hewing in pieces little Children; and generally above the Heads of all, are abundance of diminutive Folk hovering in the Air, represented with chearful Aspects, and in lively Figures. This variety of pleasant and monstrous Images, I lookt upon as no other than the several Objects of the Gentiles Worship, as each Adorer's Fancy led him to his several God, either of Terror or Delight.

*Variety of strange Figures.*

There is nothing of Beauty in the Frontispiece of this *Pagode*, or of Ornament at the Entrance into it. The Figures of these Gigantick Men, to which the Heathen have paid a profound Veneration, and Reverenc'd as Heroes or Demi-Gods

*The Heathens Fancy concerning Giants.*

formerly, (for this Island is at present in the Possession of the *Portuguese*) are the representation of the first Race of Mortals, which, according to the Account of their Chronicles, were all Gyants, but dwindled by degrees into lesser proportions, and at length, thro' the degeneracy of Manners, which caused an Universal decay of Humane Nature, they shrunk into these small proportions in which they appear now in the World.[1] So that the present smallness of our Stature, according to them, derives its declension and Decay from the Excess of Vice, and the small remains of Vertue that are left. And because the Forming of a Temple out of such hard Matter, requir'd Incredible endless Pains, therefore they would Insinuate that these Giants here expressed, were only capable of such Performances, which seem now to exceed that ordinary strength we have now to go thro' with such a Work.

*The breaking up of the* Mussouns.

About the middle of *September* 1690. when the *Mussouns* were broken up, we were order'd for *Suratt*, which was very agreeable to all on Board. In our Passage we met with a puny sort of Pirates called *Sanganians*,[2] who finding us a Ship of Force, durst not attempt upon us. But a Fortnight before this time, a small *English* Ship of no Countenance, was encounter'd by two or these *Sanganians*, and Boarded by them. This the *English* Master scarce resisted, because he

*The Fight of an* English *Ship with the* Sanganians.

[1] The figures actually represent Siva and Parvati, the Hindu Trinity, and similar subjects.

[2] These are the Sanghāras or Sanganis of Okhāmandal, in the western extremity of Kathiāwār. They claimed descent from one Sangan, and their capital was Sangan Kotra, which is an island at high tide. Hamilton, *New Account*, i. 130 (chap. xii), gives an interesting account of this pirate-state, which was, curiously enough, ruled over by a princess! These people, together with their neighbours the Vāghers, and a miscellaneous crowd of outlaws whom they harboured, scoured the Arabian Sea, attacking even British men-of-war, until they were exterminated by a number of expeditions from Bombay, described in detail by Low, *Indian Navy*, i, chap. ix. See also *Bombay Gazetteer*, viii (Kathiāwār), p. 165. A further exploit of the Sanganians is referred to below, pp. 254–9.

had fitted his Ship for a close Fight, and therefore withdrawing his Men from the Decks, prepared them with small Fire-Arms, and put the Powder Chests in order, on purpose to receive them. The *Sanganians*, who fancied all their own easie Purchase, were so warmly entertain'd, that as soon as they entered, they were repulsed, and speedily withdrew, betaking themselves to the Water, to evade the fury of the Fire on Board.

Sualy. In a little time we happily arriv'd at *Sualy-bar*,[1] and the Tide serving, came to an Anchor very near the *Shoar*. Here the *Europe* Ships are permitted to ride, but no *Indian* Vessel is allowed that freedom, they are either all of them to enter the River of *Suratt*, or to Anchor at the Mouth of it; which is distant from *Sualy* two Leagues, as *Sualy* is from *Suratt* four. Here the Ships load and unload their Goods, which are kept in Yards and Ware-houses, to be ready to be shipp'd off upon occasion. When the *Benjamin* had Unloaded her Cargo here, after a long Voyage at Sea, the Commander Order'd her to be clean'd; and thereupon he found a multitude of large, well-tasted Oysters, which grew upon the bottom of the Ship, with which he feasted his Sea-men, and all the *English* at *Suratt*.

Within less than half a Mile from the Sea are three *Choultries*,[2] or Convenient Lodgings made of Timber, for the *English*, *French*, and *Dutch* Factors, at a Bow-shoot distance each from other; and made fit for their Reception by variety of Apartments; at such times as they are called down to look after the Ships Cargoes, or to recreate themselves in the Country Air, and with fresh Breezes from the Sea. Here

[1] Swally, Suvāli, the seaport of Surat, was a village 12 miles west of the city. The anchorage was in a roadstead 7 miles long and 1½ miles broad, between the shore and a sandbank which was dry at low water; about midway was the cove called Swally Hole. Between September and March, the season when the ships from Europe arrived, Swally was a scene of lively activity. Cf. Fryer, i 210 ff.

[2] A south Indian term, of doubtful etymology, meaning a *dharmasāla* or traveller's rest-house.

therefore we came on Shore, and met with an agreeable Reception and kind Entertainment from the *English* Factors: And the *Sualy Marine* being the first Land we set Foot upon belonging to the Great *Mogul*, I shall in the first place speak something particularly concerning that Mighty Monarch, and then proceed to a larger Account of the City and Inhabitants of *Suratt.*

# OF THE GREAT MOGUL

*A general Account of* Asia.

*ASIA* we know was the first Stage of Mortals, which both for Riches and Extent, is the most considerable part of our Tripartite Continent, and enjoys a temperature of Air, by its convenient position, equally superiour to both. And as it was the first Original of Mankind, by a peculiar Favour from the Supreme Author of the World; so was it likewise of Nations and Kingdoms, of Monarchies and Empires, whose Laws as well Sacred as Civil, were formed here; and those Diviner Mysteries of the *Jewish*, as well as Christian Religion were first explain'd. But what adds the greatest Glory to the place, is, that the Sacred Author of our Faith here drew his Breath, and Restor'd lost Mankind by his Death.

*Its Excellence above other parts of the World.*

*Magasthenes*[1] Reports, that 122 several Nations were the Old Inhabitants of *Asia*, which was first Invaded by *Semiramis*, afterwards by *Bacchus*, accompanied with *Hercules*, who taught them the use of Wine, (which now they have unlearnt,) of Oil, and Architecture. And indeed all Humane Arts and Sciences, as well as Architecture had their Rise, and were first taught here, which gives it a just cause of Challenging a precedence to all other parts of the World. *India*, which is one of its Chief Kingdoms, in latter Days was Discover'd by the *Portuguese*, in the Year 1486, by doubling the *Cape of Good Hope*; and since by the *English* and the *Dutch*, who make a greater Figure now than those more Early Discoverers, are possessed of some of their principal Forts and Factories, and daily out-do them in carrying on a vigorous Beneficial Negotiation in all parts.

*The passage to* India *how discover'd.*

[1] Megasthenes was the ambassador of Seleukos Nikator at the court of Chandragupta Maurya, the great Indian emperor and grandfather of Asoka, at Pātaliputra, the modern Patna, at the close of the fourth century B.C. See J. W. McCrindle, *Ancient India as described in Classical Literature* (London, 1901), pp. 10 ff., for the legends about these early invasions of India.

And as the Riches and extent of *Asia* surpass the other Quarters of the World; so has it rais'd its Monarchs to a point of Grandeur equally glorious and Renown'd. And that spacious Body which is awed by the *Indian* Scepter, is reputed to be one of the most Famous and Greatest, not only of all *Asia*, but of all this Globe of Earth besides. And if we consider the Diamonds and other Stones of value, the Gold and other Metals, the Spices and Druggs, the Silks and Cottons, and the vast prodigious quantities of all those rich Commodities and precious Stones, with which *India* abounds, we cannot deny it that Transcendency which its Monarch pretends to, of being Superior to other Nations of the Earth, and that it yields the Palm to none besides.

*The Riches of* India.

The *Indian* Emperour, commonly stiled the *Mogul*, deduces that Title from the last Conquerors of *India*, who were White of Complexion; which is the name of a Potent People inhabiting a vast Country in the Confines of *Tartary*, from whom they derive their Name and Descent; and tho' the Native *Indians* are all of an Olive Tawny Colour, yet these are all White and Fair, and of the same Belief with their Emperour, which is the *Mahometan*: Because *Emmaupaxda*,[1] the seventh Descendant from *Tamerlane*, being once much distressed by the *Parthians* or *Tartars*, was driven to sue for Relief from his Neighbouring Potentate the Emperour of *Persia*, which was harken'd to upon these Terms, that he should Convert to the *Persian* Faith, and submit himself and Followers to that Religion.

Moguls, *from whence.*

*Their Religion.*

*Tamerlane*[2] (that is Lame, because one of his Legs was

Tamerlane *the*

[1] Emmaupaxda is evidently a corruption of Humāyuñ Pādshāh, the favourite son of the emperor Bābur, who succeeded him in 1530. He was defeated by Sher Shāh, and after many wanderings, in the course of which the future emperor Akbar was born in 1542, he fled to Shāh Tahmāsp in Persia, who consented to help him on condition that he was converted from the Sunni to the Shiah sect. It should be noted that the Moghals, as their name implies, were originally Mongolians from the Steppes of Central Asia.

[2] Timur-i-lang, or the Lame (The Tamburlaine of English

*first of the* Indian*Emperours.* shorter than the other) was the first of the Kings of *India*, from whom his Successors boast their Original. He was Born in *Samerchandia*, a place in *Tartary*, and liv'd about the Year 1398, in the Reign of *Richard* the 2*d*. And that we may not defraud this Mighty Hero of his Valour and Renown, the *His Exploits.* glory of his Conquests has certainly far out-done the noblest Exploits of any of the *Roman Cæsars*, and the Fortune of his Arms has gone beyond the Successes of *Alexander* the Great. So that all the Registers and Archieves of Ancient Heroes, and all the Annals of *Grecian* or *Roman* Atchievements, cannot furnish us with Memoirs of this nature. For he extended his Conquests from *East* to *West*, and carried his Triumphant Banners from *China* to *Poland*, whereby he made all *Asia* tremble; which was a Victory exceeding the actions of the Bravest and most Fortunate Captains of former Ages. From Aureng-Zebe *the* 11*th. from* Tamerlane. him *Aureng-Zebe* is the Eleventh, who possesseth the Crown of *India*; and well may this great Emperour exalt his Pedigree, and value his Descent from so fam'd and Glorious an Ancestor, when that Wise and Powerful Nation of the *Romans* built so much of their Honour and Renown upon two such Ancestors as *Romulus* and *Remus*. The mighty Deeds Schah-Abbas, *a mighty Emperour of* Persia. and renown'd Exploits of *Schah Abbas*,[1] the *Persian* Emperor, have likewise imprinted Eternal Characters of Fame and Honour upon his Name, which is now by vulgar use made the signification of any thing extraordinary or Miraculous; so that when any thing surpassing Excellent, or wonderful, is either done or spoken, the *Indians* presently say of it, *Schah-Abbas!*

literature), was a Barlās Turk, whose father was the first of the tribe to be converted to Islam. He was born at Kesh, fifty miles from Samarkand, in 1336. He conquered Samarkand in 1369 and invaded India in 1398. He took Delhi and put its inhabitants to the sword. His Empire stretched from China to the Volga. He died in 1405.

[1] Shāh Abbās the Great (1586–1628) was the wisest and most powerful of the rulers of Persia. He united the country, and at his court were representatives of nearly every European power.

*The Cruelty of* Aureng-Zebe.

But had *Aureng-Zebe*[1] been more Industrious in imitating the Virtues of his Progenitors, than in raising himself to a long and proud series of their Titles, and less Cruel in his Bloody Accession to the Crown; this would have added more Splendour to his Throne,[2] than all that matchless Grandeur with which it is adorn'd by Diamonds, Emeralds, Topazes and Pearls, and would have given a truer and more lasting Nobility to his Name, than to have gain'd it with Infamy and repeated Murther. The *Roman* Histories inform us, that while that People was Just and Temperate, and Religious Observers of their Laws, their Empire was establisht in its Glory, and Success attended their Arms and Designs. And concerning the *Chinese* History, 'tis affirm'd to us, that Virtue alone formed that great Empire, and that nothing concurr'd to its Confirmation more than the Virtuous Lives of their Emperours; in so much that Forty four Kings enamour'd with the Virtue of *Venvam*,[3] submitted to his Laws. But few of the *Eastern* Kingdoms besides, are qualified for such a boast as this. Their Emperors generally sheath their Swords in the Blood of all that stand Competitors for the Soveraignty, tho' they be the Sons of the same Parent, and obliged by a natural Tenderness and Compassion to the mutual Offices of Humanity and Love. For divesting themselves of these Principles, and being whetted with an innate Ambition for Empire and Command, and led by the in-bred Laws of Self-Preservation, they pursue their Claims to the Royal Dignity, either by open Violence, or secret

*The Cruelty of the* Eastern *Emperours.*

[1] Aurangzeb Ālamgīr (1659–1707) was the greatest of the Moghul emperors. He acquired the throne by imprisoning his father Shāh Jahān, and by defeating and making away with his brothers Dāra, Shuja, and Murād Baksh, and their children. His sister, Roshanāra Begum, abetted him. He was an orthodox bigot and restored the strict religious forms of the Sunni sect in place of the easy latitudinarianism of his ancestors.

[2] The reference is to the famous Peacock Throne of Delhi, made by Shāh Jahān in 1628, and stolen by Nādir Shāh in 1739. See V. A. Smith, *Oxford History of India*, pp. 392–3.

[3] Venvam is probably Woo Wang, first Emperor of the Chow Dynasty *c.* 1000 B.C.

Machinations, by private Treachery, or publick Hostility; not sparing the slaughter of their Brethren, or Pretenders to the Crown. This is the Inhumane method pursu'd not only by the *Ottaman*, but *Indian* Kings, from which *Aureng-Zebe* did not decline, in his Cruel and Treacherous Ascent to the Throne. For his Father *Cha-Jehan* he Imprison'd, till he died: The Head of his Eldest Brother, *Daracha*, he commanded to be cut off; his second Brother, *Sultan Sujah*, he put to Flight, who was slain in his Retirement; and his youngest Brother, *Morad-Bacche* had the same ill Fate with the Eldest, was Beheaded too. Nor was this enough to satiate his Cruelty, or stop his Revenge, but tho' he saved *Rauchenara-Begum*, his Favourite Sister for assisting his Designs; yet the other, *Begum-saheb*,[1] fell a Victim to his Fury, and was presum'd to be taken off by Poison, for her Fidelity to her Father in his Distress. Thus a Father and four Children were sacrificed to the Jealousie and Malice of a Victorious Brother, who by Policy and profound Dissimulation gain'd the Crown, and pursuing his good Fortune with Success, was seated and Established in the Throne of his Fathers; and notwithstanding all those execrable Villanies, he liv'd a long time full of Years, a standing Monument of the Divine Infinite Clemency and Forbearance.

*A Father and four Brethren destroy'd by* Aureng-Zebe.

*The Succession of the Crown.*

The Crown of *India* is not Intail'd by Primogeniture on the Sons, but is ravisht by Force, or carried by Craft of such as do stand in competition for it, who to facilitate the access to it, ingratiate with the *Omrahs*[2] and Grandees at Court, with the Governours of Provinces, and Principal Ministers of State, to fortify their Pretensions, and secure Parties to themselves both in the Cities and the Camp, against the time they begin to skirmish for the Royal Inheritance, and try their Wit and Valour for the *Indian* Diadem in the Field. And as the *Japanners*, in laying the Foundation of a Palace, rip up their Bowels with a Cric,[3] or Dagger,

[1] Jahānārā, Shāh Jahān's favourite daughter.

[2] *Umarā*, Ar. plur. of Amīr, a noble.

[3] Malay *kris*, a dagger.

and so sacrifice themselves, imagining that such voluntary Victims are necessary to render both the Owners of the Building and the Habitation Fortunate; so is it the Misfortune of the *Eastern* Courts, that they think not the Throne, to which they are advanc'd, secure, or settled, without laying the Foundation of their Reign in the Destruction of all Rivals to the Crown, and in the Blood of their nearest Relatives, that can pretend to the Imperial Dignity; and make such barbarous Sacrifices necessary, for repairing and securing their own undisturb'd Tranquility and Ease.

Aureng-Zebe's *Subtility.*

'Till he was possess'd of the Arms and Treasure of his Brother *Morad-Bacche,* whom he betray'd by fair Pretences of Friendship, the kindest Caresses and Expressions of Endearment; *Aureng-Zebe* pretended himself devoted to Austerity, and that he would rank himself among the Religious *Faquires,* or *Derviches* of the Kingdom, to spend his days in Poverty and Abstinence, and a private retir'd Life; by which new strain of Policy, and the Mask of extraordinary sanctity, he gain'd upon the Credulity of the People, as an holy undesigning Prince; 'till by this pious Design he craftily undermined the Opposers of his Honour and Empire, and making use of Religious Intrigues, and the help of the Planet *Mercury,* he soon became Victorious, and got *Mars* the Ascendant of his better Fortunes: And by these pretensions to uncommon Holiness, he made way for the perpetration of such execrable *Crimes,* as are not very commonly heard of. But if we may measure our Opinions by his, and the Maxims he has laid down for Empire, his proceedings will not appear so very black and criminal, since he has perswaded himself that Princes are exempt from several of those Laws which bind their Subjects, and that Soveraign Heads are not so severely Accountable for the Justice of their Actions, as the inferiour rank of Men. As if the despotick Soveraignty he exercis'd on Earth, gave him a Priviledge and Charter for the same Arbitrary Proceedings with Heaven, and that he might in some measure act as absolutely with the Supreme Lord of the Creation, as he does incontroulably with his own Subjects.

*His state Maxim.*

The unnatural methods he pursued in wresting the Crown from the Head of his Father, cautions him from giving the least opportunity for such Rebellious practices in his Sons, and to prevent all occasions for such bold and bloody Enterprizes.

*The Rebellion of* Cha-Egber *against his Father.*

Only *Cha-Egber* his fourth Son,[1] who was born of a *Resbout*, whose Sect among all the rest of the *Indian* Inhabitants are justly reputed the most valiant, was encouraged by them to attempt the Crown, and depose his Father from the Soveraignty. These *Resbouts* were engaged in an universal Revolt, formed a formidable Army, and placed *Cha-Egber*, who was descended from them by his Mother, at the head of it, that they might raise him betimes to the Monarchy of *India*, lest his eldest Brother should get the start of him, and succeed in the Government of that vast Empire, after his Father's Death. *Aureng-Zebe* not dreaming of such an Attempt, lay very open to surprisal by this Barbarous Design, for want of Forces at that time to guard and secure him.

Aureng-Zebe's *contrivance to defeat his Son.*

And therefore upon his Son's advancement to the Capital City, betook himself to Stratagem instead of Arms, and penn'd a Letter in his Son's Name, directed to himself, to this effect, *That he was too sensible of his Duty, to dare to proceed in that disturbance, which the* Resbouts *had raised against his Person and his Kingdom, and therefore he led the Ring-leaders and the rest of the Offenders towards the Capital City, to be seized on by the Guards within, that they might be deliver'd up to Justice, and condign Punishment, according to their demerits, which would prove an unquestionable Argument to satisfie his Father of his Fidelity.* This Letter was sent by a faithful Servant of *Aureng-Zebe*'s into his Son's Camp, who pretended to come from him to his Father, but was there stopp'd, and the Letter open'd and read; and, the *Resbouts* upon it were so inrag'd, that all the Protestations *Cha-Egber* could make were impossible to appease them, or perswade their Engagement of themselves any

[1] Prince Akbar was the son of Dilras Bāno Begam, and not of a Rajput lady. He went over to the Rajput side in 1681, but was defeated by stratagem and died in exile in Persia, 1704.

longer in his Service. Some therefore left him, and others refused to advance a step forwards, 'till *Aureng-Zebe* had time given him to unite his strength, and muster his Forces; whereby he vanquisht the Enemy, and forc'd his Son to a speedy flight. In this disgrace and haste he fled to *Persia*, where he was honourably entertain'd by that Emperour, with all those Lords that attended his Flight; and is since married at that Court to the Emperour's Daughter. He daily waits for some favourable Revolution when he may return to *India* again, whither he hopes to be recall'd by his Father's death; and with the powerful Alliance and Aid of *Persia*, and the united Interest of his Friends in *India*, he expects to gain the Crown he unfortunately lost, and establish his glory in that Kingdom, to which he is now forced to continue an Exile.

Cha-Egber's *flight to* Persia.

Whenever the *Indian* Emperour is proclaim'd, 'tis with Publick Jubilee, with Songs and Musick, Mirth and Revellings, with Fireworks and gawdy Shows in all parts of the Kingdom; on this day their Ships hang out their Flags and Ensigns, and expose their Pendants not only at the Top-mast-head, but deck the Shrowds with ten or twenty more. The Crown he wears is of invaluable price, and the Throne he ascends is reckon'd at 300 *Lack* of *Roupies*. Each *Lack* is one hundred thousand *Roupics*, which with us is 11250 *l.* Sterling, reckoning a *Roupie* at 2*s.* 3*d.* Neither are these Solemnities observ'd upon an Anniversary day only, according to *Eúropean* Customs, but in Citics, Garrisons, and places of note, it obtains a weekly Celebration, not with extraordinary Illuminations, and publick joyful Feasts, but with something of Mirth and Musick more than usual. *Sunday* is the day of the Inauguration of the present *Mogul*, and solemnized with the Musick of the Trumpets at *Suratt* in the Castle there; I wisht when first I saw it, that they had converted the Civil into a Religious observation of that day.

*Great Rejoycing at the Proclaiming of the Emperour.*

*The 5th of* November, *remarkable in* India.

There is another day in *India*, as well as *England*, which is eminently remarkable, the 5*th* of *November*. This day the great *Mogul* is weighed, and if it's found that he has

*The Weighing of the* Mogul.

increas'd in bulk, above what he weighed the preceding Year, this adds excess of Mirth and Joy to the Solemnity; but if he prove lighter in the Scales, this diminishes their Triumphs, and damps their chearful Entertainments. The Grandees and Officers of State prepare for this Feast, two Months before its approach, what costly Jewels and curious Rarities they can any where meet with, which they present to the Emperour at this Ceremony; either to secure his Favour, or to ingratiate with him for a more exalted station, or Honourable Employ. The *Moguls* are sometimes weighed against Silver, which has been distributed to the Poor.

*New names given by the* Mogul *to his Subjects.*

When any *Indian* Subject stands so fair in the Eye of his Prince, as to be raised to some advanc'd degree of Trust or Honour, he acquires at the same time a new Name, according to the Prince's Fancy; according to what we read in *Dan.* 1.7. Thus the preceding Governour of *Suratt* was named *Muck Teer Chan,*[1] i. e. *Lord after my own Heart*; the present is stiled *Anamat Chan*, or, *Conscientious Lord*, because of his Fidelity and Integrity. For all the Lands of *Indostan* belonging intirely to the *Mogul*, the *Omrahs* there cannot derive their Titles from their Earldoms, Lordships, or Mansion-Houses (as with us) because they are none of their Propriety, only Tenants at will, during the *Mogul*'s pleasure; and therefore the *Mogul* confers upon them such Names of Dignity, as by their personal Conduct or Accomplishment he thinks they merit. And as he bestows Titles proper to his Generals, of *Invincible*, or *Victorious*;[2] so to his *Nabobs*, or Governours, he bethinks himself of Names suitable to their Stations, or his Opinion of their Excellencies and Endowments. This is a common thing practis'd likewise in other Kingdoms of the *East*, as at *Siam*; the King there gives Names not only to his Domesticks and *Mandarins*, or Nobles, but to his very Elephants. Tho his own Name is industriously conceal'd, lest his Enemies by some Enchantment might work upon it.

*The King of* Siam's *Name conceal'd.*

[1] Mukhtiar Khān, Independent Lord; Anāmat Khan, Trustworthy Lord.

[2] Muzaffar Khān.

Thus *Pharaoh* called *Joseph*'s Name *Zaphnath-Paaneah*, *Gen.* 41. 45. and *Job* called his Eldest Daughter *Jemimah*, *i. e.* clear as the Day: The 2*d. Keziah*, *i.e.* Pleasant as *Cassia*, or sweet Spice: The 3*d. Keren-happuck*, that is Horn, or strength of Beauty.

*The flattery of the* Eastern *Subjects.*

The dependance upon the Prince's Favour makes Obsequiousness fashionable, and Flattery practis'd in all the Courts of the *East*: So that tho' they require an account of their Affairs, and expect to be informed; yet they think it a diminution to their Grandeur, to be acquainted with any thing that may disgust, or told any thing that looks displeasing. Except among the *Chinese*, with whom the liberty of Admonishing their Emperour was established by a Law, which impowred them to use importunate Applications to him upon any failure, and caus'd them instantly to remind him of taking care of his Life and Actions, and that the virtuous Pattern of his Royal Behaviour, was the best and only method for deriving Justice, Integrity, and Loyalty upon his Magistrates and People. They likewise admonished him, that if he deviated from the transcendant Virtues of his Ancestors, his Subjects would inevitably digress from their Duties of Allegiance and Fidelity to him. For it is a receiv'd Maxim among those People, *That the Subjects are like Ears of Corn, wherewith a Field is cover'd, and the Morals of their Emperour are like a Wind, which inclines them which way it pleaseth.*

*The freedom used by the K. of* China's *Subjects with him.*

But the *Indian* Emperours are incontroulable in what they say, as well as in their Actions; so far, that it is an allowed Maxim in this Court, *That if they say at Noon-day it is Night, you are to answer, Behold the Moon and the Stars!* This flattery of their Subjects has made them fancy themselves more than Demi-Gods, and vaunt themselves in the most exorbitant swelling Titles. Thus the Emperour of *Japan* calls himself Son of the Sun; and for this Reason, when the Imperial Diadem is upon his Head, will never after appear in the sight of the Moon, for fear of debasing his Greatness, and because he thinks it would Eclipse his Glory. Thus the present

*Court Flattery.*

*Proud Titles of the* Eastern *Kings.*

*Mogul's* Father stiled himself *Cha-Jehan, i.e.* King of the World: and the Name of *Aureng-Zebe* imports the Ornament of the Throne; the titles of the King of Bisnagar are no less Extravagant than the rest, they are these, The Husband of good Fortune, the God of great Provinces, King of the greatest Kings, the Lord of Horsemen, the Master of them which cannot speak, Emperour of three Emperours, Conqueror of all he sees, and Keeper of all he Conquers, Dreadful to the Eight Coasts of the World, Vanquisher of the *Mahumetans*, and Lord of the *East*, *West*, *North*, *South*, and of the Sea, which now Ruleth and Governeth this World.[1]

*The Titles of the K. of* Bisnagar.

Thus they exalt their Pomp and Vanity by these proud and Swelling Titles, and expect there an Obeysance little less than of Adoration from their Subjects and Adressors. The *Tailim*,[2] or deep *Salem*, which is the usual Salutation to the *Mogul*, is, First to kiss the Ground with the Hand, then to touch the Breast with it, and afterwards raise it to the Head; and all this thrice repeated, when any person approaches his Imperial Presence. The ordinary *Indian* Salute, is only the lifting up of the Hand to the Fore-Head, and if it be to a Person of Eminence or Superiority, to bend the Head too when 'tis touched. The *Salem* of the Religious *Bramins*, is to join their Hands together, and spreading them first, make a motion towards their Head, and then stretch them out; and the *Salem* of greatest Respect, is to take hold of the Feet, and touch them with their Head; and if this is occasion'd by the committing of some Offence, laying the Hands upon the Supplicant's Back is a sign of Pardon; and the Offender generally holds fast the Feet, till he feels it upon his Back. The *Chineses* give their Prince nine Prostrations, accounting that Number sacred and lucky. And the King of *Sciam*

*The* Indian *Salutations.*

[1] The reference is to the great Hindu kingdom of Vijayanagar, which came to an end after the battle of Talikota, 1565. See V. A. Smith, *Oxford History of India*, Book III, Chap. V. Honorific titles of the kind mentioned in the text are common in the inscriptions of the period.

[2] *Taslim*, a deep salām.

requires not only a flection of the Body, but a profound Prostration before him. This Respect a surly *English* Sailer being unacquainted with, neglected to give him when he came before him, and when he was threatned by the Attendants for not yielding to this submissive Obeysance, he boldly replyed, *That he esteem'd his own Prince as Great and Powerful as any, and to him he never gave more observance, than bowing his Body, and uncovering his Head, and he was resolv'd never to shew a greater Civility to any Prince in the World than to his own.*

*The surliness of an* English *Sailer.*

There are different Opinions concerning the number of Kingdoms which are reduc'd to the *Indian* Scepter, some reckon Thirty Nine, or Forty. *Boterus*[1] affirms there are Forty Seven, a later Author affirms the number of Provinces in *Indoston* to be only Twenty; who tells us likewise, that the Annual Revenues amount to above three hundred and thirty *French* Millions, which does more than double the Incomes of any the most Potent Monarchs on Earth.

*Divers Opinions of the number of Kingdoms in* India.

The vast Tract of Land to which this large Empire is extended, reaches near 2000 Miles in Length, some say more; which makes it necessary for the *Mogul*, whose Territories are so large, to employ a numerous Army to awe his Infinite multitude of People, and keep them in an absolute Subjection. Several hundred thousand Soldiers are the least that are maintain'd in Pay; some affirm he allows Pay for one Million of Horses, and for every Horse and Man about eighteen pounds, whose Wages seldom run on beyond a Month or two, because by them they have their only Subsistence. And did he not constantly clear their Arrears, and keep on foot continually such a Potent Army, he could never be able to command the turbulent *Rajahs*, nor prevent their

*The extent of* India.

*See the Embassy of Sir* Tho.*Roe.*[2]

[1] Giovanni Botero, author of *Relationi Universali*, 1622, four parts. *Aggiunta alla quarta parta dell' Indie* 1623. The four parts deal with Europe, Asia, Africa, and America.

[2] Sir Thomas Roe, our Ambassador at the Court of Jahāngīr, 1615–18. See his *Embassy to the Court of the Great Mogul*, ed. Foster. Oxford, 1926.

Plotts and Insurrections; who notwithstanding frequently molest his Government, pretend a right to their Conquer'd Dominions, and raise Armies against him with that Tribute which they refuse to pay. But sure it were better, instead of all those needless repeated Conquests, he could assure himself of fixing an Empire in the Hearts of Loyal, tho' less numerous Subjects.

*Frequent Revolts in* India.

The frequent Revolts in *India* render those parts very miserable, and reduce the Inhabitants to a very distressed State. For hoping to retrieve their Liberty, and regain the Kingdoms they have lost, they often declare for a *Rajah*, which is a Native *Indian* Prince, and stand by him till the *Mogul* over-powers their Forces, defeats their Rebellion, stints their Progress, and reduces them to a tame Obedience again. So that one while the *Mogul* comes upon a City, and demands the Contribution of so many Thousand Gold Moors,[1] or else he threatens the Raseing its Foundations, Pillaging the Houses, and converting them into Smoak and Flames. When he is retreated, the *Rajah's* Army flies upon them with Fury and Hunger, and storms their Towns, and threatens them with Fire and Sword as their inevitable Fate, if they offer to delay the payment of so many thousand Gold Roupies more. Or if these formidable Threats are not listned to, they take that by Rapine, which was civilly demanded, ravage the Country, and load themselves with Plunder and Spoil. Which makes Fear and Distress, Poverty and Famine the universal Air and Genius of those unquiet Abodes. This was the unhappy condition of *Suratt*,[2] An. 1664, when *Rajah Sivagy* plundred it for Forty Days together, carried off in Gold, Silver, and Jewels an Infinite Sum, without sparing any part of it, but the Habitations of the *English* and *French*, and the Castle, who defended themselves with their Canon.

*The miserable lives of the* Indians *in some parts.*

Sometimes the Conquest of one part of the Kingdom is the

[1] *Mohur*, the official name of the chief gold coin of India, equivalent to 14 rupees. Pers. *muhr*, seal. Cf. p. 132, *infra*.

[2] Sivājī plundered Surat 6–10 January—four days, not forty. See Foster, *English Factories in India*, 1661–4, pp. 296 ff.

loss of another, for that *Rajah* who without reluctancy submitted to the *Mogul*'s Power, while his Camp was near, immediatcly disclaims it, when he knows it at a distanee; which Commotions bring on the *Mogul* endless Troubles and Expence.

A mighty *Rājah*[1] is now abroad, in his Expedition to the Coast of *Choromandel*, where he expects Recruits of Men and Money; he has secur'd a strong Party upon the Coast of *Malabar*, and it's believ'd will in a short time appear in the Field with very Potent Forces. If his Martial Arms be proportionably as extensive as his Natural, they will certainly reach very far, and stretch his Authority farther than any Potentates in the *East*; for they are so long, that as he stands, his Hands reach down below his Knees. And may be the *Indians*, who upon this account are apt to harbour Superstitious Thoughts concerning him, may be the easier won to his Alliance and Designs; if this be not a feign'd Report. *A particular* Rajah'*s Revolt.* *The great length of a* Rajah'*s Arms.*

The *Mogul*'s Army are pursuing their Conquests with all vigour towards Cape *Comeron*, the Southermost Promontory of *India*, where are several Inferiour Princes not yet attempted upon, the Conquering of whom takes up the thoughts, and is the main Object of *Aureng-Zebe*'s Ambition. *The* Mogul'*s Ambition.*

Besides the vast Army which is always Incamped, and ready for any Expedition and onset, the several *Nabobs*[2] and Vice-Roys are obliged to keep continually in Pay considerable Forces, for maintaining their own Port, and the Peace of the Provinces where they preside. Soveraign Princes do not exceed some of these in point of State and Income. The *Nabob* or Governour of *Bengal* was reputed to have left behind him at his Death, twenty Courous of Roupies: A Courou is an hundred thousand Lacks, a Lack is an hundred thousand Roupies, a Padan is an hundred thousand Courous, a Nil *The* Mogul'*s Forces.* *Lacks, Courous, Padans, Nils, what they are.*

[1] The reference seems to be to Rājārām the Marātha, who succeeded Sambājī in 1680 and died in 1700. In 1691, the Moguls made their furthest advance southwards, as far as Tanjore and Trichinopoly. Sijavi was famous for his long arms.

[2] Port. for *nawāb*, Deputy, really the plural of Ar. *naib*, *nāyab*.

is an hundred thousand Padans; Lacks, Courous, Padans and Nils, rise by a gradual advancement of an hundred thousand higher one than another.[1]

Aureng-Zebe's *living in his Camp.*

*The Camp well provided with Necessaries.*

*Aureng-Zebe* seldom leaves the Camp, but both he and his *Haram* keep their Tents Winter and Summer in the Field. His numerous Army has a daily supply of all Provisions and Necessaries from all parts of the Empire, in as great plenty and order as any of its Cities can afford them; and whatever the Kingdom yields, may be with as much ease purchased here, as in any publick Fair. So that there is always in the Camp a multitude of People brought thither, as large almost as the Army, who come thither, some out of Curiosity, others out of Friendship and Relation, but the most for Sale of their Goods, which the Soldiers take off, by whom they live, and from whom they have their Subsistence.

*The Order in the Camp.*

Where-ever the *Mogul* removes his Camp, the Generals and Officers, as well as private Centinels, still pitch their Tents in the same Position and Place in respect to his, and one another, as they formerly were posted in; so that he who once knows where such a Captain had his standing, may readily be directed to it, though he has decamped from the place he left an Hundred Miles. For all are obliged to the same distance, and to the same Station and Quarter in relation to one another, and the Emperour's Tent, in whatever Ground they pitch their Tents.

*Measuring the Way, a thing customary in the* Indies.

Before the *Mogul* begins to move his Camp, to set out upon a Progress, or undertake any small Journey; and before any Omrah, or Person of Note sets forward to Travel, the way they must pass is measured out by Line, by a Servant appointed for that Trouble; and a just account both of the distance and number of Miles is brought to them, before the Journey is begun: and so exact are they in maintaining this piece of *Indian* State, of measuring the Road, that though they have travell'd that way often, and are sufficiently

[1] Lākh, Skt. *laksha*, 100,000; kror, Skt. *koti*, one hundred lakhs, or ten million; padan, Skt. *padma*, is 10,000 millions; nil, Skt. *nīla*, 100,000 millions.

knowing in all its Paths, yet without this Ceremony they are loath to stir.

*The Mogul's Elephants.*

Besides the Army, and the several Nabobs and Governours of Provinces and Cities, of Towns and Castles, which drain his Treasure, and put him upon immense Expences, the *Indian* Emperour maintains daily at least Four or Five Hundred Elephants, with Camels, Mules, and other Beasts of Burthen; some for the War, and others for his Women and Attendants, his Carriage and Provisions in the Field. The principal of all his stately Campaign Elephants has a stated extraordinary Allowance of Sugar mixt with his Provender, and Jaggary Rack,[1] which is a kind of *Aqua Vitæ*, with his Water; which consume the *Mogul* Five Hundred Roupies every Month, that is, near Sixty Pounds Sterling.

*The White Elephant respected at* Siam.

These mighty Animals are in high esteem in all the Oriental Kingdoms, especially at *Siam*, whose Soveraign is renown'd for his Respect to the White Elephant, upon the Perswasion he has of its being inspired with the Soul of some supreme Prince. And from the Bulk and Strength, the Sensibleness and Docility of that Creature, they infer commonly, that nothing less than the Soul of some Illustrious Prince, or mighty Heroe, can animate it, and be receiv'd into a Body so stately and large. The *Achen* Elephants are most looked upon for their Teeth, because that Ivory they say, maintains its Whiteness, and turns not Yellow, as other does. They say that it's thirty Years before the Elephants come to their full growth.

*The* Achen *Ivory best.*

*Two ways of catching Elephants.*

The wild Elephants, which the *Mogul* and other Princes keep tame, are taken different ways. Sometimes by digging Pits in the Ground, and covering them with false Earth, in the Paths frequented by the Elephants, which walking upon it deceives their Weight, and suddenly they drop down. But if the unweildy Animal chances to evade this Covert Contrivance, he grows very vigilant ever after, and warily with his Trunk examines all suspected Ground he is likely to tread

[1] Jaggary Rack is arrack distilled from the sap of the jagry or kitūl palm. Cf. pp. 142–3, and 230.

upon. Sometimes they decoy the Male with a Female Elephant bred up for that purpose, which leads him into a narrow Passage,[1] hedged in so strongly on both sides with Trunks of Trees, and many pieces of Timber, that he can neither turn about his monstrous Body to step backwards, nor remove with all his mighty Strength the Obstacles that inclose and barracade him, till he is chafed and spent, and thoroughly intangled. After this he is taken and led home between two others that are tame, and his Wildness presently wears off, and in less than a Fortnight's time he quietly submits to Discipline, bethinks himself, and grows familiar.

*The way that the Elephants engender.*

The Female Elephant receives the Male lying upon her Back, contrary to the Custom of other Animals; and the Male is said to carry his Testicles between his Ears. After they are taken they seldom Ingender, tho' sometimes they burn with a lustful Heat, which is not extinguished but by Fire brought near them, or the Blood of the Riders, if they chance at that time to be upon them.

*The Respect paid to the Indian Emperour, and Men of Note.*

The Princes of *Indostan* who attend the Court, and all the *Omrahs* and Principal Officers of the Crown, observe always a due Respect, and keep a convenient Distance to the awful Person of the Emperour. So that whenever he thinks fit to ascend an Elephant, and mount himself on that lofty Creature to take the Air, the *Omrahs*, in a lower Order, ride only upon Horses. When he seats himself in his Palanquin, then do they walk in a lowly Posture on Foot after him; shewing in all things a submissive Deference to his Greatness, and profound Respect to his eminently August Majesty: And till he gives the Word, no Man dares mount before him. And as if the Words of his Mouth were Oracular, no Sentence of moment proceeds from the Emperour, but the *Omrahs* greedily catch it, and cry out, *Karamat! Karamat! Wonder! Wonder!*[2] And if any Person of Note in *India* is seen by an inferiour at a distance, both on Horseback, the

[1] The *kheda* or trap used for catching wild elephants: see Hobson-Jobson, *s.v.* Keddah.

[2] *Karāmat* (P). Wonder, miracle.

meaner Person lights from his Horse, and there stands till his Superiour passes by him.

The Mahometan Religion, of which the *Mogul* is a zealous Professor, is that which is spread very far, and is chiefly countenanced in *India*; the *Mogul* never neglecting the Hours of Devotion, nor any thing, which in his Sense may denominate him a sincere Believer; insomuch that there spread a Report, a little before I left *Suratt*, that his ardent Zeal had carried him to design a long Pilgrimage for *Meccha*, to visit the Venerable Shrine of their False Prophet. His eldest Son Sultan *Mozum*[1] was to be left Inheritor of the Throne, to secure his peaceable Possession; yet would not this defend the Claims from the Royal Brothers, who are ready to dispute it with their Wit and Courage, with all the Force and Art of War. And 'tis not unlikely, whenever the Crown becomes vacant, and is under a Contest, but that *Cha-Egber*, Son-in-law to the *Persian* Emperour, will in that Martial Lottery gain the Prize, and defeat the other Pretenders. Which if it should happen, and the *English* should be assisting to his Designs at that time, either by accommodating him with Ships from *Gombrone*,[2] or befriending him at *Suratt*, they might expect very considerable Advantages in their Trade and Customs, both in *India* and the *Persian* Gulph.

*The* Mogul's *Piety.*

*The likelihood of* Cha-Egber's *succeeding his Father.*

*What Advantage the English may receive by his Succession.*

The *Mogul* delights much in Proselyting all the *Rajahs* he conquers, and bringing them to the Mahometan Faith, which has much exasperated those Grandees, and the Gentile Sects of his Kingdom. And he was so sensibly taken with a Horse presented to him by an *English* Merchant, that he commanded him to be fed near his own Apartment, and to be frequently brought forth before him, to delight his Eyes with

*The* Mogul's *Zeal.*

*His kindness for a Horse.*

[1] Prince Muazzam, Aurangzeb's eldest surviving son, was under arrest from 1687 to 1694, when he was appointed as Governor of Kābul. He succeeded his father and reigned under the title of Bahādur Shāh I, from 1707 to 1712, Prince Akbar having died in exile in 1704.

[2] Gombroon, now Bandar Abbās in the Persian Gulf, where the English had an important factory, 1616–1759.

the daily pleasant Spectacle; for no other Reason, but because he observ'd him match a Horse which *Mahomet* was wont to ride, and nearly resembled in Shape and Colour, as he somewhere read, a stately Steed of the Grand Prophet's.

*All the Land in India is the Mogul's.* The whole Kingdom of *Indoston* is intirely the Possession of the *Mogul*'s, who appoints himself Heir to all his Subjects; so that neither the Widow, nor Children of a General, can peremptorily challenge one Piece after his Decease, without the Emperour's bounteous Indulgence. He that tills the Ground, and spends his time in Agriculture, is allowed half the Product for his Pains, and the other Moyety is reserv'd for the King, which is collected by Under-Officers, who give in their Accounts to the Superiours in the Provinces, and they discount to the Publick Exchequer. Only for the Encouragement of Trade in Cities and Maritime Towns, he dispenses with the Merchants building their Houses, and the Propriety of them descending in their Families; very few are allowed Paternal Inheritances; but even all this is the extraordinary Grace and Favour of the Prince, and revocable at his Pleasure. *The Mogul absolute.* His Will likewise is the Law, and his Word incontestably decides all Controversies among them. *His Justice.* So that he is the main Ocean of Justice and Equity, and from him all the smaller Rivulets of Wealth flow, and to him they all pay Tribute, and return again. He generally determines with exact Justice and Equity; for there is no pleading of Peeridge or Priviledge before the Emperour, but the meanest Man is as soon heard by *Aureng-Zebe* as the chief *Omrah.* Which makes the *Omrahs* very circumspect of their Actions, and punctual in their Payments; because all Complaints against them are readily adjusted, and they never want jealous Rivals at Court who are willing to bring them into Disgrace with their King for any Fault.

Since the Conquest of *Viziapour*,[1] the Diamond Mines are claim'd and possess'd by the *Indian* Emperour, who for some time since thought fit to shut them up. They formerly paid

[1] Bijāpur, conquered by Aurangzeb in 1686. The diamond mines belong to Golkonda, captured in the following year.

to the King of *Golconda* so much hourly for the liberty of digging, whether they were fortunate in finding any Diamond or no; a Pagod,[1] which is a piece of Gold valued there at Nine Shillings, was the stated Price for an Hours time. We have an Account, that he reserv'd another Diamond Ground in his Country for his own Use, which yielded him daily several Ounces, whenever he imploy'd his Labourers to work, which were reckon'd to be near Six Thousand, whose very Wages consum'd a great part of the Gains.

*The Rate of digging for Diamonds.*

Those that dig the Ground are narrowly look'd to, and examin'd at their Departure, that nothing be privately convey'd or stole away; and yet they sometimes escape all Discovery, by slipping a Stone into their Mouths, or thrusting it upwards in their lower Parts, or by bribing of the Overseers. By this means we sometimes meet with large Stones very valuable. Two I saw at *Suratt*, the smaller was a sort of Table-Diamond, rated at Twelve Thousand Pounds; the other was larger, and exceeded the Price of the other almost Eight Thousand Pounds. All Stones of such a Size are Royalties, and Sacred to the Crown; and whoever finds them, or wheresoever they are heard of, they are presently seized, and taken for the use of the *Mogul*. Therefore the Owner of these Noble Diamonds solemnly engaged our Secresie, and bound us to Silence, before we were permitted a sight of them. The Stones of *India* are not so rich, or of equal Repute with those of the Island *Borneo*, whose Sparkling and Brightness gives a glorious and surpassing Splendour. The Diamonds are found rough, cover'd with a Coat or Shell, which is taken off, and then the Diamond is polish'd, and cut in such Figures, as the natural Shape of the Stone, or the Design of the Lapidary inclines to. The Art of discerning the excellence of Diamonds by the Eye, is very curious: because there is such an

*All Diamonds of such a size belong to the* Mogul.

*Diamonds from* Borneo *most fam'd.*

*The way to know true Diamonds.*

[1] The gold Pagod or *hon* was a gold coin current in South India, and worth about 4 rupees. The silver pagod, equivalent to 3½ rupees, was the standard coin prior to the introduction of the rupee in 1818. For the origin of the term, which is much disputed, *vide* Hobson-Jobson, *s.v.* Pagoda.

Affinity between the Brightness of Stones, that some eminent *Indian* Jewellers have been impos'd upon by false ones brought from *Europe*; because they shot such Rays, and the Lustre with which they shin'd was so extraordinary. But the Hammer and Scales discover'd that Fallacy, which the Eyes could not; they were softer than a genuine Diamond, and lighter than one of the same size: For no Stone comes near a Diamond in hardness; nor, of the same magnitude, in Weight. Diamonds take their Estimate from their Magnitude, Splendour, Figure, and Water; for some Persons value a Diamond of such a Water much more than of another; and some are pleas'd with such a sort of Cut, beyond any else. Thus a fair Rose-Diamond of Black Water and Diamond Cut was of general Esteem with some *Europeans* at *Suratt*, whilst a White Water gain'd a Repute with the *Dutch*, and Table-Diamonds were with them of best Esteem. The *Moors* exalt the Rate of such a Diamond, whose Surface is cut in very minute Figures, much less than what the *Europeans* affect, though in all things else the Diamond was equally good and valuable. For as the use of a Diamond, and all other Stones, is very inconsiderable, in respect of that high Value which the Fancy of Man and common Custom has put upon them; so are their Rates too very variable and uncertain, as this Instance of a Rubie will make out. A Rubie, which in Perfection is a Stone superiour to a Diamond, made this gradual Exaltation of its Rates in *India*. It was sold at first at the rate of 400 Roupies, afterwards at 600, then at 800, then at 1200; from this it rose to 1600, thence to 2000, after this it mounted to 2400, then to 2800, from which it was sold for 3000, and lately for 3200. Thus the Fancy of the Purchaser advanc'd it at length Seven Hundred *per Cent.* beyond the Original Price it was first reckon'd at. These perfect Rubies are scarce attainable, those of a deep clear Colour are rarely seen, which put Men upon a hot Chace after them when they are heard of, and inhaunces their Value and Esteem.

*The valuable Qualities in Diamonds.*

*The Excellence of a Rubie above a Diamond.*

*Several prices paid for the same Rubie.*

*The Mogul's Avarice.*

Notwithstanding all these Diamonds and immense Treasure, of which the *Mogul* is Absolute Master, yet is not his

Mind satisfied, nor his Desires abated by his Accessions, they rather stretch and swell the more, and push him on to aspire to that real Character, which his Father assum'd, of being *King of the World.* So little has either Increase of Wealth, or Extent of Power, heal'd his restless Faculties, or compos'd the unruly Turbulence of his Spirit. However, had *Aureng-Zebe* laid his Schemes of Victory only towards the *Indian* Princes, and those potent Neighbours, from whose Conquest he might expect to reap some Glory; this methinks would have carried with it a greater Air of Majesty and Grandeur, than that meaner Action which is recorded of him in *India,* of stripping the *Faquires* of their Wealth and Jewels.

It seems this Prince was minded to compass a little Treasure somewhere, and the only Method he pitch'd upon for it, was to make a Booty of the *Faquires.* These *Faquires* nearly resemble the *Romish* Mendicants in some things, their Character I shall expatiate upon hereafter. The Emperour therefore causes Proclamation to be made through all the Provinces of his Kingdom, *That all* Facquircs *should make ready to repair to a splendid Entertainment, which he design'd to prepare for them.* The News of this Royal Banquet was esteem'd so honourable an Instance of Condescention in the Emperour to these poor Men, that without any further Summons or Invitation they instantly prepar'd and flockt from all the remotest parts to come and receive it. When they were come, and had satisfied themselves with the sumptuous Feast, and overjoy'd at the Thoughts of being Guests to such a Noble Banquet, to which they had been called by the Person of their Emperour, they now adress themselves to him with grateful Acknowledgments for his Bounty in those Royal undeserv'd Favours, so far beyond what the Meanness and Poverty of their Condition would suffer them so much as to think of. And withal wishing him, that Glory and Success might be the distinguishing Characters of his prosperous Reign for many Years, they humbly craved Liberty of departing to their proper Dwellings. To which the Emperour reply'd to this Effect, *I would not have you think that I have*

Aureng-Zebe's *robbing the* Faquires.

*yet forgot the Kindness I had for you and your Profession, in my former Years. 'Tis not the being seated upon the Throne of* India, *that can make me overlook the Consideration of your Poverty, or the Relation I had to you, e'er Fortune and your Good Wishes rais'd me to the Glory of my Ancestors, and the Soveraignty I now enjoy. And therefore as you have thought fit to taste of my Banquet, and express your selves pleas'd with the Entertainment; so I expect from you likewise the acceptance of some Raiments I have provided for your Use, to prevent your Return in that ragged Dress; and that the World may see after your Departure hence, what Kindness I had for you, in conferring these more lasting Favours upon you.* At this they unanimously voted for their old Cloaths, as more agreeable to their Condition, and that he had sufficiently honour'd them by his splendid Repast. But the Servants, who stood by, immediately unstript the *Faquirs*, and brought forth fresh Garments for their old, in which were found abundance of Jewels, Gold, and Precious Stones, enough by far to overpay the Expence; as *Aureng-Zebe* by his former Acquaintance and ancient Intimacy with them could well discover. This Relation which I had from a Gentleman at *Suratt* agrees very well with *Auren-Zebe*'s Policy; but methinks it suits not well with his Honesty and Greatness.

*The Insolence of the* Portuguese *in* India.

The Insolence of the *Portuguese*, as well as *Rajahs*, gives likewise some Disturbance to this Prince, and has drawn down his Arms against their Forces, which has driven several of them from the adjacent Islands to repair for shelter to our Island of *Bombay*. The *Mogul*'s Army has made several Inroads into their Country, plunder'd some small Towns, and threatens *Basseen*.[1] For the *Portuguese* Governour of that Town inticed from a *Rajah* that lived near him a very beautiful Woman of the *Bramin* Cast, which was after a while sent for by the *Rajah*, and remanded back again by twenty or

[1] Bassein, *Vasāī*, 26 miles north of Bombay, the head-quarters of the Portuguese from 1354 to 1739, was a magnificent city when Fryer visited it. It was sacked by the Marāthas in 1739, and now lies in ruins.

thirty Soldiers. But the Lady's Charms blinded his Reason, and biassed both his Justice and Civility, made him refuse to dismiss her, and treat the Messengers with such Violence, that the *Mogul* in Vindication of the *Rajah*, encourag'd his storming of the Town.

*Three Reasons of the* Mogul's *Enmity to the* Portuguese.

Other Reasons are used for the *Mogul*'s present infesting the Country of the *Portuguese*, and for sending three several Parties of Men, pillaging, burning and destroying all before them. One is, that the *Portuguese* burnt formerly a *Cogee*[1] at *Goa*, who is a Person skill'd in their Law. Another Reason is, because the *Portuguese* proselyte the Children of all Persons deceas'd among them, whether their Parents are *Moors* or *Pagans*, and seize their Estates into the Church; which raises a loud Clamour against them, and grievous Complaints to the *Mogul*. Some ascribe the Hatred and Hostility of the *Moors* at this time to these two insufferable Actions of the *Portuguese*. Besides all this, the Religion of the *Portuguese* is very offensive to this Emperour, who carries such an invincible Antipathy to Idolatry, and all sort of Adoration of Images, that he has now suppressed the greatest part of all the Pagodes of his Dominions, where his Pagan Subjects incens'd and invok'd the Idols. Nay, this is such an Abomination to the Mahometan Belief, that the *Moguls* allow not the Representation of any Creature that has Life, even upon their Tea-Cups and China Ware, nor admit the Figure of any Animal upon their Atlasses[2] or other Silks. Therefore the *Portuguese* Religion being grossly tainted with this manner of False Worship, has render'd them very detestable to this sort of Men, as well as other things have made them odious to the *Arabians* at *Muscat*.

*1. Their burning a* Cogee.
*2. Their Conversion of the* Indians.
*3. Their Idolatry.*

*The low condition of the* Portuguese *in* India.

They that were formerly the Glory and Terror of the Eastern Seas, who flowed with Wealth, and all the Riches of the *Indian* and the *Persian* Gulph, are now as low and declining, as they formerly were powerful and in a splendid state. The *Muscatters* daily increase their Naval Forces, and prevail against them incon-

[1] Kāzi, one who is learned in Mahommedan law.

[2] Atlas (Ar.), Indian satin. Cf. p. 167.

testably at Sea, by fitting out against them Ships both of Burthen and Strength, and manning them with skilful, bold, and adventurous Sailers. Only two years since they built in the River of *Suratt* a very comely stout Ship of above a Thousand Tun, which carried at least an Hundred Guns.

*The Mogul's Age.* The *Mogul* is now past Eighty Years of Age,[1] but yet administers the weighty Affairs of his vast Kingdom, and retains a Vigour in his Discerning Faculties. *His care of what he eats.* Whatever he eats is first tasted by his Daughter, and passes under the Chops[2] or Seals of three or four principal *Omrahs*; and his Drink is *His Drink.* the Water of the River *Ganges*, which is reputed Sacred throughout all his Kingdom, and is said to sanctifie the Natives, whether they drink, or bath in it. I fancy the Native Purity of the Water may give it this Credit and Reputation, because they say it has that singular Quality of our River *Thames*, that it never remains corrupt long; and a Quart of it is lighter by much than any other Water. This Water is dearer to him, than if he had drunk *Europe* Wine; for it is brought to him over Land in Copper Jarrs, tinn'd within, upon Mens Shoulders, or upon Beasts of Burthen, several Hundred Miles. Thus the ancient Kings of *Persia* drank no other Water, than that of the River *Elæus* or *Chospes*,[3] because of the Esteem they had of its Excellence.

*His Care in taking Physick.* Whenever his Health requires Physick, he expects the Physician should lead the way, take Pill for Pill, Dose for Dose, of the same which is administred to him; that he may see the Operation upon the Body of the Physician, before he will venture upon it himself. *His Abstinence.* He never violates his Obligations to Abstinence, by tasting the Juice of the Grape, which the *Omrahs* dispense with, and are fond of, and buy it up at any rate, if they can by any private Method be accommodated with it in the Camp.

[1] Aurangzeb was born in 1618, so this is incorrect.

[2] Hind. *chhāp*, a seal or stamp. Cf. p. 149.

[3] These two rivers unite to form the modern Karun river at the head of the Persian Gulf. Susa, the ancient capital of Persia, was on the Choaspes.

He formerly admir'd the Fair Sex; but Old Age, and the Decay of Nature, keep him at a farther Distanee at present from his *Haram.* His Women are all closely guarded, not visible to any, but himself and his Eunuehs, whose Virile Parts are cut off smooth, to prevent the least Temptation from the Sex; so that whenever there is need, they are forced to the use of a Quill in making Urine. And all the Women of Fashion in *India* are elose penn'd in by their jealous Husbands, who forbid them the very sight of all Strangers. However the Watch is neither so eareful, nor their Modesty so blameless, but that they sometimes will look abroad for Variety, as well as their roving Husbands do. A Passage of which I shall here insert. A Gentlewoman, viciously inelin'd, contrives one Day to get abroad, with a trusty Familiar of her Acquaintance, though totally a Stranger to her new Husband. She freely imparts her lewd Intentions, earnestly requests her Fidelity, and withal desires she would vouchsafe to take the Message upon her self, and walk into the Bazar, and there espy what comely Person she could meet with, proper, lovely, young, and handsom, and eonduet him privately to sueh Apartments as she had provided. The Friend, thus instructed, goes abroad, views, and culls out from the rest in the Bazar the most amiable Person she could meet with, and intreating him to step aside, discovers the Intriegue, and then eonducts him to the place appointed. The Gallant it seems was Husband to the Gentlewoman that expected him, who seeing him come near the Gate, was all in Confusion, and quite confounded at the sight of his unfortunate Approach. But she found it was no time to dally, or delay her Resolutions, and therefore instantly summon'd all her Thoughts, and after a little Pause, threw her self directly upon the Cot or Bed that was by, and put the Covering over her Face. Her Husband, ignorant whom she was, and knowing for what Intent he was sent for, begins immediately to disturb her, and by and by endeavours to uncover her Face. At which she rose up in a seeming Rage, and told him, *For shame, Sir, I have often heard of your Pranks*

*The Eunuchs cut smooth.*

*A pleasant Story of an ingenious lewd Woman.*

*and loose Intricgues abroad, but my Charity made me willing to unbelieve it, till this Minute has given me an invincible Argument, for assuring me of the Truth of what was spoken. I sent on purpose to find you out, and plac'd my self as a Stranger here to entertain you; and hither you came, I find, with dishonest Resolutions, and treacherous Designs to our Nuptial Bed. Can you pretend to so much Tenderness and Affection for me, and yet listen to the least Temptation that courts or calls you from me? Was I ever unfaithful, or cool in my Affection, that might thereby drive you from my Embraces, to follow Strangers you never heard of?* At this rate she turn'd the Argument upon himself, made him the only Person guilty of these wanton Amours, and with a gargled[1] Mouth endeavour'd to wipe off all the Defilements of her Thoughts, and to render her Innocence as clear as her Excuse. She knew that a Conjugal Affection is very apt to grow jealous upon any apparent suspicion of mutual Fidelity, and that nothing sooner excites and ferments the Rage of a Man, than the apprehension of a Partner in his Bed. But yet this Jealousie is much extinct among the Inhabitants upon the Coast of *Malabar*, where the Husbands, even the prime Nobility, to compleat the Welcom of their Entertainments, offer the Familiarity of their Wives; and esteem the rejecting this Civility as an Affront. Two *English* Merchants some time before I came to *India*, were invited abroad, and after Dinner were tempted with this kind of Treat; but the Piety of one of them kept him from it, whilst the immodest Frolicks of the other intic'd him on to the use of an unlawful Pleasure. And many of their Women by their usual Custom in these cases, quite contrary to that of other Nations, have gain'd the Name of *Malabar Quills*.[2]

*Women offer'd to Strangers.*

[1] For this use of 'gargle', cf. 'gargling glib divisions in their outlandish throats', in Sheridan's *Critic*, i. 3.

[2] Probably a misprint for 'quail', a courtesan. Cf. the French *caille*, which has the same meaning. The bird was thought to be very amorous; hence the metaphor.

# THE CITY OF SURATT,[1] AND ITS INHABITANTS

THE City of *Suratt* lies in 21 Degrees, and some odd Minutes of North Latitude. 'Tis by *Ptolomy* call'd *Muziris*,[2] and is situated upon a River Ten or Twelve Miles distant from the Sea. The Name of the River is *Tapy*, or *Tindy*, which rises from the Mountain of *Decan*, and from thence falls down through *Brampore*,[3] and by *Meanders* from *Suratt* glides down gently into the Ocean. The Circumference of it, with the Suburbs, is between two and three *English* Miles, tending somewhat in its Position to the Form of a Semicircle or Half Moon, because of the winding of the River, to which half of it adjoyns. It is fortified with a Wall,[4] which is flankt at certain Distances with Towers and Battlements, occasion'd by the frequent Incursions of the Enemies; but its greatest Strength is in the Castle, which commands not only the Ships and Boats in the River, but likewise guards the City by Land.

*The Latitude of* Suratt. *Its Situation.*

The Castle is built towards the South West part of the City, having a River to defend it on one side, and a Ditch on the other. It is built square, and fortified at each Corner with a large Tower, containing various Lodgings, and furnish'd

*The Castle.*

[1] Surat, Skt. *Saurāshtra*, good country, was the great emporium and port of the Moghal Empire, and the point of embarkation of the Mecca pilgrims. It was the head-quarters of the English in Western India from 1608 to 1687, but its exposure to attack from the Marāthas, who sacked it in 1664 and 1670, the silting up of the Tapti, and the arbitrary conduct of the Moghal officials, led to its abandonment in favour of Bombay. Cf. p. 90, note 1.

[2] Muziris of the classical writers is probably Cranganor on the Malabar coast and certainly not Surat.

[3] Burhānpur in the Central Provinces, on the banks of the Tāpti river. It was once the Moghal capital of Khāndesh, and famous for its silk and other wares. Sir Thomas Roe visited it in 1614.

[4] Built after the sack of the town by the Marāthas in 1664. Cf. Fryer's description, i. 229 ff., and Thévenot, *Voyages*, iii, vii–xvii.

with all Conveniences fit for accommodating the Governour, and has several Canons mounted upon the Walls.

*The Gates of the City.* The Entrance into the City is by six or seven Gates, where are Centinels fixt continually, requiring an Account, upon the least Suspicion, of all that enter in, or pass out of the City.

*The Buildings.* The Houses are many of them fair and stately, tho' unproportionable to the Wealth of the Inhabitants, who are always concern'd to conceal their Riches, and therefore never exceed in any Luxurious Furniture, lest it should prove too powerful a Temptation to the Avarice of the *Mogul.* They are flat roof'd, or rather made a little shelving, after the manner of the Buildings in *Spain* and *Portugal,* cover'd with Tiles, and the Walls are made of Brick or Stone. The Windows are without Glass, and kept open for the Convenience of the fresh Air; and the Floors both of the lower and upper Stories are all Terrass'd to make them cool. But the poorer sort, and such as inhabit the Skirts of the City, live much meaner, in Houses, whose Walls are only Bambous at a Foot distance, with Reeds wove through them; and their Covering is only Cajan, or Palm-leaves of Trees, which gives them the common Name of Cajan-Houses.[1]

*The Streets.* The Streets are some too narrow, but in many places of a convenient breadth; and in an Evening, especially near the Bazar, or Market-place, are more populous than any part of *London*; and so much throng'd, that 'tis not very easie to pass through the multitude of *Bannians* and other Merchants that expose their Goods. For here they stand with their Silks and Stuffs in their Hands, or upon their Heads, to invite such as pass by to come and buy them.

*Castle-Green.* In the midst of the City is a spacious vacant place, called *Castle-Green*, because of its nearness to the Castle, on which are laid all sorts of Goods in the open Air, both Day and Night, excepting the *Mussoun* time. And here the *English*, *French*, and *Dutch*, with the Natives, place their Bales, and prepare them as Loadings for their Ships.

The Governour of the Castle is appointed by the *Mogul*;

[1] Malay *Kajang*, plaited palm leaves used for thatch.

and his Authority seldom stretches beyond the space of three Years, in all which time he is a real Prisoner under the appearance of a high Commander, and under a severe and strict Engagement never to pass without the Walls of his Castle; but to be continually upon his Guard, in a constant readiness for any Emergence or Surprize, all the time he is in the Government.

*The Governour of the Castle always confin'd to it.*

*Suratt* is reckon'd the most fam'd Emporium of the *Indian* Empire, where all Commodities are vendible, though they never were there seen before. The very Curiosity of them will engage the Expectation of the Purchaser to sell them again with some Advantage, and will be apt to invite some other by their Novelty, as they did him, to venture upon them. And the River is very commodious for the Importation of Foreign Goods, which are brought up to the City in Hoys and Yachts, and Country Boats, with great Convenience and Expedition. And not only from *Europe*, but from *China*, *Persia*, *Arabia*, and other remote parts of *India*, Ships unload abundance of all kinds of Goods, for the Ornament of the City, as well as inriching of the Port.

Suratt *a chief Town of Trade.*

It is renown'd for Traffick through all *Asia*, both for rich Silks, such as Atlasses, Cuttanees,[1] Soofeys, Culgars, Allajars, Velvets, Taffaties, and Sattins; and for Zarbafts from *Persia*; and the abundance of Pearls that are brought hither from the *Persian* Gulph; but likewise for Diamonds, Rubies, Saphires, Topazes, and other Stones of Splendor and Esteem, which are vendible here in great quantities: And for Aggats, Cornelians, Nigganees, Desks, Scrutores, and Boxes neatly polisht and embellisht, which may be purchas'd here at very reasonable Rates.

*Its Commodities.*

The Gold of *Suratt* is so very fine, that 12 or 14 *per Cent* may be often gain'd by bringing it to *Europe*. And the Silver, which is the same all over *India*, out-does even the *Mexico*

*The fineness of* Indian *Gold and Silver.*

[1] Cuttanee, &c., names of various kinds of piece-goods exported from India previous to the introduction of machinery in England. *Nigganee* (Niccanee) is another; *Zarbaft* (P. 'golden woven') is gold brocade or kincob. See Hobson-Jobson, *s.v.*

*No clipt or bad Money. Gold and Silver Roupies how valued. A Pice how much. Bitter Almonds pass for Money.*

and *Sevil* Dollars, and has less Allay than any other in the World. I never saw any Clipt Money there, and 'tis rare if either the Gold or Silver Coin is falsified. The Gold Moor, or Gold Roupie, is valued generally at 14 of Silver; and the Silver Roupie at Two Shillings Three Pence. Besides these they have Foreign Coyns, but not in that Plenty; and Pice, which are made of Copper, Sixty of which, sometimes two or three more or less, are valued at a Roupie. Lower than these, bitter Almonds here pass for Money, about Sixty of which make a Pice.

*The Custom paid by all strange Coins. Customs paid in* China *according to the largeness of the Ship.*

All strange Coyn, whether Imported or Exported, pays to the *Mogul*'s Officers Two and an half *per Cent.* and other Goods pay more. In some other Nations of the East, as in *China*, they take other Measures in their Customs, not according to the Value or Quantity of the Goods, but according to the Burthen of the Ship, which is measur'd and examin'd upon her first Arrival; and upon this such a Custom is charged upon her, without any Consideration of her Cargo. When this is paid, there is Liberty granted of fraighting upon the Ship what Goods Men please, those of the richest as well as the meanest Value. An *English* Ship there of 400 Tuns, paid for its Custom 1000 Dollars.

*All strange Coins melted down at* Suratt. *The Reason that Old Coin is of less value than New.*

Whatever strange Coyn comes into the Hands of the *Mogul*'s Officers, 'tis melted down, and converted into Roupies, which are stamped with the particular Characters of the Emperour then Reigning. After the Emperour's Death the value of it abates, may be a Pice or two in a Roupie, because of its Antiquity, whereby, they say, so much of its Worth is wore off; and only the new Coin passes currant without any Diminution.

*Silks sold by the Cobit. A Cobit what it is.*

The Silks and Callicoes vendible here, are either sold by the Piece, or by Cobits,[1] which is a Measure containing 27 Inches.

Their Rice and Corn, and other Commodities which are sold with us by Concave Measures, are with them sold by

[1] Cobit, Port. *covado*, cubit or ell. Fryer, ii. 127, enumerates two Surat cobits of 27 and 36 inches respectively.

Weight. The common Weight is a Sear,[1] which weighs $13\frac{1}{3}$ Ounces Avoirdupoise; and also the Maund, which contains forty Sear. Pecks and Bushels I never heard of. For as their Kingdoms, so are their Customs in these Kingdoms quite opposite in many things to ours. The Teeth of their Saws, for Instance, are made quite contrary to ours; their Locks are fashion'd and open quite different ways; and the very Dispositions of some Irrational Creatures vary from the Genius they retain with us; as at *Tunquin* the vigilant Dogs watch all Night to devour the Rats and Mice, which are there very large and troublesom; as our Cats do with us.

*Corn sold by weight.*

*No hollow Measures in* India.

*Some* Indian *Customs contrary to ours.*

*Dogs catch Mice.*

Goods are brought to *Suratt* from *Agra*, their Capital City, from *Dehli*, *Baroch*, *Amadavad*, and other Cities noted for particular Commodities, which are sold off in great quantities to the *Europeans*, *Turks*, *Arabians*, *Persians*, and *Armenians*, who above any of the rest Travel the farthest, spread themselves in all parts of *Asia*, as well as *Europe*, and are as universal Merchants as any in the World. The *Armenians*[2] are Civil and Industrious, their Language is one of the most general in all *Asia*, and they have spread themselves in vast Colonies very far, in *Anatolia*, *Persia*, the *Holy Land*, *Egypt*, *Russia*, and *Polonia*, and range by private Persons and Families, like *Jews* into all parts, and like them are as subtle and diligent in their Traffick. For they have always had a celebrated name for Merchandise; and near them in ancient times, that is, at *Phasis* in *Georgia*, was kept the Golden Fleece, which was likely nothing else but a Rich and Profitable Trade of Wool, Skins, and Furs, which the Northern

*Goods from whence brought to* Suratt.

Armenians *great Merchants.*

[1] For Indian weights and measures, see Fryer, ii. 127, with Crooke's notes. They vary enormously, the *tola*, equivalent to the weight of one rupee, being the unit. The Bombay rate is :

80 *tolas* . . . . . 1 *ser* (2 lb.)
40 *sers* . . . . . 1 *mān* (maund).

Hobson-Jobson, *s.v.* Seer, Maund, may also be consulted.

[2] There is still a large Armenian colony at Calcutta. Fryer, ii. 252 ff., and Manucci, iv. 182 ff., give interesting accounts of the Armenians at Ispahān. Ruins of the Armenian church at Surat are still to be seen, near the English Factory.

People brought thither, and to which they now drive a Trade of some resemblance in their costly Tapestries, Grograins,[1] watered Chamlets, *&c.* And *Jason*, and the Greeks being the first Discoverers of the Fleece, above all the rest of *Europe*, and encountring many Hazards and Dangers in the first Navigation; it was said to be guarded by Furies, Bulls, and an horrible Dragon, that is by men bold and well Armed.

*The Carriage of their Goods in* India.

For the Carriage of their Goods, the *Indians* seldom make use of Horses, they are generally employed in the *Mogul*'s service in War; but bring them to *Suratt* in Waggons, upon Dromedaries, Asses, and Camels: The strength and hardiness of the Camels qualifie them extremely for the weight of Burthens, and the length of the Roads. They dispatch their Journeys with some quickness, and have this advantage in making short the way, in that they are observ'd to have a Joint extraordinary in their hind Leg, which hastens and assists their Motion, by the large reach which it gives them in their walking. They cannot walk upon slippery places, and are therefore best fitted by Nature for Sandy Earth.

*A joynt extraordinary in the Leg of a Camel.*

*The manner of the Camels Copulation.*

At the time that the Camels Couple, the Female takes the burthen in her Womb in the same posture she receives the Load upon her back, for they both lie down upon their Bellies and generate backwards, because the Genitals of the Male are placed behind. When they are in case for Copulation, the Keepers are constrain'd to muzle them, and keep a severe hand over them, they are so rampant, furious, and unlucky; and at these seasons the lustful inflam'd Animal will subsist, they say, Forty Days together without Food. The Heat and vigour of their Spirits keep them sprightly and alive without any Aliment. Some of the Camels go with their young above a Year.

*A Camel when heated with Lust, will live 40 days without Food.*

*The time they go with Young.*

*The Spice-Trade in the Hands of the* Dutch.

The *Dutch* supply *Suratt* with all kind of Spices, saving Pepper, in which the *English* share with them. The Cinnamon is brought hither from *Ceylon*, and is cut off from a Tree

[1] Grograms and chamlets were among the numerous varieties of piece goods (see Hobson-Jobson, *s.v.*) exported from the East in the seventeenth century.

cloathed with three Barks, two whereof are stript off, which are the Cinnamon, the third and most inward, which incloses the body of the Tree, is never toucht, because an Incision in it kills the Tree. After three Years time the two extreme Barks are renew'd, and cover the body of the Tree again, and are fit to be pulled off. If the *Dutch* are under any apprehension of glutting the Trade of *Europe* with this fragrant Spice, and of abating its value by sending home too great an abundance, they lay it on an heap and burn as much of it as they imagin useless for their service, which Spicy Mountain sends out its fragrant Exhalations for many Leagues into the Sea.

Ceylon *the chief place for Cinnamon.*

*The Cinnamon-Tree.*

*Much Cinnamon burnt by the* Dutch.

The Cloves and Nutmegs are convey'd hither from some Islands towards *Malacca*, whither the *Dutch* send their Exiled Criminals to perpetual Slavery. Upon the Out-side of the Nutmeg is the Mace, which is cover'd again with a very thick Coat, like a green Wall-Nut; this Covering preserv'd is taken as a high Cordial, and eaten as a Restorative with pleasure. They relate a passage somewhat strange and surprizing concerning the nature of the Nutmeg-Tree, that it is never Planted, and if it be it never thrives; but such of them as Fructifie and arrive at perfection, arise from a ripe Nutmeg swallowed whole by a certain Bird in those Islands, which disgorges it again without digesting it, and this falling to the ground with that slimy matter it brought along with it, takes root and grows an useful Tree: But this may be a subtle contriv'd story of the *Dutch*, to keep Men from endeavouring to transplant them.

*Islands of* Malacca *afford Cloves and Nutmegs.*

*The Nutmeg.*

*A report concerning the Nutmeg-Tree.*

The Cloves grow upon a Tree, and before they come to maturity, are of a very delightful Colour. Before they are cleans'd, they are of such a spungy attractive quality, that they drain any Liquids that stand near them, and except the Master of the Ship, in his conveyance of them from the Islands, takes care to keep them at a convenient distance from his Liquors, a quantity of them will in two days time extract and dry up a Hogs-head of Wine or Water.

*Cloves.*

*Their Spungy quality.*

Those that Sell the Spices are not always very fair and honest in disposing of them. For sometimes they extract a

*How the* Dutch

*draw the Spirits from the Spices, and then sell them.* quantity of Oyl, or Essence, or of Spirits from the Cloves, Cinnamon and other Spices; and after this, confidently expose them for choice untainted Commodities, and raise their Rates to that pitch, as if they were fresh, and never robb'd of their Spirits: Some in *Batavia*, their Capital City in the *East*, whither the greatest quantity of Spice are brought, have large Yards fill'd with them, and kept there on purpose for this Design, first to drain them of their Essences and purer qualities, and afterwards sell them for sound Goods. For which reason we sometimes meet with several sorts of Spice that are very dry and insipid, of little Smell or Taste, pillaged of all their Oyl and Substance.

*The Governour of the City.* Besides their Governour of the Castle of *Suratt*, who is always confin'd a Prisoner within its Walls, there is another of the City, to whose management and Care is committed the Trust of all Civil Affairs. He receives Addresses from the Principal Merchants and Men of Note, and all Applications of moment from the Inhabitants are made to him. He generally keeps at home for dispatching the business of his Master, or the People under his Care; and if he goes abroad, he sometimes takes the Air upon an Elephant, seated in a Chair of State upon his back; and besides the Keeper of the Beast, carries along with him a Peon, or Servant to Fan him, and drive away the busie Flies and troublesome Musketoes: *A Horse-tail Fan.* This is done with the Hair of a Horse's Tail fastned to the end of a small stick of a Foot length, a very homely Fan,[1] but yet the only one in esteem with the Grandees, and even the Emperour himself. To maintain the dignity of his Post and Station, he maintains several large Elephants, and keeps in constant pay and readiness many Souldiers, both Horse and Foot, to guard his person at home and abroad, and to be ready for his dispatches.

He does not peremptorily Arbitrate in Cases of moment, but when any matter of consequence is brought before him,

[1] The chowry, Skt. *chāmara*, is, like the umbrella, a sign of royalty all over the East. It is really made from the tail of the yak.

he seldom determines it without the Consultation and Concurrence of other Officers of the City, the *Cogy*, the *Vacanavish*, and *Catoual*.[1]

*Officers in the City.*

*The* Cogy.

The *Cogy* is a Person skilled in the Municipal Laws, acts as Judge, and is consulted in matters relating to the Civil Customs of the Empire.

*The* Vacanavish.

The *Vacanavish* is the *Mogul's* publick Intelligencer, and is imploy'd in giving a Weekly Account from *Suratt* to the Court of *India*, of all occurrences here of Truth and moment.

*The* Harcarrah.

Next to him, and somewhat like him, is another Officer called the *Harcarrah*,[2] who harkens to all kind of News, whether true or false, listens to every thing that happens, whether of moment or of no account, and reports to the great *Mogul* whatever is done or spoke of; but with so soft a Pen, that nothing may offend, considering the profound veneration due to such a powerful Prince, whose Frowns are mortal.

*The* Catoual.

The *Catoual* is another Officer in the City, somewhat resembling a Justice of the Peace, in endeavouring the suppression of all Enormities in the City. For which reason he is oblig'd to ride the streets for prevention of Disorder, thrice in the Night, at 9, 12, and 3 a Clock, 'till 5 in the Morning, at which Hours the Drums beat, and a large long Copper Trumpet sounds aloud.[3] The *Catoual* is always attended with several Peons and Souldiers arm'd with Swords, Lances, Bows and Arrows, and some with a very dreadful Weapon, a Rod of Iron about a Cubit's length, with a large Ball of Iron at the end, which is able with ease to dash out the Brains, or break and shatter the Bones at once. When he meets with a Person guilty of petty Irregularities, or some trivial Offence, he Confines him for some time; but if his Misdemeanour be more notorious, he must smart for it by a Chawbuck,[4] or Bastinado.

*A dangerous* Indian *weapon.*

[1] Cogy, *kāzi*, judge; vacanavish, *vākiahnavīs*, news-writer; catoual, *kotwāl*, city magistrate, chief constable.

[2] Hind. *harkāra*, spy, messenger.

[3] For the noise of the *naubat* or drums at Surat, cf. Fryer, i. **213**.

[4] Hind., *chābuk*. Cf. sjambok.

Tho this City is frequented by a conflux of several Nations, and Peopled by abundance of Foreigners as well as Natives, whose mixt Concourse and mutual Conversations might be apt to raise Tumults and Disputes, yet they very rarely happen, so much as to cause even a slight Punishment. And for Capital Inflictions, there are seldom Criminals so daring as to merit or incur the Guilt of them. The In-offensive Conversation of the Gentile *Indians*, who are very apt to receive, but seldom to give an abuse; keeps them Innocent, and at a distance from all hainous Crimes, and timorous in approaching the commission of any such gross Offence, as Murther, Robbery, and such like; and for petty Failures, a drubbing is a sufficient Atonement to publick Justice.

*Capital Crimes rare in* India.

*Few put to Death at* Suratt.

I believe there has not been a Criminal for this 20 Years that has suffer'd a Capital Punishment at *Suratt.* There were, I confess, some Pirates, but all of them *Europeans*, who were guarded thro' *Suratt* in their Journey to the *Mogul*, for a Tryal of their Lives, while I stayed there.

*The power of Life and Death in the hands of the Emperour.*

The Power of Life and Death is the Emperour's Prerogative, which he hardly vouchsafes to communicate to any Civil Judge, except they be at a distance, but reserves that Authority intirely to himself, of pronouncing the Sentence of Execution; and if the Offender is at a distance, his Crime is many times transmitted by a Messenger to the *Mogul*, who determins sometimes without sending for the Offender, according to the Account of the matter that is sent him.

*Oaths administred in* India.

In Controversies and Decisions of Right, Oaths are administred and made use of here, as well as in Christendom. Tho' the timorous *Bannian* will be apt rather to venture the loss of his Cause, than the taking an Oath, because of the Infamy which swearing obtains among them. As we lay our Hands in swearing upon the Holy Bible, so he puts his hand upon the venerable Cow,[1] with this Imprecation, *That he may eat of the Flesh of that Blest Animal, if what he saies be not true.*

*The* Bannian *Oath.*

[1] The cow's-tail oath was administered to Hindu witnesses in the Mayor's Court, Bombay, as late as 1747. *Bombay City Gazetteer*, ii. 216–17.

For as the *Chinese* endeavour a perpetuation of their Laws, and the preserving their People in Obedience, by the dread and awful Respect which they Harbour towards their Dead Parents, whom they pretend are Inspectors of their Childrens Actions, and highly incens'd at their Posterity, whenever they transgress, or would contrive an alteration of those Laws which they have left them; so does the Opinion of the Transmigration awe the *Bannian* into a singular respect for all Kinds of Beasts, especially the Cow, which for their Lives they would not touch, lest they might thereby Eat the Flesh of that Animal, wherein they hope their Father's Soul has been.

*The* Foursdar.

If any Thefts or Robberies are committed in the Country, the *Foursdar*,[1] another Officer, is oblig'd to answer for them; who is allowed Souldiers and Servants under him to traverse the Country, and look after the High-Ways, to hunt out the Robbers, and keep all suspected Places quiet and safe for Passengers.

Having given this Account of the situation and Extent of *Suratt*, of its Strength and Buildings, and of its Riches and Commerce, (which are the strength of a Nation) and likewise of its Governour and Principal Officers: I shall now proceed to a Relation of its Inhabitants, especially its Natives, of their Customs and manner of living; of their Religion, their Festivals and Fasts; their Marriages and Burials; of their Language, their Learning and Recreations.

*The* Moors *at* Suratt.

I shall distinguish the Natives here into three sorts. First, the *Moors*, or *Moguls*.[2] Secondly, the *Bannians* or Antient Gentiles. Thirdly, The *Parsies* or *Gaures*. And first, To treat briefly of the *Moors*, who are allowed a precedence to all the

[1] The Fauzdār (Hind. *fauj*, army) was the chief of police.

[2] In the idiom of the seventeenth century, the Moors (Port. *Mouro*) were the Mahommedans, contrasted with the Gentoos, that is gentiles (Port. *gentios*) or Hindus. The word Bannian or Bunya, really only applicable to the Vānis or Hindu traders of Gujarat, is also used indiscriminately of all Hindus. The Parsees are called 'Gabers or Gaures', i.e. fire-worshippers, in Persia; cf. Fryer, ii. 253. This is the Persian *gabr*, *gaur*, *gor*, English Giaour, Guebre, 'infidel'.

*Respected above the* Gentiles *of their Religion.*

rest, because of their Religion, which is the same with that of their Prince, and for this reason they are advanc'd to the most Eminent Stations of Honour and Trust; are appointed Governours of Provinces, and are intrusted with the Principal Military, as well as Civil Employments. Very few of the Gentiles being called to any considerable Trust, or incourag'd any more, than just to follow their several Manual Occupations, or Merchandize. For Religion, which puts a Biass upon the Mind, Intitles them to the Court Favours, when it carries a conformity to that of their Prince. Therefore the Gentiles are little esteem'd of by the *Mogul*, and contemned by the *Moors*, and often treated with Inhumanity and neglect, because of their adhesion to the Principles of a Religion, which is different from that of the State. And yet their peaceable submissive Deportment wins mightily upon the *Moors*, and takes off much of that scornful Antipathy which they harbour against them.

*The* Moors *forbid to taste Wine, but allow'd Concubines.*

As the *Mahometan* Principles indulge an extraordinary Liberty for Women, so are they nice in the innocent allowance of Wine, and strictly prohibit the tasting of strong Liquor. The *Moors* therefore here, as in other Kingdoms, practise the Use of Concubines, according as their Fortunes and Abilities can reach towards their Maintenance; by which means they fancy not only an impunity to themselves, but something of Merit, by propagating the number and increase of the Faithful.

*Their Food.*

Yet tho' they are under a severe restraint from the Juice of the Grape, they are not debarr'd the Eating of Rich and delicate Food, nor from dressing it with such store of Spice and high Cordial Ingredients, as mightily invigorate their Spirits, warm their Stomachs, and inflame the Vital Heat. Cloves and Amber-Grese,[1] Cinnamon and other fragrant Oriental Spices, do often help to compound their Dishes of Pilau,[2] and other Meats that are in use among them, in the

[1] Ambergris, found in the whale's stomach, and widely in demand as a drug and perfume. Cf. Fryer, i. 68, and Crooke's note.

[2] Cf. p. 231, note 2.

Families of Men of Fortune and Estates. Some of whom, notwithstanding their Prophet, thro' whose Prohibition they are restrain'd from Wine, will yet privately be as Licentious therein, as other Persons who are allow'd to drink it with moderation. And many of them take the liberty of mixing Dutra[1] and Water together to drink, without any privacy or fear, which will intoxicate almost to Madness, when they are in the humour of gulping it freely; and this sometimes puts them beyond their Native tender Deportment, and forces them upon suddain Bold Attempts. 'Tis commonly observ'd concerning this Herb Dutra, that whatever Humour prevails in any person at the time of his drinking it to Excess, that Temper continues with him in the highest pitch, 'till the inebriating quality abates. If he is Melancholy, he is then rais'd to the utmost degree of Sadness; If Amorous, he is all Love and Flame; if he is Merry, he is then a perfect Antick. And pouring cold Water upon the Leggs, removes these excessive Humours, and restores them to their Senses and Sobriety again. The *English* and other *Europeans* sometimes in their pleasant Frolicks, are pleased to divert themselves with these gay Humours and strange Actions, by taking a chearful Draught or two of this Liquor.

*Dutra intoxicateing Herb.*

When any grievous Disaster happens to a Man, which he finds himself unable to sustain through disquietness of Mind and anguish of Spirit, 'tis very customary upon the Coast of *Malabar*, for such an unfortunate person to make his Application to a large Dose of this Herb for his Relief; which chafes and ferments him to such a pitch; that with a Catarry[2] or Bagonet in his hand he first falls upon those that are near him, whether Parents, Wife or Child, killing and stabbing as he goes; and then in the same mad Frenzy runs along the Streets and High-Ways, and blindly Executes the same Fate upon all he meets with, 'till at length by some Martial Hand

*Running a Muck.*

[1] Datura, *Datura stramonium*, or thorn apple, was the favourite drug of the Thugs, and is still used widely by Indian thieves and poisoners in order to drug their victims.

[2] Hind. *katār*, Skt. *kartāri*, a dagger.

he falls himself, and ends his Life in that bitter Fit. These that run thus are called *Amouki*,[1] and the doing of it *Running a Muck*. And for this reason, to prevent all Misdemeanours of Persons heated with Arak, or any strong Liquor, does the King of *Siam* forbid any one to enter into his Palace; and all that do, or are suspected, must allow the Porter to smell their Breath before they pass the Gates.[2] Those that pretend to the understanding of the derivation of this word Arak, deduce it from the *Arabick*, wherein they say it signifies Sweat, and metaphorically Essence, and by way of Excellence *Aqua Vitæ*. Of this sort of Liquor there are two kinds most fam'd in *India*, the *Goa* and *Bengal* Arak, besides that which is made at *Batavia*. *Bengal* is a much stronger Spirit than that of *Goa*, tho' both are made use of by the *Europeans* in making Punch, and are bought at both places at very low rates. Arak is distilled from Rice, and sometimes from Toddy the juice of a Tree, and is prescrib'd in healing the Griping of the Gutts. Stronger than this is another Compound-Liquor made in *India*, which is distilled from Black Sugar mixt with Water, with the bark of the Tree Baboul, this is called Jagre Arak; it is as hot as Brandy, and is drunk in Drams by the *Europeans*.

*Drunkards not to enter the K. of Siam's Palace.*

*Arak, from whence it is deriv'd.*

*Two sorts of it.*

*Its Virtue.*

*Jagre Arak.*

*Pleasant Liquors.*

But the Coco and the Palm-Tree afford a pleasant Juice from their Head and upper Branches, which the *Moors* as well as *Europeans* drink of plentifully. A Quart of it may be got for a Pice or two, and is so strong that it turns the Brain as soon as *English* Beer; for want of which the Sailers take up with this Juyce to refresh themselves, when the Ships Anchor near the Shoar; for no Malt drink is made in *India*. It distils from the Tree into Earthen Jars, which are fixt to the Branches of the Coco-Tree, when they are cut off to a Foot length; and are put to the Hole in the Palm Tree, which by incision is made one Inch deep, and three wide; and in one Nights time a Jar containing above a Quart will be filled with

[1] The word is probably Malay; *vide* Hobson-Jobson, *s.v.* *A Muck*.

[2] For a similar story cf. Jourdain's *Journal*, p. 104.

the Juyce of one Tree. When it distils into a Jar that has been formerly us'd, it suddenly taints and grows harsh, and turns sower in less than the space of 24 Hours: In the Morning it is laxative, and costive in the Evening. The name of this liquor is Toddy; but the Neri[1] which is drawn from the Arequier Tree[2] in a fresh Earthen Vessel, is as sweet and pleasant as Milk, but more lively, without any mixture of a hard or sharp Taste. Several *Europeans* pay their Lives for their immoderate Draughts, and too frankly Carousing these chearful Liquors, with which when once they are inflam'd, it renders them so restless and unruly, especially with the additional heat of the Weather, that they fancy no place can prove too cool, and so throw themselves upon the ground, where they sleep all Night in the open Fields, and this commonly produces a Flux, of which a multitude in *India* die. The securest way here for preserving Health after an excess in drinking, and an intemperate draught of any strong liquor, is to keep close after it under some convenient Covering, and to digest it by keeping warm, and sleeping out the Fermentation.

*Toddy, Neri.*

*A Receipt for prevention of Fevers being Mortal.*

The *Moguls* feed freely on Beef or Mutton, or the Flesh of any other Creature which is not accounted unclean among them; but Swines-flesh is under a dis-repute, and held among them an Abomination. Yet the Grandees will taste of this, as well as Wine, and will not stick at the Eating it at a private Collation. For an *English* Agent, by a frequent Interview with the Governour of a City, arriv'd at length to that familiarity with him, that he took the liberty of Inviting him and some Intimates more, to a friendly Entertainment of *Persian* and *European* Wines. The Governour coming to it, was so Charm'd with the welcome which he receiv'd, because the Wine had that influence on his Humour and Palate, that upon his departure he stept to the Agent and told him, he design'd him suddenly another Visit, and withal desir'd from him a couple of young Kidds of the Agent's preparing,

*Swines flesh forbid the* Moors.

*A Story of some* Moors *eating a Pig instead of a Kid.*

[1] Guj. *Nīr*, sap, water.

[2] The areca palm (*Areca Catechu*).

and whispering to him privately, he told him he meant young Piggs. The Agent expressed his humble Sense of the Honour they had vouchsaf'd him, and his satisfaction at the freedom they had taken; and withal assur'd them, that such an Evening the Kids should be provided for their coming. He instantly sent abroad his Servant, for procuring him two of the fattest Pigs that could be met with, and order'd them to be roasted against the time appointed; and pulling off their Skin, and cutting off their Heads and Feet, had them brought before the invited Guests. They rejoyc'd at the sight of them, and when they had tasted, applauded the delicacy of the Meat, eat it with abundance of delight, and boasted that they had never seen any such plump Kids, whose relish outdid any thing they had ever tasted; and heartily wisht for the opportunity of such another Repast, and the liberty of Banqueting frequently upon such Dainties. They admir'd the Christians Indulgence in such noble Liquor, and such exquisite Fare, and believ'd that the unconfin'd Luxury in Eating was equal to the pleasure of their desirable variety of Women; and that the Carnal Excesses approv'd by *Mahomet* do not outvie the unconstrain'd Liberty which the Christians take in sumptuous Repasts, and such kind of Luxurious Sensuality.

The *Moors* are only bound to abstain from Unclean Beasts, and load their Tables with Fish and Fowl, and other Fare.

Bannians, *no Butchers.*

And it is only among them that the Butchers kill the Meat, and sell it to strangers; for the *Indians* will scarce look upon a mangled Carkass. A Butcher with them is little less than a Murtherer, but of all Vocations that is the most odious with them.

*The Fast Ramezan.*

The *Moors* with a very rigid and avowed Abstinence, observe every Year one Month, a Fast, which they term the *Ramezan*;[1] during which time they are so severely abstemious, that they stretch not their Hands to either Bread or Water, 'till the Sun be set, and the Stars appear; no, not the

[1] This is the ninth Mahommedan lunar month, the month of the Fast, or Lent.

Youths of 12 or 13 Years of Age. Which makes the Penance so much the more rigorous and troublesome, in that a draught of Water in those warm parching Climates is so very necessary, and so refreshing to such as are ready to faint with Thirst. This Fast is not kept always at the same Season of the Year, but begins its date Annually more early by Eleven Days. When I was at *Suratt*, this mortifying Custom was about the Month of *September*, at which time the *Moors* would begin to refresh themselves about the close of the Evening, and Eat then freely; and by an Early Collation in the Morning, before the dawning of the Light, prepare themselves for the drought and heat of the following Day. The Almighty, they told us, requir'd from *Mahomet*, that his followers should be oblig'd to this Austerity, the whole Circuit of the Year; but that the Holy Prophet, in compassion to the Faithful, obtain'd from God the confinement of it only to a Month, which would therefore highly aggravate their Crime, if they neglected the Dedication of so small a Portion of the Year to this Religious Abstinence, tho' the observance of it had been injoyn'd after a more rigorous manner than it is. And to add to the Sanctity of this Celebrated and solemn Fast, their *Mullahs*,[1] acted with a sacred Zeal, and lively concern for the Souls of the People, will at this time spend whole Nights in the *Musseets*,[2] in chanting aloud alternately their Divine Hymns, 'till the approach of day breaks up their Devotions : And so they compleat their Fast, according to the strictest Rules of the most rigid *Ascetichs*, by mixing Prayers and Watchings with their Abstinence; in which, as well as in their Publick Prayers and Religious Worship, they tie themselves up to a very nice and devout strictness, and behave themselves with all those decencies of Respect, with that astonishing Reverence in the *Musseets*, as not to defile them with either their Eyes or Lips; not daring so much as to turn their Heads to gaze about, or utter the least word to one

*A story concerning* Mahomet.

*The* Mullahs *Devotions*.

*Their decent Religious Behaviour*

[1] Hind. *mullā*, one who reads the Korān, a doctor of the Law.

[2] Hind. *Masjīd*, a mosque.

another. Which profound Respect casts an obloquy and deserv'd Reproach upon some Professors of a much purer Religion, and more Holy Faith, whose careless Deportment and familiar Address discountenance all the Religious decorum of Prayers, and might tempt those Heathens to conclude, that our Devotions were rather some light Diversion, than the effects of serious and sacred Thoughts.

*The Funerals costly.*

The *Moguls* are very profuse in their Funeral Expences; as well at the time of their Friend's deeease, as at several others within the compass of a Month, when they think themselves ingag'd at their publick Invitations to lavish away immoderate Cost to their Friend's Memory, enough almost to sink a rich Fortune. Besides the solemn yearly Celebration of an Expensive Feast for all the Friends and Relatives, in Honour of the Departed; that they may revive the kindness they entertain'd for the Virtues and Affection of him they lament, and that they may keep up the Idea of his Person and Endowments. At this time too the Tomb is deckt with Lamps, and beset with bright Illuminations, as Emblems of his shining Excellencies and Perfections.

*The* Moors *manner of Burying.*

The dead Corps is carried after our manner on a Bier upon Mens shoulders, decently drest and beautifyed with Flowers, and attended with the company of Friends and Relations to the place of Burial. The Grave is Arched under Ground so high, that a Man may sit under its Roof; to this Intent, that when the Angel at the Day of Judgment shall come and ask them, Whether they are *Mussulmen?* They may sit up in their Graves, and answer, *Yea.* Some of them are reported to be skilled in preserving a Corps from Putrefaction a considerable time, only with the Repetition of some few Words, and without the Art or Expense of *Egyptian* Embalming, to keep it from Corruption, only with a Verbal Charm.

*A Charm to preserve a Corps.*

*Their Tombs placed contrary to ours.*

And as their Minds are wrought into an Aversion against ours, by the Contrariety of their Faith, when they were alive; so they would seem to continue that Antipathy even beyond the stroke of Death, to the very Confinement of the Grave, by placing their Corps in a quite contrary Position to ours, which are laid from East to West, as theirs are athwart from North to South.

*The* Moors *Language wants Characters.*

The Language of the *Moors* is different from that of the ancient Original Inhabitants of *India*, but is oblig'd to these Gentiles for its Characters. For though the *Moors* Dialect is peculiar to themselves, yet is it destitute of Letters to express it; and therefore in all their Writings in their Mother Tongue, they borrow their Letters from the Heathens, or from the *Persians*, or other Nations.[1] The Court Language is *Persian*, which obtains with all the Honourable *Omrahs*, and with all Persons of Ingenuity and polite Conversation through the Empire, which creates an Ambition of dressing their Speech as well as Writing in that favourite Style. For Foreign Languages in *Asia*, as well as *Europe*, invade the use of the Mother Tongue with Princes, and their Ministers of State; as here the *Persian* prevails; in *Persia* the *Ottoman* Language; and at the August Port the *Arabian* Tongue.

*The Court Language* Persian.

'Tis observable that the Introduction of a Language concurs towards compleating the Conquest of a Nation; which yet the *Moguls* have not been able to effect in *India*, neither totally to reduce the old Natives to a chearful undisturb'd compliance with the Government: But a potent *Rajah* is tempted to raise new Factions now and then to disturb the Affairs of the *Mogul*, and give Diversion to his Army. And zealous of the Tradition of their Ancestors, maintain not only their own Tongue, but as much as possible their ancient Customs and Opinions, and start new Objections against their present State, the better to assert their Primitive Liberty again; and the ancient Possession of those Kingdoms, which their Progenitors for so many Ages by immemorial Custom had formerly retain'd.

*Factions now and then in* India.

Indeed the *Bramins*, who are deriv'd from *Bramon*,[2] who

*The* Bramin *Language.*

[1] Fryer, ii. 103, 122, makes the same observation. Hindustani or Urdu, was, as the name implies, a bastard dialect, which sprang up among the camp-followers of the Moghals in India. It is a mixture of Hindi and Persian, and was written in Persian or Nāgari characters indifferently.

[2] Brahmā, the Creator. From the root *brih*, to increase.

(they say) was one of the first Men that inhabited the World, have a Language used among them, but very difficult to be attain'd, which several of themselves therefore understand not. It is the Learned Language among them, called the *Sanscreet*, and is the same with them as Latin is with us. In this the Records of their Nation, the Mysteries of their Theology, the Books of their Religion and Philosophy, and the Fables of their Priests, are writ; wherein are several weak and loose Opinions, discovering their Ignorance both of the Duration of this World, and the State and Condition of the next. I wanted that opportunity I wish'd for, of enquiring more particularly into the several Mysteries of their Religion. Besides, few of the learned *Bramins* live near *Suratt*.

*The Paper-Books in* India.

The Paper-Books, in vulgar use among the Inhabitants of *India*, are long Schrowls of Paper, sometimes Ten Foot in length, and a Foot broad, sowed together at the upper end, as many long Sheets as the occasion of the Writing requires.

*Their Pens.*

The Pen they write with is the ancient *Calamus*, or Reed, about the thickness of a large Goose Quill.

*Their Standishes.*

And some of their Standishes[1] are made long and square, and above an Inch broad, and of sufficient length to contain both Pens, and a place for Ink.

*Their way of writing.*

Their manner of Writing is neither directly forwards nor backwards, nor in a streight Line downwards, like the *Chinese* from the upper to the lower part of the Paper; but it is a Medium between both, from the uppermost Corner of the left to the lowermost Corner of the right, slanting gradually downwards; especially when they write any Notes or Epistles to one another.[2]

*The Paper.*

Their Paper by its Slickness and Smoothness appears shining, which is of ordinary use; but that which they write upon, either to the Emperour, or Persons of Consequence, is gilt all

[1] Inkstand, Hind. *kalamdān*, from *kalam* a reed-pen. Gk. κάλαμος, cf. Lat. *calamus*, a reed.

[2] This is incorrect. All Hindu languages are written in the ordinary manner, from left to right.

on the Surface, as ours is only on the edges, with some small Flowers interspersed here and there for Ornament.

*The Covering for Letters.*

For the Security of Letters sent abroad to the principal Ministers, or the Emperour, they are inclos'd in a large hollow Bambou of a Foot length, at one end of which is a Head or Cover two Inches long, which after the Letter is put in, is join'd close to the Bambou, and upon that joining the Seal is fixt, to prevent taking out the Letter without breaking the Seal. This preserves the Letter neat and clean, unsullied by Rain or Dust, or being carried from Hand to Hand; so that let the Journey be never so tedious, this Respect always accompanies the Letter to him it was sent to, that in opening of it, he finds it as neat and fair as it was when it was first sealed up. The Covers of Paper which are put upon our Letters in *Europe*, bear some resemblance to the Civility of the *Indian* Bambou.

*No Coats of Arms in* India.

Upon their Chops, as they call them in *India*, or Seals engraven, are only Characters, generally those of their Name, upon Gold, or Silver, or Cornelian Stones.[1] Coats of Arms in *India* are not heard of; for no Man is hereditary there, either to Estate or Honours, those all depend upon the Breath and Pleasure of the *Mogul*, who is the sole Fountain of Honour and Riches, who blasts the Fortune of his Subjects, or raises them by his Favour, as he thinks fit. There every Man's Title and Estate are as mortal as himself, die with him, and return to the Disposal of the Soveraign.

*No Posts here.* [*Patimār*, courier.]

The *Indians* in sending their Letters abroad have not learnt the convenience of the quick Dispaches of our Posts: A Pattamar, *i. e.* a Foot Messenger, is generally employ'd to carry them to the remotest Bounds of the Empire. So that whenever the *English* are under a necessity of writing to *Bengal*, *Maderas*, or any other part of *Indostan*, a Person is sent on purpose upon the Errand.

*No Printing here.*

Neither have they endeavour'd to transcribe our Art of Printing; that would diminish the Repute and Livelihood of their Scrivans, who maintain numerous Families by the Pen.

[1] Cf. p. 126, note 1.

But they can imitate a little the *English* manner of Binding Books.

*No Improvement of the Language.* They have not many Learned among them, to remove any Defects that might be found in their common Stile, or to improve their Language, so venerable for Antiquity, and preservation of its self for so many Ages without any known Alteration. It is otherwise in *Europe*, where Foreign Words are naturalized for embellishing the Elegancy of Speech, which has been more particularly design'd in *Germany*; and for compleating which the Emperour founded the *Swan-Society*, as Censors of the Language, to correct and refine, to alter and amend whatever they found unpolish'd or amiss.[1] But *Dr. Kempfire*,[2] an ingenious Traveller, and *German* Physician, who told me this, told me likewise, that they exterminate all exotick Words, however proper or specifick, by a Confinement to those of their Mother Tongue, tho' loaded with Circumlocutions. This Method, methinks, cannot so much refine, as debase the Speech; which being an Instrument of conveying the Ideas of things to the Mind, must needs increase its Excellence, by how much the more particular and distinguishing Characters it represents them by; and this Excellence depends upon the Idiom of Words.

*Fine Horses.* In Journeying, or in taking the Air, the *Moors* are not only accommodated with delicate Horses bred in *India*, but have convey'd hither from *Persia* and *Arabia* Horses so well turn'd, and of such admirable Shapes, that a Thousand Roupies is easily sunk in the Price of one of the more ordinary that are brought hither. Some of them are train'd up, and excel in Management as well as Shape; but their Care of them is equal to neither of these Excellencies; for in the shooing of them, 'tis commonly done so inartificially, that

[1] During the early part of the seventeenth century, several literary societies, in imitation of the Italian academies, were started in Germany in order to set up a standard of pure speech. The earliest was the 'Fruchtbringende Gesellschaft' founded by Prince Louis of Anhalt-Köthen, 1617.

[2] For Dr. Kaempfer, see p. 34, note 2.

they easily batter their Hoofs, and expose them to surbating[1] with a very moderate Journey.

*Oxen rid upon commonly instead of Horses.*

The Vulgar are not mounted on these stately Steeds, but they are pleas'd with getting upon a small Ox, as their Pad, to carry them in the Town, or round the Country. They ascend them as we do our Horses, equipp'd with a soft Cushion instead of a Saddle, and a long Rope thrust through the Cartilage, which separates the Nostrils, knotted on each side, which supplies the use of a Bridle. And thus at a good round easie rate they travel upon the ambling horn'd Beast, either longer Journeys, or shorter Stages, as they please.

*Hackeries drawn by Oxen.*

*A large Bump between the Shoulders of the black Cattle.*

*Buffoloes.*

*The Horns of the Oxen set off with Silver.*

Their Hackeries[2] likewise, which are a kind of Coach with two Wheels, are all drawn by Oxen, which though they are naturally heavy Beasts, and slow in their Motions, yet by constant and long Exercise they acquire a great Facility and Speed of Foot in drawing the Hackeries, so as to vie with one another in Swiftness for Wagers in running Races. Some of their Oxen are very large and tall; and all their black Cattel, both of this kind, and the Buffoloes, are remarkable for a big piece of Flesh that rises above Six Inches high between their Shoulders, which is the choicest and delicatest piece of Meat upon them, especially put into a Dish of Palau.[3] The Buffolo is generally larger than an Ox, but a very sowr untractable Animal, by which means he is useless to the Natives in the convenience of Riding, or of Hackeries, and is generally employ'd in carrying large Bags of Fresh Water on each side, from the Tanques to the Houses. They affect no gaiety or Trappings or of Harnass upon their draught Oxen, but delight to see their Horns set off with Brass or Silver made hollow, of three or four Inches length, fixt to the tip of them, with a long Chain of Silver reaching from the end of each Horn to the middle of the Head, and there fastened.

[1] Becoming footsore.

[2] A light cart or *ekka*. Perhaps from Hind. *chhakrā*, 'a two-wheeled chariot drawn by swift little oxen,' says Fryer. Another suggested derivation is Port. *carreta*, a cart.

[3] 'Bullock's Hump' salted is a well-known Anglo-Indian joint.

*The Description of a Hackery.* The Hackeries are made of a square Figure, as our Coaches, but the Seat is flat, not rais'd with Cushions to lean upon. They can carry three or four persons, and are all open on the sides, but supported at each Corner, and in the middle by Pillasters. Some of better fashion are hung round, with an Imperial over Head to fence off the scorching Rays of the Sun, and with a Carpet spread under to sit upon.

*Palanquins.* Those whose Wealth is able to support it, are pompously carried upon Men's shoulders in Palanquins, whose carriage is as easie and pleasant as that of our Chairs in the Streets of *London*, but far surpasseth them in point of State and quick dispatches of a Journey. Four or Six Servants support the Palanquins, with others that attend and relieve them by turns, who will with ease carry it twenty or thirty Miles a Day. It hangs like a Cradle upon a Bambou five or six Inches in Diameter, and near four and twenty Foot long; Arched in the middle for the convenience of him that sits in it, and sustaining the Hangings with which it is cover'd; but it is streight above five Foot at each end, where the Servants carry it upon their shoulders. Ballisters of four or five Inches thickness support it; the sides of it are curiously wrought, and richly plated with Gold or Silver; the Covering is made of fine Silk; the Cushions within are generally of rich Zarbaft,[1] with the choicest Carpets spread under them. Here the great Men stretch themselves at ease, as it were upon a Couch, and hereby they avoid that Heat and ruffling of their Spirits, which either the motions of a Horse or a Hackery might cause, and which in these Kingdoms is so very troublesome. The Antient *Romans* us'd something like a Palanquin, as *Juvenal* in his first Satyr, tells us,

*Zarbaft is a kind of Silver or Gold Brokade.*

[Juv. 1. 32.] *Causidici nova cum veniat lectica Mathonis*
*Plena ipso.*

When they take the Air, either in Palanquins or otherwise, they usually frequent the coolest Groves, and the pleasant Gardens adjacent to the City, refresht either by the River

[1] Gold brocade. See p. 131, note.

*Tappy*, or by Water convey'd into their Tanques, or Ponds. And here the Dancing Wenches, or Quenchenies,[1] entertain you, if you please, with their sprightly Motions, and soft charming Aspects, with such amorous Glances, and so taking irresistible a Mien, that as they cannot but gain an Admiration from all, so they frequently Captivate a zealous Rich Spectator, and make their Fortunes and Booty of the Inchanted Admirer. *Dancing Wenches.*

*——ut Gaditana canoro*
*Incipiat prurire choro, plausuq; probatæ* [Juv. *Sat.*
*Ad terram tremulo descendant clune puellæ.* 11. 163.]

One of the principal Persons about *Suratt*, was thus surpriz'd and insnar'd while I was there, and lost both himself, his Fortune, and his Friends, in their eager Admiration. For they are Educated in the Improvement of all that is gay and entertaining, they set themselves off with such advantage, by a Rhetorical Look and taking Air, wherein they shew an unparallell'd Master-piece of Art, that a grave *European* will scarce adventure himself in the sight of their insinuating Temptations, and charming deportment.

Among the Men, whose Imployment it is to divert Spectators with amazing Shows and Sights, some, they say, will take in their Hands a Clew of Thread, and throw it upwards in the Air till it all unravels, and then climbing up themselves by this tender Thread to the top of it, presently fall down piece-meal upon the Ground; and when all is dropt, unite again the parted Members. Others are said to raise a Mango-Tree, with ripe Fruit upon its Branches, in the space of one or two Hours. To confirm which Relation, it was affirmed confidently to me, that a Gentleman who had pluckt one of these Mangoes, fell sick upon it, and was never well as long as he kept it, 'till he consulted a *Bramin* for his Health, who *Strange Shows.*

[1] Hind. *Kanchanī*, a Nautch Girl; either the name of a caste, or 'gilded', 'decorated', Hind. *Kanchan*, gold. *Vide* Hobson-Jobson, *s.v.*

prescrib'd his only Remedy would be the restoring of the *Mango*, by which he was restor'd to his Health again.[1]

*Dancing Snakes.* Dancing Snakes kept tame in Baskets are every where common; their Keepers use them as familiarly as we do Puppies, take them in their Hands, and sometimes force them to bite their Flesh without any consequent harm. He that carries them about, plays upon a Pipe when he exposes them, at the noise of which the Snake will hiss, spread his Head and throw it about.

*A large Fowl swallowed by a Snake.* We had brought into our Factory once a tame Snake, of that bigness and length, that one of the Fowls of the largest size was swallowed whole by it, with all the Feathers on, in my sight; it first began with the Head of the Fowl, and then twisting its Body about the Body of the Fowl, squeezed it close, to facilitate the Passage. The Fowl Screeched once at the first seizing, and afterwards lay dead: The Snake strugled sometime with the Bulky part of the Body before it could get it down; but as soon as it was once swallow'd, it found a speedy passage to the middle of the Snake, which lay there strecht and swell'd, 'till the natural Heat, in less than 24 Hours, had digested both the Bones and Feathers. This was an extraordinary Morsel, and far surpassing that ordinary Food upon which the Snakes do commonly feed. But there is much more danger than diversion from these Serpents in *India*, where they are so numerous, that the unwary Traveller is often expos'd to the fatal effects of their sudden Venom. For a Peon of mine, named, *Gemal*,[2] walking abroad in the Grass after the Rains, was unfortunately bit on a sudden by one of them. The latent Snake twisted unawares about his Leg, and in a short time brought him to the Ground, by causing in him an immediate deliquium of Spirit, almost even to Expiration. The Servants who were

[1] Fryer, ii. 104, gives an account of Indian jugglers. Entertaining extracts will be found in Hobson-Jobson, *s.v.* Mango trick. Ibu Batuta, *c.* 1340 A.D., saw the Rope trick, but no modern first-hand accounts of it exist.

[2] Jamāl, a Mahommedan name.

standing by, amaz'd at the accident, called immediately upon an *English* Merchant, who hasten'd towards him with a special Medicine for his Recovery. The thing which he carried about him, and which instantly applyed, is a Specifick against the Poison of Snakes, cured him, and therefore obtains the Name of Snake-stone.[1] It is a small artificial Stone, almost flat, only with a little protuberance in the middle, and of a gray Colour. The Composition of it is Ashes of burnt Roots, mixt with a kind of Earth, which is found at *Diu*, belonging to the *Portuguese*; and those are burnt together again, out of which Paste the Stones are formed. They are not all alike Colour'd, but those that have receiv'd more of the Fire, are thereby inclin'd to a lighter Gray, the *The Snake Stone.*

[1] Various medicinal stones played an important part in the seventeenth-century pharmacopœia, and fetched fabulous prices as articles of trade with the East. The snake-stone was apparently made of charred bone. The bezoar stone (Pers. *pādzāhr*, expelling poison) was a concretion found in the bodies of goats, monkeys, and other animals. Both were porous, and when applied to a snake-bite were believed to absorb the poison. The Goa stone was a secret preparation of the Jesuits, being the invention of Fr. Antonio, a lay brother of the order. A little of it powdered was said to cure a variety of diseases. See the interesting passages quoted in Hobson-Jobson, *s.v.* Bezoar Stone, Goa Stone, Snake-Stone, and Fryer, ii. 11, 141, 193, 200, 363; iii. 15, 99, 322. The following reference to Ovington's account of the Snakes-tone is taken from an anonymous *Account of the Island of Bombay*, now attributed to Burnell, 1711–12, in the Orme Collection, India, vol. ix, pp. 2126–7 : 'The common antidote in India to expel their [snakes'] poison is the Snakes-tone, made of a Buffelo's horn, tho' Mr. Ovington saith of earth found at Diu and the ashes of certain herbs mixed, being made into a paste and burnt, becomes of a porous nature; and indeed I must own it seemeth to stand most with reason. Of these I have had several, being about the bigness of the top of one's thumb, flat, and of a black or greyish colour. When they are used, they are placed to the part afflicted, where (being of a spungy nature) they suck out all the venom the wound hath imbib'd. Then, being thrown into milk, it presently disgorgeth what it hath received, and is instantly fit to be applied to suck out the remainder, where it sticks 'till it hath fill'd it's pores and then falls off like a Horseleech.'

*Its Virtues.* others are a little more dark. This Stone Cures by the application of it to the part invenom'd, to which it immediately sticks fast, and by its powerful Attraction sucks back the infus'd Venom, 'till its Pores are full. Then like a glutted Horse-Leach it falls off, and disgorges the replenisht Pores in Milk (the properest liquor for this purpose) which by discolouring, it renders livid. Upon this it recovers new strength, and its Alexipharmick quality again, and is speedily prepar'd for a fresh Draught of Poison, if any remains in the affected part, 'till it quite extracts whatever the venomous Serpent had immited; which makes those Counter-Poisons in great esteem against all external Attacks upon the Body; as the Cordial Antidotes are most valuable for expelling or subduing any Poyson inwardly receiv'd. The double Excellence of this Stone recommends its worth very highly, in that a little of it scraped off, and mixt with Wine, or some other proper vehicle, and inwardly taken, is reputed one of the most powerful Medicines against any Malignant Fevers or Infectious Diseases, that is known; and much excels the deservedly fam'd *Gasper Antoni*, or Goa Stone. The *How to try the Snake Stone.* trial of these Stones is made by fixing them to the Roof of the Mouth, to which if they stick fast, 'tis a sign they are genuine, if they easily fall off, fictitious. Another method for knowing the true Stones from the Counterfeit, is to immerse them in a Glass of Water, where, after a while, if some light Ebullitions rise from them, and ascend through the Body of the Water, this likewise is an approv'd Sign that the Stone is not spurious. The *Europeans*, for the Security of themselves against the Danger of these Serpents, which are every where so common in *India*, carry always about them one of these Stones inclosed in a Heart of Gold, fixt to a Golden Chain, which hangs about their Necks.

*The Virtue of burning Coal.* A burning Coal is boasted to be able to effect the same Cure, as the Snake-Stone does; and to heal the Venom of Serpents, or stinging of Scorpions, by gradually drawing out all the Poyson, when it is applied very near the Wound; which is not easily vext or incommoded by the Fire, by reason that the acuteness of the Venom abates the sensibleness of the Heat of the Fire, and keeps it off.

As the Kingdom of *Indostan* is very much annoy'd by the multitude of these venomous Creatures, which lurk in all Coverts and secret places, so is it stockt with Medicines extraordinary against their Harm. The wise Designation of Heaven providing all things for the Convenience, as well as Necessity, both of Nations and particular Creatures, by suiting Remedies peculiar to each ones Exigence, and appropriating agreeable Circumstances to the particular Natures of all. Therefore as inward Poysons prevail in these parts, as well as outward; so do Medicines likewise, which are available for abating and expelling both of them. For besides several Poysonous Herbs which grow in *India*, the old Natives of *Bengal* affirm, that if Sugar be kept for Thirty Years, it is as dangerous, as quick, and effectual Poyson as any. *Sugar long kept is poysonous.* One of the Antidotes, above all the rest, is the celebrated *Maldive* Coco-nut,[1] of which this Encomium is given by *Piso*, *The* Mal*dive Coco-Nut.* in his *Mantissa Aromatica*, at the latter end of *Bontius*, *Vera cum Gloria prædicare non dubito, Antistitem Alexipharmacorum Coccum nostrum esse, experimentis indubitatis non fallacem.* That is, He can truly boast by many infallible Experiments, that there is no Alexipharmick goes beyond the *Maldive* Coconut. He prescribes four Scruples, or from half a Drachm to a whole, to be taken in proper Liquor, which he affirms prevails miraculously to the Cure not only of Internal *Its Virtues.* Poysons, but mightily helps forward Women in Labour, as he would prove by an Induction of many Particulars. It

[1] The Coco de Mer, or double coconut of the Maldive Islands, was formerly credited with all sorts of amazing qualities. It was said to grow under the sea and cure all kinds of diseases, and fetched extravagant prices. The Maldive name is *Tava-kārhi.* The Dutch botanists Piso, *De Indiae utriusque Re Naturali et Medica*, Bontius, *Hist. Nat. et Medic. Indiae Orientalis*, Amsterdam, 1658, and Rumphius, *Herbarium Amborense*, Amsterdam, 1693, are responsible for many of these fables. It is said that the Emperor Rudolf II offered 4,000 florins for one that had been given by the King of Bantam to Admiral Wolfert Hermanzen.

cures the Bloody Flux, the Pestilence, and Malignant Fevers, Poysons, Falling Sickness, Palsey, Convulsions, and frightful Tremors of the Spirits: So great are its Virtues, that the use of it, as he elsewhere tells us, is consecrated by a certain Priviledge of Nature to the support of Life, *p.* 207. Which made *Rudolphus*, a certain *Roman* Emperour, understanding its Excellence, purchase it at the price of Four Thousand Florens.

*This Nut found in several parts of* India.

The Name of this Nut with the *Maldives* is *Tavarcare*; and tho' it has appropriated the Name of *Maldive*, yet is it found in other parts of *India* besides, though probably the first, or most of them, are met with there. It is conjectured to be the same with the Land Coco-Nut, and that when the Ocean invading the Main Land of *Asia*, made a Breach of the *Maldives* from it, these Nuts were cover'd under the Water, which now and then are taken up in it floating, or washt upon the Shore.

*A strange Cure perform'd by the* Maldive *Coco-Nut.*

The *Indians* are very fond of it, and strongly maintain its Medicinal Virtues against Poyson; in Confirmation whereof, an old *English* Master of a Grab,[1] or small Vessel, *George Toach*, has frequently repeated this Story to me, 'That in his Voyage to *Patta*,[2] which lies near the *Red Sea*, upon the Coast of *Africa*, in the time of the Sale of his Cargo there, the King's Son of the Place was poysoned to that degree, that his Skin was bloated and swollen upon him like a Bladder: He presently betakes himself for a Remedy to the *Maldive* Coco-nut, several of which are found there. This he rubbed upon a hollow Stone, containing five or six spoonfuls of Water, till the Water was well tinctur'd by it; and in the same manner rubb'd a piece of a Rhinoceros Horn,[3] and then drank the Water off. And repeating this Medicine for three or four

[1] Mar. *Gurāb*, galley, corvette.

[2] A small island off the coast of British East Africa. Cf. p. 72.

[3] This was another extraordinary remedy. See the learned note by Crooke to Fyrer, ii. 298, and cf. Ben Jonson, *Every Man in his Humour*, v. 4, 'Had you no unicorn's horn, or Bezoar's stone about you?'

Days, the Humours sensibly asswaged, and in that time were all drawn off by so powerful a Purgation, that though it had rack'd and examin'd every part of his Body, yet he recover'd in that short space of time; the Swelling abated, and his Skin fell, and hung loose about him like a Garment.' I brought one of these Coco-nuts with me from *Suratt*, which was graciously accepted of by the late Queen, of Glorious and Immortal Memory.

*The Virtue of the Rhinoceros Horn.*

They ascribe very much likewise to the Rhinoceros Horn in *India*, as it is an Antidote against all poysonous Draughts, and hugely extol in it that Medicinal Excellence and singular Quality. The Character of this Horn prevail'd so far with a former President of ours at *Suratt*, that he exchang'd for a Cup made of this Horn a large capacious Silver Bowl of the same bigness.

*The* Indians *play at Chess.*

The Heat of the Country about *Suratt*, will scarce permit that eager Prosecution of Sports or Recreations, which a cooler Climate does encourage; but a Game at Chess in their Houses, or in the Shades of the Streets, will invite them to spend some Hours at it: I did not hear of their Expenses otherwise, I mean of their Goods or Money. For they seldom are heated into Passion, or ruinous Adventures, by the Polemick Traverses of that intricate puzling Game. Their Frolicks reach not to that pitch of Folly, as to exchange their Pastimes into Punishments, or to make them hazard the loss of their comfortable Subsistence for ever, for diverting themselves for some Hours or Minutes. And to me it seems more rational, the Penalty of the *Japanners* upon Gaming, who have decreed it a Capital Crime to play for Money; than the Liberty taken by the *Siamese*, in playing away not only their Estates, but Families, and sometimes themselves too. How many fair Estates have been squandred away in one Night's time, by the Votaries of Fortune, who have both ruin'd themselves and their Families, by the Effects of this Vanity, and the bewitching Love of Gaming? And by running their Estates upon unhappy Destinies, by a cross turn of Fortune, or an unlucky Chance, have made themselves Suppliants for

*Gaming for Money capital at* Japan.

part of those Possessions, of which they were intire Masters before.

*Hunting of wild Beasts.* The variety of Wild Beasts afford the stouter *Indians* abundance of other Game, and divert them with more manly Pastimes. Insomuch that in some of our *English* Factories, particularly *Carwar* upon the Coast of *Malabar*, Deer, Antilopes, Peacocks, wild Bulls and Cows, are almost the daily Furniture of their Table, brought home by the Peons, without any further Expence than that of Powder and Shot. *Suratt* abounds not with that Plenty; however, Hares and Peacocks, Deer and Antilopes, are sold here at easie Rates; though Provisions are not quite so cheap as at *Bengal*, where Forty Fowls, or Fifteen Ducks, may be bought for a Roupie.

*English Dogs valuable there.* A considerable Value is set upon any of our *European* Dogs, either Spaniels, Greyhounds, or Mastiffs. A Water-Spaniel, in the River of *Tappy* after a Duck, will call forth the whole City to the Pastime; and 'tis with them upon this score so very amazing and delightful, because they have none of that Breed among them; nor indeed any other, that I ever saw, but Currs; into which our fiercest and most lively Dogs degenerate, after a Litter or two, by the constant unallay'd heat of the Country. The Grayhounds and Hounds are likewise equally valuable and divertive, and live for some time, if they run them not in the Heat of the Day; but if they chance to hunt with them about Noon, the ambient Air mixing with the Natural, when it is fermented and chafed, commonly proves too strong for their Constitutions; so that they frequently expire upon the spot, and rarely live out any number of Years or Months.

*The Irish Wolf-Dogs much esteem'd of.* A couple of *Irish* Wolf-Dogs were so prized in *Persia*, that they were taken as a welcom and admired Present by the Emperour himself. Two more of which (which were given to me by the Earl of *Inchequin*, when we put into *Kingsale*, after the Voyage) I dispos'd of to the *East-India* Company, who dispatcht them in their Ships immediately to the *Indies*, to be there bestowed in some of the Eastern Courts.[1]

[1] Cf. Introduction, p. xii.

*A Quarrel about an English Mastiff.*

A large *English* Mastiff, given by a Merchant, was look'd upon as such a Rarity and Favour by a Noble *Omrah*, that he engag'd himself and Six Hundred of his Followers, in a hot Dispute concerning his Property in the Dog, with another as potent a Grandee who claim'd a Right in him. For the Decision of this Controversie, they each led forth a like number of Men, to determin their Right by a bloody Contest. Till one, a little wiser and more cool than the other two, intreated their respite, and bespoke their Audience, and told them the case might be easily remitted to the *English* President, who was able to give a just determination in it. This by their joynt consent and application kindly prevented the Design'd Quarrel, and the *English* President Arbitrated fairly in justice to him to whom the Dog was given.

And because the *Moors* have invented peculiar Arts and methods in their Recreations, from what obtain among us; I shall instance in some of their diversions, which will not be ungrateful to the Reader, especially if he be a Man of Sports.

*The Hunting of Deer with Leopards.*

In hunting their Antilopes and Deer, as they are destitute of Dogs, so they endeavour to supply their want by tame Leopards, train'd and brought up for that purpose, which warily leap upon the Prey, and having once caught it, hold it fast.[1]

*Deer Hunted by Hawks.*

In *Persia*, in the room of Dogs and Leopards, they bring up Faulcons to hunt their Antilopes and Bucks, which are brought to *India* from thence, and are train'd to it after this manner. Whenever the Hawk they breed up to it is hungry, they fix its meat upon the Nose of a Counterfeit Antilope, and from thence only feed it, without allowing it any Meat but what it Eats there. After this they carry one or two of these Falcons into the Fields, and flying one of them at an Antilope, it fastens just upon his Nose, which so blinds and stops the Antilope, by the force and fluttering of its Wings, that he can neither well espy his way, nor find his Feet as nimbly as he would; and this gives a very easie admittance to the Men or Dogs to come in and catch him. If this Hawk

[1] The hunting-leopard or cheetah (Hind. *chītā*).

is beaten off, which is sometimes done with much ado, another aloft stoops and lights upon the same place, and strikes him backwards with his Talons, 'till at length he is made a Prey: For one of the Hawks always mounts as the other stoops.

*Another way of Hunting the Game.* Sometimes a great company of Men range the Fields, and walk together into the Inclosures, to look after their Game; when once they have espy'd the place where they fancy the Game lies, they inclose the Ground, and stand in a Ring, with Clubs or Weapons in their Hands, whilst they employ others to beat up the Ground, and raise it for them.

Nor are they destitute of ingenious Inventions, when they recreate themselves with Fowling, any less than they are in their Hunting Sports. For in the room of our stalking Horses, *Stalking Oxen.* they make use of stalking Oxen, which are manag'd and bred up to the purpose, even to admiration. I have seen a *Moor Indian* shoot at once five or six Ducks under one of their Bellies, without the least starting, or surprisal to the Ox; and the quiet temper of this laborious Animal renders it, I believe, as easily brought up to it, and as proper for this Game as any Horse. Some of the *Indians* maintain themselves very well by this Art.

*An Ingenious way to catch Wild-Fowl.* But they use another ingenious method for catching Wild Fowl, which is very pretty. The Fowler when he is in quest of his Game, espying at length his sport at a distance, prepares a Man to go before him toward the place where he sees his Game, and carry in his Hand the boughs of Trees, so artificially wrought and joyn'd together, that they perfectly resemble a small Bush or Hedge, which is a shelter both to the Fowler and him that carries it. By this contrivance, the Fowler passes altogether undiscover'd towards his sport, and gains the convenience not only of shooting at what distance he pleases, but sometimes approaches his Game so near, that he takes it almost in his Hand. *Another ingenious contrivance to catch Wild-Fowl.* If the Wild Fowl be at a distance upon the Water, he then contrives another method for coming near them, and surprizing them with his Hands. He takes a Pitcher or Earthen Jarr, so large that he fits it to his Head, which he covers all over, and decks it with the

Feathers of what Water-Fowl he thinks convenient; and making holes in it for him to breathe and look thro', he then fastens it upon his Head, and being expert in swimming, ventures into the Pond where he sees the Fowl, and moves towards them, without any thing visible but the Pitcher above the Water; when he comes near them where they swim about, he catches them one by one by their Legs, and silently pulls them under Water, and there fastens them to his Girdle. They all this while fancy the moving Feather'd Jarr a living Fowl, and those that were pluckt under the Water to have been Diving, 'till sometimes the Fowler catches the whole Flock.

*The* Bannians.

Next to the *Moors* the *Bannians*[1] are the most noted Inhabitants at *Suratt*, who are Merchants all by Profession, and very numerous in all parts of *India*. They are most innocent and obsequious, humble and patient to a Miracle; sometimes they are heated into harsh Expressions to one another, which is seldom; and this Tongue-Tempest is term'd there a *Banian* Fight,[2] for it never rises to Blows or Blood-shed. The very killing of a Fly with them, is a Crime almost inexpiable. They cannot so much as endure hot Words, as they call them, from the *Europeans*; but if they see them exasperated, and in a Rage, retreat for a day or two, 'till they give them time to cool; and when they find the Passion asswag'd, form their Addresses in the most affable manner, and obliging Respect.

*Their Temper and obsequious deportment.*

The Orientals are generally much more tender and insinuating in their Language, and more prompt & easie in their Deportment, than those that are bred in the Tempestuous Regions, and Northerly Air of *Europe*, which has a certain Influence upon their Spirits, to render them boisterous and irregular, in respect of that submissive temper and affable Carriage of the Eastern Nations. He that has convers'd for any time among these, can hardly bear the roughness, or be

*The Tempers of Men alter by the Climate they live in.*

[1] This is the *Vāni* or trading class of Gujarāt. Cf. *Bunya*. But the word, like Gentoo, is often used indiscriminately of Hindus in general. Cf. p. 139, note 2.

[2] Sir G. Birdwood says that the phrase is still current in Bombay.

brought to digest the rudeness of the others. For the sudden Changes, and uncertainty of the Weather in all Seasons of the Year, affect both the Heads and Hearts of such as are Conversant in these uneven Climates; it makes them suddenly heated into Passions, and as hardly brought to any warmth of Affection; it makes them both unlike other Nations, and inconsistent with themselves, by raising unequal Humours, and unconstancy in the Passions, unfixt Desires, and uncertain Ends. And were the *Bannians* to be transported hither, who hold a Transmigration,[1] they would be apt immediately upon their Arrival to conclude, that many of the Men had really invaded the Natures of some of the most savage Brutes, were animated with no other Souls than those of Tygers and Bears; and that the *Irish* and *French* Opinion of the *Lougaroos*,[2] or Men turn'd into Wolves, was as true and authentick a Notion, as any that prevail'd among them.

*The Reasons of the soft Temper of the* Bannians.

But that Opinion of the *Bannians*, which possesseth them with an Horror of Blood, does quite discourage them from all Hostile Attacks and thoughts of War; and their Despotick Government breaks their Spirits, and the feeble phlegmatick Aliments, with the consumptive Heat of the Sun, all contribute to weaken and effeminate their Constitutions, to the producing a tractable Disposition, and smooth regular Deportment.

*Much given to Riches.*

They are mainly addicted to prosecute their Temporal Interest, and the amassing of Treasure; and therefore will fly at the securing of a Pice, tho' they can command whole Lacks of Roupies. I know those among them computed to be worth an Hundred Thousand Pounds, whose Service the Prospect of Sixpence Advantage will command to traverse the whole City of *Suratt*. For they are always upon the

[1] All Hindus believe in the transmigration or wandering (*samsāra*) of the soul from body to body until it finds *Moksha* or Release. Its next incarnation is determined by its *karmā* or deeds in a former life.

[2] Fr. *loup-garou*, werewolf, λυκάνθρωπος.

Thoughts of increasing their Wealth, and plodding for Gain, which they lay hold on upon the least occasion, tho' by never so minute and inconsiderable Advantages. By which Diligence they generally secure a comfortable Subsistence; and some of them amass a prodigious Treasure.

The *Bannians* are by much the most numerous, and by far the wealthiest of all the Pagans of *India,* whose Distinction in Religion argues a difference of their various Vocations; and each single Trade is diversified by some particular Opinions; the Goldsmith, and Scrivan, the Joyner, Barber, and Merchant, *&c.* as they have different Employments, so are they of divers Sentiments, and distinguished in the Ceremonies of their Worship; and mix no more in their Sacred Sentiments of Religion, than in their Civil Arts. Therefore all their Arts are Hereditary, and their Employments confin'd to their own Families. The Son is engag'd in the Father's Trade, and to maintain the Profession of it in his Posterity, it is transmitted always to the succeeding Generation, which is obliged to preserve it in a lineal Descent, uncommunicated to any Stranger. Upon this account all Marriages are restrain'd to one Sect, and contracted only between Persons of the same Perswasion and Profession. The Merchant is debarred from entring into any League of Love with the Daughter of a Goldsmith, Shoemaker, or of any other different Employment; and all Persons are under a strict Confinement, in their Matrimonial Ties and Addresses to direct their Passions and Affections to those only of their own Opinion and Trade. Which Custom has formerly prevail'd even in the most Western Island of this Hemisphere; and several Great Men in the Septs of *Ireland,* had heretofore their Physicians, Poets, Smiths, and such like, who always continued in the same Races.[1]

*Each Trade of a different Opinion in Religion.*

*No Persons whose Parents are of contrary Trades, marry together.*

[1] Ovington's account of the Hindu caste-system is mainly correct. Caste was originally a trade-gild, like the gilds of medieval Europe, crystallized by centuries of custom. Each caste has its *dharma* or duties. There are thousands of castes, which fall into four great groups: Brahman, Kshattriya, Vaisya, Sudra. V. A. Smith, *Oxford History of India,* pp. 34–43.

*The* Indians *Ingenuity.* The *Indians* are in many things of matchless Ingenuity in their several Imployments, and admirable Mimicks of whatever they affect to copy after. The *Bannian*, by the Strength of his Brain only, will sum up his Accounts with equal exactness, and quicker Dispatch, than the readiest Arithmetician can with his Pen. The Weavers of Silk will exactly imitate the nicest and most beautiful Patterns that are brought from *Europe*. And the very Ship-Carpenters at *Suratt* will take the Model of any *English* Vessel, in all the Curiosity of its Building, and the most artificial Instances of Workmanship about it, whether they are proper for the Convenience of Burthen, or of quick Sailing, as exactly as if they had been the first Contrivers. The Wood with which *A sort of Wood that never splinters.* they build their Ships would be very proper for our Men of War in *Europe*; for it has this Excellence, that it never splinters by the Force of a Bullet, nor is injur'd by those violent Impressions, beyond the just Bore of the Shot.[1] The *The* Indian *Tailers.* Tailers here fashion the Cloaths for the *Europeans*, either Men or Women, according to every Mode that prevails; and fit up the Commodes, and towring Head-Dresses for the Women, with as much Skill, as if they had been an *Indian* Fashion, or themselves had been Apprentices at the *Royal Exchange*. But they are tainted with a superstitious Fancy, that mending old Cloaths in a Morning, is of very ill abode; and therefore they rather are willing to employ that time in fashioning of New, and reserve the Afternoon as most proper for the other.

The *Indians* have not yet attempted an Imitation of our Clock-work in Watches; and may be it is, because they

[1] Ovington's remarks are prophetic. In the early years of the nineteenth century, Bombay became famous for the line-of-battle ships designed by the veteran Parsi naval architect Jamsetjee Bomanji. His masterpieces were two magnificent eighty-four-gun vessels, the *Ganges* and the *Asia*; the latter afterwards carried Codrington's flag at Navarino. They were fifty per cent. cheaper than English-built vessels, and teak, as Ovington says, stands shot better than oak, and is more durable. The Lowji Wadia family were also great Bombay shipbuilders.

seldom continue their just Motions for any long time, by reason of the Dust that flies continually in the Air, which is apt to clog and stop the Wheels. But the *Chinese* have undertaken to take our Clocks and Watches in pieces, to form new ones themselves, and may be in some time produce some fresh Improvements in those Mechanical Operations. The *Siamese* measure their time by a sort of Water-Clock, not like the Clepsydra of old, wherein the Water descended from above, but by forcing it upwards through a small Hole in the bottom of a Copper Cup, plac'd in a Tub of Water. When the Water has sprung up so long that the Cup is full, it sinks down, and those that stand by it forthwith make a noise with Basons, signifying that the Hour is expired.[1]

*The* Chinese *imitate our Clock-work.*

*The Water Clock at* Siam.

In some things the Artists of *India* out-do all the Ingenuity of *Europe, viz.* in the painting of Chites[2] or Callicoes, which in *Europe* cannot be parallell'd, either in the brightness and life of the Colours, or in their continuance upon the Cloath. The Gold Stripes likewise in their Sooseys,[3] and the Gold Flowers in their Atlasses, are imitated with us, but not to Perfection. And the Cornelian Rings with double Chains of Gold about them, meeting at several Distances, where small sparks of Diamonds, Rubies, or Saphires are inlaid to beautifie the Ring, surpass the Skill of any other Nation to arrive to. I cannot boast of the Lack upon Scrutores and Tables at *Suratt*, which is but ordinary in respect of that at *Japan*.[4] They make it, as I was told by Mr. *Prescot*, one of the Council at *Bombay*, invulnerable to all Impressions, so hard and thorowly firm, that if you will but rise to the price of it, they will venture it with a Bagonet, and forfeit it entirely, if the sharpest Point shall pierce it very deep. But yet

*The extraordinary Ingenuity of the* Indians *in some things.*

*A Report concerning the Lack at* Japan.

[1] A water-clock of this kind, called *ghati*, is still used in Hindu marriage ceremonies. It takes 24 minutes to fill the pot.

[2] Chintz, printed cotton-cloth. Calico, cottons from Calicut.

[3] Hind. *sūsi*, a silk fabric. Atlas, Indian satin; cf. p. 125, note.

[4] Lac, lacquer, Hind. *lākh*, the resinous incrustation on the trunks of certain trees caused by the puncture of a small insect. A scrutor is an escritoire or writing-table; cf. p. 131.

all the Wood among them which is Lackt, is not of this impenitrable Hardness; and yet all of it is laid on both deeper, and made much firmer, than the Lack of *Tunquin*,[1] which sometimes yields to the Force of the Nail of ones Finger pressed upon it; and is one way of trying its Excellence. This Varnish grows upon Trees very common in the Woods of *Siam*, which distils from them like a Gum, and is transported to *China*, *Japan*, and other Kingdoms.

*A way of trying Lack.*

*The Lack grows at* Siam.

*24 Casts of* Bannians.

Among the *Bannians* are reckon'd 24 Casts, or Sects, who both refrain from an indiscriminate mixture in Marriages, and from eating together in common. They all maintain a Transmigration of Souls, and Abstinence from the Food of any Living Creature, according to the Doctrine of *Pythagoras*, who is presum'd by some Learned Men to have borrowed his Opinion from them. This *Philostratus* relates of *Jarchas*, a Principal of the *Bramins*, how he told *Apollonius Tyanœus*,[2] that he himself had formerly been *Ganges*, *Apollonius* had been an *Egyptian* Mariner, and an Attendant that waited upon them had been *Palamedes*, and in new Bodies had represented themselves to the World. Which Opinion spread it self as far formerly as our Nation, among the Druids, who for this reason taught and prescrib'd an Abstinence from Flesh. They fancy that every Man, according to his Demerits in his Life-time, shall animate a noble, or more infamous Animal after Death. And him they pronounce compleatly happy, whose Soul, after its departure out of the Body, can fortunately escape into that of a Cow, and inform the Body of that blest Creature, which above all the rest of the Animal Generations, is of singular Esteem and greatest Respect, even almost to Adoration: A solemn Address is paid to this Creature every Morning; and he that is destitute of one at home, makes his Visit to that of his Neighbours. They admire it for the Excellence of its Nature, for which it is conspicuous in those extraordinary Benefits which Man-

*They hold the Transmigration.*

*Eat no living Creature.*

*The Druids hold a Transmigration.*

*Their great Esteem for the Cow.*

[1] *Vide* p. 76, note.

[2] A famous miracle-worker, born in the first century A.D. at Tyana in Cappadocia. See McCrindle, *Ancient India*, pp. 191 ff.

kind receive from it in the support of their Lives; and for the Convenience of it after Death, in conducting them over a broad deep River, which they are ingaged to pass, which would be impassable, were it not for the Cow's Tail, which the *Bramins* tell them, they are to take hold of in getting over.[1]

Besides these, there are other Reasons for the profound Respect they have for the Cows; for they believe, with the *Mahometans*, that the Foundations of the Earth are supported on the Horns of these Creatures; and that the Cows extraordinary fast Motion causes Earthquakes. They tell us likewise, that *Mahaden*,[2] being greatly provok'd by the Crimes of the People, and resolving upon it to destroy the World, he was appeas'd by a Cow, who reconcil'd him, and sav'd the Earth from utter Ruin. Therefore did the former Kings of *Malabar*, whenever they created a Nairo[3] or Knight, after their embracing him, enjoyn'd his Kindness to those two especially, the *Bramins* and the Kine. And whatever Opinion some present Philosophers have of Brutes, who deny them not only the use of Reason, which others have ascrib'd to them, but likewise that of Sense, by degrading of them into meer Machines; the Ancients had better Thoughts of them; and the *Egyptians* and *Persians*, as well as *Indians*, had them in universal Esteem. The *Egyptians* form'd the Images of their Gods in the Similitude of Beasts, or Birds, or Fishes; as that of an Ox, a Crocodile, or other Creature, to affright the Vulgar by these Sacred Symbols from hurting the dumb Animals; and that struck with a Sacred Reverence, they might abstain from the Death of any living Creature. And thus the Disciples of the *Persian* Magi receiv'd an Alteration of their Names into those of Beasts, or Birds; and were called Lions, Panthers, Hawks, or something else, to form in them a likeing to those Creatures; and by resembling them in the various Figures with which their Garments were

Bramins *and Cows most respected.*

*The* Egyptian's *kindness to living Creatures.*

*And the* Persians.

[1] For the worship of the Cow, see *Bomb. Gaz.* ix, Part i, pp. 372 ff.

[2] Mahādeva, Siva.

[3] Nairs, Skt. *Nāyaka*, the ruling caste in Malabar. Cf. p. 192.

painted, to bring them to entertain a certain Friendship and Affection to them; thereby insinuating this *Indian* Perswasion of the Transmigration of Souls, and that the Spirit of Man is liable successively to animate all kinds of Bodies.

*The Respect which a certain* Bannian *paid to a Snake.*

The *Bannians* are of so firm a Belief in this matter, and so far gone in this Assertion, that if either Bird or Beast be seen to frequent their Habitation, it must consequently be the Spirit of some lately departed Friend. *Moradash* [1] a *Bannian*, and Scrivan or Secretary [1] to the *English* Brokers, was some few Years past sorely afflicted for the Death of his Father, and in deep melancholy Sighs had long bewail'd his Misery and Loss. Till at length a large Snake appearing in the House some time after, where his Father died, became a Refuge to his sorrowful Thoughts, and reliev'd the Troubles of his Mind. *Moradash* fixing his Eyes upon the crawling Snake, and attentively considering its Windings and Motions for a while, revolv'd in his Mind how it found out its way thither, having never seen't before. And therefore strengthening his Opinion by his Affection, concludes that this could be nothing else but the Soul of his ancient Father, who in this Shape applied himself to his Son for Relief and Nourishment. Upon which his Superstition wrought so powerfully, that nothing now could alter this new Opinion, but he must carefully nourish this Snake, and so religiously continues a filial Respect to it, appointing it daily a certain Allowance of Rice and Milk. The Snake lodges in a Hole of the Wall, and after taking his Repast and Liberty in the Room, retires into his Apartment, till Hunger calls him forth to a fresh Meal; and is now both by the Scrivan and his Family as carefully attended, as if his Father were alive.

*The same* Bannian's *kindness to Rats.*

This fond indulgent *Indian* is as profuse in his Favours to some Rats, which lodge in his House, and are grown as familiar as Cats; for to these he allows some daily Food, because he is certain they harbour the Souls of some departed Relations.

[1] *Moradash* = Morār Dās. *Scrivan*, Port. *escrivão*, clerk, writer; cf. *scrivener*.

Some Men think that this Opinion of the Metempsyeosis takes its Original from the Transformation of *Nebuchadnezzar* into a Beast, whieh is mentioned in the Book of *Daniel*; and that when his Soul passed into that of a Brute, when he was under a eorporal Transformation, the Souls of other Men might undergo the same Fate after Death, as a Punishment for their Crimes, as his was. For the aneient *Gauls* maintain'd the Immortality of the Soul, and its shifting eontinually from one Body to another; and that aeeording to its Deportment here, sueh and sueh Bodies were appointed it by God, more or less painful, and suitable to its Condition. *Claud. in Ruff. Lib.* 2

*An Opinion concerning the Transmigration.*

*Muta ferarum*
*Cogit vincla pati, truculentos ingerit Ursis,*
*Pracdonesque Lupis, fallaces vulpibus addit,*
*Atque ubi per varios Annos per mille figuras*
*Egit, Lethæo purgatos flumine tandem*
*Rursus ad humanæ revocat primordia formæ.*

He made them wear the silent Yoak of Brutes, some that were Cruel, he lodged in the Bodies of Bears and Wolves; those that were Crafty, in Foxes, and others in other Animals, 'till after the sueeession of a thousand Years and Shapes, at length they are re-plae'd into Human Shapes, when they had been well purg'd in *Lethe*'s Flood.[1]

But to strengthen this Consideration the more eoneerning *Nebuchadnezzar*, they observe, that this wonderful Transformation of that great Monareh, happen'd at or about the very same time that *Pythagoras* was at *Babylon*, whither he travell'd to gain the Eastern Learning; but this may be a small mistake in time. Henee he brought the Report fresh with him, and being of a faneiful Genius, thought the best way to solve that strange oeeurrenee, was to assert a Metempsyehosis. But tho' there is no mention of the Soul's

[1] Claudian (*c.* 400 A. D.), the last of the Latin poets of antiquity, was an Alexandrian. His poems are mostly panegyrics, particularly of his patron Stilicho, the minister of Honorius.

*The ancient Opinion of the* Chinese, *of the Transmigration.*

Transmigration more ancient among the *Greeks* than *Pythagoras*; yet among the *Chineses*, whose Antiquities are said to be stretcht backwards above four thousand Years, there is this Opinion yet current among their Learned Men, as well as among the *Indians*, and is agreed to be of ancient Date: That the Souls after Death are Subject to a Transmigration. And it is not improbable that much of the *Phœnician*, as well as *Grecian* and *Egyptian* Institutions, were deriv'd from the ancient and remote Fountains of Learning, the *Indies* and *China*: Especially, if we consider not only the Opinion of the Soul's Transmigration, but of the Eternity of Matter; the four Cardinal Virtues, the Indolence of Body, and Tranquility of Mind, Abstinence from living Creatures, and several others, which seem to be intirely Oriental, and brought from thence by *Pythagoras*, *Democritus*, *Lycurgus*, and others, who travell'd into those distant parts.[1]

*The* Bannians *Days of Devotion.*

The Days set apart for the publick Devotion of the *Bannians*, are only two in a Month, about our ninth and twenty fourth; in which, by a very strict Discipline, they abstain from all things eatable 'till the Evening most Religiously.[2] And inculcate this severity upon their younger Children, in their Infant Growth, to induce the observance of it with facility upon them, and to render the Abstinence tolerable and less troublesome in their riper Age.

*Their Abstinence.*

*Holy Ballads Sung all the day long.*

The Pagans, who are bred to labour and Manual Occupations, consecrate each Day in the Week, and every thing they take in Hand thus far; that they fill their Mouths with a pious Song at the first dawning of the Morning, as soon as ever they ingage in their several Employments and Manual Occupations, and never cease their Secular Vocation without concluding with the mixture of a Holy Rhime. When a Company of Labourers are employ'd together about the same Work, this sacred Ballad is repeated by them sometimes

[1] The legends about the visits of Greek philosophers to Babylon and India are late traditions dating from neo-Platonic times.

[2] The Ekādashi, or eleventh day of each half of the Hindu month, is observed as a strict fast by orthodox Hindus.

alternately, sometimes by single persons, the rest answering in a Chorus, all the Day long, without the intermission of one quarter of an Hour. The Lascars or Sea-Men upon the Water, all the while they handle the Oar, divert themselves by turns with this tuneful Melody. This piece of Religion they are so solemnly and constantly inur'd to, that if they design'd the undertaking any work in secresie and un-observ'd, the custom they have acquir'd in singing would be apt by some sudden Eruption to betray their Privacy, and discover the silence and obscurity they desir'd. I fancy the warmth of the Air, which is apt to stupifie the Spirits, and render them unweildy and dull, was as likely a Reason for introducing this melodious Diversion, which is apt to keep them active and awake at their Work, as it was to exercise the Devotion of their Thoughts. The Introduction of this Custom was probably design'd by him, who writ the second Volume of the five principal ones that are extant in *China*; which is a Collection of Odes, and several other little things of that nature.[1] For Musick being greatly esteem'd and much used in *China*, and whatever is publish'd in this Volume, having respect only to the Purity of Manners, and practice of Virtue, those that wrote it compos'd it, in Verse, to the end that every one being inabled to sing the things therein contain'd, they might be in every ones Mouth. And from thence it might spread it self, for this very reason, as far as *India*.

*A Conjecture at the reason of this Singing.*

*Its rise, used in* China.

*Aureng-Zebe*, upon an implacable destestation to the Idolatry of the *Bannians* and other Gentiles, has forbid in a great measure their Pagodes, and commanded both a defacing of them, and suppressing the Solemnities of their publick Meetings, which thereupon is not so common as formerly, and that which is conniv'd at, is generally in some distant Priviledg'd Parts.[2]

Aureng-Zebe's *restraining Pagan-worship.*

They repeat their Devotions, especially the *Moors*, in the

*The* Indians.

[1] The reference is apparently to the famous Chinese classic, the *She King*, or Book of Odes.

[2] For Aurangzeb's religious bigotry, see V. A. Smith, *Oxford History of India*, p. 437 ff.

*very publick in their Devotions.* Corners of the Streets, and upon the House tops, in the High Ways, and where there is commonly a publick Concourse of People; as if they were ambitious of opportunities of demonstrating their Zeal to the God they worship, whom they always approach with Postures most submissive, and suitable to the respect of that awful Majesty they implore. *They show great Reverence at Prayer,* After they have bended the Knee, they in the most profound Prostration kiss the Ground frequently with their Fore-heads, express their fervency in Devotion with the most ardent pathetick Aspirations, in the Mornings especially, and with the setting Sun.

*Their constant Ablutions.* They are constant in their washings, either in the River *Tappy*, which runs by the Walls of *Suratt*, or in their own Houses before they stir abroad; at which time they cannot endure the least touch from any Stranger's Hand upon their naked Bodies, 'till they have finisht their Lustrations. And *Their cleanliness.* all their Infants, even in their tender Years, are washt all over both Morning and Evening. When they are called upon by the Necessities of Nature, they always carry in their Hands a small Jarr of Water, which they use to wash themselves clean with; and this Office is never perform'd but *The* Banians *Superstition in Drinking.* only with the Left-Hand. They never drink out of the same Cup with a Christian, or any Person of a different Sect; nor defile their Lips with the same Water that has been touch'd by any Stranger; whereby all their Water-Pots are reserv'd entirely for their own Use, nor are ours ever desir'd by them. Therefore they carry about with them Kousers[1] or Jarrs of Water when they go abroad, to quench their Thirst, and pour it into their Mouths at a certain distance, according to the *Thracian* manner of taking full draughts without winking, without either shutting the Mouth, or fetching Breath. See *Horace*, Book *the first, Ode* 36.

——— ——— *multi Damalis meri*
*Bassum Threicia vincat amystide.*

*Kousers.* The Kousers are made of a sort of Earth, which preserves

[1] Pers. *kuza*, an earthen water-pot.

the Water cool and palatable, and so porous, that once only in a minute or thereabouts, a single drop distils thro' the body of it, which falls into a Bason underneath, and acquires a little pleasing Coolness, as well as Rarefaction, by the Distillation.

*Their Entertainments.*

When any *European* is invited by a *Bannian* to a Collation, the Repast is little else but variety of Sweet-meats laid upon the green Leaves of Trees, which after the Entertainment are thrown away. Sometimes a Dish or two of rich spic'd Palau may come in to make up a complete Banquet. Sherbet, that is Wine, Water, and Lemon; tis the best Drink they indulge themselves, or allow others commonly to partake of. For Wine they abominate as well as Flesh, and hate it as much as *Manes*, the Author of the *Manichees*, who pronounced it to be the Blood of Devils.[1]

*Their tenderness to living Creatures.*

*India*, of all the Regions of the Earth, is the only publick Theatre of Justice and Tenderness to Brutes, and all living Creatures; for not confining Murther to the killing of a Man, they Religiously abstain from taking away the Life of the meanest Animal, Mite, or Flea; any of which if they chance wilfully to destroy, nothing less than a very considerable Expiation must Atone for the Offence. This Precept was comprehended in that Short System of Injunctions laid down by *Draco* and *Triptolemus*, the most ancient Law-givers among the *Athenians*, to *Honour their Parents, and neither to kill Man nor Beast*. And 'tis observ'd, that the Benefits which the *Barbarians* fancied they received from Beasts, made them less Cruel and severe towards them, and sometimes Consecrate them; which *Plutarch* thus excuses in the *Egyptians*, saying, *That it was not the Cat, the Ox, or the Dog which they adored; but that in these Beasts, they ador'd some resemblance of the Divine Perfections; in this, the Vigilance, in that the Patience and Utility, and the Vivacity in the other.* But however a Civil Regard, tho' no Veneration, is enjoyn'd as a

[1] Manes, the founder of the Manichean heresy, a curious farrago of Zoroastrian, Christian, and Buddhist elements, was born at Ecbatana about A.D. 215.

common Duty of Humanity, which forbids an Arbitrary Violence, a Cruel or Wanton Malice towards them. Therefore the *Romans*, pleas'd with the Vigilance of the Geese, by publick Voice took care of their Nourishment. And beyond this, the *Athenians* Decreed a liberty of Summering it up and down, and taking their Choice and Range in any Pasture, Hill, or Valley, to the Mules that were Employed in Building the Temple, called *Hecatompedon*. [The Parthenon.]

*The unreasonableness in their Opinion of killing young Creatures.* But that which most of all amuses and disturbs the *Bannians*, is our destruction of living Creatures in their growing Years; for in this they condemn us of Folly, as well as Cruelty, in preventing that greater advantage which we might promise our selves by their Increase in Bulk and Age; and denominates it, in their Opinion, a disadvantagious, as well as barbarous Action in those that kill them. And therefore they mightily decry our Inhumanity, and inveigh severely against our Imprudence in slaughtering Kids, Lambs, Chickens, &c. *A Calf their Darling Animal.* But above all, the Calf is the Darling Animal among them," as the Goat is the Idol ador'd by the *Bonzes* of *Tunquin*, whose Life they seldom fail to Ransom, and that sometimes at an immoderate rate, when they find it is in danger. Therefore the Gentiles near *Goa* used to divide the meat, when it was ready, into three parts; the first was given to the Poor, the second to the Cow, and the third to the Family. The Young Factors at *Suratt* divert themselves with this fondness of the *Bannians* to the dumb Creatures, and make an advantage of their tenderness and respects to them; for the *English* Caterer is cautious in buying a Calf for Slaughter, lest some *Bannian*, Friend to the Factory, should beg the Life of it, or some way molest or prevent him in taking it away; tho' at other times he makes himself a gainer by its Redemption. *The young Factors at* Suratt *in their sports imposing upon the* Bannians. Sometimes the Young Men enter with a Gun or small Fowling-piece into the Fields and Inclosures adjoining to the Habitations of the *Bannians*, and there make a show of shooting Sparrows, Turtle-Doves, or other small Birds among the Trees, which when the *Bannian* observes (as it is design'd he should) he runs in haste, as it were for Life, to bribe the Fowler, not only with courteous Expressions and fair Speeches, but with ready Money, not to persist in his Diversion; and drops in his Hand a Roupie or two to be gone, and not defile the Ground with the effusion of any Blood upon it; for all kind of Fowl are as dear to them, as ever the Dove was to *Semiramis*, or the Swan was unto *Philip*; and they entertain all their fellow Animals with a singular Esteem and kind Respect; and are at considerable Annual Expences for preserving their Lives from Inhumanity and Death.[1]

*A Hospital for old Cows, Horses, &c.*

For within a Mile distance from *Suratt* is a large Hospital, supported by the *Bannians* in its maintenance of Cows, Horses, Goats, Dogs, and other Animals diseas'd, or lame, infirm or decay'd by Age; for when an Ox, by many Years Toil grows feeble, and unfit for any farther Service; lest this should tempt a merciless Owner to take away his Life, because he finds him an unprofitable Burthen, and his Flesh might be serviceable to him when he was dead; therefore the *Bannian* reprieves his Destiny, either by begging him from the Owner, or by buying of him at a certain Rate, and then places him in the Hospital, where he is rescued from any other Death, but what is due to Nature, and is there attended and fed, 'till he spins out the appointed customary term of Life. This Charity which they extend to Beasts, is accounted by them an act of great Reputation and Virtue; nor can they be reconcil'd to that inhuman Cruelty, which destroys those Creatures which are the Nurses of our Lives, and by whose labour we live at Ease.

*A Hospital for Buggs, Fleas, &c.*

Near this Hospital is another built for the preservation of Buggs, Fleas, and other Vermin, which suck the Blood of Men; and therefore to maintain them with that choice Diet

[1] The killing of animals, especially cows, has been a perennial source of trouble in India. In Surat, the Hindus paid a fixed sum to the Mahommedans in return for sparing the cows. In 1608 a riot was caused at Surat by a drunken sailor, one Tom Tucker, who killed a calf. Similar occurrences at Kārwār and Honāwar led to outbreaks, in one of which the whole factory was murdered. Anderson, *English in Western India*, pp. 107-8.

to which they are used, and to feed them with their proper Fare, a poor Man is hired now and then to rest all Night upon the Cot, or Bed, where the Vermin are put, and fasten'd upon it, lest the stinging of them might force him to take his flight before the Morning, and so they nourish themselves by sucking his Blood, and feeding on his Carcass.[1]

*A Feast for Flies.*

Once a Year the charitable *Bannian* prepares a set Banquet for all the Flies that are in his House, and sets down before them, upon the Floor or Table, large shallow Dishes of sweet Milk and Sugar mixt together, the most delicious Fare of that liquorish little Creature.

*Their Charity to the Pismires.*

At other times he extends his Liberality to the Pismires, and walks with a Bag of Rice under his Arm, two or three Miles forward into the Country, and stops, as he proceeds, at each Ant-Hill that he meets with, to leave behind him his Benevolence, a handful or two of Rice straw'd upon the Ground, which is the beloved Dainty on which the hungry Pismires feed, and their best reserve and store in time of need.

*No tasting of Flesh.*

Therefore they never taste the flesh of any thing that has breath'd the common Air, nor pollute themsleves with feeding on any thing endued with Life; and are struck with astonishment at the voratious Appetites of the Christians, who heap whole Bisks[2] of Fish upon their Tables, and sacrifice whole Hecatombs of Animals to their Gluttony. They cannot be tempted, either by the delicacy of the Food, or for prevention of either Sickness or Death, to so enormous an Offence as the tasting of Flesh. Vegetable products, and the Milk of Cattle, Rice, and other sorts of Grane, which Nature affords in plenty, and they with Innocence can enjoy, is the lawful Nourishment they delight in; nor will they be induced, by the meer indulgence of their Appetites, to make their Tables Altars of Luxury and Excesses, no more than the original Inhabitants of the World, whom Antiquity supposes

[1] These animal hospitals or *pinjrapols* date back to the days of Asoka.

[2] A rich soup or potage, made by boiling down birds, &c.

not to have been Carnivorous, nor to have tasted Flesh in those first Ages, but only to have fed upon Fruits and Herbs.

The Prohibition of Flesh being eaten with the Blood, was an ancient Sanction of the *East*, and is very universal to this day. It was forbidden by Moses, because he plac'd the Life in it; nor is it dispens'd with by the *Mahometans*. Some ancient Philosophers, as *Empedocles*, plac'd the seat of the Soul in the Blood, and *Democritus* assign'd it the whole Body: And tho' the *Bannians* are under restraint from the Blood of either Animal, or that of the Grape, yet will they freely taste the Grapes themselves, and entertain themselves Luxuriously with their Juice, while it is innocent and harmless. We have Grapes brought to *Suratt*, from the middle of *February* 'till towards the end of *March*; some from *Amadavad*, some from a Village called *Naapoure*,[1] four days Journey distant from *Suratt*. They feed likewise upon Pine-Apples, Custard-Apples,[2] so called, because they resemble a Custard in Colour and Taste, and many other sorts of Fruit unknown to *Europe*. But the Mangoes are of principal esteem, and the most common Fruit of *India*: They have a Stone in the middle, by which and their outward shape, they come nearest to the form of our long Plums of any Fruit, only they are generally much larger; they attribute many medicinal qualities to this sort of Fruit, and ascribe to it those Virtues which free them from all Diseases incident to that Season of the Year, and sometimes those Chronical Distempers they labour under. They are of exquisite Taste when they come to Maturity, and are Eaten then in vast quantities by the *Indians* and *Europeans*, as well for the Security of their Health as for pleasure and delight. When they are Green, they are Pickl'd there and sent abroad, and make that Mango Achar,[3] which we taste in *England*.

*The Season of Grapes.*

*Mangoes much eaten.*

[1] Navapur.

[2] *Anona squamosa*, probably introduced by the Portuguese from the New World. See Hobson-Jobson, p. 284.

[3] A Portuguese word, meaning a pickle, relish, or chutney.

*Cucumbers much eaten.* The cold quality of the Cucumber is here so prepar'd and digested by the Sun's Heat, that the *Bannians*, without endangering their Health, will feed upon them as plentifully as we do upon Apples. And the Water-Melons are very large, delicious, and easily purchas'd, and very refreshing cooling Fruit in the warmer Season. *The delicacy of the Musk-Melons.* But the Musk-Melons from *Amadavad*, highly deserve that fragrant Name, being inriched both with a flavour and a taste superiour to any of that kind in the World.

*Tea and Coffee drunk by them.* The *Bannians* are not restrain'd from the liberal Draughts of Tea and Coffee, to revive their wasted Spirits, any part of the Day; but in those they may Revel uncensur'd, as long as they please; and have there more inviting Temptations to drink them plentifully, than with us. *Great Art in making Coffee.* For the Coffee, when it is truly boiled and prepared, carries a kind of yellow Oil upon the head of it, by which it acquires a soft, pleasant Relish, and requires so much Art in bringing it to this Perfection, that it ingages some who affect this sort of Liquor in the expence of a skilful Peon, on purpose to look after it in the Preparation. This Berry is of very common growth in *Arabia*, especially about *Mocha*, and from thence is transported to the remotest Regions of the *East* or *West*. Coffee is said to be good for Cleansing the Blood, for helping Digestion, and quickening the Spirits.[1]

Tea[2] likewise is a common Drink with all the Inhabitants of *India*, as well *Europeans* as Natives; and by the *Dutch* is used as such a standing Entertainment, that the Tea-pot's seldom off the Fire, or unimploy'd. *Tea healthful in* India. This hot Liquor it may be suppos'd might not seem so proper and agreeable to so hot an Air, and yet we find is very convenient for our Health, and agreeable to the Habits of our Bodies. And even all the Arak Punch which is drunk there, is seldom toucht, 'till by a

[1] For Coffee cf. p. 271.

[2] Ovington took a great interest in tea, and did much after his return to England to popularize its use by means of his *Essay on Tea*, which he published in 1699. This essay achieved considerable notoriety at the time, and was recently reprinted.

heated Iron, or Wedge of Gold, it is made luke warm. This both supplies the Vapours which are continually exhal'd from the Body, and helps the prevention of Fevers by keeping the Pores open.

Tea, with some hot Spice intermixt and boiled in the Water, has the Repute of prevailing against the Headach, Gravel, and Griping in the Guts, and 'tis generally drunk in *India*, either with Sugar-Candy, or, by the more curious, with small Conserv'd Lemons. And a Dram of double distill'd Arak, is prescrib'd likewise as an Excellent Remedy against the Gripes, and such inward Twistings of the Bowels. The frequent use of this Innocent Tea, and the perpetual perspiration caus'd by the Heat, which is augmented by this Liquor, are the reason why the Gout and Stone, Agues, Rheumatisms and Catarhs are rarely heard of in these parts. The Heat indeed abates the vigour of our Spirits, and thereby induces a languid Faintness, which is the general, but withal a very tolerable Infirmity, in respect of those acute Distempers. The *Chinese*, among whom the Tea grows, take abundance of this Drink before their Meals, and are generally very plump and in very good likeing.

Our *English* President enquir'd much for the Flower of Tea, among those who had been Conversant in *China*, but could never obtain a sight of any; and it seems very doubtful whether that Shrub bears any Flowers at all upon it.[1] For a *Chinese Mandarine*, who arriv'd at *Suratt* in the quality of an Envoy from *Limpo*,[2] brought with him several kinds of Tea, but no Flower; some of it was so valuable in *China*, that a single Catte[3] of it was reputed a noble Present for the chief Ministers, and it was very rarely to be found, however he brought with him a Taste of it for our President, among several other kinds, wherein he gave him a Morning Entertainment. And a Learned Physician, who for some Years

[1] Wrong: the bush has a small white flower.

[2] Ling pao, in the Shan-si province.

[3] Catte or Catty, a Chinese weight of $1\frac{1}{2}$ lb. It survives in 'tea-caddy'.

had lived in *China*, spoke nothing of this Flower of Tea, only gave this Account of three other sorts that grew there, and were most frequently drunk among them, *viz*. Bing, Singlo, and Bohe. Bohe is a small Leaf and very young, and by its moisture, upon the score of its under-growth, requires more than an ordinary frixure, which makes it acquire that blackness visible in it, and which discolours the Water to a kind of Redness. The second is Singlo, which is a larger Leaf, because more grown. The third, which is Bing, is the largest of all; and is in *China* of a proportionable larger rate than the other two. Singlo obtains most among the *Europeans*; but Bohe among the *Chinese* has so much the esteem and precedence above the other two, that in their Sickness they totally forbid them, but in their most dangerous Distempers instantly make use of this; and Experience convinces them of the Choice and Utility of that Leaf in their Extremities. They all proceed, he told me, from a Shrub about the height of our Gooseberry or Curran Bushes. The Leaf is first green, but is made crisp and dry by frying twice, or oftener, in a Pan; and as often as it is taken off the Fire it is roll'd with the Hand upon a Table, till it curls. This Preparation is cautiously conceal'd from all Strangers, and was accidentally known to him by the opportunity he once had of peeping through the Crevice of a Door when it was a preparing. He found it growing in the Latitude of 51, as well as in a warmer Air; which gives a probable Conjecture for its thriving in our Kingdom; for *London* lies near the same Parallel.[1]

*Three sorts of Tea.*

*Bohe the best Tea.*

*How Tea grows.*

*The way it is prepar'd*

As Musk and Amber grease are said to damage Pearl, so is Tea prejudic'd by the approach of unsavory Smells, and par-

[1] Ovington's account of tea is generally correct, *pace* Hamilton. See the long notice, with quotations, in Hobson-Jobson, and Anderson, p. 36. Tea appeared in London about 1658, and a tax of 8*d*. per gallon was imposed upon it in 1660. On 25 Sept. of that year, Mr. Pepys sent out for a cup of tea 'a China drink, of which I never had drunk before'. It was first imported by the Company in 1664, when we find 'for 22¼ lbs. of *thea*, at 50*s*. per lb., £56 17*s*. 6*d*.'

ticularly of *Assa Fœtida*,[1] and is so delicate and tender, that it is injur'd by the very Breath of only the common ambient Air. For preventing which it is inclos'd in Pots of Totaneg,[2] or in strong large Tubs of Wood, and in them is safely sent abroad.

The *Bannian* seldom drinks of the common Water of the Wells or Rivers, only what falls from Heaven in the time of the *Mussouns*, which is preserv'd in large Tanques and Cisterns made on purpose to receive it, and keep it ready for their use the following Year. For in this, as well as his Diet, he is very squeamish; and therefore he confines his Draught to those Heavenly Showers, which he esteems a more pure and Etherial Liquor for descending from above. *Rain Water commonly drank by the* Bannians.

*Dye*[3] is a particular innocent kind of Diet, fed upon by the *Indians* for the most part about Noon. It is sweet Milk turn'd thick, mix'd with boil'd Rice and Sugar, and is very effectual against the Rage of Fevers and of Fluxes, the prevailing Distempers of *India*. Early in the Morning, or late at Night, they seldom touch it, because they esteem it too cool for their Stomachs and Nocturnal Delights. Dye *a sort of Food.*

*Kitcheree* is another Dish very common among them, made of *Dol*,[4] that is, a small round Pea and Rice boiled together, and is very strengthening, tho' not very savoury. Of this the *European* Sailers feed in those parts once or twice a Week, and are forc'd at those times to a Pagan Abstinence from Flesh, which creates in them a perfect Dislike and utter Detestation to those *Bannian* Days, as they commonly call them. Kitcheree *an* Indian *Dish.*

Wood is the only combustible matter in *Suratt*, which is commonly made use of in the Kitchin, either by *Indian* or *European*, for boiling and roasting their Victuals. Some of the more poor Natives make Fires of dried Cow-Dung. There *No Coals in* India.

[1] The repulsively smelling condiment, beloved by Hindus, known in India as *Hing*, Latin *silphium* or *laserpitium*.

[2] White metal or pewter.

[3] *dahi*, curd.

[4] *khichri*, a mess of rice, butter, and *dāl*, pulse or split pease.

is not any Necessity of Fuel in private Apartments, the great Globe of Light is the universal Fire all over *India*, which cherishes and keeps them warm without any Expence of Chimneys or of Hearths in their Lodging-Rooms. The Fire-Wood is bought in the Bazar by Weight, for so much the Seer, and is brought home by Servants. And every Roupie which the Servant lays out in buying either this or any other Goods, he peremptorily demands back for his own use a Couple of Pice from the Seller.

*Wood here bought by Weight.*

Bannians *curious in what they eat.*

The *Bannian* is very curious in dressing his Meat, and preparing his Victuals; and therefore least some unclean Hand should have touch'd what is sold already cookt in the Shops or the Bazar, he seldom buys any from thence, but eats what is dress'd only by his own Domesticks. In their solemn Entertainments they are kind and communicative, to the meanest Attendant of any Person of Consequence or Rank whom they invite to their Houses; and like the Great Men at *Tunquin*, will provide almost for the very Dogs.

*A Caravansaray.*

In the middle of the City is built a noble spacious Caravansaray, or Inn, for the Convenience of Merchants that are Strangers, and resort hither for Traffick, where they may decently repose at Night. For here are no Publick Houses for the Entertainment of Guests or Travellers, lest the Jealousie of the Husbands should be rais'd concerning their Wives and Daughters, by the frequency of such Temptations. And upon this Account, all Men whose Affairs call them into the Country, either take care of providing their own Victuals, or commit that Charge to their Peons and Attendants, to make it ready for them at their Resting-places by Day, or in the Fields where they sleep at Night.

*No Houses of Entertainment.*

As the heat of the Sun, when it is in the Meredian, is very apt to pall the Appetite, and dissipate that warmth and Heat of the Stomach, which is proper for Digestion; so the *Bannians* and *Moors*, to prevent that inconvenience, change their Repasts to other Seasons of the Day, and take their Collations about 8 or 9 in the Morning, and at 4 or 5 in the Afternoon. And often at Midnight, after their nocturnal

*Their times of Eating, are the Morning and the Evening.*

Embraces, they recover their Spirits by some nourishing Food, to excite them again to fresh Amours.

The Heat of the Day is spent in Rest and Sleeping, to refresh their exhausted Strength, sometimes upon Cotts, and sometimes upon *Bechanahs*,[1] which are thick Quilts, spread the breadth of a Room, and the Length of a Man, with Bolsters at the Head, where Eight or nine may sleep together. They seldom take their Repose without a Wench in their Arms, that is a small Pillaber [2] upon their Stomack to defend it from the ambient Vapours that might be apt to annoy it; and seldom use any other Covering but their Shirts and Drawers, except it be a Sheet or slight Callico spread over them.

*The Heat of the Day spent in Rest.*

*Bechanahs.*

The Garments which the *Indians* wear, are generally made of white Callico, fashion'd into Caba's,[3] that is, outward Coats, somewhat like our Frocks, turning over their Breasts as far as the Shoulders, and from thence tied with strings down to the middle; with a Puggaric,[4] or Turbant upon their Heads. It was very surprizing at first, to view so many People passing up and down, most of one coloured Cloaths, and those white. For a distinction between the *Moors* and *Bannians*, the *Moors* tie their Caba's always on the Right side, and the *Bannians* on the left; and if any *European* thinks fit to dress himself, and take upon him the *Indian* Garb, he therein compliments the *Moors*, and pays his Respect to their manner of wearing and putting it on. The length of their Breeches, which descend to their Heels, serve them instead of Stockins; which is the reason that their Language has no word for our *Stockins*, so that they thrust their Feet always bare into their Shoes, which are very neatly Imbroider'd with Gold; or Silver, or Silk Flowers.

*White Callico the common* Indian *Garment.*

*The difference of Garments between the* Moors *and* Bannians.

*No Stockins in* India.

No Man in *India*, no not the *Mogul*'s Son, is permitted the

*Umbrellas permitted*

[1] Hind. *bichhāna*, bedding.

[2] Pillow-case, Chaucer's pilwe-beer, *Prol.* 694.

[3] Cabayá or Caba, Port. from Ar. *kabā*, vesture, a long coat or tunic of muslin.

[4] *pagrī*, a turban.

*to be used by none but the* Mogul. Priviledge of wearing a Kittisal[1] or Umbrella, let the Sun's Beams be never so scortching, but a Peon goes before the great Men, carrying a small Skreen made of Ostrich Feathers, to shade his Eyes. The use of the Umbrella is sacred to the Prince, appropriated only to his use.

*The Stale of a Cow, drunk by the* Bannians. The *Bannians* observe several Fasts; but one more solemn in the Year is much remarkt, when they drink nothing in the Morning but the fresh Stale of the Worshipful Cow, which they fancy is abstersive, and endow'd with a kind of lustral quality, apt to purifie the Defilements of a *Bannian*; as one of themselves was pleas'd to tell me.[2]

*Their Religious observations convenient upon a natural account.* Their constant Ablutions and daily Washings, their Abstinence from Animals and from Wine, had doubtless a prospect more than what was merely Religious in it; they were not imprudently design'd upon a Civil Account, to keep their Organs clear, their Spirits lively, and their Constitutions free from those Diseases, which a grosser Diet is apt to create in these warm Climates, and to preserve their Bodies Neat and Clean by frequent Bathings and Lustrations. For there is not one of these Customs which are fasten'd upon them by the Rules of their Religion, but what comport very well, and highly contribute to the Health and Pleasure of their Lives. And for this end they are much addicted to sweet Smells and fragrant Exhalations, and generally each Night procure a Necklace of Jessemy Flowers to sleep with, for at that time they more sensibly emit their Fragrant Vapours. The scent of Flowers is much abated on the day time, being dissipated by the great Heat; which is the reason why the Streets of *Suratt*, tho in many places over-spread with the Excrements of Men and Beasts, yet never molest those that pass thro' them, by an unsavoury Smell, because the Sun's attenuation of the Vapours, diminishes their strength from annoying the Sense.

*Ill Smells not so offensive in* India.

[1] Port. *quita-sol.* The *chhatri* (umbrella) is an emblem of royalty.

[2] Cow's urine, *go-mutra*, is used by orthodox Hindus for various purificatory ceremonies. Perhaps Ovington here refers to its employment at the time of changing the Sacred Thread (*srāvani*). It is similarly employed by the Parsees.

Under their abstemious mortifying Diet, the *Bannians* maintain as good a Habit of Body, are as comly and proportionable as other People, and live to reckon as many Years as those that pity their spare Food. But in their Thoughts they are often more quick and nimble, by that course of living they chuse to delight in, which renders their Spirits more pure and subtle, and thereby greatly facilitates their Comprehension of things. Besides, this Religious abstinence very much disingages their Affections to the World, disintangles their fears of Death, and Passions for these momentary things; it sets their Spirits upon the Wing, ready without reluctancy to quit this Life, in expectation of a better; and makes many of them pass as chearfully into the invisible World, as they would take a Journey from their own Kingdom to another Country.

*The* Bannians *live to a good* Age. *They are quick of Thought.*

*They die easily.*

Their Wealth consists only in Cash and Jewels, the distinction of personal and real Estate is not heard in *India*, and that they preserve as close and private as they can, lest the *Mogul*'s Exchequer shou'd be made their Treasury. This curbs them in their Expences, and awes them to great secresie in their Commerce, especially in their receiving, or Payments of Money, for which they either make use of the darkness of the Night, or of the obscurity of the Morning, in conveying it to the place of Payment. For should the *Mogul's* Officers see the Chests and Bags of Gold and Silver carried as publickly here, as they are in the Streets of *London*, they would be apt to change their Owner, and be deliver'd to him who calls himself the Original Proprietor. And yet the conditions of these *Indians* is not so vile and lamentable by much, as that of the Commonalty at *Tunquin*, where the vulgar Mechanicks are Slaves for one part of the Year, and work three Months for the King, and two for the *Mandarins*, and are only allowed the rest of the Year for themselves, for supporting of their Wives and Families. This is called there *Viecquam*, that is the condition of a Slave.

*Cash and Jewels are their only Estate.*

*Their Wealth kept Secret.*

*Viecquam.*

But I was told of a Noble *Bannian* at *Amadavad*, who, by bribeing the *Nabob* into a connivance, did on publick

*A* Bannian *poison'd for living splendidly.*

Festivals, and times of Jubilee make his Entertainments in Dishes and Plates of solid Gold. But poor Man, his splendid living did not hold out long, before it rais'd the Envy of a neighbouring *Moor*, who could not endure this repeated Magnificence in a Gentile, and therefore dogging the Merchant as he rode one day out of the City, he followed him at a distance, and shot him dead with a poison'd Arrow. Sumptuousness and State suit not very well with the Life and Condition of a *Bannian*; they must not both flourish long together. This keeps our Brokers at *Suratt*, who are *Bannians*, from all costly disbursements, tho' they are reckon'd by some to be worth 15, by others 30 Lacks of Roupies, and causes a Contraction of their Expences, and a retrenchment of their Tables to three or four Thousand Roupies a Year, without any show of a luxurious Garniture, either on their Dishes, or in their Houses.

*The* Bannian *Women very richly attir'd.*

Their main Cost is expended upon their Women, who ambitiously affect a Gayety in their Dress and Cloathing. Jewels and Ornaments are the very joy of their Hearts, (as they usually call them) with which they are deckt from the Crown of the Head to the very feet. Their Toes are adorn'd with Rings, and their Legs with Shackles of Gold, or Silver, or some other Metal, which are sometimes above two Inches in Diameter, wreath'd and hollow. The Women that carry the Water about the Streets, will not walk abroad without these Ornaments upon them. Some tie up the Hair of their Heads, and put it under a hollow large piece of Silver, rais'd somewhat like a Bell, gilt, and neatly embellisht on the outside, and fasten'd to the Crown of their Heads. Some wear Ear-rings all round their Ears, which for Ornament's sake will dangle sometimes almost down to their Shoulders, and have Bracelets about their Necks and Arms, and Rings about their Wrists, and on every Finger. Some adorn themselves with Breast Jewels, form'd in Fashion of a Heart, compos'd of variety of Diamonds, Rubies, Saphirs, and other Stones of Esteem; and on their Fore-Heads wear a Gold Bodkin, broad at the end, beset with glittering Diamonds, or some other precious Stones. And as they are much taken with this gawdy Attire, and delight in these splendid Ornaments themselves, so they think them a kindness to the very Brutes; and shew their Affection to a Darling Cow, or Favourite Goat, by fastening large Rings of some Metal or other about their Legs. Nor will they spare their Ornamental Favours to the Fruit-Trees in their Gardens, but shew them their profuse Respect in adorning them with a Painting of divers Colours. *Beasts and Trees adorn'd by the* Bannians.

The meanest Female in *Suratt* is not wholly destitute of Ornaments upon her Body, though she be able to spend no more than two or three Piee a day. For Herbs (which are the common Food of the Poor) are here in plenty, and bought at very low Rates, which encourages the daily Labourers to work for very low Wages. And the moderate Barber (which is not the meanest Profession) shaves the Beard, and cuts the Hair, picks the Ears, and pairs the Nails, all for one Piee or two. *All things cheap at* Suratt.

The Love of Women, which is rooted in Mens Hearts by Nature, and which discovers it self in People of all Ages, Nations, Qualities, and Constitutions, is cherish'd betimes by the *Bannian*, who courts and sometimes marries his Mistress at Six or Seven Years of Age, and cohabits at Eleven or Twelve, or sometimes sooner.[1] And some of the Gentile Sects, before they feel any great Warmth of this amorous Passion, are by their Parents join'd together in their very Infancy, at three or four Years of Age. From which time they endeavour mutually to kindle this tender Passion, till the growing Years blow it up into a lively Flame. And by a thousand little Tricks and Arts of Love they endeavour to stamp their Affections upon their Infant Souls, which like melted Wax are pliant and easie to receive the Impression, and so they are insensibly captivated by each others Snares. The young Lover wins upon his Mistresses Passions by *Marriages at 6 or 7 years of Age.*

[1] Orthodox Hinduism demands that girls should always be married before the attainment of puberty. For Hindu domestic ceremonies and beliefs in Gujarat, as described by Ovington, compare *Bomb. Gaz.* ix, part i, *passim*, and Forbes, *Rās Mālā*, Book iv. Ovington is usually astonishingly accurate.

frequent Visits, large Presents, and munificent Gifts, whilst her soft Looks and Innocent Air form his Mind into kind and amorous Inclinations towards her. And thus being happily prepossessed with a mutual good liking, even as it were from the Womb, as if they had been born Lovers, they are taken off from all Objects, and freed from the Disappointments of fickle Mistresses, and from being wearied with whining Addresses to coy Damsels. Which, besides others, may be some Reason why the *Indian* Wives committed themselves with so much chearfulness into the Funeral Flames with their Dead Husbands; because their Sympathetick Minds, linked together from their Infancy, were then fed with such early Tastes of Love, as became the Seminary of those strong and forcible Inclinations in their riper Years, and made the Pains of Death become preferable to a Life abandon'd [by] the Society of those they so entirely lov'd. For what could fix their Affections more thán the cherishing of them in their tender Years, and digesting them with their Mother's Milk? Or form their Embrio Passions into more Strength and Duration, than confining them early to such an Object, as might receive their entire good liking, before ever they were distracted by various volatile Affections? [1]

*A Reason why the* Indian *Women freely burn with their Husbands.*

But the Reason alledg'd by them for these Infant Marriages, is, because they esteem it a matter of more Decency to approach their Brides in their purer state, before they come to riper Years. And for hastening the young Mistress's Maturity for the Conjugal Embraces, great Care is taken of a proper Diet, and that she feed plentifully upon Milk, boil'd two or three Quarts into one, which they find by Experience is very nourishing, and ripens them for being fit to come together at Eleven or Twelve. The Husband drinks largely of melted Butter, which he finds very apt to invigorate his Spirits, and makes use of it as Oil to his Flame.[2]

*Milk very nourishing.*

*Melted Butter drunk by the* Bannians.

[1] This is *Sati*, literally the True Wife. The custom of widow-burning was abolished by Lord Bentinck in 1829. See Hobson-Jobson, *s.v. Suttee.*

[2] *ghī*, clarified butter, plays a large part in Hindu domestic life and ceremonial.

*No Women allow'd second Marriages.*

Second Marriages, which are indulg'd to the Men, are solemnly prohibited the Women, because this engages their Fidelity so much the more to the first Lovers, in that they are debarr'd all Hopes and Prospect of all others. But with this Additional Severity upon the young Maids, whose Husbands die before they cohabit, that they are obliged to a disconsolate Virginity all the Days of their Lives; and must never contract with another Man, tho' they are unfortunately Widows at Six or Seven Years of Age.[1]

*Polygamy permitted to the Husbands.*

Polygamy likewise, besides second Marriages, is allowed the wanton Husbands, who notwithstanding are not often so very Amorous as to prosecute that Liberty, or rather Thraldom, to more Wives than one at once. The nature of the Climate inclines them much to this Amorous Passion, which stings them with impatient Desires, and makes them restless by Delays; and yet tho' Marriage upon this account is so very necessary and agreeable, they do not think that the variety of Women will compensate for the double Burthen and Inconvenience of them in a Family; nor do they imagin that it's worth their while to satisfie the fervour of their wandring Desires, that is attended with such a train of mischievous Consequences. A merry *Bannian* was wont often to complain of this Folly, of engaging with two Wives at once, and venturing too hastily upon a double Marriage, because the fondness of the two Wives provoked them to continual Feuds and Jealousies. For he could never enjoy the one without disturbance to the other, whose Passions were presently alarm'd upon any token of Kindness extraordinary. When he was wheedled into a liking of the one, the other would pout and ask him if he meant to forsake her? And if he was going that way, would hold him by the Coat, and pull him back to her. This urg'd to him, that she was the Wife of his Youth, that they had contracted a long and intimate acquaintance, and his first solemn Engagements were made to her: The other replies to him, that she now ought to partake

*The inconvenience of Poligamy.*

[1] There is no remarriage of widows among the higher Hindu castes.

more liberally of his Favours, and his Thoughts should incline more kindly towards her, since the other possess'd him so long before. Thus the distracted Husband was twitted on both sides, and at a stand many times which way to turn for his own tranquility and their satisfaction, and often in his *Indian* English confest, *English fashion, sab,*[1] *best fashion have, one Wife best for one Husband.* And 'tis seldom but among a multitude of Wives, there will now and then happen Debates and Contests. We read of a Custom among the Ancient *Britains* which seems peculiar to themselves, and not found in the Stories of any other Nations, either Civil or Barbarous, not of many Wives belonging to one Husband, which is the case of many Heathen Nations, but a Society of Wives among certain numbers, and by common consent. Every Man married a single Woman, who was always after and alone esteem'd his Wife: But it was usual for five or six, ten or twelve, or more, either Brothers or Friends, as they could agree, to have all their Wives in common. But neither did this method preserve an entire Amity and Affection among them, but sometimes Encounters and Disputes happen'd.

*An odd English custom concerning many Wives in common.*

*The* Nairos *Women great esteem of Matrimony.*

The *Nairos* Women hold Matrimony in such singular esteem, That they think it sacred, and so necessary in this Life, that if they chance to die Virgins, they are debarr'd from entring into Paradise. And are therefore extreme sollicitous of not neglecting the happy opportunity of the Marriage state, which is reckon'd by them a necessary introduction to so much Bliss.

*No private stoln Weddings.*

*The gay solemnities of Marriages at* Suratt.

Clandestine Marriages and stoln Brides are things unheard of at *Suratt.* For both the Bridegroom and the Bride, and their several Attendants, appear publickly in the Richest Garments, in the gayest Equipage and splendour, which they can either purchase for their Money, or procure by their Friendship. Flags, Flambeaus, Musick, State-Coaches, and Led Horses, are all too little for this Day's Solemnity. The Pretty Bride then puts on her costly Jewels, and is trimm'd

[1] *Sāheb*, (Hind.) Sir.

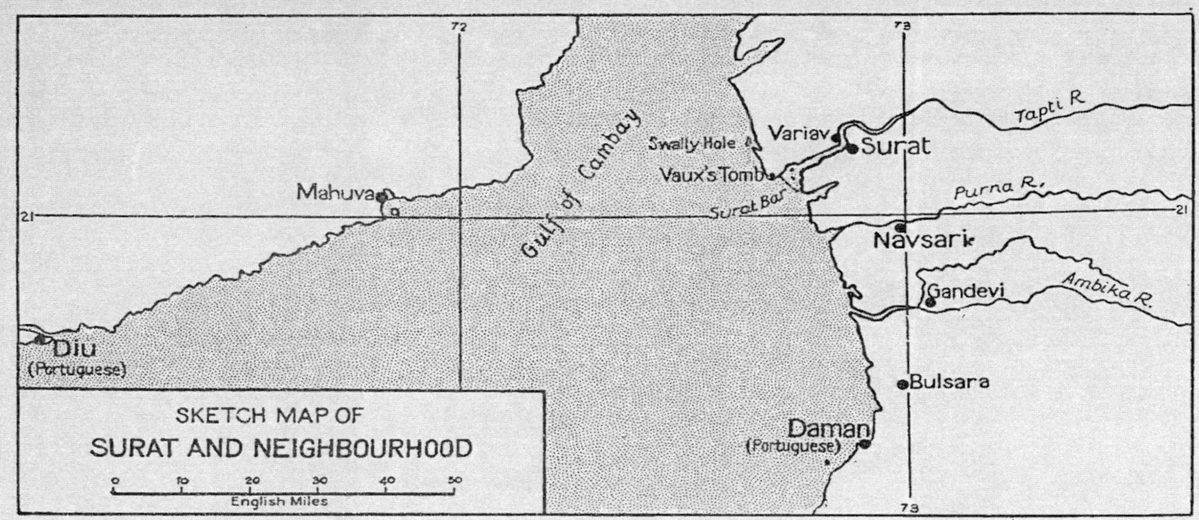
SKETCH MAP OF
SURAT AND NEIGHBOURHOOD
0 10 20 30 40 50
English Miles
72
73
21
Tapti R
Variav
Surat
Swally Hole
Vaux's Tomb
Gulf of Cambay
Surat Bar
Purna R.
Navsari
Gandevi
Ambika R.
Bulsara
Daman
(Portuguese)
Mahuva
Diu
(Portuguese)

with all the finest Silks; sits Queen of the Ceremony, carried in Triumph through the Streets of the City. The Bridegroom likewise is set off with all the advantage of rich Cloaths and Trappings; and there is nothing great and noble in *Suratt*, but is purchas'd for them, according to their Abilities, to give credit to the Nuptials, and adorn the Solemnity; which is perform'd after this manner. When the Joyful Bridegroom and the Bride, with their costly Equipage and Pompous Train, have marcht thro' the principal places of the City, in publick view of all Spectators, seated upon some delicate *Indian* Horse, or *Persian* or *Arabian* Steed, ambitiously courting the Eyes and observance of all as they pass along, to take notice of that honourable state they are now proceeding to: When with a blameless undisguis'd Assurance they have finish'd their stately Progress thro' all the noted places of the Town, they turn about to the Bride's Habitation, where they enter, and are seated opposite to one another in two Chairs, with a Table put between them. Then stretching forth their Hands to each other over the Table, they join them together, and the *Bramin*, standing by, covers each of their Heads with one large Hood or Pamarin,[1] which is spread over them about a quarter of an Hour, 'till he has finisht his Prayers for their Happiness, and made an end of his Benediction; and then loosing their Hands, and uncovering their Heads, the Ceremonious part of the Marriage is concluded. And now the Mirth and Festivity follow; now they begin to scatter about their Perfumes, to sprinkle their Guests with Rose Water, poured upon them out of Silver Cruets, and so refresh them with sweet smells. The Caba's and Puggaries,[2] *i.e.* all their exteriour Garments, are wet with Unguents, and Coloured yellow with the rich and fragrant Essence of Saffron,[3] which remains upon their Cloaths for a Week, to

*The particular Ceremony at Weddings.*

*The Guests at Weddings sprinkled with Rosewater and Perfumes.*

[1] Mar. *pāmari*, a silk scarf. At a Hindu wedding, a cloth is held between the bride and bridegroom until the *Joshi* or astrologer declares that the auspicious moment has arrived.

[2] *Vide supra*, p. 185, notes 3, 4.

[3] Saffron (*halad*), really turmeric (especially when made into the powder known as *kanku*), is used for a variety of purposes such

declare their presence at this joyful meeting. For the nature of Saffron being very Cordial, and apt to exhilarate the Mind, is sprinkled outwardly as a token of their inward Mirth and Gladness. And to complete this sumptuous jollity, the Guests are all invited to lie down to a large and costly Banquet.

*A Superstitious Observation of days for Marriages.*

In the Celebration of these Marriages, they are much addicted to the strict observance of particular days, and only upon those that are accounted lucky, will they undertake the Celebration, because their pitiable foolish Superstition has laid severe Restraint upon their Consciences, from Marrying upon any days of bad Omen.[1] Upon those which they account Lucky, will sometimes be solemniz'd more Weddings, than in two or three Months at other times, sometimes two or three hundred on a day. Such as are Wealthy, continue the sumptuous Festival Entertainments above the space of a Week, which with the large Expences at their Funeral Feasts, drains their Fortunes, and keeps them low; and if they are Poor, never suffers them to grow Wealthy. These Charges upon their Estates, the *Mogul* encourages on purpose, by this Artifice to break their Spirits and Fortunes, that he may keep them servile and less able to Rebel against him.

*Funeral expences, and costly Marriages design'd to keep the People poor.*

*The Wives in some measure servile.*

When once the Husband and the Wife come to cohabit, she is then under great distinctions of Respect, and in a manner oblig'd to a kind of servile Attendance upon his Person; however in Language and Deportment the Man appears very kind and obliging, and shews a tenderness to the Partner of his Bed.

*The great Civility which the* Siamese *Language shews to Women.*

But among all the Nations of the *East*, the *Siameses* excel in Civility of Expressions to the Female Sex. For their Language (as we are told) admits no distinction of Masculine and Feminine in their Genders, which is the cause, that

as dyeing clothes, and anointing the forehead on occasions of rejoicing, on account of its auspicious colour.

[1] Auspicious days and hours for weddings are fixed by the *grām joshi* or astrologer in accordance with the horoscope of bride and bridegroom. Marriages can usually only take place between the months of Magh and Jyestha (January—June), when Jupiter and Venus are in conjunction with the Sun.

whenever they would Express a Woman, they add young to the Masculine, to imply the Feminine; whereby their Language hinders a Woman from ever growing Old, by affixing always Youth to the Female; as when, for Example, they would name an Empress, they would say young Emperour.[1]

*The* Bramins *Marry.*

The *Bramins* Marry, as well as the other *Indians*; and treasure up sometimes abundance of Wealth, which is bequeathed to their Families, for maintenance of their Widows, and to portion their Children. One of the *Bramins*, who had been straitned in his Abilities from giving a competent Portion with his Daughter, which was then closely Courted, contrives this Stratagem to squeeze some hundreds of Roupies from the People for that purpose. He ascended a Tree, which stood without the Gates of his City, and then declar'd, that there he would fix his Habitation; there he would stay and starve, and never come down, 'till they contributed among them to make up the Sum. The affrighted Inhabitants, who are tender of the Life of any Animal, thought it not fit to dally with that of their Priest, but lest his obstinate Resolution of continuing there might endanger the welfare of him they so highly esteem'd, and involve them in the guilt of Sacred Blood, therefore with united Hearts they clubb'd together to make up a common Purse, which was deliver'd to the Damsel as a Dowry. The crafty Priest upon this descended from perching aloft in the Boughs of the Tree, and was kindly congratulated at his coming down for sparing his Life, which he had taken private Care of that it should not be in any Danger, by engaging an Accomplice to convey to him secretly what Nourishment might be necessary for his Subsistence.[2]

*A* Bramin'*s Craft to get a Portion for his Daughter.*

*A strict sort of* Bramins.

One sort of *Bramins* at *Suratt*, which are by much the

[1] This is not correct. In Siamese, the words *chi* and *ying* are added to indicate gender in the case of persons and *phoo* and *mia* in the case of things.

[2] This was evidently a form of the Gujarāti custom of 'sitting Dharna', i.e. sitting at the debtor's door and threatening suicide. See Hobson-Jobson, *s.v.* Dhurna, Trāga.

strictest Sect among them, do far exceed the rest in Abstractions from Sense, and abstemious living, and refrain from entring the Conjugal State, lest some Animals, as they tell us, might be crusht to Death by their mutual Embraces. And therefore to keep up the Succession of this Priesthood, if any Lay-Person of their Tribe has two or three Sons, one of them is chosen from among the rest to be consecrated to this Order. This sort of *Bramins* are sparing of their Speech, and will rarely speak, for fear of killing some invisible Creatures, which they affirm float in the Air, and which some of their Holy Men have seen, though others cannot. They also sweep the places where they rest with a Brush, lest they should crush some Animal by sitting upon it. And for this end a Cloath is always tied cross their Mouth, and fastned at each Ear, to prevent all invisible volatile Creatures approaching their Breath, lest it might prove fatal to them. And though Ablutions are so necessary in *India*, so universally practis'd, and so solemnly enjoin'd, yet cannot this sort of *Bramins* be brought over to this convenient Discipline, to wash their Bodies, and cleanse themselves with Water, for fear of murthering some Creatures which they fancy live in that Element. Nor will they drink cold Water till it's boil'd, because they say it has Life in it, and that would destroy it.[1] They neither cut their Beards, nor shave their Heads; but notwithstanding all the Pain of it, pull all the Hair up by the Roots, as fast as it grows on those parts of their Bodies. And wholly careless of the Future, and never anxious for to Morrow's Concerns; they take all chearfully that happens each Day, and of the Provision which Providence sends them, if any Overplus remains, they liberally distribute to such as want it, and trust the same Providence for the following Day. Thus they live *ex tempore*, and as little sollicitous for the World, as if they had been intimately acquainted with our Saviour's Rule, *Take no thought for to morrow, but let the*

Bramins *that never wash their Bodies.*

*Nor cut their Hair.*

*Nor make any Provision for the future.*

[1] These statements really apply to orthodox Jains rather than to Brahmins, and are due to exaggerations of the *Ahimsā* doctrine.

*morrow take thought for the things of it self; sufficient unto the Day is the Evil thereof.*

*The Ceremony of naming the* Bannian *Children.*

The *Bannians*, at the naming of their Children, which is about Ten Days after the Nativity, perform that Ceremony after this manner. They call together about a Dozen Children, and put into their Hands a large Sheet, which is spread, and they standing round, take hold of it in a Circle, and bear it up from the Ground. The *Bramin* standing by, has brought to him thither two or three Sere of Rice, which he pours into the middle of the Sheet, and upon the Rice lays the Child to be named. The young Boys that hold the Sheet shake the Child and the Rice together to and fro, for a quarter of an Hour or more. The Father's Sister then steps near, and has the right of naming the Child; but in case of her Absence, or Death, this Priviledge devolves upon the Father or the Mother of the Infant. When the Child has thus receiv'd its Name, it continues so for the space of a Month or two, after the expiration whereof they proceed further towards its perfect Initiation into the *Bannian* Religion; and then it is brought to the Pagode, where the *Bramin* is ready, and mixes some Shavings of Sandalwood, Champhire,[1] Cloves, and several other sweet-scented Perfumes, and puts them upon the Child's Head; after which it is esteemed a Member of their Religion, and commences compleat *Bannian*.[2]

*Women in Child-bed not toucht.*

The Mother, till Ten Days after Child-bed, is toucht by none but a dry Nurse, nor is she allowed her self to put forth her Hands for the Dressing of any Meat till Forty days be past after lying in, and she be perfectly past her Purification.

*Hanging-Cradles.*

The Cradles for the Children in *India* are much easier, and more convenient than ours, that are plac'd and move upon the Ground. For theirs are hung in the Air by strings ty'd to each end, and fastned to a Beam or Post above, and so swing to and fro with a soft quiet Motion by the slightest

[1] *Champhire* = camphor, Hind. *kafur*; *sandal* = Hind. *chandana*, ground into a paste, and used for anointing the body.

[2] The Naming Ceremony is still celebrated in this way in Gujarāt. See *Bomb. Gaz.* ix, 1, pp. 34 ff.

touch of the Hand. And this was answerable to the Tenderness and Care they had for their Children's Temper, even whilst they were carried in the Womb; who provided such convenient Food and innocent Diversions, such pleasing Entertainments of their Senses and Fancy for the Teeming Women at that time, that the Minds of the Children might participate thereby of those Delights, might be chearful and serene, and free from all dismal Impressions from their Parent; and so their Lives afterwards might be composed and exempt from all anxious Thoughts, from all turbulent Desires, and vexatious Agonies of Spirit. And from hence I will proceed to one of the last things I shall take notice of concerning the *Bannians*, and that is their Burials.

*Women with Child always kept chearful.*

As every Man's coming into the World necessarily infers his going out of it, and consequently a Separation of Body and Soul; all the World therefore seems much concern'd, what will become after Death, of that other part of themselves, in the Sepulture of their Bodies. And as there have been five ways of disposing of the Dead; one, to put them into the Ground; another, to cast them into the Water; the third, to leave them in the open Air; the fourth, to burn them; the fifth, to suffer them to be devoured by Beasts: So of these Five, two have principally obtain'd in the World; that, of committing their Bodies to the Earth; and the other, to the Flames. The last of these is made choice of by the *Bannians*, who carry their dead Bodies to a Pile of Wood near the Water-side, not far from *Suratt*, which is presently kindled after the Corps is laid upon it; and when the Flame has reduced it to Ashes, the Remains are thrown into the River. They likewise, if they are able, burn some fragrant Wood of great Value with the Corps, to sweeten the Air, and mix its Perfumes with the black Exhalations. And were it not for the Tyranny of Custom, it seems more Honourable to have our Bodies consum'd by that lively Element, than to have them devour'd by Worms and Putrefaction; whereof Fire being an Enemy, and the Emblem and most sensible Hieroglyphick of Immortality, there can be no better Expedient

*Five ways of disposing of the Dead.*

*The* Bannians *burn the dead Bodies near the Waterside.*

*Fragrant Wood burnt with the Corps.*

*Burning more honourable than burying.*

to secure our Friends from Oblivion, than that of burning their Bodies, whereof we have either the Bones or Ashes Left, which may be preserved whole Ages. The several Nations of the World had Customs of their own, which commencing upon uncertain Principles, have been deriv'd to their Posterity, and receiv'd with a Religious Fancy; and they would rather die, than do an Act of Violence to them, and believ'd it the greatest Impiety in the World to break them. Whereof *Herodotus* gives a full Instance in a Trial made by *Darius* to the *Indians* and *Greeks*. He askt the *Greeks*, what they would take to do as the *Indians* did, who eat their dead Parents and Friends, and accounted it the most honourable Burial? They answered, They would not do it at any Price. And when he askt the *Indians*, upon what Account they would be induced to burn the Bodies of their Fathers, and not to eat them? They desired him not to speak to them of any such horrid Impiety, as to burn their Fathers Carkasses, and to deny them the Honour of a Natural Burial in the Bowels of their dear Children. This shews how Custom is the Spirit and Genius of a Man's Actions, and introduces a Nature and Religion it self: and were the Prejudice of that remov'd, other civiliz'd Nations might doubtless be as zealous for burning their dead Friends, as the *Bannians* are now-a-days.[1]

*Custom a second Nature.*

The Four Elements were formerly worshipped by the ancient *Siamese*, who committed their Bodies, when dead, to what they ador'd when they were alive. He therefore that worshipped the Earth, made choice of that for his Interrment; the Fire consum'd the Corps of its Adorers; the Worshippers of the Air were expos'd to the Birds to devour them; and those that reverenced the element of Water, were drowned in it at their Burial. This Care of Mens Bodies after Death seems natural to Mankind, and almost universal; which *Osiris* King of *Egypt* taking notice of, made use of as an Encouragement to Vertue, and an Argument for the

*Four ways of disposing of their Dead among the* Siamese.

*All Nations take care of their Dead.*

[1] For Hindu funeral ceremonies in Gujarāt, cf. *Bomb. Gaz.* ix. 1, pp. 47–51.

practice of Morality among his People. Those whose Vertues were Illustrious, and whose Characters were unblemisht, were appointed by him to be buried in Beautiful Fields, near *Memphis*, verdant with all manner of Flowers; whilst the others were assign'd to places of Punishment and Ignominy, whose lives had been Dissolute and Vicious.

*The Corps Burnt sometimes before 'tis quite dead.*

The *Gentiles* of *India*, as if they were weary of their Friends when alive, and loath to harbour them when dead, burn the Body sometimes before it is quite dead, and when they think it past recovery. A *Bannian*, who was Broker to the *English*, was thus hurried away to the burning Place, as he was just expiring; but being happily met by the *English* Surgeon, who felt his Pulse, and gave some hopes of Recovery, some kinder Friend among the rest, disswaded the Company from proceeding, and in a little time, by the application of a few Cordials, he was recover'd to his Health, and by that Miraculous chance evaded an untimely end.

*The manner of carrying the Dead to be Burnt.*

The Corps is carried upon a Bier, according to the Custom of the *Moors*, attended by Friends and Relations, who as they pass along the Road, are incessantly repeating *Ram! Ram!* that is, in their Language, God! God! For *Ram*, they say, was formerly the name of a mighty Prince among them, and is now invoked by them, as if he were God, or the name translated to the Almighty.[1]

*Shaving the Hair a token of deep mourning.*

If a *Rajah* dies, his Subjects and Dependants cut off all their Beards, and shave their Heads, as tokens of the deepest Mourning for his Decease; which is such a solemn sign of Grief and extraordinary Sorrow, that this nakedness and want of Nature's Covering and Ornament of the Head and Face, is never shown, but for a Prince, a Parent, or some nearest Relation.

*Funeral expences costly.*

Upon the Death of any Friend, the *Bannians* are not sparing of their Cost, but spend profusely in Banqueting and Feasts, which are kept publickly for the two or three days following; then they observe upon the same account, the Twelfth, the Twentieth, the Thirtieth, and the Fortieth,

[1] p. 210, note 5.

besides once each Quarter of the succeeding Year, 'til the Annual Solemnity returns. And he who at these times is parsimonious, and endeavours to contract his Expences, is accounted, if he be a Man of Wealth, the most sordid Miser in the World.

*The Reason which the* Indians *had for burning themselves.*

The Impious Opinion which the *Indians* formerly entertain'd, of having a power over their own Lives, as they were Masters of themselves, caus'd many of them to venture upon Death at pleasure, and as advantagious to the Soul, by securing it some degrees of Felicity and Virtue. And for this reason the loving Husband inamour'd with his kind or beautiful Wife, would sometimes burn himself with her in the Funeral Pile, in expectation of a happy future Enjoyment of her. But this was seldom. For it generally fell to the Wives lot to be committed to the Flames with the dead Husband. And this Heathenish Custom was introduc'd, because of the libidinous disposition of the Women, who thro' their inordinate Lust would often poison their present Husbands, to make way for a new Lover. This was so far incouraged by the Politick *Bramin*, who was always a Gainer by her Death; that if any Woman refus'd to burn, her Head was order'd presently to be shav'd, that she might appear Contemptible and Infamous for ever after. For all the Jewels she put on, who deckt her Body for the Flames, when she was resolv'd to die, were carefully lookt after by the Priest, and made his Propriety after her Death; because he only had power to touch the Ashes, and rake therein for Gold and Silver.

*Sometimes the Husband would burn with his dead Wife.*

*The Reason why the Wives were burnt with their Husbands.*

*This custom incouraged by the* Bramins.

*This Custom restrain'd by the* Mogul.

Since the *Mahometans* became Masters of the *Indies*, this execrable Custom is much abated, and almost laid aside, by the Orders which the *Nabobs* receive for suppressing and extinguishing it in all their Provinces. And now it is very rare, except it be some *Rajahs* Wives, that the *Indian* Women burn at all; and those that do, obtain the liberty by costly Presents and powerful Applications to the Governours; by which the Women who are forc'd to survive their Husbands by a superiour Authority, evade that Ignominy and Contempt which would otherwise be cast upon them. This foolish desire of Dying with their Husbands, is exprest by the Poet in these Verses. *Propertius* L. 3. Eleg. 11.

*Namque ubi mortifero jacta est fax ultima lecto*
*Uxorum fulsis stat pia Turba comis:*
*Et certamen habent lethi quæ viva sequatur*
*Conjugium, pudor est non licuisse mori;*
*Ardent victrices, & flammæ pectora præbent,*
*Imponuntque suis ora perusta viris.*

'Tis from this barbarous perswasion of a Power they have of disposing of their own lives, and those that belong to them; that the *Tunquinese* poyson each Year one of the Fruits of the *Araguer*,[1] and gives it to a Child to eat, imagining that by the death of that innocent Child, they shall thrive the better the succeeding Year. And indeed it is an unaccountable Folly in the *Indians* to be so profligate of their own lives, and yet so sparing of the Life of any the most insignificant living Creature; as if the life of a Man were of less consequence and consideration than that of a Beast. The usefulness indeed of some Brutes may gain them an esteem, and the kindness and fidelity of others, as of the Dog *Hircanus* belonging to *Lysimachus*,[2] who leapt, as we read, into the Fire with the Body of his dead Master, and was burnt for Company; and Tyranny even to any Creature argues a savage inhumane Nature; but then it argues the pitch of stupidity and madness, for a Man to destroy and cast away himself in a vain fit of Fancy or of Humour; who is by the dignity of his Nature advanc'd so far above the rest of the Animal World.

*The unreasonableness of this Custom.*

*Some* Gentiles *in* India *are Intomb'd.*

Tho' all the *Gentiles* do for the most part consume the Corps of their Dead by Fire, yet some small Tombs are seen here and there, where their Bodies have been immur'd;[3] but

[1] Areca, *Areca Catechu*, L., Port. *Arequeira*, and spelt in various ways by the older travellers (*arach*, *arrach* in Fryer). Poison was commonly administered mixed in betel nut. *Vide supra*, p. 143.

[2] Lysimachus, son of Agathocles, one of Alexander's generals, was killed in 281 B.C.

[3] Actually these are cenotaphs, erected on the site of the cremation.

all of them very small and mean in respect of the rich and stately Monuments erected by the Principal *Europeans* near *Suratt*. For the *Bannians* are not of the Opinion of the *Egyptian* Kings, who fancyed that the Souls after Death were delighted to hover about their Bodies, and to keep as intimate a Correspondence with them as they could; the *Bannians*, I say, never dreamt this, and were not therefore sollicitous for any stately Receptacle for their Bodies after Death, as those Monarchs were, who erected those stately Pyramids, as Palaces of their last Repose; which neither the fury of the Elements, nor the Assaults of Time were able to Demolish; and where their Souls might live with their Bodies solitary and undisturb'd, by the approach of any rude Guest or vulgar Spirit.

*A tedious Pestilence at* Suratt.

Six Years are now elapsed since a violent Pestilence first broke out among the *Indians* at *Suratt*, and has raged without interruption from the time of its first rise, tho not always with equal fury; for as it had some sort of Interval, in the times of the *Mussouns*, which cool'd the Air; so its greatest Paroxysms were always immediately before, and after that Season of the Year. Before the Rains fall, the Air is extreme dry and parching, and when they are fallen, such store of hot unwholesome vapours are rais'd and scatter'd in the Air, that they give Birth to more Diseases, than all the Year besides produces. Above an Hundred *Gentiles* in one of these Seasons were carried out of the Gates of this City one Morning to be Burnt, besides the *Moors* which were carried off by the Plague, and those of both Casts which died in the Suburbs; which by a very modest Calculation will amount to the number of 300 a Day. And yet the Inhabitants are very numerous still, the Streets populous, and there is but little appearance of any such violent Destruction of the Natives. Before the Eruption of this Pestilence, there happen'd a small Earthquake, which alarm'd the People, but without the Ruin of Houses, or mortal effect to any Inhabitant. But that which creates the greatest Admiration in the *Moors*, and not a little Joy in the *English*, is our escaping all this while the

*An Earthquake.*

*The wonderful Preservation of the* English *from the Plague.*

direful Influence of this mortal Disease, so that not one *English* man was ever yet affected by it. This makes the Heathens cry out, that God is among us, whilst they observe whole Families of their own swept away, without the least Infection touching any one of our Nation; they observe those menial Servants that attend us, both constantly in our Chambers, and in all publick places, falling Dead within a few Hours after they have left our presence; and both the Wives and Children of these persons that wait upon us, languishing at home of this Pestilential Sickness, whilst we all escape its horrid Mortal Blasts. And tho' I cannot in this case but ascribe something to second Causes, to the generous Wines and costly Dishes, to the strength of that Aliment whereon we feed; yet when I consider how languid and feeble several of the *English* are at sometimes of the Year, and notwithstanding their Food, much less vigorous and Athletic in their Bodies than the *Indians*, and therefore less able to repel a contagious Disease; I think there is some Reason for the Pious Opinion of the *Indians*, and that the Almighty displays an extraordinary Power in our Preservation.[1]

*A violent Plague at* Balsera [Bulsār].

From *Balsera* we received Advice, in the Year 1691, that Two Hundred Thousand People, in Eighteen Days time, were taken away by a sweeping Pestilence; but it soon abated its Rage, and the violence of it shorten'd its continuance.

*Feavers common in* India.

The common Distemper that destroys the most in *India*, is Feavers, which the *Europeans* with difficulty escape, especially if they have boild up their Spirits by a solemn Repast, and been ingag'd in a strong Debauch. Besides this, the Mordechine[2] is another Disease of which some die, which is a violent Vomiting and Looseness, and is caus'd most frequently by an Excess in Eating, particularly of Fish and

*The* Mordechine.

[1] The first recorded outbreak of bubonic plague in India was in 1616. For other epidemics see V. A. Smith, *O. H. I.*, pp. 381–2.

[2] Cholera. The word is often written *mort de chien* or *mort de Chine*, but it appears to be derived from Mar. *moḍashi*, through the Port. *mordexim*.

Flesh together. It has been Cur'd by a Red-hot Iron clapt to the Heel of him that is sick, so close that it renders him uneasie by its nearness, whereby it leaves a Scar behind it. Another Distemper with which the *Europeans* are sometimes afflicted, is the Barbeers,[1] or a deprivation of the Use and Activity of their Limbs, whereby they are rendred unable to move either Hand or Foot. This arises sometimes from the neglect of guarding the Limbs from the cold Vapours of the Night, and securing them from the Moistness of those Nocturnal Mists which are sometimes felt in these Parts. And nothing contributes more to the Recovery of the benum'd Limbs, than frequenting the Humhums, which are here in great plenty.

*The Cure of it.*

*The Barbeers.*

*The Cure.*

The general Ease and Cure which the White Powder in *India* gives to Feavers, makes that a very common and acceptable Receipt there; and it has, with very good Success, been administred in *England*, sent from thence by the *Indian* Physicians. And all their Medicines here are generally of the cooler sort, because of the Heats to which the Climate naturally inclines them.

*The White-Powder good against Feavers.*

Tho' Theology is the proper Profession of the *Bramins*, yet some of them are skilled in Arithmetick, Astrology, and Physick; and make pretensions to the Prediction of Events, the Calculation of Nativities, and Cure of Diseases. But such as addict themselves to the Practice of Physick, are bound to pay an Annual Fine to the rest of their Sect, because Physick is both Advantagious and Foreign to their Profession.

*Some* Bramins *Practice Physick.*

A *Bramin*, who had spent some Years in studying the Art of Physick, was invited to visit an *English* Gentlewoman, labouring under a Chronical Disease, who when he came desir'd a sight of her Urine, and pouring it into a small *China* Cup, he let fall upon it one drop of Oyle, upon which he made this Remark in my presence. That if the Oyl sank to the bottom, it inevitably betoken'd Death; the spreading of it self immediately upon the Urin, prognosticated an Increase

*A* Bramin *Physician's Observation upon Urine.*

[1] A kind of paralysis, caused by sleeping in the open, or exposure to the NE. 'land wind'. *Vide infra*, pp. 72, note 2, 85, note 1.

of the Distemper; but if slowly, and by little and little, an abatement of the Disease.

*The best cure for Feavers.* Cooling Herbs, and Congy,[1] that is, Water with Rice boil'd in it, and Abstinence, are the best Receipts they prescribe for mitigating Intestine Fervors of the Spirits, and allaying the Heat of the Blood, which they think is better preserv'd and cool'd within the Veins, than let out, if it boils too fast.

*The Chinese's skill in the Pulse.* I could never learn that our *Indian* Physicians could pretend to that wonderful Knowledge in the Pulse, which those of *China* confidently boast of, and presume to so much Skill in it, as to tell not only the Term of a Man's Disease by it to a Day or Hour, but how many Years, excepting Violence and Accident, a Man in perfect Health may live.

For Astrology, and Natural Physick, the *Indian Bramins*, account themselves however still very eminent and renown'd, by which they foretel such distant Occurrences, and effect such strong Operations, as seem to Men very wonderful and astonishing, and not to be done without some secret Recourse to the Invisible Spirits, or Familiarity with Supernatural Powers. We read the same of some excellent ancient Philosophers, so learn'd in the Works of Nature, as thereby to point out the times both of Eclipses in the Planets, and Commotions in the State, Earthquakes and Inundations, Storms at Sea, and Plagues at Land. And that the Reader may see that their extraordinary Skill in Magical Operations *The Story of a strange Prediction of a* Bramin. is not yet vanisht, I will here relate a Story of them, which I remember was often publickly repeated by the last President at *Suratt*, *Bartholomew Harris*,[2] concerning a *Bramin*, in the time of the Presidency of Mr. *Aungers*,[3] who foretold the Arrival of a certain *English* Ship several Months before she

[1] Hindi *kānji*, rice-gruel.

[2] Bartholomew Harris, President of Surat and Governor of Bombay, 1690–5.

[3] Gerald Aungier or Angier, President of Surat and Governor of Bombay, 1669–77. He was the founder of Bombay, and the greatest of the early servants of the Company. See Hunter, *History of British India*, ii. 214 ff.; Malabari, *Bombay in the Making*, chap. iv.

came to the Harbour. President *Aungers* being under a Disturbance of Mind, and oppress'd with some perplex'd Thoughts for want of Intelligence from *England*, was desir'd by the *Bramin* Physician, who observ'd his Grief, and the melancholy of his Spirit, the Reason of his Concern and dejected Looks, with a chearful Tender of his Service, and Willingness to administer to him in any thing that might contribute to the removal of his Malady, and to his Cure. The President told him, that it was beyond the Power of Physick to heal his Disease, or abate that Distemper he labour'd under; that no Cordial could revive his Thoughts, but News from *England*; or chear his Heart, except it were the sight of an *English* Ship, which he had long expected, but now despairs of. *If an* English *Ship then*, says the *Bramin*, *is your only Cure, be pleased to give me leave to be absent for three or four Days, and I question not by that time but to remove your Trouble, and bring you undoubted News of that Medicine you long for.* Upon which the President consented to his Departure for that time, and withal promis'd him as an Encouragement to his Skill, a rich Paramin,[1] or Indian Mantle, for a Reward. Within Four Days the *Bramin* returns, and addressing himself to the President, assur'd him, that at such a time an *English* Ship would arrive at *Suratt* River's Mouth, with such a particular Person, who had formerly been in *India*, on board her; and that on such a particular Day of the Month he would arrive at the Custom-House of *Suratt*, before Eleven in the Morning. The President pleas'd with this Assurance, and this confident Relation of the *Bramin*, diverted himself with the thoughts of it for some time, and a little after rehears'd it jocularly at a publick Dinner to all the Factors. The Young Men who heard this Discourse, did sometime after recollect with themselves, as they were walking down the Banks of the River to enjoy the Morning Breeze, that this was the critical Morning foretold by the *Bramin*, when an *English* Ship should arrive, and such a

[1] A misprint, occurring also on the following page, for *pamarin*, for which see p. 193, note 1.

particular Person in her. The thoughts of it hasten'd them back again towards the Custom-House, to enquire if there were any *English* News; and upon their Return were surpriz'd at the sight of an *English* Boat, which they espyed was rowing up the River; and were no sooner arrived at the Custom-House, but they found the *English* Man who had been expected in her. The News of this was very grateful to the President, and not ungrateful to the *Bramin*, who received a curious Paramin from the Hands of the Governour, whom he had oblig'd with so faithful and particular a Prophetick Relation.

And the worthy President Mr. *Harris*, who had himself been sometimes in distress for *English* News, has likewise told me of a *Bramin*'s Proposals to him, of bringing him undoubted Intelligence, how the Companies Affairs in *England* stood, within the space of four days. But that he durst not accept of the Proposition, because he was confident that it depended upon the Assistance of a Familiar. And surely those sprightly Beings can easily dispatch a very tedious Voyage in a very short time. For if we only consider the nimble Progress of Light thro' the Air, with what swiftness it darts its bright active Atoms from *East* to *West*, and flies thro' the immense Expanse from the lofty Regions of the Skie; we cannot with any great Reason deny this same or greater Power to the active Spirits of Darkness, who are stript of all the Clogs of Matter, and void of all material Substance.

*The reproach of being slipper'd.*

The *Bannians* are far from any thing of Severity, and not prone to the inflicting any Corporal Punishments, and have a perfect Antipathy to those that are Capital; but the ignominious Punishment which they all sorely dread, is Slippering; that is, when any Person, who has been offended by a *Bannian*, takes off his Slipper, spitts upon it, and then strikes the *Bannian* with the sole of it. This is more detestable and abominated by them, than for any among us to spitt or throw dirt in another's Face; for it is not only esteem'd the most hainous Abuse, but the redemption of the

Affront is very eostly, and the disgraee is not wiped off without difficulty and Expenee. This touching the *Bannian* with the sole of a Slipper, is as unsufferable and odious in *India*, as touching with the Hand the Head of a *Siamese*; for that being the highest part of the Body, is with them aeeounted of prineipal Honour, and never to be stroakt or toueht without the greatest Offence and Affront. Insomueh that the King himself permits no Person to dress his Head, but is so far his own Valet, that he puts the Covering upon it himself.

*An Affront to touch the Head at* Siam.

This is the Substanee of what I thought might eontribute to fill the Aeeount of the *Bannians*, of whom I have discours'd eoncerning their Natural Tempers, and Religious Opinions eoncerning their Abstinenee, and Days of Devotion; their Diet and Ingenuity in their Vocations; their Attire and Ornaments; their Marriages; Naming of their Children, and their Burials; and have Coneluded with a Relation of some of the eommon Diseases of *India*, and of the tedious Plague at *Suratt*. And shall now endeavour to entertain the Reader with a Deseription of the strange Manners of the *Indian Faquirs* near *Suratt*, and with an Aeeount of the *Parsies*, and *Halalchors*.

# THE FAQUIRS[1] NEAR SURATT

*Pulparrock, frequented by the Faquirs.* TWO Miles distant from *Suratt*, is a very delightful place, nam'd *Pulparrock*,[2] adorn'd with pleasant Walks and Groves of Trees, near the gentle Streams of the River *Tappy*.[3] The Ground is all very even, except only near the Banks of the River, where the rising Hills enlarge the prospect upon the Water. And the Hot Air is temper'd by the shady Walks under the spreading Branches, and the nearness of the Current of the Water gliding by. For these Religious *Santones*[4] here, as well as in *Europe*, are industrious in culling out the most delightful Habitations in the Country, and taking up their Abode where ever either Art or Nature Invite their Residence by a commodious pleasant Dwelling. For there is not any place near *Suratt*, that yields either the Beauty, or the Delight that *Pulparrock* affords.

*The Original of the Faquirs.* The Original of these Holy Mendicants is ascrib'd, according to their Account, to a certain Prince named *Revan*, who quarrell'd with *Ram*,[5] a Knowing and Victorious Prince; and being Conquer'd and depriv'd of all by a certain Ape named *Herman*, or *Hanneman*, which was his Assistant on Earth, spent the remainder of his Days in Pilgrimage, and rambling, without any Maintenance either to himself or his Followers, but what was given them in Charity: It was for the good

[1] This word only properly applies to a Mahommedan religious mendicant, but it was loosely used of Hindu ascetics, properly speaking Yogis, Sanyāsis, Sādhus, &c.

[2] Pulpāra, a suburb of Surat, on the banks of the Tāpti, still a favourite resort of Sanyāsis. It is mentioned by Fryer, ed. Crooke, i. 255, and by Forbes, *Or. Mem.*, second edition, i. 176, 184.

[3] *Tāpi*, Skt. 'hot river', is the more correct form of the word.

[4] Guj. *Santa*, a saint, ascetic.

[5] The reference is to the story of the great Hindu epic, the *Rāmāyana*. Ravana, the demon-king of Lanka (Ceylon), carries off Sitā, the wife of Rāma, Prince of Ayodhya. She is rescued with the help of Hanuman, the leader of the monkeys. Cf. *supra*, p. 200.

Services done to *Ram* in his Life time by the Apes, that they are in so great Esteem both with the *Moors* and *Gentiles* in the *Indies*; and this arch unlucky Creature is in that Repute among them all, that they seriously declare, *were the Blood of one of them spilt upon the Ground, the Earth would suddenly become unfruitful, and the Judgment upon it would be at least a Years Famin.* And therefore when a large Ape had broke loose from the *English* Factory at *Suratt*, and skipping to and fro' had snatch'd away several things of value, and in his Anger had bit a Child or two so sorely, that they afterwards died of the Wounds, (as it was reported,) yet was it an inexcusable Crime at the same time for any violent Hand to touch him.

*The Indian's respect for Apes.*

These Philosophical Saints have since the first forming of their Order, assum'd a liberty of taking that by violence, which they find is denied their civil Requests, and sometimes force a Charity from the People, when Intreaties cannot prevail, especially in the Country Villages. For their numbers render them imperious, and upon pretension of extraordinary Sanctity, they commit a thousand Villanies unbecoming their Profession. They imitate the *Romish* Orders in Vows of Piety and Celibacy, and in their Pretensions to a strange Intimacy, and prevailing Interest with Heaven. Thus they endeavour to raise their Veneration and Respect; thus they acquire constant Homage and Address, daily Applications, and large Presents from the People. And some, by a seeming neglect of themselves, indulge their Bodies, and pamper their Ambition the more.

*The Rudeness of the* Faquirs.

They are called *Faquirs* by the Natives, but *Ashmen* commonly by us, because of the abundance of Ashes with which they powder their Heads, and mix with their Hair, which falls down sometimes to the middle of their Backs. They use no Pillabers[1] to repose their Heads on, but lay them unconcernedly upon the Ground, where they gather a constant supply of Dust and Filth, which makes them (in their Opinion) of a very becoming appearance, because it is

*Their filthiness.*

[1] See p. 185, note 2.

squalid, but gives the Ascetick or votary in our Eyes a very disagreeable and sordid Aspect.

*The Immodesty of some* Faquirs.

Of this Persuasion and kind of life, are several sorts both among the *Gentiles* and the *Moors*; some of whom shew their Devotion by a shameless appearance, and walking naked, without the least Rag of Cloaths to cover them. And even at Mid-day, and in the heart of the City, and places of chief Concourse, will they walk the Streets, as shameless and unconcern'd, as if they were Cloathed all over. The constant sight of them in the City, which offers it self at every turn, abates that bashfulness in the Spectators, which such an immodesty might be apt to create, and diverts neither Sex from their Society, from a familiar Conversation and Intimacy with them; and Custom has wore off all that Coyness even in the Women, which would be startled at such an immodest Spectacle at first.[1]

*The several tormenting Postures of these* Faquirs.

Others make solemn Vows of continuance in such and such kind of Postures all the days of their life, and will never move from them to alter them, tho' the Pains are never so violent, which seem to be attended with so much Torture, as would even force them to forbear. For these are Penitentiaries in earnest, without any Mask or possible appearance of Deceit, and voluntarily mortifie their Limbs, and distort their Joints to a perfect Dislocation. For by the Delusions of Satan, these infatuated Votaries are possessed with a wretched Opinion of making themselves unspeakably happy hereafter, by these insufferable Torments here: And the Enemy of Mankind, impatient of Delays in exercising his infernal Cruelty, persuades them to undergo these Torments which will end in making them Meritorious Saints, and that

[1] For parallel passages cf. Hobson-Jobson, *s.v.* Jogee. Ascetics, especially those of the Śaiva sect, wear a minimum of clothing, and formerly went stark naked. They are the Gymnosophists of the Greeks. The same custom was practised by the Digambara Jains. The self-tortures practised by these ascetics are for the purpose of subduing the senses in order to attain *Yoga*, union with the Supreme Being. Cf. Hastings, *Encyc. Rel. and Ethics*, *s.v.* Asceticism (Hindu).

by these horrid Punishments they may secure a future larger Bliss.

Among these violent Postures, some I observ'd with both their Arms stretcht out toward Heaven continually, which they never let fall, and are therefore by long use grown so much into that Position, that by long continuance it begins to grow Natural, and without Violence they cannot move them downward. The Nails from their Fingers too, are grown beyond the Paws of any Lyon, into three or four Inches length, (by an Opinion which they have imbibed, like that of the Emperour of *Japan*, who, after his Coronation, is deterr'd from permitting either Razor or Scissers to come near his Hair or Nails,) upon a Persuasion that it is a kind of Sacriledge in those cases to cut them.

Others, as devout as these, gaze with their Eyes continually toward Heaven, by holding their Faces directly upwards. They throw their Heads so far backwards between their Shoulders, that their Eyes can never behold any other Object but the Stars and Sky, whither with unwearied Earnestness they look continually, delighted as it were with the pleasant sight of the blessed Regions above, and loath to cast their Eyes upon any thing of this vile and wicked World. But before their Eyes can be thus fixt, and their Heads setled in this Posture, the *Faquirs* run thro' much Uneasiness and Trouble, molested both in the Utterance of their Words, and in receiving any Food. And both those who extend their Arms continually towards Heaven, as if they were reaching at that place; and those whose Eyes are constantly fixt upwards, are rendered thereby wholly unserviceable to themselves, and are therefore attended always by a Servant or two, who administer to them in their Necessities, and conduct the gazing Saints to different places of Abode.

Others there are with their Right Arm brought round the Neck over the left Shoulder, and the Left Arm over the Right Shoulder, and their Fingers clasping one another before their Breasts, with the Palms of their Hands turn'd outwards. This twists the Arms, dislocates the Shoulder-bones, and therefore vexes the Patient with inexpressible Torments.

Some of the *Faquirs* neither sit, nor ever lie down, but constantly either walk or lean. They lean upon a small Pillow, or Quilt, laid upon a Rope, which hangs down from the Boughs of a Tree, where the two Ends are fastned above, and swing in that posture to and fro Day and Night. But when these *Faquirs* prepare themselves to pray, they change this Gesture, and fasten their Feet in two Ropes that hang down from the Boughs of a Tree, and with their Heels upwards, and their Heads down, as if they were asham'd to lift up their Eyes to Heaven, they pour out their powerful Supplications. And from the Prayers of these humble Saints are expected to flow considerable Blessings, and the prevention of many Mischiefs.

Some of these devoted Mendicants extend only one Hand toward Heaven, others turn only one Arm round their Shoulders. But they are all in singular Esteem, and religiously resorted to by the Vulgar; and by these Distortions of their Bodies they gain the Repute of Men of perfect Hearts and of upright Minds.

*A savage Custom near* Carwar.

Besides these painful unnatural Postures near *Suratt*, a savage Custom is still maintain'd by the Gentiles near *Carwar*, in offering Sacrifice to the God of Plenty, at the Season of the growing Corn. The *Bramins* at this time kill a Cock, and make an Oblation of his Blood, as was usual with other Heathens; while the People that are concern'd in it are struck with amazing Horror and Consternation, their Faces are writhed, and their Looks ghastly; their Flesh creeps upon them, and their Joints tremble; and to all Men they appear frightful, as if they were possessed; and they own too, that the Devil at that time inhabits them, and acquaints them with several strange things. After the Sacrifice is past, Six Men, and an equal number of Women, are appointed to perform a Ceremony very dreadful. Upon each side of the Back-bone of the Men are stuck two Iron Hooks into the Flesh, by which they are lifted up to the top of a Pole standing out like a Gibbet, above 20 Foot high. This Gibbet is fasten'd to an Engine with four Wheels, which is drawn upon the Ground above a Mile, with the Men hanging upon the Tenters all the way. The Women have each of them a sort of Bason upon their Heads, upon which are set Six Cups as large as Tea-Cups, one upon another, with Fire in each of them, which being very tottering, makes the Women exceding careful how they tread; lest if they slip, and thereby any Cup falls, or the Fire be shaken out of any, the Woman forfeits her Life, and is sentenc'd to immediate Death. But if with Care and Dexterity they go thro' with the Walk as far as the Men, they then are safe, and the Solemnity ceases. And notwithstanding all the tediousness of the Passage, and the jogging of the Carriage whereon they hang, which one would think would force the Hooks to tear the Flesh in pieces; yet will the Men, poor miserable Wretches! take Swords and brandish them in their Hands, as it were, in defiance of their Torments all the way.[1]

The *Faquirs* resort sometimes together in great numbers, and live upon the Spoil and Alms of the Country, as they pass in their Pilgrimage. If they find the People unwilling to give, they audaciously demand, and that not in the humble strain for a Pice or two, but sawcily beg a Roupie. One of these Mendicants in a petulant Humour, impudently requested from an *English* President, whom he met abroad, twenty Roupies. The President to humour his Forwardness and Impudence, offer'd him Nineteen, which he magnanimously refused, because he thought it unbecoming his Greatness, to sink a Farthing below his first demands.

*A story of a sawcy* Faquir.

Of these Imperious Godly Beggars, I have seen an hundred (at least) of them in a Company, seated under a shady Grove of Trees, rejoycing at a publick Entertainment, which was prepar'd by a leading Man of their Company. I observ'd that

[1] The horrible custom of hook-swinging (Band or Charakh Puja), now abolished, is described by Hamilton, *New Account*, i. 269, Abbé Dubois (ed. 1906), p. 598, and many other writers. See Crooke's note to Fryer, *East India and Persia*, ii. 77–8.

they drunk very freely of Bang,[1] steep'd in Water, while I stood among them, whose Intoxicating quality is very apt to disturb the Brain. Which made me enquire whether such Jovial Meetings were not apt to end in Madness and Quarrels; and the Excess of that Liquor, by kindling an unruly Heat, disturb their Spirits, and convert their friendly Meetings into feuds and discords, and mischievous Debates? To which they answer'd, That they took care of preserving Peace and Amity, and as much decency and order at these times of Mirth, as at their ordinary Meetings; for which end, they chose a number from among themselves, who were totally debarr'd from Drinking, and were Censors upon others, to inspect their Carriage, and interpose in their Disputes, to restrain them from all exorbitant Mirth, and excessive Drinking.

*The* Faquirs *very orderly at their Feasts.*

*The* Persies.

Besides the *Moors* and the *Bannians*, and these *Faquirs*, which belong to both Professions, the *Persies*[2] are a Sect very considerable in *India*, of whom the Tradition is, that coming from *Persia* in a Tempest, at the time that *Mahomet* and his Followers gave Laws to the *Persians*, (which they were unwilling to submit to) they were driven to that distress, that they almost despair'd of Life, 'till hearing a Cock Crow, and espying Fire at Land, they recover'd their hopes of safety, and gain'd a speedy Arrival. The Cock therefore is as much esteem'd by them, as the Cow is by the *Bannians*, of the lives

*Their Respect to a Cock and to Fire.*

[1] Bang or Hashish, Indian Hemp (cannabis Indica), a well-known intoxicant.

[2] The Parsis (Old Persians or Iranis) were the followers of Zoroaster, who fled to the coast of Western India to escape forcible conversion to Mahommedanism when the Sassanian Empire was overthrown. They landed at Sanjan, 88 miles north of Bombay, in A.D. 716, and made a compact with the Hindus. In A.D. 1142 they settled in Navsāri, eighteen miles from Surat. Before the advent of the British rule they were employed as agriculturists and weavers. They were first described by Henry Lord, *Display of two forraigne Sects* (1630). Gerald Aungier, who first encouraged them to settle in Bombay by allowing them to build a *dakma* or Tower of Silence (*c.* 1672), calls them 'an industrious people and ingenious in trade'.

of both which, they are the zealous Patrons and Protectors. For the Worshipping of Fire seems to be the Ancientest instance of Idolatry in the World, inasmuch (as some think) that *Cain*, after he was banished from the Presence of the Lord, turned a downright Idolater, and then introduced the Worship of the Sun, as the best resemblance he could find of the Glory of the Lord, which was wont to appear in a flaming Light. And in after-times, they Worshipped Fire in the Eastern Counties, as the best Emblem of the Sun, when it was absent. Nor was the Vestal Fire ever more Sacred, than all other Fires are with the *Persies*, the extinction of which, if it is voluntary, is a Crime as hainous, as if the vital Heat of the Cock, or some other beloved Animal were destroy'd; so that if their Houses were on Fire, they would sooner be persuaded to pour on Oyl to increase, than Water to asswage the Flame. If a Candle is once lighted, they would judge the Breath of him more than Pestilential, that durst attempt to blow it out. And a *Persy* Servant, who is commanded to bring a hot Steel, and warm with it a Bowl of Punch, will plead his Excuse, and that he dare not hasten the coolness of the Steel by a violent abatement of the Heat. The active Flame must be allow'd to live, whilst there's any Fuel for it to feed on; if the Fire is once kindled, all care is taken that it comes to a natural Expiration, and no violence allow'd to bring it to a period sooner: Another account we have for their respect of Fire, is, that their great Law-giver, *Zertoost*,[1] was taken into Heaven, and brought from thence Fire with him (*Prometheus* like) which he commanded his Followers afterwards to Worship.

They have other Fables concerning *Abraham*, that he was once in the Devil's Power, who expos'd him to the Flames, but the kind Fire would not fasten on him; from which they

[1] Zardusht is the later form of Zarathustra, the Greek Zoroaster, the founder of the Parsi religion. His date is uncertain. He lived at the court of Vishtāspa or Gushtāsp, King of Bactra or Balkh, who is sometimes identified with Hystaspes, the father of Darius the Great. See A. V. W. Jackson, *Zoroaster, the Prophet of Ancient Iram*, New York, 1899.

infer the great unreasonableness of destroying that Element, which was so averse, (notwithstanding all its Fury) from hurting *Abraham* their Friend; the Reason of this may be, because that *Abraham* came from the Land of *Ur*, which signifies Fire,[1] which might give the occasion for the Fable of his Escaping the Fire.

*Their days of Devotion.* They own and Adore one Supreme Being, to whom, as he is the Original of all things, they dedicate the first Day of every Month, in a solemn observance of his Worship. And enjoin, besides these, some others for the Celebration of Publick Prayers.

*Eating in common.* At their solemn Festivals, whither an hundred or two sometimes resort, in the Suburbs of the City, each Man according to his Fancy and Ability, brings with him his Victuals, which is equally distributed, and eat in common by all that are present. For they shew a firm Affection to all of their own Sentiments in Religion, assist the Poor, and are very ready to provide for the Sustenance and Comfort of such as want it. *The* Persies *kind to their own Cust.* Their universal Kindness, either in imploying such as are Needy and able to work, or bestowing a seasonable bounteous Charity to such as are Infirm and Miserable; leave no Man destitute of Relief, nor suffer a Beggar in all their Tribe; and herein so far comply with that excellent Rule of *Pythagoras, to enjoy a kind of Community among Friends.*

*Their Transportation to* India. These *Persies* are by another Name term'd *Gaures*,[2] or Worshippers of Fire, because of their Veneration for that Element; and were Transported into *India*, when *Calyf Omar*[3] reduc'd the Kingdom of *Persia*, under the Power of the *Mahometans*; and they profess the Ancient Religion of the *Persians*. But their Religion spread it self more Westerly, it seems than *Persia*; for the *Babylonians*, who by their Religious Discipline, were engag'd to the Worshipping the Sun,

[1] Ur means Council. The story cannot be traced.

[2] Cf. p. 139, note 2.

[3] The second Caliph, A.D. 634–44, and conqueror of Egypt and Persia.

did likewise under the Names of *Nego*, and *Shaca*,[1] Adore the Fire and the Earth. And the Parents of *Gregory Nazianzene*,[2] who was born in the Fourth Century at *Arianzum*, an obscure Village belonging to *Nazianzum*, a Town of the second *Cappadocia*, were of a mixt Religion made up of Judaism and Paganism, or rather some select Rites of both; for with the *Gentiles* they did honour to Fire and burning Lights, but rejected Idols and Sacrifices; and with the *Jews* they observ'd the Sabbath. But I believe what remains of this Cast, are most of them in the Kingdom of the *Great Mogul*. But we read of some in *Persia* of great Antiquity. For near *Yesd* in the Province of *Ayrack*, (or *Hierack Agemi*)[3] which yields the richest and Fairest Tapestries of all *Persia*, and of the World; and on the Mountain *Albors*,[4] there are yet some Worshippers of Fire, who are said to have used it above 3000 Years.[5]

*Superstitious in eating and drinking.*

They are not quite so Abstemious in their Diet as the *Banians*, but Superstitiously refuse to drink after any Stranger, out of the same Cup. Some *Hindoes* will eat of one kind of Flesh, some of another, but all refrain from Bief, out of respect to Kine.

*Many of the* Persies *Weavers.*

In their Callings they are very Industrious and diligent, and careful to train up their Children to Arts and Labour. They are the principal Men at the Loom in all the Country, and most of the Silks and Stuffs at *Suratt*, are made by their Hands.[6] The High-Priest of the *Persies* is called *Destoor*, their Ordinary Priests *Daroos*, or *Harboods*.[7]

1 Apparently the Babylonian deities Nebo and Sakkuth are meant.

2 St. Gregory Nazianzen, born A.D. 329 at Nazianzus, in Cappadocia, died *c.* 389 at Arianzus, was one of the four great fathers of the Church, a famous preacher and scholar, a disciple of Origen and Athanasius and an opponent of Arianism.

3 Irāq Ajami.

4 Elburz.

5 An unfavourable account of the Guebres or remnant of the original Parsis at Yezd, in Persia, is given in Fryer, ed. Crooke, ii. pp. 252 ff.

6 The stuffs known as *Doti* and *kinkāb* are specially made on the looms of the Parsi weavers of Gujarāt.

7 The Parsi priesthood is divided into three classes—Dasturs or

*Their dead Bodies expos'd to the Birds of Prey. The Ceremony used by the* Persies *in their Burials.*

I shall not mention their Marriages, which much resemble the manner of the *Bannians*, but proceed only to a Description of their way of Burying, which is this. The noblest Sepulture which they fancy they can bestow upon their deceased Friends, is exposing them to be devour'd by the Fowls of the Air, and bestowing their Carcasses on the Birds of Prey. After the Body is for some time dead, the *Halalchors*[1] (which are a sort of sordid *Indians*) take and carry it out upon a Bier into the open Fields, near the place where it is expos'd to the Fowls of Heaven. When 'tis there decently deposited upon the Ground, a particular Friend beats the Fields and neighbouring Villages, upon the hunt for a Dog, 'till he can find one out; and having had the good luck to meet him, he cherishes and intices him with a Cake of Bread, which he carries in his Hand for that purpose, 'till he draws him as near the Corps as he is able; for the nearer the Dog is brought to the dead Body, the nearer are its approaches to Felicity. And if the hungry Cur can by bits of Cake be brought so nigh the Deceased, as to come up to him, and take a piece out of his Mouth, 'tis then an unquestionable Sign, that the Condition he died in was very happy; but if the timorous Dog startles at the sight, or loaths the Object, or being lately well fed, has no Stomach to that ordinary Morsel, which he must snatch out of the dead Man's Jaws, the Case then with him is desperate, and his state deplorable. The poor Man whom I saw, was by these Prognosticks, very miserable; for the sturdy Cur would by no means be inticed to any distance near him. When the Dog has finisht his part of the Cere-

High Priests; Mobeds, the middle class of priests; and Harbads, the lowest rank. The office is hereditary, but a priest may become a layman. Daru is an ordinary prefix to a priestly name.

[1] It is incorrect to say that the Parsi dead are removed by halalchors or scavengers. The work is done by the *nasā sālārs* or corpse-bearers. Before the body is taken to the Tower of Silence (*dakma*), a dog is brought to gaze on it, in order to drive away the fiend (*druj*). This ceremony is known as *sagdād* or dog-sight. See Hastings, *Encyc. Rel. and Ethics*, art. Death and Death Ceremonies (Parsi), iv. 502.

mony, two *Daroos*, at a Furlong's distance from the Bier, stand up with joined Hands, and loudly repeat for near half an hour, a tedious Form of Prayer by Heart; but with such a quick dispatch, that they scarce drew Breath all the while, as if they had been under some invincible necessity of running over the Words in such a time. All the while they were thus gabling, a piece of White Paper[1] fasten'd to each Ear, o'erthwart the Face, hung down two or three Inches below the Chin; and as soon as they had ended their Petitions, the *Halalchors* took up the Corps, and conveyed it to the Repository, which was near; all the Company ranking themselves by two and two, and following it with joined Hands. The place of Sepulture is in the open Fields, within a Wall built in form of a Circle, about twelve Foot high, and about an hundred in the Circumference; in the middle of which was a Door of Stone about six foot from the ground, which was open'd to admit the Corps. The Ground within the Walls is rais'd above four Foot, and made shelving towards the Centre, that the Filth and Moisture which are drain'd continually from the Carcasses, may by an easie passage descend into a Sink made in the middle to receive them. The Corps therefore was left here, and all the Company departing thence, betook themselves to a Rivolet that run near the place for Ablution, to cleanse themselves from what defilements, on this Melancholy occasion, they might have contracted; and retir'd afterwards to their proper Habitations in the City, from whence this place is distant about a Mile. But within the space of a Day or two after, some of the nearest Relatives return again hither, to observe which of the Eyes of their deceased Friend was first pickt out by the hungry Vultures; and if they find that the right Eye was first seis'd on, this abodes undoubted Happiness; if the left, they then are sorrowful, for that's a direful sign of his Misery.

*The Burying of their Hair every Year.*

The *Persies* are very nice in the preservation of their Hair, and careful to preserve whatever is cut off their Heads or Beards, that nothing of it be lost or carelessly thrown

[1] Really a white cloth, tied over the mouth and nose.

about, but once a Year be decently laid in their Burying place. A description of which, tho' it be drest with nothing but Horrour, yet may here properly be inserted.

*The* Persies *horrid Burying-place.*

The Burying-place of the *Persies* is an Object the most dreadful, and of the most horrid Prospect in the World, and much more frightful than a Field of Slaughter'd Men. It contains a number of Carcasses of very different disagreeable Colours and Aspects. Some are seen there bleeding fresh, but so torn by the Vultures that croud upon the Walls, that their Faces resemble that of a Death's Head, with the Eyeballs out, and all the Flesh upon the Cheeks pickt off. And on the Fleshy part of the Body, where the Ravenous Bird tasted a more delicious Morsel, are eaten several large Holes, and all the Skin on every part is mangled, and torn by the sharp Beaks of these devouring Creatures. Here was a Leg, and there an Arm, here lay half, and there the quarter of a Man. Some look'd as if they were partly Jelly, others were harden'd like Tann'd Leather, by the various operations of the Sun and Weather upon them; Here lay one pickt as clean as a Skeleton, near that, another with the Skin in some parts Green, in others Yellow, and the whole so discoloured, as if all within were Putrefaction. A sight terrible enough almost to afright an hungry Vulture from his Prey. But these Birds are most delighted with these dismal Objects, and that noisom smell which evaporates from the dead Corps affords a pleasant Odour to their Senses. The stench of the Bodies is intolerable, and of malignity sufficient to strike any Man dead that would endure it; and yet the Vultures chuse to sit to the Leeward upon the Wall, luxuriously to suck up and indulge their smell with these deadly foul Vapours. Some of these glutted Birds were so cloy'd and cramm'd with Humane Flesh, that they seem'd scarce able to take Wing, and the Feathers of others were much moulted away, by this kind of rank feeding.

Besides this manner of Burying, in use with the *Persies*, near *Suratt*, there are other Eastern Nations who have peculiarly affected the Intombing their dead Bodies in Animals.

The Inhabitants of *Pegu* reckon him happy, whose Fate it is to be devour'd by a Crocodile. And the Natives formerly, near the Mouth of *Ganges*, if weary of this Life by Sickness or Old Age, committed themselves to be devoured by the Dog-Fish, as the safest passage to their future Felicity.

*Two odd ways of Burying.*

The *Halalchors*, (whom I occasionally mention'd a little before) are another sort of *Indians* at *Suratt*, the most contemptible, but extremely necessary to be there. They are term'd *Halachors*, by the *Moors* and *Indians*, in the *Persian* Language, which signifies *Eat-alls*, or *Eaters at large*. They will indulge themselves with Wine, as well as drink Water; they Eat all kinds of Fish or Flesh, and without any scruple of Conscience or of Appetite, will feed upon either Horse or Cow, and will satisfie their Stomachs as well with a piece of Carrion out of a Ditch, as with the freshest Meat that can be bought in the *Bazar*. These are the Persons employ'd in sweeping the Houses, and cleaning the Streets, in carrying away the Dirt and Dung, in washing the dead Bodies, and conveying them to their proper places of Sepulture, which makes them absolutely necessary in these parts, because such Employments as these are an Abomination to the *Moors* and defile the *Bannians*, and are only ingag'd in by these poor People, who for this Reason are accounted Vile and Mean, the most abject and Scandalous of all the Inhabitants of *Suratt*. One of the greatest marks of Ignominy, when any Person is reflected on, is to be called *Halalchor*. Yet these despicable Persons take all in good part, cringe and bow to all they pass by, Eat whatever is offer'd them from any Hand, and go thro' with their Drudgery without noise and concern. The *Halalchor* industriously avoids the touching of any Person for fear of Offence; he is separated from all the rest of the *Casts*, as a thing Unclean; for if he happens to come too near a *Bannian*, he defiles him by his touch, and puts him to the trouble of some Purification, to wash off the Defilement he contracted upon it. Therefore are they shunn'd by all, and endeavour to keep at a distance from all.[1]

*The Halalchors a sordid sort of People.*

[1] Halālkhor literally means one who eats what is *halāl* or law-

I have now finisht my Discourse of the City and Inhabitants of *Suratt*, of its Government and Trade, and of the Customs and Religion; the Language, Arts and Recreations of the Natives; with a particular Account of the Mendicant Friars, or *Faquirs*, of the *Persies* and *Halalchors*, and shall conclude all my Thoughts of *India*, in a brief Description of the *English* Factory at *Suratt*, and of the Troubles which happen'd to the *English* while I was there.

fully killed by Mahommedan law. Hence, one to whom all things are lawful, or perhaps an ironical perversion of *harām khor*, one who eats forbidden food. The word is said to be an invention of Akbar's.

# AN ACCOUNT OF THE ENGLISH FACTORY AT SURATT[1]

THE *English East-India* Company (from an Account we have of it in a Pamphlet concerning their Trade) are at the Annual Expence of one hundred Thousand Pounds. For they esteem it necessary, as well for the Honour of the *English* Nation, as facilitating of their Traffick, to maintain their principal Servants in *India*, not only in Decency, but Splendor, as is visible to any that has travell'd either to *Suratt*, or the *Fort* of St. *George*, to *Gombrone* in *Persia*, or *Bengal*. These are the chief places of Note and Trade, where their Presidents and Agents reside, for the support of whom, with their Writers and Factors, large Privileges and Salaries are allowed. *The yearly Expence of the Company.*

The several parts of *India* have each their peculiar Commodities proper to them, which are bought up, and made ready by the Companies Servants, to load upon their Ships at their Arrival. And were not the *English* constantly upon this Account kept in those parts, the other *European* Nations would soon fill up all our vacant Factories, and so monopolize the *Indian* Trade, that not only the Spice Islands would be their darling Propriety, but all *Indian* Commodities as well as Spices, Silks, Callicoes, Drugs, Precious Stones, *&c.* *The necessity of* English *Factors in* India.

[1] This account of the English Factory at Surat should be compared with that of Fryer, ed. Crooke, i, pp. 210 ff., and the anonymous letter, probably by Streynsham Master, in Yule, *Hedges Diary*, ii, pp. cccv. ff. Other accounts are quoted in Rawlinson, *British Beginnings in Western India*, chap. ix, *passim*. An engraving of the Factory (from Mandelslo, 1638) appears as a frontispiece to Foster, *English Factories*, 1634–6. For the exact position of the original Factory, which is probably not the building at present shown to tourists, see the authorities quoted by Crooke, on Fryer, i, p. 214, note 2, and Foster, *English Factories*, 1661–4, pp. 296 ff.

should (within a while) be apt to bear what Rates in *Europe* they thought fit to lay upon them. For accomplishing which design, some People have already some time ago, profer'd to the *Great Mogul* the advancement of his Customs at *Suratt*, to a much higher Rate than now they are at, upon condition of Establishing that intire Trade upon them. And both by large Presents, and by raising of the Price of Pepper upon the Coast of *Malabar*, they have indefatigably endeavour'd a total subversion of our Trade therein among the Natives. Therefore the continuance of Factors in *India* by a Company, seems very necessary and just; and were this practice once withdrawn, the *Indian* Trade to *England*, would probably soon be remov'd too. For other means would soon be projected for accomplishing what Bribes and Presents to the *Mogul* and his Officers could not effect, by which those that secur'd the Trade for themselves, would soon find a Way of stopping all Traffick from the *Indies*, but what came through their Hands. Therefore are our Presidents oblig'd continually to watch their Motions in *India*, and observe their Designs, to countermine their Projects, and gratifie not only the *Mogul* now and then, with grateful Gifts, but likewise to be always upon the same method with the *Omrahs* and Favorites at Court, ingaging a continuance of their Favours.

This makes those that are concern'd in the Trade of *India* think fit, that this necessary Expence of Factors for continuance of the *Indian* Trade to *England*, should be recompens'd with some publick Priviledges for its support. And that therefore the private Advantage which grows from this great Care and Cost, should not easily be checkt and discourag'd, especially considering likewise that the securing the Traffick in the power of the *English* from Foreign Designers, contributes not a little to the common good, especially if thereby their Ships be enabled to come home in good Fleets, as the *Dutch* do, which would thereby the better secure them from the common enemy the *French*, that they might not be so easily Seiz'd to the publick Damage of the Nation.

THE ENGLISH FACTORY AT SURAT IN 1638

*The House where the Factors live.*

The House provided for the Entertainment of the *English* at *Suratt* belongs to the *Mogul*, and is fitted with the best Accommodations of any in the City. It is situated in the *North-West* part of it, and is able to give convenient Lodgings to forty Persons, besides several decent Apartments to the President. Our Land-lord *Aureng-Zebe* is extreme kind and liberal in permitting us to expend the Rent, which is 60*l*. Yearly, either in Beautifying, Repairing, or in additional Rooms to the House, so that he seldom receives much Rent from us. It is built with the Convenience of several Cellars, and Ware-houses, of a Tanque of Water, and an Humhum.[1]

*The Priviledge of Traffick allow'd the President and Factors.*

The President of the Northern Parts of *India* resides here, who is dignified frequently with the Government of *Bombay*, and invested with the Title of Honourable. A few Years stay here has rais'd several of the Presidents to Plentiful Estates, who besides their Salaries, which is 300 *per An*. and several Advantages by the Ships, are permitted a free Trade to all the parts of the *East*. This is indulg'd likewise to all the Companies Servants of what station soever, which is a Favour attended with considerable Benefit, suits well with the freedom of an *English* Subject, and is a profitable Blessing for which the *Dutch* Factors are earnest Supplicants, and from which they are very strictly restrain'd.

*The Council.*

The Accountant succeeds the President, next to him is the Store-keeper, and to him the Purser Marine. These four constitute the Council, among whom the President has a double Vote; and all Cases and Affairs relating to the Company, or their Servants, are debated and determin'd by them.

*Advancements according to every ones standing.*

The Secretary, tho' none of the Council, yet always attends their Orders and Consultations, and stands Candidate for the first Vacancy among them; to which all are gradually advanc'd according to the Seniority of their time or Station; except the Authority of the Company interposes in their Earlier Exaltation, which they seldom attempt, because as the other method is most equitable, so they find it most suitable to their Affairs and Interest.

[1] Ar. *Hammām*, a Turkish bath.

The Chaplain, who is respected as third in the Factory, the Senior and Junior Factors, the Writers and Apprentices make up the rest. These all remain in their various Stations, for three or five Years, or as many as they and the Company have agreed upon at their first coming out, before they rise to new Degrees, as from Apprentice to Writer, from Writer to Factor. And every step they take in Promotion, the Company raises their Salary, and allows them some new Privilege. They all have given to them their Diet and Lodging gratis by the Company, besides Wages, and the advantagious liberty of Trafick to all parts, wherein from *China* to *Suratt*, they commonly make *Cent per Cent*; they can sometimes make 50 *per Cent.* from thence, if they only carry out Silver and bring home Gold: And those among them that are Persons of Credit and Esteem, but of small Fortunes, may borrow from the *Bannians* Money for *China* at 25 *per Cent.* and that only to be paid upon the safe Arrival of the Ship, which if it miscarries in the Voyage, they are exempt from all damage. To some parts their Gains amount to more, to some they are less, according to the distance of Ports, and opportunities of Trade.

*Several Peons main-tain'd by the Company.*

For dispatching of the Companies Affairs, and attending on the President and Council, there are kept always in the Companies Pay, Forty or Fifty Peons,[1] who wait daily upon the President in the Morning, that they may receive his Commands for the Service of the Day; and appear before him in a Body in the Evening, to pay him their Homage, who then (at his pleasure) with a Nodd dismisses them to their Homes in the City. Besides these, the President is allowed for his personal Attendance several others, the Accountant or second is allowed two, the Minister, and the rest of the Council, and the Secretary, each of them one.

The whole Business and Concern of all is zealously to promote the Honour and Interest of the Companies Affairs, in maintaining their Reputation, and vending their Commodi-

[1] Port. *peão*, 'footman', an orderly, messenger; cf. 'pawn'.

ties at as high Rates, and buying for them others at as low as they can.

*The Salaries and Wages of the Companies Servants.*

The President and all the rest of the Society are paid their Salaries once a Year; the Second 120*l.* the Senior Factors who are of the Council, 40*l.* the Junior Factors 15*l.* the Writers 7*l.* Besides which, the Council and Secretary have several advantagious Perquisites belonging to their places. The Peons receive their Wages every Month, which are four Roupics to each, and six to their Captain. At the beginning of the Month they give their Attendance, and respect; address themselves first to the Moon, and then to the President, who then appoints the Steward to discharge their Accounts.

*The honesty of the Peons.*

Lest any thing of value might be lost in the Factory, thro' this multitude of Peons who are called to their Service there continually, the Butlers are injoin'd to take an account of the Plate each Night before they depart home, that they might be examin'd before they stir, if ought be wanting. But their Honesty is our security from being damag'd by any Theft, which has not been charg'd upon them in the Factory these many Years: Nay, such is the approved Honesty and Fidelity of these Servants to our Affairs, that whenever the President designs to run the Custom of a considerable Sum of Gold or Silver, he commits the secret to some of these Peons, who manage it dextrously, and are Faithful to a Roupic.

*None permitted to lie without the Factory.*

Without Liberty from the President, none are permitted to leave the Factory, to lie abroad, or depart into the Country; and the Porter who attends the Gate both Day and Night, keeps all from Entring into our Precincts, whose admittance he judges may not be proper. But each *Thursday* Night he craves leave of going home, because he is a *Moorman* and Married, and he fears that the neglecting a Visit to his Wife for more than a Week, might give an occasion of Complaint. Therefore on this Night the Poor Men that beg in the Streets commonly do it in the prevailing Stile of *Jimroot sab, Jimroot sab*;[1] intimating as much as, Sir, since this is *Thursday* Night, let me (I pray you) partake something of

[1] *Jum'ā rāt* (Urdu), Thursday.

your Bounty, as a means the better to inable my Kindness to my Wife.

*A publick Table.* Each Day there is prepar'd a Publick Table for the Use of the President and the rest of the Factory, who sit all down in a publick place according to their Seniority in the Companies Service. The Table is spread with the choicest Meat *Suratt* affords, or the Country thereabouts; and equal plenty of generous *Sherash* Wine, and *Arak* Punch, is serv'd round the Table. Several hundreds a Year are expended upon their daily Provisions which are sumptuous enough for the Entertainment of any Person of Eminence in the Kingdom; and which require two or three Cooks, and as many Butchers to dress and prepare them. But *Europe* Wines and *English* Beer, because of their former Acquaintance with our Palates, are most coveted and most desirable Liquors, and tho' sold at high Rates, are yet purchased and drunk with pleasure. A Wealthy *Indian* who was curious to see our manner of Eating, and desirous to please himself with the Pride of our Entertainments, was strangely amaz'd and surpriz'd at the opening of a Bottle of Bottled Drink, when he saw it froth and fly about. The President askt him what it was that struck him with such Admiration? which was not, he told him, the sight of the Drink flying out of the Bottle, but how such Liquor could ever be put in.

*The President and Council only meet at Supper.* The President and Council only meet at Supper, for the maintenance of a Friendly Correspondence, and to discourse of the Companies Business, and prevent all Jealousies and Animosities which might obstruct the publick Affairs from that Progress, which a joint Unanimous Affection might carry them on with. For the Current of the common Interest has been sometimes very much lessen'd and diverted by the unhappy Intervention of private misunderstandings and Quarrels. And tho' it has been a repeated Contrivance of some leading Men, to play their Servants in *India* one against another, and to set them as Spies of each others Actions, yet I'm sure the publick Affairs have suffer'd when the Design has been unmask'd, and the Jealous Eye has been awaked.

For nothing vexes a Man of Honour, and who is conscious of his own Integrity more, than to find himself suspected of Dishonesty, and Designs laid by those to intrap him in his Actions, who have the least Reason in the World to distrust his Fidelity.

Both before and after Meals, a Peon appointed for that purpose, attends with a large Silver Ewer and Bason, for those that sit down to wash their Hands; which at both times is a Decency in all places, but here necessary, because of the Heat and Dust which are so very troublesome. All the Dishes and Plates brought to the Table are of pure Silver, massy and Substantial; and such are also the Tosses[1] or Cups out of which we drink. And that nothing may be wanting to please the Curiosity of every Palate at the times of Eating, an *English*, *Portuguese*, and an *Indian* Cook, are all entertain'd to dress the Meat in different ways for the gratification of every Stomach. Palau,[2] that is Rice boil'd so artificially, that every grain lies singly without being clodded together, with Spices intermixt, and a boil'd Fowl in the middle, is the most common *Indian* Dish; and a dumpoked[3] Fowl, that is, boil'd with Butter in any small Vessel, and stuft with Raisons and Almonds, is another. Cabob,[4] that is, Bief or Mutton cut into small pieces, sprinkled with Salt and Pepper, and dipt with Oil and Garlick, which have been mixt together in a Dish, and then roasted on a Spit, with sweet Herbs put between every piece, and stuft in them, and basted with Oil and Garlick all the while, is another *Indian* Savory Dish. Bambou and Mangoe Achar, Souy the choicest of all Sawces,[5] are always ready to whet the Appetite. The Natives at *Suratt* are much taken with *Assa Fœtida*, which they call Hin,[6] and

*All the Dishes and Plates pure Silver.*

*Several sorts of* Indian *Dishes.*

[1] Pers. *tās*, a cup.

[2] *pilāv*, a dish of rice and stewed meat; cf. pp. 130, 151.

[3] Pers. *dampukht*, 'air-cooked', baked, a boned and stuffed fowl.

[4] Hind. *kabāb*, 'roast'.

[5] Pers. *āchār*, 'pickle'. Soy is a sauce made of the Soy bean, *Soya hispida*.

[6] *Hing*, asafœtida; cf. p. 183, note 1.

mix a little of it with the Cakes that they eat, which tho' very unpalatable and unsavoury, yet because they esteem it beyond all things healthful, the *English* are tempted sometimes to taste it. The whole City sometimes smells very strong of the nauseating Vapours which flow from that abundance that is eat in it.

*The Great Entertainments on publick Days.*

Upon *Sundays* and publick Days, the Entertainments keep up a Face of more Solemnity, and are made more large and splendid, Deer and Antilopes, Peacocks, Hares, Partridges, and all kind of *Persian* Fruits, Pistachoes, Plumbs, Apricocks, Cherries, *&c.* are all provided upon high Festivals; and *European* as well as *Persian* Wines are drunk with Temperance and Alacrity. Then the King's Health, and afterwards that of the Companies, are sent round the Table to the lowest Writer that sits down. When the Banquett is past, they generally divert themselves for a while with some Innocent easie Recreation.

*The state the President goes abroad in.*

The President upon Solemn Days generally invites the whole Factory abroad to some pleasant Garden adjacent to the City, where they may sit shaded from the Beams of the Sun, and refresht by the Neighbourhood of *Tanques* and Water-works. The President and his Lady are brought hither in Palanquins, supported each of them by six Peons, which carry them by four at once on their Shoulders. Before him at a little distance, are carried two large Flaggs, or *English* Ensigns, with curious *Persian* or *Arabian* Horses of State, which are of great value, Rich in their Trappings, and gallantly equipt that are led before him.

The Furniture of these, and several other Horses, whereon the Factors Ride, is very costly; the Saddles are all of Velvet richly Embroider'd, the Head-stalls, Reins, and Croupers are all cover'd with solid wrought Silver. The Captain of the Peons at this time ascends his Horse, and leads forty or fifty others after him, which attend the President on foot. Next the President follow the Council in large Coaches, all open, except their Wives are in them; the several Knobbs about them are all covered with Silver, and they are drawn by a

Pair of stately Oxen. After them succeed the rest of the Factors, either in Coaches, or Hackeries, or upon Horses, which are kept by the Company to accommodate their President, and People at these times, or whenever they fancy to take the Air. In this pompous Procession does the President, when he goes abroad, travel thro' the Heart of the City.

The Evenings and the Mornings being allay'd with moderate Breezes, and cool and temperate in respect of the Heat when the Sun is at the Height, invite the Factors daily almost to the Groves or Gardens near the Water side, there to spend an Hour or two with a Bottle of Wine, and cold Collation which they carry with them. And neither the Chaplain nor any of the Council stir without the Walls of the City without the attendance of four or five Peons upon the Coach. This creates a Respect from the Natives as they pass along, strikes them with a Regard to the *English* whenever they meet them; makes them value our Friendship, and place an Honour in our Intimacy and Acquaintance. The Probity and Grandeur of the *English* Living hath formerly rais'd the Presidency of *Suratt* to that Veneration and Esteem, among the Native Inhabitants, that it has Eclips'd the greatness of their own Government, by incouraging the Injur'd and Distress'd *Indians*, to apply themselves for Relief, rather to our President, than their Governour.

*The Natives respects to the* English *because of the state main-tain'd by them.*

The Factors when they eat at Home, do it after the *English* manner, but abroad they imitate the Customs of the *East* in lying round the Banquet upon the *Persian* Carpets which are spread upon the Ground, twenty or thirty Foot in length.

*The Factors sometimes eat lying.*

For the Buying and more advantagious disposing of the Company's Goods, there are Brokers appointed, who are of the *Bannian* Cast, skilled in the Rates and Value of all the Commodities in *India*. To these is allow'd three *per Cent.* for their Care and Trouble. And once a Year, which is their Grand Festival Season, called the *Dually*[1] time, they have a Custom, much like that of our New-Years-gifts, of presenting

*The Companies Brokers.*

*The Dually time.*

[1] Divāli, the Feast of Lamps, a great Hindu festival usually occurring in November.

the President and Council, the Minister, Surgeon, and all the Factors and Writers with something valuable, either in Jewels or Plate, Atlasses, or other Silks, according to the Respect which they owe to every Man's Station. Whereby the Young Factors besides their Salaries, Diet and Lodgings, are supplyed likewise with Cloaths sufficient for their Service a great part of the Year. Which things prevent their Necessity of any great Annual Expence, and happily contribute towards giving them a Life of Delight and Ease. Besides these Gratuities, the Minister and Surgeon seldom fail of the President's Bounty at the Christmas Season; and whenever there is occasion for either of their Services, they commonly meet with very liberal Returns.

*A Doctor and a Surgeon provided for the Factory.*

If either a Disease, or any unlucky Casualties should happen to any in the Factory, the President has provided an *Indian* Doctor of Physick, and an *English* Surgeon to take care of them. The Surgeon, whose Salary is about forty Pounds a Year, gains considerably too by his outward Practice and Traffick. And whatever Medicinal Drugs, or Unguents, Balsoms, or Spirits are thought necessary for prevention or healing of Diseases and Sores, they are presently acquir'd, and charg'd upon the Company's Account; that their Factors might in all things be nicely taken care of, and not destitute of any thing for the support of either Life or Health.

*A Minister of the Factory.*

And that their Souls might not be neglected amidst all this Affluence and Ease, and care of their Bodies, there is a stated Salary of an Hundred Pounds a Year appointed for a Minister, with Diet and convenient Lodgings, a Peon to attend him in his Chamber, and the command of a Coach, or Horse, at any time he thinks fit to use them. Besides many private Gifts from Merchants and Masters of Ships, who seldom fail of some valuable Oblation to him, or Rarity of the place they come from; and the noble large Gratuities which he constantly receives for officiating at Marriages, Baptisms, and Burials. And that nothing might be wanting to the making of either his Life happy, or his Function Venerable, he is injoin'd from all a civil Deference and Deportment, and a Precedence next to the second in the Factory. And indeed such is the constant obliging Carriage of all to a Man of his Character, that were he the Principal Man of the Province, or Primate of *Indoston*, he could not wish for more Respect.

*The Ministers Duty.*

The Minister is oblig'd to a publick Discourse once, and publick Prayers thrice on *Sunday*, and to read Prayers Morning and Evening in the Chappel, each other Day on the Week, *viz.* about six in the Morning, before the Factors are called forth to Business, and at Eight at Night, when all is past. He is ingag'd to Catechize all the Youth; to visit the subordinate Factories upon the Coast of *Malabar*, at *Carwar*, *Calicut*, *Ruttera*,[1] &c. and to give Instructions for their Administration of Divine Service in his Absence.

*The Chappel.*

The Chappel, where they meet at Prayers, is within the Factory, decently Embellisht, so as to render it both neat and solemn, without the Figure of any living Creature in it, for avoiding all occasion of Offence to the *Moors*, who are well pleas'd with the Innocence of our Worship.

For want of a Minister qualified for the Administration of Baptism among the *Dutch* at *Suratt*, they request that Favour from the *English*, who performs it for them in their Chappel; which at first sight might be very well taken for a Guard-Chamber, because they keep their Arms in it.

*The stately Burying places of the* Europeans.

The *English* and all the *Europeans* are priviledg'd with convenient Repositories for their Dead, within half a Mile of the City.[2] There they endeavour to outvie each other in

[1] Ruttera (Mal. *randu*, two; *tara*, village) is another name for Covalam in the Trivandrum division, Travancore State. It is 'a very small village port with a bay which affords a tolerably safe landing in the fine season. It is now used as a sanatorium. It was once the seat of an English factory.' *Travancore State Manual*, ed. 1906, iii. 583. Cf. *Madras Manual of Administration*, iii, *s.v.* Rand, Travancore.

[2] These curious and, to modern taste, ugly structures may still be seen by the visitor to Surat. They were evidently built in rivalry to the great tombs of the Mahommedans at Sarkej near Ahmedabad and other places. See Rawlinson, *British Beginnings in Western India*, Appendix I, p. 135, and *Bomb. Gaz.*, vol. ii (Surat and Broach), pp. 323 ff.

magnificent Structures and stately Monuments, whose large Extent, beautiful Architecture, and aspiring Heads, make them visible at a remote distance, lovely Objects of the sight, and give them the Title of the Principal Ornaments and Magnificencies about the City. The two most celebrated Fabricks among the *English*, set off with stately Towers and Minorets, are that which was Erected for Sir *John Oxonton*,[1] and the other for the Renown'd and Honourable President *Aungers*. The two most noted among the *Dutch*, is one, a noble Pile rais'd over the Body of the *Dutch* Commissary, who died about three Years ago;[2] and another less stately, but more fam'd; built by the order of a Jovial *Dutch* Commander, with three large Punch-Bowls upon the top of it, for the Entertainment and Mirth of his surviving Friends, who remember him there sometimes so much, that they quite forget themselves.[3]

[1] This is a curious slip. Ovington evidently refers to the tomb of the great Sir George Oxenden, President of Surat 1662–9, and of his brother Christopher, who died in 1659. Both repose in the same huge mausoleum. See Rawlinson, *British Beginnings*, Appendix I, pp. 135 ff. and illustrations. For an account of the funeral, see Streynsham Master in Yule Hedges' *Diary*, ii, cccv, quoted in Rawlinson, *op. cit.*, p. 134. Gerald Aungier, the founder of Bombay, succeeded Sir George Oxenden in 1669, and died 30 June 1677. His grave was originally without an inscription. It has now been conjecturally identified and a marble tablet to this effect has been affixed. *Prog. Report, A.S.W.I.*, 1916–17, p. 42.

[2] This is the gigantic pile erected over the remains of Baron van Reede, Commissary of the United Netherlands East India Company, who died on his way to Surat, 15 Dec. 1691.

[3] Ovington's humorous account of the Dutch tombs at Surat is evidently suggested by a passage in Thévenot, *Voyages aux Indes Orientales*, third ed., 1727, Amsterdam, vol. v, p. 71. Thévenot was a friend of Tavernier, and landed at Surat in January 1666. Ovington had evidently read him carefully.

'Il y en a une entr'autres d'un certain Beuveur qui avoit été relegué dans les Indes par les Etats Generaux, et qu'on disoit être parent du Prince d'Orange : On lui a élevé un monument comme aux autres gens de marque; mais pour faire connoître qu'il savoit bien boire, l'on a mis au haut de sa pyramide une grande tasse de pierre, et une au bas à chaque coin du Tombeau, et auprès de chaque tasse il y a la figure d'un pain de sucre; et quand les Hollan-

Lest all the Care and Instruction of a Minister might be inavailable for reclaiming the Dissolute and Refractory among the *English*, the Company have interpos'd their own Authority, and publisht their Orders and Injunctions in these following words.

*The Governour, Deputy, and Committees of the* East-India *Company, having been inform'd of the disorderly and Unchristian Conversation of some of their Factors and Servants in the parts of* India, *tending to the dishonour of God, the discredit of the Gospel of our Lord Jesus Christ, and the shame and Scandal of the* English *Nation; And being desirous, as much as in them lies, for the future to prevent the like, and reduce all their People in their several Factories and Colonies, not only to a Civil, but also to a Religious and Pious Comportment, that may render our Nation Honourable, and the Religion we profess amiable in the sight of those Heathens, among whom they reside: Have thought fit to require and enjoin a strict observation of the ensuing Rules and Orders, to which they do expect from all their Factors and Servants a due compliance.* *The Company's Instructions.*

Then after some Rules enjoining a strict Observance of *Sundays*, and of publick and private Prayers, this follows.

*That the Agents and Chiefs in their several Factories, take care to prevent all prophane Swearing, and taking the Name of God in vain by cursed Oaths; all Drunkenness and Intemperance, all Fornication and Uncleanness; and that if any will not be Reform'd, and do not abstain from these Vices, but after Admonition and Reprehension, shall be found faulty again, that then such Punishment shall be inflicted on them, consisting with the Laws of God and this Kingdom, as the Agent and Council shall find their Crime to deserve. And that if after such Punishment inflicted, he or they will not amend, or be reform'd, then the Agent is strictly enjoin'd and requir'd, to send home for* England *by the next Ships, such Person or Persons so unre-*

dois vont se divertir auprès de cette Sepulture, ils font cent ragoûts dans ces tasses, et se servent d'autres plus petites tasses pour tirer ce qu'ils ont appreté dans ces grandes, afin de le boire ou de le manger.' The punch-bowls have now disappeared.

*claimable, that they may not remain in* India, *to the dishonour of God, the Scandal of Religion, the discredit of our Nation, and perverting of others.*

And that both the Company and their Servants may be constantly blest with the Favours of Heaven upon them in their respective Stations, therefore they have ordered a Form of Prayer to be used daily in their Factories, for the obtaining a common Blessing upon them all; which is as follows,

*The Prayer for the Company.*

*O Almighty and most Merciful God, who art the Sovereign Protector of all that Trust in thee, and the Author of all Spiritual and Temporal Blessings, we thy unworthy Creatures do most humbly implore thy goodness for a plentiful Effusion of thy Grace upon our Employers, thy Servants, the Right Honourable* East-India *Company of* England. *Prosper them in all their publick Undertakings, and make them famous and successful in all their Governments, Colonies, and Commerce both by Sea and Land; so that they may prove a publick Blessing by the increase of Honour, Wealth and Power to our Native Country, as well as to themselves. Continue their Favours towards us, and inspire their Generals, Presidents, Agents and Councils in these remote parts of the World, and all others that are intrusted with any Authority under them, with Piety towards thee our God, and with Wisdom, Fidelity and Circumspection in their several Stations; That we may all discharge our respective Duties faithfully, and live Virtuously, in due Obedience to our Superiours, and in Love, Peace and Charity one towards another: That these* Indian *Nations among whom we dwell, seeing our sober and righteous Conversation, may be induc'd to have a just esteem for our most holy Profession of the Gospel of our Lord and Saviour Jesus Christ, to whom be Honour, Praise and Glory, now and for ever.* Amen.[1]

[1] This prayer may be Ovington's own work. At a meeting of the Court, on 16 December 1698, we find: 'The titles were read of three prayers for this Company—one to be used at home, another to be used in their factories abroad, and a third to be used on board their ships—approved by His Grace the Archbishop of Canterbury and the Lord Bishop of London. Ordered that 1,000 of the said three prayers be printed and that Mr Ovington supervise the press.' Introduction, p. xiii.

# THE TROUBLES

## Which the English Suffer'd from the Moors at Suratt, in the Years 1691, 1692.[1]

*AUGUST* the 27*th* 1691. All the *English* in the Factory of *Suratt* were under a close Confinement from the *Moors* Governour of the City, and surrounded with a Guard of Horse and Foot. Nor were the *French* or *Dutch* permitted to pass without the Walls. The occasion of it was a Report spread abroad, that a Rich *Moor*-ship belonging to one *Abdel Gheford*,[2] was taken by *Hat-men*,[3] that is, in their Dialect, *Europeans*; and therefore 'till Restitution is made by them of nine Lacks of Roupies, which exceeds the value of 100000 *l.* Sterling, no liberty must be granted. The Ship was in her Passage from *Mocha* to *Suratt*, and tho' the *Indians* were averse from Fighting, or hazarding their Lives for four Roupies a Month, yet the *Turks*, who had a valuable Cargo of Goods on Board, behav'd themselves with redoubted Valour, 'till after the loss of some of their Lives, they were overpower'd by Men, and forc'd to surrender.

*The Confinement of the* English.

*The occasion of it.*

The Accusation run against all the *Europeans*, because the Pirate shew'd both *English*, *French*, and *Dutch* Colours, and a Restitution was expected from them all; especially too,

*All the* Europeans *Accus'd.*

[1] The imprisonment of the Surat factors by the Mogul authorities as reprisals for the conduct of interlopers and pirates who seized their ships was a perennial occurrence. Bartholomew Harris was actually in prison when called upon, 4 February 1690, to succeed Child, because Child had seized some Mogul shipping. He and his companions were released in April of the same year, only to be once more imprisoned in August 1691. The factors were again in trouble in 1695–6, owing to the depredations of the notorious pirate Avery. This led to the decline of English interest in Surat, for the Company now determined to make themselves an independent power at Bombay. See Forrest, *Selections from State Papers*, Home Series, vol. i, p. xxiii, Introd., and *infra*, p. 271.

[2] Abdul Ghafur.

[3] Hind. *Topi vālā.*

because the *Moor*-ship which was taken, sailed from *Suratt* River with all their several Passes.

*The* English *Presidents Defence.* Our Honourable President *Bartholomew Harris* made his Defence to the Governour after this manner. That for the certainty of the Fact, tho' it might be disputable, because our grand Accuser *Abdel Gheford* had been found formerly faulty in such a case, wherein he suborn'd a Multitude of Sailers, who afterwards confest his Bribery and their Perjury; yet admitting it true, he thought it unreasonable for us to be charg'd any more with the payment of Money taken by the *Pirates* at Sea, than the *Mogul* is for Robberies at Land. However thus far he will ingage his Honour for satisfaction of the Piracy, if it can be fairly prov'd, that the Ship belong'd to his Master, the *East-India* Company.

*The Governours Letter to the* Mogul. The Old Governour finding the *Mogul*'s Customs begin to sink, by reason of the Embargo, which was as well upon our Ships, as our selves; and knowing that the Advancement of them was the great Instrument of his Promotion; and unable to remonstrate any thing material to our Presidents Reasons, directs a Letter to *Aureng-Zebe* to this effect. That since the late Wars the *English* Merchants at *Suratt* have traded fairly, and liv'd peaceably; that much of the Money due to the Merchants upon the Accounts of the Wars was already paid, and the rest would follow; and that for the Pirates at Sea, they were neither Authoriz'd by the Company, nor were they within the reach of their Command: All which things might justly plead the Innocence of the *English*, excuse their payment of any Money, and give them therefore a Release. But the exasperated *Turks*, and the violent *Abdel-Gheford* prevail'd for a closer Confinement of us, not only to the Walls of the Factory, but our very Chambers, had not the vigilant Industry of our President opportunely repealed that severe Decree. Our Enemies, likewise, incessantly urg'd the Governour to menace and disturb our President, that he might be thereby wrought upon to their Designs. To which the sage Governour mildly reply'd, That he knew Mr. *Harris* too well, to value any Threatnings which were Injurious to the Com-

*The Governours Character of the* English *President.*

pany's Interest or Honour; and that tho' he suffer'd much, he would endure much more, rather than yield to an unjust Compliance.

*The* Turks *threaten the Lives of the* English.

The inraged *Turks* finding their Machines would not work, and that they could get no ground upon us this way, began now to threaten our Lives, because the loss of our Liberty did not appease them, so much that the Governour as he formerly set a Guard upon us to shut us in, now increases it to keep our Enemies out.

*The* Turks *private Discords.*

In the mean time, the Providence of God so contriv'd for our Innocence, that the *Turks* began to clash among themselves, and heated with some private Dissentions, became their own Accusers. For some of them came to *Dungevora*,[1] a famous *Persy* Merchant, and Friend to the *English*, and inform'd him that all their Allegations against us were built upon Falsehood and Malice, and their Charge was all a contriv'd Design, in as much as they were all satisfied in their own Minds, that the *Pyrates* were *Danes*, and not *English*. But this they durst not discover to the Governour, for fear of a publick Examination, which if they submitted to, their lives would be exposed to the Fury of the rest of the Confederates. Neither durst we encourage them with any Present of Money to proceed in their Depositions, lest we should find it a Stratagem of theirs, thereby to insnare us.

*The* Danes *found to be the Pirates.*

*November* the 1*st*. arriv'd a Pattamar or *Courrier*, from our Fakeel,[2] or Solliciter at Court, acquainting us that the *Mogul* had News from the *Danes* themselves, of their taking and plundering the *Moor*-Ship, and that they resolv'd upon a continued Enmity to the *Moors*, 'till their Demands were fully satisfied for the Injuries which they formerly sustain'd from them. The Letter was directed to *Isa Cooly*,[3] Principal of the *Armenian* Merchants at Court, who by making a noise, which is the method for obtaining Audience, was called upon by the *Mogul*, to read his Letter upon a publick Court day.

[1] Danji Vora. [2] Arab. *Vakīl*, an attorney. [3] Isa Quli,

*The Mogul's Letters for our release.* This brought down the *Mogul*'s Letters to the Governour, requiring a speedy Respect and Civility to the *English*, with a permission and Encouragement of Trade. But the Pishcashes[1] or Presents expected by the *Nabobs* and *Omrahs* retarded our Inlargement for some time notwithstanding. For

*The Reason of the English's longer Confinement.* the strong Contest and Application which was made for the Government of *Suratt*, which was then said to be dispos'd of, put a stop to the Emperours more absolute determinations. The *Mogul*'s Resolution of continuing the present Governour, frustrated all the Court Interests for themselves, which mov'd *Salabet Chan*,[2] a Bosom Favourite, to wave the Solicitations he had begun for his Son, and end them for the Governour. For he design'd to send his Son to *Suratt*, Invested with the Command of the City, and the Messenger of this welcom News to us, which would render him thereupon more acceptable to the *English* Nation, and would be apt to gain him some costly Present from us at his Entrance upon his Authority.

*The English released.* Therefore *December* the 2*d*. in the Evening, word was brought by the Brokers to our President, of a *Cosset*'s[3] Arrival with Letters from Court to the *Vacinavish*,[4] injoyning our immediate Release; and the day following the *Chocadars*[5] or Souldiers, were remov'd from before our Gates.

*A generous Arab.* *Sheak Jemme*,[6] a brave and hearty *Arab*, who had all along wisht Prosperity to our Affairs, was so transported at the hearing of our Inlargement, that he gave to the President's

[1] Pers. *pesh-kash*, a present.

[2] Salābat Khān. He was the son of a nobleman who held the office of *Mir Bakhshi* or Paymaster-General in the time of the Emperor Shāh Jāhān, and was stabbed in the presence of the Emperor by a Rajput chief, named Amar Singh Rathor, son of Gaj Singh, on the evening of Thursday, 25 July, A.D. 1644, in the Fort of Agra. Amar Singh was pursued and cut down near one of the gates of the Fort, which is called after his name the Amar Singh Gate.

[3] Arab. *kāsid*, a courier.

[4] Arab. *vākiahnavīs*, news-writer, intelligencer. Cf. p. 137.

[5] Hind. *chokīdār*, a night-watchman.

[6] Shaikh Jammu.

Peon, who carried him the News of it, a rich flower'd Coat.[1] And when this generous *Arab* was called upon by one of the *Mullahs* or Priests, and authoritatively demanded why he would countenance the *Cafries*,[2] or Unbelievers, meaning us, against the *Musoulmen*, or true Believers? Bravely answer'd that it was his principle to Encourage Truth wherever he found it; and that he knew the *English* innocent of the Fact, which the *Turks* insisted upon against them. That none were so much *Cafries*, in his Opinion, as those that were false in their Words, and Dishonest in their Actions, and that the best Believers should always act the best things.

*The second Confinement of the* English.

*The Reason of it.*

In *September* the Year following, which was 1692, did *Abdel-Gheford*, our Old Implacable Adversary, revive his Enmity, upon a Report he forg'd, that some of his Ships from *Mocha* were seiz'd on by some *English* Pirates; and upon this pretence, secur'd us in our Factory under a Guard of *Chokadars*, 'til the latter end of *October*. The Governour upon this sent for the *English, Dutch, and French* Presidents, the two latter of which disputed that Precedence which they allow'd to the *English*, but the *French*, unwilling to raise any Contest in the Governours Presence, immediately departed. He insisted upon a Restitution for the Damages which were sustain'd by *Abdel-Gheford*, and menac'd them with a Prohibition of Traffick. Which they told him they were willing to relinquish, rather than be liable to the Payment of such unjust Demands.

Abdel-Gheford's *baseness to the* English *discover'd.*

The Villany of *Abdel-Gheford*, and the Baseness of his Actions were after a while made apparent to the whole City. For part of the Money which he charg'd upon us, was convey'd from on Board his Ship, into a Garden near that of *Nocha Damus*'s[3] by the River side. Four Thousand Checkins[4] he privately tyed to the Flooks of an Anchor under Water; and some he hid within his Tanques on Board, and

[1] Arab. *khil'at*, a robe of honour.
[2] Arab. *kafar*, pl. *kofra*, an infidel.
[3] Nava Dumas, a village near the mouth of the Tapti.
[4] Sequin, a Venetian gold coin worth four rupees.

in the Ballast of his Ship. The rest was put privately into a Palanquin, which the Souldiers observ'd to sway very heavily as it past the Gates, and searching it upon the mistrust, found the Gold in it. So the Injury he would have laid upon us, was fixt with a scandalous Note of Infamy upon himself; and we were before *November*, fortunately released.

*The Releasement of the* English.

I shall now take leave of these Misfortunes, which in some measure compensate for their Uneasiness, by the Pleasure which they afford in a Relation; and before I proceed to *Cape Bone Esperance* in *Africa*, will make some stay in *Arabia Felix*, in a Description of two of the most Fam'd Emporys and other parts of that Kingdom, *viz. Muscatt* upon the *Persian* Gulf, and *Mocha* which lies upon the *Red-Sea*.

# THE CITY OF MUSCATT[1]

## IN ARABIA FELIX.

*The Situation of* Muscatt.

*MUSCATT* is a City in *Arabia Felix,* which lies to the *Eastward* of that Kingdom, situated upon the *Persian* Gulf. Tho' none of the *Arabia's* are equally fruitful as many other parts of the World that are less fam'd, yet this part of *Arabia,* because of its Pleasantness and Fertility, in respect of the other two, has obtain'd the name of *Hyaman,*[2] which signifies Happy. For besides the great increase of Cattle which is here to be seen; the Soil in some places is Rich and Fruitful, and Corn and Wine, Fruits and fragrant Spices are produc'd in great plenty. It abounds with many useful and Beneficial Commodities, with several kinds of Druggs, with Balsom and Myrrhe, Incense, Cassia, Manna, Dates, Gold, Frankincense and Pearl, and maintains a constant Trade of rare and valuable Goods to *Persia, Egypt, Syria,* the *Indies,* &c. And *Muscatt* above all those places which are situated near the Gulf of *Ormus,* is the Principal Town of Traffick between the *East,* and that part of *Arabia the Happy*; only at one Season of the Year, which is in *June, July* and *August,* the Pearl-Fishing of the Island *Baharem,*[3] which lies higher up in the Gulf, renders that place of more Note and Fame, yielding to the *Persian* Emperour yearly, the value of Five hundred Thousand Ducats,[4] besides one hundred thousand more, which are suppos'd to be diverted.

Arabian *Goods.*

[1] Maskat, the capital of Omān, on the sea-coast, 23° 40′ N., 58° 25′ E., is an ancient town, perhaps the Moscha of the *Periplus.* Its importance began with the Portuguese occupation (1508–85).

[2] Yemen, the 'right-hand', i.e. lucky or fortunate land,—Arabia Felix (δεξιός, εὐδαίμων).

[3] The Bahrein Islands.

[4] So called from the inscription *Sit tibi Christe datus quem tu regis iste ducatus.* See Roberts, *Merchant's Mapp of Commerce,* 1638, whence we infer that there were two ducats, worth 3*s.* 4*d.* and 4*s.* 2*d.* respectively.

Muscatt lies under the Tropick. *Muscatt* is Situate between the Capes of *Raz al-Gate* and *Moccandon*[1] in 23 Degrees, 30 Min. *North* Latitude, exactly under the Tropick of *Cancer*. 'Tis about three Miles in its *Its Extent.* Circumference, built at the bottom of a small Bay, encompassed with high Rocky Mountains, and guarded with a strong Wall. Besides it is fortifyed with five or six Castles and Batteries, and lies very convenient for Trade by its nearness to a safe Harbour.

*The great Heat here.* Tho' this City lies at the utmost Bounds of the Suns progress towards the *North*, yet it is infested with a more intense Heat than several places that are nearer the Line. The Desart Ground and high Mountains reflect the warm Rays of the Sun with so much vigour, that it may as justly challenge a Title to the name of the *Torrid Zone*, as any place between the Tropicks; for some would perswade us that it has a Title to the most literal meaning of these words, and that a small Fish laid in the hollow part of a Rock, where the Sunbeams reflect from every side, in the heat of the Day, and when the Sun is in the *Zenith*, will be half Roasted in a little time by the Heat. *Rains fall seldom.* It rains here but seldom, and in some places of *Arabia*, not above twice or thrice in two or three Years; but the abundance of Dew which falls at Night refreshes the Ground, supplies the Herbs with Moisture, and makes the Fruits excellent.

*The nature of the Inhabitants.* The *Muscatters* (for the most part) are lean, and of a middle Stature, very swarthy in their Complexion, and not of very strong Voice. They are stout and manly, and expert at the Bow and Dart, and since their ingagement in the War with the *Portuguese*, are excellent Marks-men, and very dexterous and ready in the exercise of Fire-Arms, in which they Employ always some part of the Day.

The Ground yields them variety of excellent Fruits, as Oranges, Lemons, Citrons, Grapes, Apricocks and Peaches, *Dates the chief Commodity.* and most sorts of Roots and green Herbs: But the Staple Commodity of the Country is Dates, of which there are whole Orchards of some Miles together. They have so much plenty

[1] Ras el Hadd and Ras Musandin are apparently meant.

of this Fruit, for which they have so ready a vent in *India*, that several Ships are sent thither loaded from hence without any other Cargo.

The Hills are generally all steril and bare, and he that takes only a prospect of them would conclude the Land quite uninhabitable, and unable to afford either sustenance for Man or nourishment for Beast. For the Soil there languishes for want of Moisture, and the ground is dried up like a barren Wilderness; the Earth brings forth neither Grass nor Flowers, nor Trees with either Leaves or Fruit. But casting his Eyes down into the Valleys, he sees them all flourishing and green, and cover'd with Vegetables fit for the Pleasure and Refreshment of Animals, and very Beautiful to Admiration. There are Arable Fields and green Pastures, Fruit-Trees that look neither wither'd nor faded; nothing there is Barren or Unprofitable, but bountiful Nature compensates with the fruitfulness of the Valleys for the nakedness of the Hills; so that here, if upon their Topps, a Man would be apt to think himself among the *Lybian* Wastes; yet let him but descend lower, and he would fancy himself in the pleasant Fields of *Tempe*. All this is due to the Industry of the People, who for want of Rains, are forc'd to water their Gardens every Morning and Evening, by the labour of the Ox, who draws the Water twice a day to the Root of every Tree in their Gardens. There are several Channels cut out in the ground for the Water to run thro', and at the Banks of these Canals, the Trees are Planted near the Water for Moisture and Nourishment of the Roots, which together with the Mists that descend in the Night time, preserve them fresh, and green, and very Fruitful.

*The Hills are bare.*

*The Valleys fruitful.*

*The Watering their Trees.*

Having spoke thus much of *Arabia* in general, of the Extent and Situation of *Muscatt*, and the quality of its Climate, of the Stature and Complexion of the Inhabitants, and nature of the Soil thereabouts; I will now relate one thing observable concerning the Food of their Cattle, and will then proceed to an Account of the Temperance and Justice of the *Arabians* of *Muscatt*, for which two things they are more remarkable than any other Nation this day in the World.

*Fish the Food of their Cattle.*

Their Cattle here are fed with Fish, which is a sort of Food that seems as Unnatural for them as for Fish to live upon Grass, which is the proper Meat for Cattle. But the Fish which they eat is not fresh, and just taken out of the Sea, but when a great quantity of it is caught, the *Muscatters* dig a large Hole in the Ground wherein they put it, 'till it remains so long that it rotts and comes to a kind of Earth. After this it is taken up, and boil'd with Water in great Earthen Pots, which makes a kind of thick Broth; and standing 'till it is cool, it is then given to the Cattle, by which they grow extreme Fat, and yet their Flesh is very savory, not tainted with either an ill Taste or Smell.

*The Food of the Natives.*

The Inhabitants of *Muscatt* feed promiscuously upon either Fish or Flesh; they eat Beef, Mutton, Goat and Deer, and the Flesh of Camels is admir'd by them, and is in repute for a Healthful sort of Meat. But they are very nice and curious in killing those Animals on which they feed, and which they refuse to taste 'till the Meat is cleans'd and washt from the Blood.[1] They abound too in many sorts of Fish, and are scrupulous in Eating of some kinds of them, such especially as have no Scales, from whieh they totally refrain, and esteem the Food of such as well as of Blood, an Abomination. The Soil affords abundance of Wheat, which might be properly made use of for their Bread, but the Dates are so plentiful, so pleasant and admir'd, that they mix them with all their Food, and eat them instead of Bread, through all these parts of *Arabia*, both with their Fish and Flesh.

*The great Abstinence of the Natives.*

But of all the Followers of *Mahomet*, and zealous Admirers of his four principal Doctors, *Abu Becre*, *Osman*, *Omar* and *Hali*,[2] none are so rigidly Abstemious as the *Arabians* of *Muscatt*, as well from the Juice of the Grape, as other more

[1] The reference is to the *halāl*, or ritual for slaying and bleeding an animal to be used for food.

[2] The reference is to the first four Khalīfas or Successors of the Prophet: Abu Bakr, Omar, Othman, and Ali.

common and innocent Liquors. For Tea and Coffee which are judg'd the privileg'd Liquors of all the *Mahometans*, as well *Turks*, as those of *Persia*, *India*, and other parts of *Arabia*, are condemn'd by them as unlawful Refreshments, and abominated as Bug-bear Liquors, as well as Wine. He that would turn Advocate for any of these sorts of Drink, and commend the Use of them as convenient for their Stomachs, as fit to chear their Hearts, and chase away Melancholy from their Spirits, would be look'd upon as a vile Contemner of their Law, and an Encourager of Libertinism and Intemperance. They abhor likewise the smoaking of Tobacco, and the warm intoxicating Fumes of that *Indian* Weed, and constantly burn all that they can find brought into their Country. Sugar, Water, and Orange mixt together, which they call Sherbet,[1] is their only Drink; such is their Antipathy to all Liquors that are warm and strong, that in perfect Indignation they rased a *Jews* House to the ground, that had only made some strong Waters. Therefore they call themselves the strict *Arabs*, the Chaste *Mahometans*, the only true Professors of the *Mussulman*-Law, and genuine followers of the Prophet. To this degree of Abstinence they are all bred up, who are Natives of this Region hereabouts; thus they abstain from all those sensible gratifications of their Palates, which may any way inebriate their Faculties, and render the Mind dull and unactive; and shun the Taste of any thing that may disturb their Person, or raise up in them any irregular Appetites.

*Their Extraordinary Justice and Civility.*

Nor is the Justice and Civil Conversation of the *Arabians* at *Muscatt*, less remarkable and to be admir'd, than their extreme Temperance and Sobriety. The Governour of the City, who is nearly related to the King of the Country, takes care that a strict Watch be kept in the Castle every Night, for the safety of the City, and prevention of all Disorders that might happen. And will not allow any Boat to go, or come ashore,

[1] Arab. *sharbat*, draught, corresponding to our 'lemon-squash', the only beverage of its kind permitted to the orthodox Mahommedan.

or to row from Ship to Ship, either before the Sun rises, or after it is down; to the end that all that Traffick may do their Business while it is Day, that no man might dispose of his Goods secretly, and shelter himself by the obscurity of the Night.

*No private Correction in Families.*

They forbid all Despotick Authority in private Families, and the Arbitrary proceedings of either Masters or Parents towards their Domesticks. So that if either a Child or a Servant chance to transgress, let the Crime be what it will, either more heinous, or less villanous, Publick Justice must determine the Punishment, and the Magistrates must interpose in awarding the Penalty, and no man must lift up his Hand to punish any that offends in his own Family. By this Oeconomy in their Affairs, the Inferiours are freed from the violence of all Splenitick Disgusts, and unreasonable Severities of their Superiours. A Revengeful Master cannot vent his Passion at his Pleasure upon his Servant, nor an unnatural Parent Beat and Chastise his Son at his will: Complaint must first be made to the Magistrates of the place, who being dispassionate and unprejudic'd in their Tempers, examin the matter with a still Mind, and Arbitrate calmly in the Case. No private Punishment is ever inflicted in *Muscatt* and the adjacent parts; they cannot there think that any Corrections are so equitable, as those that proceed from the deliberate Sentence of unbyassed Men.

*The way of punishing Malefactors.*

If Murther or Theft, or any such execrable Crime is at any time committed among them; which are seldomer here than in any other part of the World, the Malefactor is never Punished with sudden Death, nor does any fatal hand touch him, but his Sentence is, to be Immur'd, where he leasurely dies, between two Walls. For they hate by any violent direct Death, to take away the life of any Offender.

*Justice speedily administred.*

They are never dilatory in their Administrations of Justice, nor vex the Clients with tiresome Delays, but quickly determin in the Case, and dispatch all matters that are brought before them. The Governour with fifty or sixty more sit openly to the publick view, whenever they do justice, which is not by plurality of Voices, but all unanimously consent to the Sentence that is pronounced.

These *Arabians* are very courteous in their Deportment, and extreme Civil to all Strangers; they offer neither Violence nor Affront to any; and tho' they are very tenacious of their own Principles, and Admirers of their own Religion, yet do they never impose it upon any, nor are their Morals leven'd with such furious Zeal, as to divest them of Humanity, and a tender Respect. A Man may travel hundreds of Miles in this Country, and never meet with any abusive Language, or any Behaviour that looks Rude. And if you happen to be loaded with any Money in your Travels, you need no Arms to defend your Person, nor any Guards to secure your Purse; for you may sleep with it in your Hands in the open Fields, or lay it by you with safety as you repose your self in the King's High-way. Captain *Edward Say*, who had liv'd among them at *Muscatt* for several Years, and who affirm'd all this Relation to be really true, had passed from one part of the Country to another, some hundreds of Miles, and never was troubled by any Person, tho' he slept sometimes in the Roads and Fields, neither heard he of any that had been pillag'd by Robbers all that while.

*The extraordinary honesty of the* Arabians.

In fine, these are a People naturally Temperate and Just, and endued with those excellent Qualities which the *Grecian* Philosophers and *Roman* Moralists endeavour'd to inspire into their Subjects, tho' they miss'd of their aim. For these are directly opposite in their Temper and manner of Life to those wild *Arabs*, that haunt the Banks of *Tigris*, and sculk about near the River of *Euphrates*, that live by Rapine, spoil and violence. I shall relate only one remarkable Passage more, concerning the Justice and Kindness of these *Arabs*, and leave this Theme.

*The* Arabians *great kindness to Captain* Say, *after his Shipwrack.*

When the forementioned Captain *Say* had unluckily lost his Ship on the Island of *Macira*,[1] which is near this Coast of *Arabia*; he and his Mariners were so fortunate that they sav'd all their Lives, and got on Shoar, tho' naked and in a

[1] Masira, on the Hadramaut Coast, a long way south of Muscat.

very distress'd forlorn Condition. The sight of this deplorable Accident mov'd the *Arabs* to Pity and Compassion towards them, and made them offer their Service, by such Signs, as they thought might be most Intelligible, for assisting them in the Recovery of those Goods that were on board the Wrack. They were perfect strangers both of them to each others Persons and Language, and therefore one among the rest, who lookt like the Governour, rais'd a heap of Sand, as they sat near one another, upon the Shoar, which he divided into three parts, reserving two to himself, and offering the other to the Captain. But the Captain esteeming it unequally proportion'd, shook his Head, in token that he dislik'd the Bargain. The Governour seeing this, adjusted the matter with more equality, and divided the Heap of Sand into two parts only, one of which he took to himself, and gave the other half to the Captain; which because he thought it very fair, they shook Hands upon it, as a sign they were both well contented. The Money which was brought on Shoar, and saved from the Wraek, was twelve or fourteen Thousand Pounds, which they contriv'd to divide in this manner. They tyed to a Stick two Baskets instead of a pair of Scales, and made them as equipoize as they could, and by these they weighed each parcel that was brought off from the Ship with great exactness; if there appear'd any seeming advantage in either Ballance, the Governour forc'd that always upon the Captain, so that he was not injur'd one Mite, nor in all that Account lost a Farthing that was his Due. If the Inhabitants upon all the Coasts of *Europe* were as Hospitable and Just to all Persons of their own Perswasion, as these *Arabians* were to those of a strange Faith, and distant Nation, those that do narrowly escape with their Lives from the Dangers of the Sea, would not so often by a merciless People be barbarously depriv'd of them at Land. The King too in Compassion to his Miseries, requir'd only 2 *per Cent.* for his Goods, whilst he made other Strangers pay 4.

The *Portuguese* formerly were receiv'd by the *Arabians* at *Muscatt*, with abundance of Civility and Candor, and allow'd not only the freedom and Exercise of their Religion, but encourag'd to build a stately Church, and erect a College, and were no way stinted in the Profession of their Faith, and ostentation of their Pompous Worship. The King granted them the freedom of the Port, by which they grew very Powerful and Wealthy, and by that means Indulg'd themselves in Ease and Luxury, built many fair Houses in the City to dwell in, and at length began to be so Insolent and Unruly, that they openly abus'd that Civility which had entertain'd them so friendly, despis'd that Government by which they had been Protected, and endeavour'd to wrest the Authority out of the Hands of the Civil Magistrate, and set up their own instead of it. The *Arabs* who are naturally Civil and obliging, bore the repeated Insolencies with great Patience, and were loath to be drawn into any Quarrels or Debates with them, notwithstanding all this turbulent Carriage of the *Portuguese*; 'till allarm'd with the danger of their City, and unable to endure their Affronts any longer, the King himself appear'd in Person with a numerous Army of resolute *Arabs*, with whom he set down before the City. The *Portuguese* defended themselves against him with great Courage for a long time, and shut themselves up in their Church and College, which were converted into Cittadels for their Safeguard, because they were strong. But the *Arabs* at length blocking up all the Avenues whereby they might expect any Succour either by Sea or Land, and placing themselves upon heights which overlook'd the Fortifications of the Enemy, who receiv'd no Relief either from *Goa* or *Cong*,[1] as they expected; the *Portuguese* at length betook themselves privately to two or three of their Ships which lay in the Harbour, and made their Escape that way. The Holes of the Gun-shot which the *Arabs* made in the Church and College of

*The Reason of the War of the* Arabians *with the* Portuguese.

[1] Congo Bunder (Kang Bandar) was a famous mart for Bahrein pearls, where the Portuguese set up a factory after the fall of Ormuz. It is on the north shore of the Persian Gulf, about 100 miles west of Gombroon. Hamilton, *New Account*, (1744 edn.) i. 92 *seq.*

the *Portuguese*, during the time of the Siege, are yet visible. Since this Rebellion, there arose an invincible Hatred between these two Nations, that were thus at variance; so that they are always designing upon each others Lives and Estates where-ever they meet. The *Arabians* are a Stout, Couragious, Hardy Nation, and will in nothing, give place to the *Portuguese*, and generally are Victorious, and prevail against them as often as they Attack each other at Sea. The *Portuguese* are mightily sunk, as well in their Courage, as in their Fame and Fortune, and are found to be such contemptible Enemies, that they are seldom discours'd of, but with Reproach, by the name of *Gallina's*,[1] *i.e.* Hen-hearted Fellows. The *Arabs* carry in some of their Ships above 500 Men, go out in Fleets, and are so very strong in their Naval Forces, that the *Portuguese* generally endeavour to avoid them, and never dispute it with them but with great Advantage on their side.

*The* Arabs *kindness to their Enemies.*

All the Prisoners of War are made Slaves of on both sides; and those that are taken by the Inhabitants of *Muscatt*, are used so very kindly, that they are tempted almost to be in love with their Confinement, and are never us'd with any such Hardships, so as to be forct to attempt an Escape by Flight. They neither correct them like Slaves, nor impose upon them any servile work, but maintain them in Ease and Idleness, with a certain allowance of Provisions every day. Of such inconquerable Generosity are these *Arabians* even to their very Enemies! And tho' they sometimes perswade them to their own Faith, and to turn *Mahometans*, 'tis never but with Mildness, with gentle Allurements, and Hopes of Reward.

I will here insert a short Account of the taking of Captain *Edward Say* by the *Sanganians*,[2] who Inhabit a Country

[1] Terry repeats the gibe, '*Gallinas dell Mar*, the hens of the sea', *Voyage* (1777 edn.), p. 153. For Portuguese degeneracy, see Rawlinson, *British Beginnings in Western India*, pp. 16 ff.

[2] For the Sanganians, see p. 99, note 2. Another version of Captain Say's adventures is given in Hamilton, *New Account*, i. 56. His ship was the *Merchant's Delight*, and the date 1684.

opposite to the *Arabian* Shoar, and then pass over to the other Coast of *Arabia* the *Happy*, which borders upon the *Red Sea.*

This Commander, after his Shipwrack upon the Island *Macira*, and a tedious stay among the *Arabians* at *Muscatt*, set Sail from thence to the Island of *Bombay* in the Company of eighteen or twenty Ships bound for *Suratt*, and other parts of *India*. After they had been some time at Sea they parted Company, and the Ship wherein the Captain had imbarked, espyed a little after, two Sail to windward of them, as far as they could see from the top-Mast-Head, which made all the Sail they could after them, and thereby forc'd them to bear away right before the Wind with all the Sail they had; and to lighten their Ship so as that she might the better escape them, they cut away their Boat which was tow'd a stern, and threw abundance of valuable Goods over-board. But the two Ships notwithstanding this, outsaild them, and as they came up towards them, the Black Sea-men descried them by their Colours, to be *Sanganians*. They gave the Captain Chase all the Day long 'till four a Clock in the Afternoon, who fir'd the Stern-Chase with his four Guns all the while; at length they shot his Man at the Helm thro' the Head, and laid him on board in the Midships, entring 70 or 80 Men with Sword and Target. The Black Sailers, who were thirty, leapt over-board to save their Lives, leaving the Ship to the Captain and his two Servants. The Throat of one of them was immediately cut, and as they came in fury to hew down the Captain, and slay him instantly, as they had done his Servant, he fended off the fatal Blow by receiving it on his Hand, which was cut half off thro' the dint and violence of the Stroke. While they were thus eager for his Destruction, and intent in taking away his Life, they espyed a Rich Prize which diverted their Fury and Design; for the Captain wore a sett of Gold Buttons upon his Coat, which they presently flew at upon the first sight, and were so zealous for the Purchase, that he ransom'd his Life by the price of his Gold. They stript him as naked as an *Indian Faquir*, excepting

*Captain Says Captivity by Pyrates.*

only a small piece of a shirt to cover his Nakedness, and left him in that Santone-like[1] Condition for two Months, without either Hat to his Head, or Shoe to his Foot. One of the *Sanganian* Ships which had made them a Prize, was of some Force, she carried ten Guns and 150 Men; the other was only a small Galley of no more than four Guns and 50 Men, whereby the Captain who had resisted them stoutly for some time, being easily overpower'd, was forc'd to surrender. The *Sanganians* after the Dispute was over, finding no more resistance, grew compassionate and kind, and refresht the Captain with Water and Opium, which was the Nourishment they found most proper for themselves after any hard Labour or Languishment of Spirit, and the speediest Relief for decayed Nature. They were much concern'd too for the Cure of his Hand, which was in danger of being lost by the deepness of the Wound, and apply'd to it Loaf Sugar to stop the Bleeding, and something else to keep the Wound clean; after which the Wool of a Sheep's Back, and the Oil of their Lamps, without any other Medicines, in a short time thoroughly perfected the Cure.

*Opium a refreshment.*

The Ship was taken near the Island of *Bombay*, which made them spend a Month in Sailing before they Arriv'd in their own Country. When they drew near *Aramra*,[2] which was the Port to which they design'd, they according to Custom, fir'd a Gun belonging to the Captain's Ship, to salute their Country and Relations; in which the Captain had hid 1500 Venetians,[3] to secure them from the Rapine of the *Pyrates*, thinking them safe in that strong Hold, but were by this means unluckily lost; which made it a very costly Salute to our poor Commander, of whose Money they discharg'd near 700 *l.* at one Shot.

The Queen of the Country, after she heard of their Arrival,

[1] i.e. naked like an ascetic (*santa*), *vide supra*, p. 210, note 4.

[2] Near Beyt on the extreme western extremity of Kāthiāwār. Ovington is wrong in saying that it is at a little distanee from Diu. *Infra*, p. 257.

[3] i. e. Sequins. Cf. p. 243, note 4.

sent a Messenger for the Captain to bring him up to Court, whither he travell'd for two or three Miles without Covering either to his Head or Feet, very ill equipt to appear in the Presence of a Queen. When he came in this distress before her Majesty, she spoke to him by a *Portuguese* Interpreter, who inquir'd of him by the Queen's directions, which of her People they were that had his Moneys; which he answer'd he could not tell. Then she threatned to keep him a perpetual Exile from his Country, and for his further Comfort, would allow him only Salt Water to drink.

It happen'd about a Month before this time, that a *Portuguese* Ship with a Priest and his Images had been taken and brought into this Harbour, which because they were devoutly Rever'd by that Nation, therefore did the Queen imagin, that all *Europeans* had them in the same Religious Esteem: And because that the Captain was inflexible to her other Menaces, she order'd the Image of the Virgin *Mary*, with those of two or three Saints more, about a Foot high, to be brought before him, and told him if he would but yield to kiss them, she would give credit to what he said. The Captain who was a very Rational Man, and bred out of the Road of Romish Superstition, was neither so sparing of his Civilities, as to forbear a Complement to the piece of Wood, nor of such unrefin'd Principles as to give it a Religious Adoration, but was ready either to kiss or burn it, which they pleas'd, since he had an assurance of his Release upon such easie terms, and therefore kiss'd it very freely; and after two or three days stay here, where he fed upon Rice and Water, and lay in the Night time with the Cattle, he was dismiss'd. A while after they sent him aboard his Vessel for a day or two, which lay in the Harbour, and gave him along with him about twelve Pints of Wheat, the Sweepings of the Ship, to sustain him in his Voyage to *Suratt*; but he imbark'd upon an *Arabian* Ship which was then loading for *Muscact*, in which he was carried to that City. *The Captains release.*

*Aramra*, where the Captain was brought in Prisoner, lies opposite to the *Arabian* Shoar, between *Sindy* and *Cape* Aramra. [Sind. Jagat.]

*Jugatt*, a little distance from *Diu*, which belongs to the *Portuguese*. The Country of these *Sanganians* lies between those vast Empires of *Persia*, which is on the *West*, and *Indoston*, which borders upon it on the *East*. They are great *Pyrates*, and live by those Prizes which they take at Sea, where they range from the Streights of *Ormus* to the Gulf of *Cambay*, and down the *Malabar* Coast, Cruising about from one place to another, where any hopes of Booty invites them forward. They infest all the Western Coasts of *India*, and tho' their Ships are of no great Force, yet they are seldom taken because they are made so well for Sail, that they are ready to run when they see a Vessel of any Countenance; and those they think they are able to Encounter, they endeavour to make of them a Prey.

*An instance of Justice in these* Sanganian *Pyrates.*

Tho' the Principles of these *Sanganians* are so far leven'd with Fraud and Injustice, that they wholly devote themselves to a life of Piracy, and subsist by the Spoil of the Innocent Traffickers at Sea, yet have they not all divested themselves of their obligations to all kinds of Justice, but are very faithful to what they promise, and inviolable observers of their Word; as our Captain had occasion to try by an Experiment very successful and advantagious. For being robb'd of all his Wealth, but an hundred Checkins which were privately hid in some part of the Ship, his Cook came to him and acquainted him, that the Boatswain of the Man of War, who was put in Commander in chief on Board them, would ingage to return him half of what ever Money was committed to his Custody. The Captain deliver'd to him an hundred pieces of Gold, which the Boatswain tied in a small bit of Cloath, with a small Line to it and a Bouy at the end of it, and threw it over-board. For every Man was searched before they went ashoar, and not suffer'd to come from aboard, 'till the Vessel was unladed. The day following, the Boatswain went overboard in quest of the Bag he had dropt in the Ocean, and after a little search found it, and deliver'd half of the Gold to the Captain; at which the Captain was so well pleas'd, being wholly at his Mercy, and in that distress, that he offer'd him ten pieces as a gratuity, which the Boatswain rejected for this Reason, because he told him he would keep his word according to his Promise.

I shall now proceed to an Account of *Mocha*, and other remarkable places situated upon the *Red Sea*, according to the Method I lately proposed.

S 2

# MOCHA

## And other Remarkable Places upon the Red Sea.[1]

*The Introduction.* I SHALL here give the Reader a short View of *Mocha*, and other places of Note and Traffick, which border upon the *Red Sea* on the *Arabian* side, in the full extent of it from the Island of *Socatra*, where it begins to mix with the Oriental Sea, or *Indian* Ocean, to the very Head of it, which reaches to that Isthmus, or Neck of Land which divides *Asia* from *Africk*. I shall not detain him with any tedious Description of these places, or run into expatiating upon their Government and Laws, the Manners and Customs of their Inhabitants, or their Strength and Polity, but only lead him along the Shoar, and give him a view of the Harbours as we Coast along, to prevent all Miscarriage at his first entring into these Ports, many of which are scarce known to the Navigators of *Europe*. A fuller Account of these Parts may be expected from another Hand; from Mr. *Edward Clyve*, who by his Personal Observations is qualified not only for confirming all this Relation, but also is furnished with such Remarks, as inable him for a larger performance, in a clear and ample Account of what is yet unknown, and very worthy the publick Notice, among these People.

I shall observe no other Method in this Relation, than what Nature has chalkt out to us in the Situation of the Towns, which shall briefly be describ'd according as they lie upon the Sea-Coast.

*Why called the Red Sea.* And shall begin with the *Arabian Gulph*, or *Red Sea*, the reason of which Name is perplext with variety of Opinions, and different Conjectures; for Antiquity (we find) did not confine the Name of the *Red Sea*, only to that narrow Channel

[1] This account of the Red Sea is based on report, not on personal experience. Ovington was never there. It should be compared with Hamilton, *New Account*, i, chaps. i–ix, which is the result of personal observation.

which divides *Arabia* from *Africk*, and gives a boundary to some parts of those Ancient Kingdoms, but included also the *Persian* Gulf and all the Seas about *Arabia*, and all that vast Tract of Ocean which extends from *Cape bone Esperance*, even beyond the River *Ganges*: And the later Western Writers have limited it only to this Gulph, because it lies the nearest, and was first discover'd to them. Therefore they contend, that because King *Erythros*, who was Master of this Sea, was interr'd in one of its Islands, it obtain'd the Name of *Mare Erithrœum*, which signifies the *Red Sea*, and the *Latines* and others from thence, have retain'd the same Appellation. Some fancy that the redness of the Sand or Corall, which lie at the Bottom, or the redness of its Waters; and others affirm that the strong reflexion of the Sun's Beams upon the Surface, or the redness of the Neighbouring Hills, might justly occasion the imposition of this Name. *Herodotus* takes notice of a place hereabouts, called *Erythrobolus*, or the Red Soil, which might Countenance another Opinion. In the *Hebrew* this Sea is called *Suph*, or the Sea of Weeds, because according to *Kimchi*, there grew abundance of Weeds upon the sides of it.[1] ['Ερυθρόβωλος.]

*The length of the* Red Sea.

This Gulph runs from 12 Degrees No. Latitude to 29, and farther, most of it along the Shoar of *Arabia the Happy*, which is a large Peninsula, as it stands divided from the other two *Arabia*'s.

*The time of the Ships coming towards* Mocha.

The Ships from *Suratt* that Sail for the *Red Sea* take their departure generally about *March*, and Arrive at *Mocha* towards the latter end of *April*, or before the 20*th* of *May*; at which time, (or as the Moon Changes, or is in the Full) the Winds vary, and prevent any more Ships entring into the Sea that Year. In their Passage at that time of the Year, they generally make the Island of *Socatra*, and keep under

[1] The term Erythraean Sea was applied by the Greeks and Romans to the Indian Ocean, with its adjuncts the Red Sea and the Persian Gulf. Agatharchides, *De Mari Erythraeo*, § 5, refers it to a king Erythras and not to the colour of the water. David Kimchi was a celebrated Rabbi of Narbonne, A.D. 1155–1235.

Cape *Guardifeu* and the *Abasseen* Coast, to escape the danger of those impetuous Currents that run strong on the *Arabian* Shore.

Socatra. The Island of *Socatra*[1] lies 12 Deg. 30 M. No. and is subject to the King of *Casseen*,[2] one of whose Sons is always plac'd in the Government, whose main Revenue arises from the Aloes, Dragons-Blood, and Goats and Cows Skins, which are sent every Year either to *Seer* or *Casseen*. The Road here is very good, when once the Danger is past in entring into it, and that is easily evaded by the Pilots, who are always ready to conduct the Ships with safety into the Harbour. To the *Eastward* of this Island is very good Anchorage, but the Water is neither Healthful, nor is there any great store of Provisions. They exceed all their Neighbours in the quantity and Art of making Butter, and furnish with it *Casseen* and *Seer*, sometimes *Mocha* and *Aden* with that valuable Commodity. Their Ships for Traffick are very few, not above 6 or 7 Grabbs or Gelva's[3] belonging to the Island, most of which are imploy'd upon the King's Account. The Natives are of a swarthy Complexion, and of civil Demeanour, and would gladly invite the *English* to a settlement among them, but the meanness of the Trade will not permit them to accept the Profer.

*Cape* Guardifeu. Opposite to this Island upon the Main of *Africa* is Cape

[1] Socotra, *Sukhādara Dvīpa*, Isle of Bliss, was for many centuries dependent upon the sultans of Kishīn on the neighbouring Arabian mainland. It was ceded to Britain in 1886. Its chief exports are aloes and Dragon's Blood, or cinnabar, the latter being a resin exuding from the *Pterocarpus Draco*, and used as a dye, a varnish, and a drug.

[2] Seer and Casseen, i.e. Shihr and Kishīn, are on the Hadramaut coast, between Dhāfar and Aden. Hamilton, *New Account*, i. 54, says that Kishīn lies 'almost under the meridian of Cape Guerdafoy, and under the prodigious high mountains of Megiddo, on the coast of Arabia'. He also describes the government and trade.

[3] The grab (*gurāb*) or corvette was, on account of its light draught, a type of warship commonly employed on the west coast of India. The jalba or gelva is the galley; cf. English 'jollyboat'. Hobson-Jobson, *s.v.*

*Guardifeu*, which is very remarkable Land, and lies in 12 Deg. No. Lat. The Reason of mentioning this Cape is, because most Ships that come for this Sea in *April*, or later, desire for their safety to make that Land or Promontory. Near this is *Mount Felix*, which is only a small Mountain, but shews it self in appearance at a distance, like a small Island, yet joins the Main by low Land; and the Ships keeping their Course along this Shore for about 150 Miles Westward from the Cape, at length they espy a small white Island, from whence they cross the Gulph towards *Aden* on the *Arabian* Shore, which now follows in order to be describ'd. Mount Felix.

Upon this Coast of *Arabia*, are variety of places noted for Traffick, the first of which that I shall here take notice of is *Dofar*,[1] which is situated towards the Eastern part of this Sea. The King of this place Ingages now and then in small Skirmishes, and Martial Disputes with his Neighbouring Princes, the Kings of *Seer* and *Casseen*, but their Contests are seldom very Bloody. And his People are inur'd but very little to the Laws of Hospitality and Kindness, but are injurious in their Commerce, and Villanous to Strangers. The Country produces only some Olibanum,[2] Coco-Nuts and Butter. The Religion of the Natives is *Mahometan*, of which they are such zealous Admirers, and are heated with such extatick Warmths, that they are not asham'd sometimes to pretend even to Inspiration, especially when they are seiz'd with a fit of Dancing. For among them prevails a particular Custom of Dancing[3] with so much pains and Zeal, so much fervency and Passion, that their strength decays, and their Spirits fail them Dofar. *The nature of the Inhabitants.* *A violent Enthusiastick sort of Dance.*

1 The modern Dhāfar. Hamilton says (p. 55) that it has not much trade, but is 'more noted for barbarity'. An English ship was plundered and burnt there in 1705.

2 Arab. *al luban*, incense. This is the resin of various trees of the order *Boswellia*. The chief port for the export of incense has long been Dhafar, the Dofar of the text, and probably the Sapphara Metropolis of Ptolemy, on the coast of Hadramaut.

3 The dancing of the dervishes (*darvīsh*), by which they attained a kind of trance or ecstasy, akin to the Hindu *yoga*, is referred to.

thro' these violent Motions, and being at length quite spent, they fall as it were quite dead upon the Ground. All the while this merry Humour does possess them, they cry aloud, *God is a great God, the only God, and* Mahomet *his Prophet,*[1] and fill the Air with such like pious and devout Expressions of their Law, 'till they are not able any longer to speak or stand. While they lie thus lifeless, as it were, and intranc'd upon the Ground, they talk, they say, with God and the Prophet, who Communicates to them Divine Revelations; and the credulous Multitude who are easily perswaded to give assent to what they say, firmly believe that they are Heavenly Inspir'd. This is done in imitation, as I conceive, and to countenance the Practice of their False Prophet, who wisely contriv'd that a Bodily Disease should pass for the Infusion of the Spirit; and being subject to the Falling Sickness, declar'd that those Swoonings were Heavenly Raptures, in which he convers'd familiarly with the Angel *Gabriel.*

Casseen. Next to this place Westward is *Casseen*, which stands in 15 Deg. No. The Road here in the Western *Mussouns* is very safe, but it lies open to the Eastward. The Town looks mean, and is no way beautified with stately Edifices, nor made strong by Fortifications, only 'tis dignified sometimes with the residence of the King, when his Revenues come from *Socatra.* For as his Royalties are very small, and his Income inconsiderable, because his Subjects are both Poor and Slavish; so is he hereby debar'd from maintaining a Princely Pomp, or making a show in any Magnificent Appearance, and therefore very often turns Merchant himself, for hopes of Advantage, and for supporting his Royal State and Grandeur. *Its Commodities.* Several Gelva's come hither freighted with Rice, Dates, Camlees,[2] which are a sort of Hair Coats made in *Persia*, and Red and White Callicoes; which are barter'd for Olibanum, Aloes and Butter. For the Necessities of the Natives incline

[1] This is the Azān, or call of the *muezzin*, La ilāha illa-l-lāh, Muhammadur-Rasūlallāh.

[2] Hind. *kamli*, a coarse blanket. See Hobson-Jobson, *s.v. cumbly.*

them rather to an Exchange of Commodities, than a Traffick for Silver, which loses its Esteem here, as much as it is Idoliz'd in other parts. Some Coins however are current among them, *viz.* Dollars, Abassees,[1] and Mamoodees.[2] That which is here esteem'd instead of Money, is a sort of Seed, which passes in the room of small Coins, and is distributed commonly by handfuls. Here the Natives are mainly addicted to those mean Vices of Cozenage and stealth, and think, they make a good purchase of any thing, which they can compass by Fraud and Cheating. Another sin to which they are often given, is so vile, that the foulness of it I cannot without Immodesty mention. The proper Season of the Year for Trade is *May*, *June* and *July*. *Seed used here instead of Coin.*

A place next to this, much more noted both for the Civil Deportment of the Natives, and for the Convenience of a Port, for a greater concourse of People, and for Traffick, is *Seer*, which is much frequented by Ships from several Ports, *viz. Muscatt*, *Gombroon*,[3] *Suratt*, and *Gella*, and some other places on the *Abasseen* Shore; from whence they bring Butter, Myrrh and Slaves; and those from *Muscatt* and *Suratt* transport with them Olibanum, Aloes, and what the Port affords. Seer.

*Aden*,[4] which is situated in 12 deg. 20 *m*. *No*. is one of the Ancientest, Fairest and most Pleasant Cities of all *Arabia*, surrounded with Walls on one side, and Mountains on the Aden.

[1] A Persian coin, worth about a rupee, named after Shah Abbas the Great. See *Num. Chron.*, 1927, and Thévenot, *Voyages*, Part iii, chapter ix.

[2] *Mahmudi*, half an *abassi*, or eight annas.

[3] The old name for Bandar Abbas, *supra*, p. 119. Gella is Zeila or Sela on the Somali coast.

[4] Aden, the Arabia Felix of the Romans, and the capital of Yemen, was from early times a great centre of the spice trade and an *entrepôt* of commerce between Europe and Asia. It was captured by the Portuguese early in the sixteenth century, but they were expelled by the Turks, who conquered Yemen in 1638. In later years Turkish rule relaxed and Aden was under a line of independent Sultans until its conquest by Britain in 1839. For a contemporary description, see Hamilton, chap. vi.

other. It was formerly in the Possession of the *Portuguese*, when they were renown'd for their Conquests in the East, but by Treachery, the *Turks* made themselves the Masters of it, after some time, 'till the puissant King of *Hyaman* became Victorious over the *Turks*, and seiz'd it for his own Inheritance. This Prince is here Invested with the Title of the King of *Hyaman*, (or *Yeoman*, as the Natives seem to pronounce it) which signifies *Arabia Felix*; not that his Dominions stretch so far, but because the extent of his Territories and vast Treasures, do much exceed all the rest of the Kings that inhabit *Arabia*. For his Kingdom reaches near 400 Miles on the *Red Sea*, from *Aden* as far as *Geron*.

*Formerly Noted for Traffick.* *Aden* formerly surpass'd all the rest of the Neighbouring Ports upon this Shore, was a famous Magazine for the various Commodities of *India*, *Persia*, *Arabia*, and what was brought hither by the *Abasseens*; and was Inhabited by a Miscellany of People, *Turks*, and *Arabians*, *Persians*, *Indians* and *Ethiopians*, who resided here for the Advantages of that mighty Trade. The Houses were built both neat and strong, and the Castles from the top of the Mountains afforded a curious divertive Prospect: Nature gave it such a fortified Situation, that it was a Garrison without Art, and was able to defend it self with a small Force, from a potent Enemy that might Invade it, either by Sea or Land. 'Till the Eastern Luxury which is more intent upon Indulgence and Ease, than building Forts and raising Sieges, made them neglect their Fortifications, and leave it open and defenceless for the first bold Assailant. *Months proper to Trade in.* The proper Months for Trade here, are *April*, *May*, *June*, *July*, and some part of *August*, at which time all the Ships in the Sea take their Departure, because of the Change of the Mussouns, which always happen towards the end of that Month. They carry nothing from hence, but Coffee, Aloes, Olibanum and Myrrh; the three last of which are not the product of the Country.

I should now take leave of this place, and proceed to give some account of *Mocha*, were it not convenient, before my departure, to insist a little upon the Discovery of some Ports and Passages hereabouts, to instruct such as design to Travel into these Seas.

The Land of *Aden*, because it makes like an Island, was formerly reputed to have been one; from whence steering *W.* and *W.* by *N.* you will come to the *Babbs*, which in the *Arabian* Language, signifies Gate or Door. The *Babbs* is a small Island opening to the *Red Sea*, and made in form very like a Garr-Fish, being low and flat. Between this and the Main Land, is a safe Passage, if you keep the Mid-Channel, where is 10, 11 and 12 fathom Water. But the great Ships for better Security, chuse rather to go on the outside, where is seldom less than Forty Fathom, 'till they hale in for Shore, which is commonly done, as soon as they are past the *Streights*. Here are seven Islands, but none of them so remarkable as the *Babbs*. The *Streights* here are commonly called those of *Babel Mandel*, which are about 7 Leagues over from main Land to main Land, about 20 Leagues from *Aden*, and 12 or 13 from *Mocha*. The Course from the *Babbs* is about *N.* by *West*, and *N. North West*. *The* Babbs. Babell-Mandell.

Before you come to these *Streights*, you will make a very high Table Land, and an opening to the Southward of it; which appears very like the passage into the *Red Sea*; but then you will discover the said *Babbs* Island to rectifie you, thro' which steering *North*, or *N.* by *W.* as you see occasion; there is opening to the Southward of the said high Land, a great River that leads to *Gella*, which is the greatest Port on the *Abasseen* side without the said *Babbs*.

Steering up the *Arabian* Coast before the Arrival at *Mocha*, is a seeming Wood, which is several Date-Trees and Gardens, to the Northward of which is *Mocha*, which yields a more beautiful prospect at Sea, than on Shore. Here you must not come into less than 7 Fathom, nearer are so many dangerous Over-falls, that they will be apt to scare a young unexpert Pilot. When the Southernmost Mosque is once brought to bear, *E.* by *S.* the Ships may luff up, or bear into the Road, and Anchor in 4, 5, 6, or 7 Fathom. Before this Road lies a long Ridge of Sands, which has seldom above two Fathom

Water, which renders it dangerous for those that enter to go in, 'till they have the Bearings above said.[1]

Near the Southern Fort is a Channel, for the Grabbs that use these parts, that gives them a passage in or out; but is dangerous for *Europeans* without the assistance of Pilots.

Mocha, *its great Trade.*

*Mocha* lies in 13 Deg. 30 M. *North*, and has been of late the principal Port in the *Red-Sea*, and to which Ships Traffick from *Suratt*, *Cambay*, *Dieu*, *Malabar*, and other parts of *India*. Hither also come the Ships from several parts of *Europe*; *England*, *Holland*, *France*, *Denmark*, *Portugal*; as also from *Casseen*, *Socatra*, *Muscatt*, and all the Gulph of *Persia*, which bring hither the Products of their several Countries; and are met by the Merchants of *Barbary*, *Egypt*, *Turkey*, by the *Abasseens*, *Arabians*, &c. who buy off their Goods for ready Money, and make little other Returns but Coffee, Sena, and some Aloes, Hepetica, and other small things of no great moment.

*The Custom upon Goods.*

The Custom paid for their Goods by the *Europeans* is 3 *per Cent.* both out and in, and they are priviledged to lay their Goods in their Houses which they vent here, without being constrain'd to bring them to the Custom-House. The Goods of all other Merchants are Examined, and the Customs stated, which are 5 *per Cent.* that is 2 *per Cent.* more, than what is requir'd from the *Europeans*. This was formerly done in favour to those Merchants, but is of late turn'd much to their prejudice.

If the *Europeans* bring hither any Cloath or piece Goods, they are some of them open'd to discover what kind they are of, and that a just Account of them may be carried to the Governour. But the Custom for them is paid according only to what they are sold and bought at, which is accepted by the Governour; but then if the Broker falsifies in his

[1] Mocha is fully described by Hamilton, chap. v. It owed its importance to the coffee trade, of which it was the great *entrepôt*. The patron saint, Sheikh Shadali, was, according to legend, the founder of the city, its law-giver, and the father of the coffee trade.

Accounts, and is ever found guilty of fraudulent Returns, he smarts severely, and is fleec'd for it after the Ships departure.

Whatever Commodities are bought or sold by Weight, must be brought to the Scales at the *Custom-House*, by which both Parties must be determin'd. The Weights here are those that follow, *viz.* *The Weights and Measures.*

| | *C.* | *Q.* | *L.* |
|---|---|---|---|
| Bahars are *English*, | 3 | 3 | or 420. |
| Frassells are 15 to one Baharr | | | 28 |
| Manns 10 to one Frassel. | | | |
| Fuckeas 40 to one Mann. | | | |
| Coffila's 10 to one Fuckea. | | | |

*Dry Measure are these*, viz.

Teman is 40 Memeeda's.
Medeeda is 3 Pints *English*.[1]

By this Medeeda they sell Oil, Butter and Liquids; but it yields not above two Pints and ½ of Corn, &c. in dry Measures. They measure their Cloath, Silk, *&c.* by a Covit or Guz,[2] which is 24 Inches, and Buy our Cloath by the Piece, of which they measure 4 or 5 together, and take our Accounts and Packers Marks.

Their Coins are Dollars of all sorts, but they abate 5 *per Cent.* on the Pillar Dollars,[3] because they esteem their Silver *The Coins.*

[1] Hamilton, in his 'Table of Weights, Measures and Coins' at the end of his *New Account*, gives the following list of weights used in Mocha for gross goods :

| | |
|---|---|
| 1 cafilla . . . | 16 kerrats |
| 1 vakea . . . | 10 cafillas |
| 1 maund . . . | 40 vakeas |
| 1 frasella . . | 10 maunds |
| 1 bahaar . . . | 15 frasellas. |

N.B.—A Frasella is 29½ lb. Avoirdupois.

The Bahar was usually equivalent to 3 pikuls or 400 lb. avoirdupois. See Hobson-Jobson, *s.v.* Frazala.

[2] Covit, cubit or ell, Port. *covado.* Juz, Persian *gaj*, a yard-measure.

[3] The Spanish dollar, or peso, 'piece-of-eight', valued at 4*s.* 6*d.* sterling, so called because it bore the figure of the Pillars of Hercules.

not very pure. The Dollar Weight with them is 17 Dr. 14 Gr. as it is only 17 D. and 12 Gr. with us. All their Coins are taken by Weight, and valued according to their fineness, and of Gold they have several sorts, *viz.*

The Ducket of { *Venice.* / *Germany.* / *Barbary.* / *Turkey.* / *Egypt*, &c. }

The Comassees[1] are a small Coin valued according to the Governments Pleasure; but they keep their Accounts by an imaginary Coin of Cabeers, reckoning 80 to a Dollar.

*The Reason of the decay of Trade here.* The Natives were very civil and courteous to the *English*, especially 'till the Year 1687, when the War commenc'd between the *English* and the *Mogul*, which was so severe among the poor *Moor* Merchants, and such a disturbance and loss to the Innocent *Indians* that Traded hither, that it has quite (in a manner) destroy'd the Traffick of this Port, and driven the Trade to several other parts in this Sea. This War has since occasion'd the utter Ruin of several *Indian*, *Turkey*, and *Arabian* Merchants. For when the *English* Sailers at that time perceiv'd the softness of the *Indian Lascarrs*; how tame they were to all their Cruelties, how patient and submissive to their Force and Arms, and how willingly they endured the spoiling of their Goods, rather than ingage their Lives in a bloody Contest; they no sooner return'd for *England*, but they Imbark'd again upon a new Design with some more *Europeans* to turn Pirates, and rob these harmless Traffickers in the *Red Sea*. And accordingly in the Year 1691, they took from the Merchants that Traded between *Mocha* and *Suratt* to the value of 120000 *l*. The succeeding Year they did the same; and at this time there are two or

[1] Cf. Hamilton, p. 2 of his Table: 'The Coin current is the *Cammassie*, which is heightned and lowered at the *Sheriffs* or Bankers Discretion, from 50 to 80 for a current Dollar, which is but an imaginary species, being always reckoned 21½ *per cent.* lower than *Spanish* Dollars.'

three small Ships more upon the quest for Rich Prizes, and making seizure of those Ships they meet with; which has so impoverish'd already some of the *Mogul*'s People, that they must either cease to carry on a Trade, or resolve to be made a Prey. Tho' the *Mogul* cannot justly charge the *E. India* Company with the barbarous Actions of these Pirates, yet the unhappy occasion of it may be very apt to excite in him very Ireful Resentments, because of the Misery of so many of his Subjects. And the *English* at *Suratt* have been already made sensible of some Inconveniences and Hardships consequent upon it, by their Imprisonment in their Factory twice in two Years, while I stay'd there.[1]

Coffee is the only Commodity in repute in this Port, of which there is no scarcity at all.[2] It grows in abundance at *Beetlefuckee*,[3] *Sonany*, *Asab*, and other parts; but from these it seldom comes grabled, or well packt, which puts the Buyers upon a new Trouble. It may be bought one Year with another, at about 45 Dollars *per* Baharr, and shipt. It is ripe at a proper Season of the Year, and is subject to Blasts, as our Corn and Fruits are. It thrives near the Water, and grows in Clusters like our Holly-Berries; the Berry it self resembles a Bay-Berry; two of which are inclos'd in one Shell, which separates when it is broken. The Leaf of it is like a Lawrel's in bigness, but very thin. The Tree it self neither shoots out in largeness, nor is very long productive of *Coffee.*

[1] See the note on p. 239 ff., *supra*.

[2] Coffee, the Arabic *kahwa*, was introduced from Abyssinia to Yemen in the middle of the fifteenth century A.D. by Shaikh Shihābuddīn Dhabhānī. It is mentioned by all the early travellers, but did not reach England till 1652, when one Pasqua Rossie, servant of Mr. Edwards, a Turkey merchant, set up the first Coffee House in London. Cf. p. 180.

[3] *Bait al Fakih*, 'tomb of the saint', the coffee-mart of which Hodeida is the port. It is about thirty miles inland from Hodeida and 100 miles from Mocha. Hamilton (p. 37) describes it as the greatest coffee-mart in the world. It shipped in his day about 4,000 tons of berries yearly to Europe, of which half went to England.

Fruit, but is still supplyed by new planting of others. This Commodity is proper only to these Parts, and, as the *Arabs* tell us, is by the Bounty of Heaven given only to them, as a means to procure for them all those Necessaries, which they stand in need of from other parts. Few Commodities of any value are here besides, except Sena, some quantity of which may be bought, and very cheap; as also Aloes Hepetica. From *Casseen*, *Seer*, and *Socatra*, come Aloes Socatra, and Olibanum; from *Gella* and other parts on the *Abasseen* Shore, Mirrh; from *Socachim*, Elephants Teeth, and Gold Dust, which are bought by the Merchants of *India*.

Moseck. *Moseck* is distant *N.W.* from *Mocha* about 10 Leagues, and is of no importance for Trade, except it be for Salt, since *Mocha* drew the *Indian* Merchants from it, and drein'd its Commerce; for the City of *Mocha* cannot boast of its Foundation above two hundred Years. This Port is situated near *Zebid* and *Beetlefuckee*, but *Hodeeda* is supply'd with Coffee from several places of Note for that Commodity.

Jutor. *Jutor* was formerly a burning Island, and is at present uninhabited, and is distant from *Mooseek* about 3 Leagues.

Hodeeda. *Hodeeda* is plac'd in about 14 d. 50 m. and is distant from *Mocha* about 60 Miles. In this is a Creek very convenient for Building Grabbs or Gelva's, and it is likewise very happy in a Port, in which is shipp'd abundance of Coffee for *Judda*, *Mocha*, and other places. It is under the Government of *Lohia*, the next Port of moment upon the Main.

Comoran. *Comoran*,[1] is an Island which is blest by Nature with a favourable Soil and advantagious Situation, but unfortunate in the Entertainment of Villanous Inhabitants, who are Characteriz'd with no better Names, than that of Robbers, or Bandittoes. It lies in 15 Deg. 20 M. and is about 10 Miles long, and two broad. Ships of the greatest Burthen may Anchor safely, in a Bay or Road which lies on the Eastermost side of it, not subject to any danger by violent frets of Wind, or Tempestuous blustering Weather. It is Fortified with a Castle, in which are some few Guns and Men; and it produces

[1] Kamaran.

no Commodities of considerable Advantage, but supplies the Ships with good Water, Goats and Fish. The Passage from hence to the Main, is not above an *English* Mile.

Since the Port of *Mocha* was disturb'd by the *English* Ships in the *Indian* War, and the Merchants Goods which were bound for *Suratt*, were there seiz'd on by Captain *A———s*, This struck such Terrour in all those People that were formerly wont to Trade thither, that they declin'd the Port, and remov'd the Trade to a Town not very remote from it, nam'd *Lohia*, which is situated in 15 Degr. 4 m. and is now grown into that Credit which *Mocha* had, and draws to it both the adjacent Merchants, and the Ships from *India* and other parts. The entrance into the Harbour here, is difficult and dangerous without Pilots, but the Port is noted for its Convenience and Trade in small Vessels, and Ships for *Judda*. It is honour'd too with the Residence of the Governour of all this part of the Country, and the Island before mention'd. Lohia.

*Gezon*,[1] which lies in 17 Deg. *No*. is the last Town of Note upon this Coast, appertaining to the King of *Arabia Felix*. 'Tis eminent for its Trade of Pearl-Fishing, which is manag'd by *Bannians*, with that Advantage, that they raise themselves thereby to very great Estates. The Island *Fersham*, which is situated from hence about 3 Leagues, is most remarkable for this Fishing, wherein the Natives are imploy'd by the *Bannians*. The Town it self is small, and only considerable for this Pearl-Fishing, and for sending a great quantity of Corn to all parts of *Arabia Felix*. From hence to *Comphida*, is no Port of Moment, or that is any way remarkable for Traffick; and if there were some convenient Harbours in this distance, the Wild *Arabs*, who are expert Robbers and live by Spoil, and inhabit those parts, would certainly divert all Merchants from coming near them. Gezon. Fersham *famous for Pearl-Fishing.*

The next place as we ascend towards the Head of the *Red Sea*, is *Comphida*,[2] which lies in 19 Deg. 5 M. It was formerly subject to the *Turks*, and its present Governour commands Comphida.

[1] Jizan. [2] Kunfuda.

only about 50 Souldiers, which carries only a Face of Command to keep the People in awe, but is more probably design'd for prevention of the stealing of Custom, because many persons chuse to land here, and from hence travel by Land to *Mecca*.

Judda. *Judda*[1] is the principal Port in this Sea, belonging to the Grand Signior, lying in about 21 Deg. 30 M. This Port is inviron'd with dangerous Sands, which make the Passage into it difficult to Strangers, but is very safe for Ships when they come to an Anchor. The Air is healthful, and its Provisions sound and plentiful, for it affords choice Mutton, Beef, Fish, Grapes and other Fruits. It is the Sea-Port to *Mecca*, a place Renown'd for the Nativity of *Mahomet*, the vile Impostor, who first drew Breath in this Barren Soil. And indeed the Land about that place is so useless and unprofitable, and unfit for any Improvements, that it seems to be accurs'd by Nature, and debarr'd of Heaven's Blessings, by a constant scarcity of all things, unless they are imported from other Kingdoms. Therefore is the Grand Signior oblig'd to very great Expences, for its support, to furnish out a Maintenance for it yearly from *Egypt*, and send from thence 20 or 25 Sail of large Ships, laden with Provisions, Money, &c. for its subsistence and the support of Trade.

Mecca *very Barren.*

*Judda* flourishes in a constant Traffick from *India*, *Persia*, other parts of *Arabia*, and the *Abasseen* Shore; it is subject to the *Turkish* Government, and defended by their Arms and Valour; for its Fortifications otherwise, are but very weak, being only surrounded by Mud-Walls. There is a passage into this Town three ways, by so many Gates, two of which are not considerable, but the third which is the Principal, and leads toward the celebrated Birth-place of the Prophet, is so sacred, that no Christian must pass thro' it without forfeiture of his Religion, and Converting to the Profession of the *Mahometan* Law: Except he be a Man of Wealth, and then his Soul is not so valuable as his Money, which will freely be

*A Gate thro' which no Christian must pass.*

[1] Jiddah, 45 miles from Mecca, is now of importance as the port where the pilgrims disembark.

taken in Exchange for it, and makes all Offences venial here.

Hither the *Arabians* bring their Coffee, which is bought here by the *Turks*, and shipp'd for the *Sues*. The Dollar [Suez.] weight here is 17 D. 10 Gr. Hither likewise resort every Year several Hoggees[1] from all parts of the *Mahometan* Countries, who come hither as Pilgrims in a Spirit of Devotion, to visit their Fam'd City *Mecca*. And as soon as they are Arriv'd here, or at *Yamboe*, which is a Port a little higher in this Sea, they instantly strip themselves, out of a humour of mortification, and set out in a holy Pilgrimage for *Mecca*, with only a Longee[2] about their middle, which is a piece of Callicoe about 3 Yards length. But I leave off from any Description of these Customs, being ingag'd only to proceed in an Account of their Ports. From hence therefore the Ships Sail in *November* and *December* for the *Sues*, to which the Passage is render'd very tedious by their coming to an Anchor every Night. For Rocks and Sands, which are very numerous between these two Places, must needs be very dangerous to Pilots, that trust only to their outward Senses, and are guided by the Eye, without any use of either Lead or Line, or Compass. They place themselves upon the Ships Fore-Castle, to espy the Colour and Ripplings of the Water, and to direct them clear of all the Shoals. The Anchoring places all along this Coast are very good, but the Towns are few, because the Country is much disturb'd by the Wild *Arabs*, whose Life is a Pilgrimage of Rapine and Spoil. Therefore if the Wind shifts at Noon, or if they cannot reach their Port before the Night comes on, they certainly bear away to the Port from whence they came, if there is no Harbour nearer.

From *Judda* to *Yamboe*,[3] which is the next Port of any note, Yamboe. is reckoned above 10 Leagues, for it is situate in 25 Deg. 10 M. The Harbour is safe for Ships when they have once escap'd

[1] Hājj, Hāji, one who has made the Hajj, or Pilgrimage to the Holy Places.

[2] Hind. *Lungi*, a waist-cloth.

[3] Yanbo el Bahr.

the Passage into it which is dangerous, by reason of the many Shoals and Sands. The Castle with which the Town is fortified, is rather built for a Terror to the petty Insolencies of the *Arabs*, than as a Fort of Defence against a powerful warlike Enemy. This Town, which is reputed very Ancient, has lost abundance of its former Glory, in that it once was dignified with the Title of Chief Port for the City *Mecca*, but is now confin'd a Sea-Port only to *Medina*, the Burying-place of their Victorious and Triumphant Prophet; from which it is distant about four Days Journey. The adjacent Country produces little but Grapes, for the use of the Natives, and of the Ships; therefore Stores and Provisions for *Medina* are here unloaded, that are brought for that end in Ships from *Sues*.

From hence is nothing remarkable besides the Barrenness and strangeness of the Country, 'till we come to the narrowing of the Sea which is next Mount *Sinai*; the Cape of which Sea is called *Ross Mahomed*, or the Head of *Mahomet*; from which to *Tor*, which is the Port of Mount *Sinai*, is about seven Leagues, and about the same distance from the *Egyptian* Shore.

Tor. *Tor* is the Sea-Port of Mount *Sinai*, distant from it about 40 Miles, wherein is a Castle of small Force, under the Government of the *Turks*.

At *Sinai* live the Caloyers,[1] or a Convent of Religious *Greeks*, who give a friendly Reception to all sort of Pilgrims that resort thither. This Monastery is said to have been built by *Justinian*, and Dedicated to St. *Catherine*. The *Greeks* distribute their Charity promiscuously, as well to the *Arabians*, as those of their own Nation, both to the Christians and the Mahometans. The *Greeks* here injoy too, a large Plantation of Date Trees, the Fruit whereof is generally consum'd by the *Arabs*, who behave themselves imperiously towards these Christians, and mightily inslave them, meerly for allowing them the liberty of injoying their Monastery at the Mount.

Hummum Mosa. Near *Tor* is a Bath called *Hummum Mosa*, or the Bath of

[1] Greek monks, from Italian caloiero, Gk. καλόγηρος, 'venerable'.

*Moses*, the Water whereof is warm as New Milk. And at their return from *Mecca*, the Caravans in their passage stop here.

From *Tor* to the Head of the *Red Sea*, which may be about 100 Miles; nothing is to be seen very considerable, but that place which is so remarkable in the History of the Holy Scriptures, and which these Natives, as well as the *Turks* and *Greeks* say, was the very place where the Children of *Israel* passed the *Red Sea*, in their flight from *Pharaoh*, which is about 40 or 50 Miles distant from the Head of it. The Passage is not above 15 Miles broad, and the Midd-Channel is about 35 Fathoms deep. *Josephus* giving an Account of this Wonderful Escape of the *Israelites*, tells us, *L.* 2. *c.* 7. how that *Alexander*'s Army had such another Passage through the Sea of *Pamphilia*, which divided it self to give way to his Souldiers, in his Expedition against the *Persians*, because there was no other way to come to destroy them.

*The Passage of the* Israelites.

The *Egyptian* Shoar all along that Coast which is opposite to this, is observ'd to be very steep, except it be a part of it, thro' which the Children of *Israel* journey'd, which is a very fine Descent about eight or nine Miles down to the Sea. On each side of which are impassible Mountains, like so many high Walls, which are called *Gibbal Pharoon*, or the Hills of *Pharaoh*. So that except the Sea had open'd for the safety of God's People, they had no where to turn, either to the right Hand or to the left, but must have inevitably perisht by the Hands of *Pharaoh*'s Army.

[Gebel Farun.]

*Sues*[1] is an Ancient Town at the very Head of the *Red Sea*, and lies nearest the Latitude of 30 D. It is defended by a Wall and a Castle of some Force, design'd rather as a small Bulwark against the Incursions of the wild *Arabs*, than to guard it from the Arm of a potent Assailant. It is the Sea-Port of *Egypt*, and under the Government of *Grand Cairo*,

Sues.

[1] Hamilton also describes the ancient port of Suez (*New Account*, i. 33), which he identifies with Ezion Geber, the port from which Hiram's ships set out for Ophir. Ezion Geber, however, was the modern El Akabah, at the head of the eastern arm of the Red Sea.

from which it is distant about 50, or 60 Miles. The best Ships belonging to the Port are bought at *Suratt* by the *Turks*, who carry on the sole Trade of this place, tho' some Vessels of very good Burthen are built here too, tho by very unskilful Artists. *Pliny* in his *Nat. Hist. L.* vi. cap. 29. mentions a Town called *Suasa*, so called, as some think, from *Shuak*, one of *Abraham*'s Sons by *Keturah*, *Gen.* 25. 2. and says it lies in that part of *Arabia* which is next to *Egypt*. This probably must be the same.

I have now finish'd these Travels upon the *Arabian* Shore, all along the *Red Sea*, as far as from *Babell-Mandell*, which is the opening into the *Indian* Ocean to *Sues*, which is at the Head of that Gulph, lying nearest *N.W.* and *S. East*, and distant above 1200 Miles. And have principally describ'd only the Ports on the *Arabian* Coast, without insisting much upon other matters, to give some light to Sailers, and such as Travel into some of those unfrequented parts, where they may find convenient Ports, and what is the Condition of their Harbours, and something of their Trade.

# THE CAPE OF GOOD HOPE[1]

*The Benjamin's return for England.* *The Chagoes.*

*FEBRUARY* the 14*th* $169\frac{2}{3}$, did the *Benjamin* set Sail towards the *Cape* of *Good Hope*, on her homeward bound Voyage, whither the Passage was safe and pleasant 'till we were driven upon the *Chagoes*[2] by some undiscernible Tides, which are a company of sharp Rocks visible to the Eye, as we sailed along upon the shallow Water; the sight whereof for the space of half a Day, and the distance we were at from any Land, had we unhappily miscarried, struck us with very formidable Apprehensions of the extreme Danger we were expos'd to all that while. But having fortunately made our way through those perilous Craggy Shelves, we kept our Course with good Success 'till our Arrival at the *Cape*.

*Signs of approaching the Cape-Land.* *The Variation of the Compass.*

The Sailers have commonly notice of this Land before they Espy it, by the Soundings which run out sixty Leagues into the Ocean, and the Almitrosses[3] which is a large Sea-Fowl, and never fly very far from Land; and the Manga Voluchoes,[4] another Sea Fowl that keeps thereabouts. On *May* the 15*th*. 1693, when we approacht the *Cape*, in the Evening, the Amplitude made 9 D. 45 Min. *N.Wly. variat.* In the Morning 10 Deg. 14 Min. and by the *Azimuth* 10 Deg. 6 Min. In the Morning the Table-Land bore *E* $_2$ *S*. The variation at the *Cape* alters much, for in the Year 1689, when we came out, the variation then was eleven Degrees, in the Year 1670 it

[1] The voyage round the Cape and the habits of the Hottentots are favourite subjects in the older travellers' narratives. See particularly Terry, *Voyage to East India*, p. 13. The story of the discovery of the Cape and the subsequent voyage to India by the Portuguese is summarized, with referenees to original authorities, in Rawlinson, *British Beginnings*, ehap. i.

[2] A group of attols in the Indian Ocean, 300 miles from the Maldive Islands. *Encyc. Brit.*[11] v. 300.

[3] The Albatross.

[4] Cf. Mandelslo, p. 248 : 'Mangas de velludo (Port. = velvet sleeves), a kind of sea-mews, being white all over the bodies and having black wings.' Pyrard de Laval, i. 21.

was only six. At *Java*, the variation has not alter'd these hundred Years, as is evident from Journals of that date.

*Our Arrival at the Cape.*

On *May* the 16*th*. about ten at Night we came to an Anchor at the *Cape*, but the Commander being a Stranger in the Bay, fir'd two Guns, to signifie we were in Distress, which presently brought two *Dutch* Masters on board us, who told us that we Anchor'd in bad ground; whereupon we weighed and stood near the Shoar, and there dropt our Anchor in better.

*The prodigious advantage of the* Dutch *E.I. Company.*

We found in the Road ten *Dutch East-India* Ships,[1] most of them of good Burthen, richly laden, bound for *Europe*; these staid expecting two or three more from the *Indies*, and six had sail'd a little before from thence to *Holland*. And every Year the *Dutch* Trade to the *Indies*, employs near 20 Ships, and as many return home; which with the Trade that they drive there, where they Traffick with at least an Hundred Sail, advances their Profits to some hundred Thousands, I had almost said some Millions every Year. For by their very Commerce at *Suratt*, which is inconsiderable, in respect of the Advantage which they reap from several other Factories in *India*, that not exceeding the twentieth part; they reckon an Annual Gain, after the deduction of all Expences of their Factory, of fifteen hundred thousand Gildars, which in *English* Money rises almost to an hundred and fifty thousand Pounds. This Account I had from one intimately acquainted with those Concerns.

*The Harbour of the* Cape.

The Harbour here is very safe and commodious for Ships, free from all inconvenience and Danger; except it be towards mid Winter, which is there in *June*, at the Suns approaching the Tropick of *Cancer*; then the *North-West* Winds blow sometimes so very fierce, that the Ships are unable to ride against them. For by a violent Gust from that Quarter, in *A.* 1692, about the latter end of *May*, two *Dutch*, and one

[1] Cape Colony was first colonized by the Dutch under Jan van Riebeeck in 1652. In 1686 the European population was augmented by a number of French refugees, after the revocation of the Edict of Nantes. Cf. Hamilton, *New Account*, i, chap. i.

*English* Ship, not able to bear up against the fury of the Weather, were driven upon the Shoar and Foundred.

*The Convenience of the* Cape *to the* Dutch.

All the *Holland East India* Ships, both those outward and homeward bound, touch in here for fresh Provisions, and furnish the place with plenty of all Commodities, both from *India* and *Europe*. By which means there is scarce one part of all the Tripartite Continent, that is furnisht with that abundance of Conveniences, which the *Cape* can boast of. And that I may present the Reader with a more regular Account of this famous Promontory, and give him a more methodical Idea of the place, I shall insist upon the following Description of it in this manner. First, in observing its situation, its pleasant Air, and fertile Soil. Secondly in considering the Nature and Customs of its Original Inhabitants. And thirdly, in shewing the Profit and Convenience, which this Plantation affords the *Dutch*.

*The method of this Discourse.*

*The Situation of this* Cape.

First therefore the *Cape* of *Good Hope* is situated between thirty four and thirty five Degrees of *South* Latitude, and is the furthermost Tract of our Continent towards the most *Southern* part of *Africa*, and esteem'd by all, the most Renown'd Promontory in the World. The *Greeks* and *Latins*, as far as we can see, have had no certain knowledge of it, much less those before them; yet from some Ancient Authors it is evident, that the *Barbarians*, that is, the strange Nations have made, or caused to be made the Circum-navigation of *Africa*, which could not be done without knowing of this *Cape*. *Bartholomew Diaz* was the *Portuguese*, who first discover'd it in *A*. 1486, which occasion'd *Emanuel*, King of *Portugal*, to give it the name of *Cape Bone Esperanse*, because he hoped a Passage would be open'd to the *E. Indies* by the doubling of it; which accordingly happen'd to the mighty inriching of his Kingdom, and of his Subjects who settled there.

*Its Discovery.*

It was the second time discover'd by *Vasco da Gama*, in *A*. 1497, at the command of *Don Emanuel* King of *Portugal*. And was at those times esteem'd so dangerous a Promontory, that the Navigators were wont to call it the *Lyon of the Ocean*, or the *Tempestuous Cape*, because of the ruffling Weather and boisterous Winds; which used to discourage their touching upon it, unless they were constrain'd by some Necessity. The Thunder and Lightning, and Impetuous Storms, which have been observ'd upon the *Cape Sierra Leona*, have made some conjecture that this place was called by *Ptolomy* and *Hanno* of *Carthage* the *Chariot of the Gods*. And to this day, if the Ships from *India* are retain'd beyond their proper Season of returning, they sometimes beat the Ocean at the *Cape* for a Week or a Fortnights space, and after all that Toil and Danger are forc'd upon retiring to the Island *Mauritius*, 'till the Winter is past.

*The storms at the* Cape.

The inaccessible Heights and craggy Clifts of some of the Mountains towards the *South*, have made the *Portuguese* give them the name of *Os Picos Fragosos*, *i. e.* sharp-pointed, because they rear their lofty forlorn Heads so high in the Clouds.

*The Reason of the coolness of the Air at the Cape.*

The Neighbourhood of *Cape Bone Esperance*, to that vast Ocean towards the *South*, cools the Air to some Degrees beyond what the proportion of that Latitude might otherwise seem to give. For in the same Degree *North*, as Mariners observe, particularly where there is not the Extent of so wide an Ocean, the coolness of the Air is not so perceptible. The reason of it may be the spacious spreading Tract of Sea, which gives the Air once agitated, more liberty to continue its motion, and constantly to increase its Coldness; which on the contrary, is straitn'd and repress'd on Land, by the meeting of Mountains, Trees, Houses, and other Obstacles, and therefore not so impetuous; neither so Cold, because the Sulphureous Vapours which arise from the Earth, and make fiery Exhalations, often intermixing with the Nitrous, which make Wind, qualify them in some measure. As at *Suratt*, the Winds are by much Hotter, which fly over the Land to us, than those that come from the Sea. The *South* Winds here therefore are observ'd to be the coolest, because they blow from the great Sea. The Air however, is not scorching here for this Reason; nor very Cold, because of its nearness to the Fountain of Heat. It has no excesses, but what are tolerable to Children, nor any thing offensive to Old Age. 'Tis temperate and sweet, healthful and pleasant; and is very agreeable to the Constitution of the *Dutch*, as well as the Natives, to whom it gives Activity and Vigour. It quarrels with no kind of natural Temper, and cherishes all sorts of Animals, as well as Plants. Nor did I ever know any that had been in this Paradise of the World, who denied it the Character of one of the loveliest Regions they had ever seen. *The modera-tion of the Climate.*

And this fair Country which the Blacks inhabit, is blest with a Soil as pregnant as the Days are pleasant, and pre-par'd for any Improvements. Beeves and Sheep, Hogs and Goats feed here upon the Herbage of the Field, which makes them flesht, and very well tasted. And all those sorts of Grain which are proper for Food, or for making strong Drink, thrive here, and grow in that plenty, that no part of *Europe* can abound with them more. Which is all to be ascrib'd to the indefatigable Diligence and Industry of the *Dutch*, who being forc'd to a good Husbandry of the Ground by the scantiness which they live upon at home, continue their thrifty Cultivating humour, when they are remov'd to a Soil where they may Cultivate what quantity they please; for they are a People remarkable for Improvements, for their commendable Pains and Care where ever they Inhabit. *The fruit-fulness of the Soil.*

But here grows the fruitful Vine, as well as the Wheat and the Barley, and the *Dutch* delight themselves in the double variety both of *French* and *English* Liquors, of Beer and Wine of their own growth, with the sprightly Juice of the one, and the healing Oily quality of the other. The Rivers and Ponds are full of Fish, of great variety and very delicate. The Country is cover'd with Woods and Forests, which abound with store of Beasts and Fowls, as Deer, Antilopes, Baboons, Foxes, *&c.* Ostriches, whose Eggs are transported to various Countries, Herons, Partridges, Feasants, Pelicans, Geese, Ducks. Tygers and Lions are very numerous, and so bold, that they range sometimes within Gun-shot of the Fort, and for that reason seldom return back, and do often prey upon the Cattle, for which cause they are kept within shelter in the Night.

*Two French Ships taken at the* Cape.

Two *French* Ships returning from the *Indies* in *A.* 1689, with very rich Cargoes, were invited to touch at the *Cape*, by the store of delicate Provisions which they heard were there. But the taste of that fresh Mutton cost them both their Ships and Men. For the speedy Intelligence which the active *Dutch* had sent abroad of the Eruption of the War that Year, arriving at the *Cape* before any News could reach the *French*, betray'd them to the vigilance of the *Hollanders*, who seized their Ships as soon as they were well Moored in the Bay.

*The Ancient Inhabitants of this* Cape.

*The reason of their Name.*

The next description which I come to, *Secondly*, is of the Ancient Inhabitants of this Promontory, in what relates to their Nature and Customs. They retain the vulgar name of *Hotantots*, because of their constant repetition of that word in their hobling Dances.

There is a vast difference between the nature of these People that dwell upon this place, and the Country they Inhabit; for of all parts this affords a Dwelling most neat and pleasant, and of all People they are the most Bestial and sordid. They are the very Reverse of Human kind, Cousin Germans to the *Halalchors*, only meaner and more filthy; so that if there's any medium between a Rational Animal and a Beast, the *Hotantot* lays the fairest Claim to that Species. They are sunk even below Idolatry, are destitute both of Priest and Temple, and saving a little show of rejoicing, which is made at the Full and the New Moon; have lost all kind of Religious Devotion. Nature has so richly provided for their convenience in this Life, that they have drown'd all sense of the God of it, and are grown quite careless of the next.

*The Bestial nature of the* Hotantots.

*Their outward form.*

They are more Tawny than the *Indians*, and in Colour and Features come nearest the *Negroes* of any People, only they are not quite so Black, nor is their Cottony Hair so Crisp, nor their Noses altogether so flat. For Nature pleases her self as well in the variety of Individuals of the same kind, as in a great number of Species of all sorts of Animals.

It might seem here a rational Conjecture for the reason of

*A Discourse concerning the* Negroes *blackness.*

the *Negroes* Blackness, that they are burnt by the Sun's Beams, which we experimentally find tinctures the fairest Complexions, when it comes near them, which recover again by withdrawing to a cooler Air. And therefore that those who are most expos'd to the Sun's Heat should always be the Blackest. For Blackness and Whiteness are not suppos'd natural to any People whatever, 'tis presum'd to be the effect of the Climate, because those that are Fair by living a long time under or near the Line, shall in two or three Generations as 'tis affirm'd, become tawny and Black, tho' they Marry only with fair People. But methinks there is something in Nature which seems to thwart this current Opinion. For under the same Parallels are People of quite different Colours; as for instance, the *Hotantots*, who live between thirty four and thirty five Degrees are Black; the Inhabitants of *Candie*, who are under the same Elevation of the Pole, are White. The People of *England* are white, and the Natives near *Hudson's Bay*, which is as Cold and *Northerly* a Climate, are Black. And neither the Colony of the *English* near *Hudson's Bay*, nor the *Dutch* at *Cape Bone Esperanse* receive any alteration in their Colour, but are fresh and fair as in *Europe*, and yet the Natives in both parts are Olive-colour'd. Some are apt to ascribe this to the Air and Climate or Earth, which in some places produces Patagons, who are Giants, as in other, Pygmies; but this seems weak and unaccountable. Others resolve much of it into the effect of Food and Diet, which I believe may be of some power, and efficacy in this matter upon this Account. Because at *Suratt*, I observ'd a young *Indian* very Black, taken into the *English* Service, who by tasting Wine and Eating Flesh, grew paler sensibly than he was before. The strong Aliment by a frequent mixture of its lively Juyces with the Blood and Spirits, which for a long time had been kept low by a Phlegmatick Nourishment, did actuate and purify them by degrees, and thereby shew'd in sometime the effect of their fermentation by a faint Varnish upon the Face. Besides, it is a Remark of the Ancients, but not methinks very sound, whereby they took notice, that 'tis the Humidity of the Elements, which defends the *Indians* against that Action of the Sun, which burns the Complexion of the *Negroes*; and makes their Hair grow like Cotton; whereas some of the *Indians*, whose Hair is long and uncurled, live as near the *Æquator*, and endure as intense a Heat as the *Hotantots* and several Negroes of *Africa*, whose Hair is crisp and frizl'd. And therefore something must be added besides the Sun's Heat, for distinction of Complexion and of Hair under the same Parallels. *Lewenhoock*[1] observes that the Blood of the *Negroes* is of a different Contexture from ours. And *Malpighi*[1] observ'd a small Membrane not transparent between the *Cutis* and *Cuticula*, which caus'd the Blackness.

*The filthiness of the* Hotantots.

The *Hotantots* are as squalid in their Bodies, as they are mean and degenerate in their Understandings. For they are far from being Curious either in their Food or Attire, any further than what they find Nature reaches forth to them. They think it a needless Toil to spend time in dressing of the Hides of Bulls, or in Spinning and Weaving the Wool of Sheep, for Ornaments and Covering to their Bodies. They are satisfied with the same wrought Garments that Nature has clad the Sheep with, and therefore without more Labour or Art, they take them from the Backs of the Sheep, and put them presently upon their own, and so they walk with that Sheep-Skin Mantle about their Shoulders, or sometimes thrown like a Hood over their Heads, which seem to be the Ancientest Garments, according to *Gen.* 2. 21. *unto* Adam *and his Wife did the Lord make Coats of Skins.* They generally turn the Wool inwards, that the outside of the Garment may defend them from Rain, and the inside from the impressions of Cold. The Ornaments about their Heads are small Shells, or little pieces of Lead or Iron fasten'd to their friz'ld Hair, or put into their Ears. The Hair of their Heads, and all their Bodies are besmear'd with Kitchin-Grease, tho' never so

[1] Leeuwenhoek (1632–1723) of Delft, and Malphigi (1628–94) of Bologna, were two pioneers of microscopy, who share with their contemporary Harvey the discovery of the circulation of the blood.

stinking and Loathsome, which when dissolv'd and heated by their Bodies, sends from thence such an unsavoury Smell, as may be scented at a Furlongs distance, and nearer hand it never fails of a strong Emetick to a weak Stomach. Stinking Grease is their sweet Oil, and the Dust of the Streets the Powder of their Hair. They Anoint their Bodies to render their Nerves supple and active, and to fortifie the Pores against the Violence of the ambient Air. For they are both nimble and swift of Foot, and of Courage to outface and worst a Lion. Before their Nakedness hangs a small Skin about a foot broad, tied by a string about their middle, which the motion of their Bodies, or of the Air, sometimes turns aside.

The Apparel of the Women upon the upper part of the Body is the same with the Men's; but round their Legs are twisted Sheeps Guts two or three Inches thick, which are serviceable upon a double account, both for Food and Ornament. The Guts, which are made more savoury by the Dirt which sticks to them, affords them as good a Meal as the Flesh of the Sheep, and are eaten with as good a Gusto.

*Their Huts which they dwell in.*

The Huts they dwell in, which are made of Bul-Rushes, or Branches of Trees, are fashion'd round almost like a Bee-hive, reaching about five Foot high, and nine broad, with a small Passage in the side to creep in at, and a Hole in the middle for the Fire.

*The Wives penance for a dead Husband.*

They disallow Polygamy in all, but in their Chief, who may entertain three Wives at once. And the kind Wives, after the Death of every Husband, if they Marry again, cut off a Joint from the little Finger, and proceed to the middle, if they Bury many. The same is imitated by some fond Indulgent Husbands, but on neither of them is there any incumbent necessity, only as they are led by Humour at those times.

*The Castration of the Males.*

The Male Children at Eight or Ten Years of Age, are Cut in their Privy Parts, and depriv'd of one of their Testicles. The same is likewise done at *Cape Comoron*, for increasing their Valour and Activity. But here, I believe upon another Score, *viz.* For prevention of a too Luxuriant Increase by Generation; because when their Children Increase beyond their Desires, and the just number which they design, to prevent a heavier Charge upon the Parents, they dispatch the Supernumeraries to the other World, without any Remorse for the horrid Crime, or Consciousness of the execrable Sin of Murther, which is the Reason, I presume, of the *Hotantot*'s losing part of their Virility, that they may debilitate that Native Heat, which powerfully prompts them to Propagation. This Barbarity has prevail'd amongst a much politer People than the *Hotantots*, even the *Chineses*, who hold a Transmigration, and alledge this Reason for killing their Children, when they abound with them, which is, to make them spring up the more Happy. When the King of *Sciam* too has any Design upon the Honour or Estate of a *Mandarin* or Great Commander, he causes him to undergo a total Castration, that their Titles and Riches, for want of Issue, may fall into his Hands.

*The reason of it.*

*The Murder of their Children.*

*The* Hotantots *no Hermophradites.*

There is a vulgar Opinion which has formerly been receiv'd that the Natives of this *Cape* were *Hermophradites*, which was founded only upon Conjecture; for two Gentlemen, who were resolv'd not to be liable to this Errour, assur'd me the Report was false, upon the Curiosity they had of knowing the Reason of it, which was because the Female Parts were cut in the Fashion of small Teats hanging down.

*Their Laziness.*

Those that can be induc'd to labour, and undergo any Toil among the *Hotantots*, are made Slaves of by the *Dutch*, and imploy'd in all servile Drudgeries. But their Native Inclination to Idleness and a careless Life, will scarce admit of either Force or Rewards for reclaiming them from that innate Lethargick humour.

Their common Answer to all Motives of this kind, is, that the Fields and Woods afford plenty of Necessaries for their Support, and Nature has Amply provided for their Subsistence, by loading the Trees with plenty of Almonds, which grow in the Forests, and yield them Food; and by dispersing up and down many wholsome Brooks and pure Rivolets to quench their Thirst: So that there is no need of Work, when such innocent Diet offers it self daily without Pains, and on which they can live without Care. And thus many of them idly spend the Years of a useless restive Life. But the Governour of the Fort, and several *Dutch* Inhabitants of the Town prevail upon some of them, and make Converts of them to labour and hardships. Thus the *Hotantots* have degenerated into the strangest kind of Rationals, and have successively surviv'd the Noble and common Instincts of Humanity; but in their Innocence of Life, the Customs of the Ancient *Britains* did in many things resemble the Inhabitants of this Promontory, in their drinking Water, and the simplicity of their Food, which was upon Acorns or Berries, or such natural Productions; sometimes upon Milk, or what they could gain by Hunting. A great part of their Bodies too was uncover'd, especially their Arms and Legs, and their Cloathing was the same with that of the *Hotantots*, made generally of the Skins of Beasts.

*The Advantage which the* Dutch *reap by this* Cape.

The *Third* thing observable at the *Cape*, was the Profit and Advantage which that Plantation affords the *Dutch*. As this Climate is most delightful, and the Native Turf capable of producing any thing that may administer either to the Exigence or Delight of Man; so is it suited with the greatest convenience imaginable to the important Negotiations of the *Dutch*, whose Ships that Design for *India*, and those that return from thence to *Holland*, are refresht here with all Conveniencies, as in the mid-way between those two distant Regions.

The Industry of the *Hollanders* has inlarg'd their Borders so far upon the main Land of this Delightful Fertile *Cape*, that were they ever put to those straits as to be forc'd to Decamp, and leave their Native Country, here they might fix in a Soil of so much more desirable Habitation, that they might thank the Fates that caus'd the Change, and bless the Authors of their Misery. Here they might live without any danger of the Seas Incroaching upon their Banks, to threaten continually a second Deluge, and free from all dread of Invasion from any Neighbouring Land-Tyrant. And might spread themselves over spacious Plains, which would afford them Work sufficient for all their Husbandry, and Pastures Pleasant and large enough for all their Cattle. And because nothing can please these People so much as Trade and Traffick, therefore here they might find convenient Harbours for their Ships, by which they might keep up their Spirit of Merchandizing, and establish their Commerce to the *Indies* and other parts of the World. The Refugees of *France*, who are received here with the same priviledge the *Dutch* enjoy, acknowledge the happiness of their Transportation; and boast that their Misfortunes are turn'd into their Felicity, since they are blest here with peaceable Dwellings and kind Accommodations, who had not formerly where in safety to lay their Heads.

*The Encouragements to such as settle here.*

The Encouragements of such as come hither to Cultivate the Land for their own Livelihood and Benefit of the grand Proprietors, is thus stated, as I understood it. Those that design to settle here, are allow'd their Transportation from *Holland* gratis. After their Arrival they are invited to range and view the Country, and survey such parts as lie wild and unmanur'd, where they may choose such a Portion as they fancy they are able to stock and Manure, and will yield them a Commodious settlement for their Families. This is to be a Patrimony intail'd upon their Children, without any Rent or other Acknowledgment to the *Dutch East India* Company, but the Sale of their Goods to the Governour, and at his Price. This by the way presses hard upon the Tenants and keeps them under, by running the chief Profits of what they possess into the Company's hands. The Governour and Council agree with the Country-man for his Goods and Cattle at a very low rate, and sell them again to the Ships that put in there, as dear as they please; because all Men are 'strain'd from vending any Commodities to Strangers without the Council's leave. But however the Industrious Planters want neither plenty of Wine for their Tables, nor variety of Tame and Wild Fowls for their ordinary Entertainments, of which they have often rather too much Store than any Scarcity, because the Company has no occasion for them, and therefore they lie dead upon their Hands. Some upon this account quit the place, and very few of any Substance but easilier may increase their Goods than their Treasure.

Those whose Poverty renders them unable to stock their Land, the Kindness of the Governour provides with Necessaries 'till their Abilities can reach a Payment. Which has mightily increased the number of Inhabitants within a few Years. For whereas about nine Years since, they could scarce reckon above four or five Hundred Planters, they can now number almost as many Thousands; abundance of whom were sent hither by the *French* Persecution, who are much delighted with the Convenience of their Dwelling.

*The space of Land which the* Dutch *at present inhabit.*

They have stretcht their Plantations in the Country above seventy five *English* Miles, and see still a vast space of untill'd Land before them. In this District they rear their Cattle, sow their Corn, plant Vines, and sedulously improve all things of worth to the best advantage. So that within the Revolution of a few Years, many valuable Commodities will be Exported thence, to the other Quarters of the Universe.

*The* Cape *Wine.*

Their very Wines, in which they will suddenly increase both to a great plenty and variety, are now able to supply their Ships, and to furnish the *Indies* with some quantity, where they sell it by the Bottle at a Roupie. 'Tis Colour'd like Rhenish, and therefore they pass it under that specious Name in *India*, but the Taste of it is much harder and less palatable; its Operations are more searching, and the strength of it more intoxicating and offensive to the Brain.

*The great Taxes upon Liquors.*

The Impositions which are laid upon Wine and other Liquors that are sold by Retail, seem almost incredible, especially when the small number of People that are presum'd to drink them, is consider'd. For in the Town of the *Cape* are not reckon'd above 500 Inhabitants, besides those that are brought in Ships and come out of the Country; and yet the Annual Impost upon *Europe* Beer and Wine is four thousand

Gilders; upon *Cape* Wine four thousand one hundred; and Brandy, Arak, and distill'd Waters, pay twenty Thousand Gilders Yearly to the Governour of the place for a License to sell them. All which Taxes summ'd together, make up above twenty eight Thousand Gilders Yearly, which according to our Accounts, raise between two and three Thousand Pounds, for the liberty of selling Liquors by Retail. This exorbitant Fine upon the Taverns and Tipling Houses makes them exact extravagant Rates from the Guests that drink the Liquor, who are indeed the People that pay it. For he that resolves to drink Brandy must pay at the rate of ten Shillings a Bottle for it; and the *Cape* Wine which in the Cask is sold for less than six Pence a Quart, is in the Tavern half a Crown, and such proportionably are the excessive Prices of the rest. A tame submission is the only Remedy for these Impositions, from which there is no Appeal or Relief, which is apt to imbitter the Lives of the People, nor can any be very happy, who are subject to the Tyranny of a Government that is under no Restraint. The Arbitrary Proceedings of the *Dutch* Commissaries in *India*, have been much resented, and have likewise rais'd loud *complaints* against them by the *injur'd Factors*, but have met with very little *redress*.

*The Governour of the Cape.* The Governour of the *Cape*, *Min Heer Simon Vanderstel*, labours much in Improvements and Accommodations for the Inhabitants and Sea-men, and to render it valuable to the Company. The Sailers are well furnisht with fresh Water and fresh Provisions; and in the Bay is caught great store of Fish, which is Pickled and put up in Barrels, and sent home instead of Pickled Herrings. *A delicate Watering-place.* The Watering for Ships is contriv'd with such Convenience, that it is scarce equalled by any in the World. For from the Mountains are convey'd in narrow Channels clear Water down to the Shoar, from whence in Leaden Pipes it is carried above Forty Foot in the Sea, and there rais'd so high above its Surface, that the Ships Long-Boats can row under the Pipes, and fill their Vessels with much Ease.

The fam d Garden abundantly supplies the Ships with

variety of Roots and green Herbs, which contribute not a little to the Health, and even preservation of Life, in these tedious *Eastern* Voyages. Here is that variety of Excellent Fruits, of Pulse and Roots, which either *Europe*, or *Asia* afford. Here are those large Walks, those stately Hedges, and Alleys of Cypres, and Beds of Flowers, which make it Beautiful and Pleasant as the Garden of a Prince, and useful as that of a Peasant. The Conveniencies it abounds with may denominate it a Kitchin Garden, but its Delights a Garden of Pleasure. It is of large Extent, at some distance from the high Mountains, but cut out upon a rising Hill, water'd with pure Springs descending from the Mountains, which make their Passage thro' various Channels that are cut out in every Quarter. The Garden in all its Walks is kept so very neat and clean, that even in the Winter Season, scarce a Leaf is seen upon the Ground. The Trees are Curiously Prun'd, and the Hedges Trim'd with such exactness, that no one irregular Excrescence appears, or Branch shooting out beyond his Fellow. Much of the Fruit in it comes to maturity twice a Year, and many Trees by their nearness to the Sun, are verdant and Beautiful all the Year. Three and Thirty Slaves, besides *Europeans*, are daily imploy'd in looking after it. This forc'd a Confession, even from the *Jesuits*, in their *Siam Voyage*, of allowing it an equality, if not precedence, to their most celebrated Gardens they had in *France*. *The Garden at the Cape.*

That the Inhabitants might be subject to no surprisal from any Enemies nigh their Plantations, the Governour with a few Attendants and Victuals necessary for such an Enterprize, travell'd by Compass for several Weeks, to find its Northerly bounds and Situation, 'till he was stopt by impassible Mountains, which forc'd a Return from any farther progress that way. In this Journey he travell'd over vast Tracts of Land, very fit for Agriculture, but all Waste and Untill'd; and was very well satisfied, that those inaccessible heights of Mountains which he saw, would stand as immoveable Bulwarks against all In-land Invasions; so that nothing was to be dreaded, but Attacks upon them from the Sea. *The Governours Travels in the Country.*

*The Fort.* For their Defence from any Onsets by Water, is built a strong Fort near the Sea, with Bastions and Guns mounted for its security, and Officers and Souldiers to guard it from an Enemy. 'Tis beautified with stately Convenient Lodgings within; as well as fortified without.

*The Town.* Near the Fort is a small Town, consisting of about an Hundred Houses; strong and neatly built with Stone Walls and pretty Apartments.

*The state which the Governour lives in.* The present Governour, who lives with his Council in the Fort, is a very kind and knowing Person, is maintain'd in Grandeur, and lives Honourably. His publick Table wants no plenty either of *European* or *African* Wines, or *Asian* Liquors; and whatever the Land or Water, or Air affords in that place, is serv'd up in his bountiful Entertainments. To Complete the Magnificence of which sumptuous Fare, all the Dishes and Plates upon the Board are made of Massy Silver. And before the departure of their Fleets, the *Dutch* Commanders are all invited to a publick Repast, where they Drink and Revel, bouze and break Glasses, what they please; for these Frolicks are the very life of a Skipper; and the Governour by indulging these Wild licentious Humours, ingratiates with them more, than by any thing else he could devise.

I have now consider'd the Situation and Air of this pleasant Promontory; the Nature and Customs of the *Hotantots*; and the Profit and Convenience which this Plantation affords the *Dutch*; and should now leave it, only a passage or two may divert the Reader, which happen'd while I was there.

*A passage concerning three* Spaniards *at the* Cape. While we staid here, we met with 3 *Spaniards*, who came from the *Moneiloes* to *Batavia*, and from thence imbarkt upon a *Dutch* Ship that was loosing from thence to the Cape. The Principal of these Spaniards was sent out privately by the K. of *Spain*, in the Imployment of Visitor General. He was free in his Discourse, and not easily warm'd into Passion, and could well discern both other Mens Failings and dissemble his own. But he was very zealous in Proselyting all he discours'd with, with the Assurance of Ease and Wealth in *Spain* while they liv'd, and Immortal Happiness after Death. But he Corrupted his Parts by false Maxims, which he borrow'd from an insufferable Pride, which not being Contradiction proof, could not well bear opposition from an Heretick.

This Ancient Gentleman was hot in converting us by his Arguments, whilst another young one endeavour'd it mightily by his Relicks, which were hung in a small Box about his Neck, and were sacred Preservatives against all Perils and Misfortunes. They were such as these. A piece of St. *Leonards* Thumb, of St. *Peter*'s Nail, and a little of St. *Bridgets* Hair. Which things tho they seem'd to us inconsiderable, yet were of Value and Esteem for those Excellencies that were found in them. For as Barbarous Nations commenc'd Civil upon their Infranchisment at Antient *Rome*; so things Contemptible and Prophane, become August and Sacred by their Adoption into the *Romish* Church. However the Relicks had as little Charm in them towards us, as the Arguments. But at length the young Gentleman produc'd a *Tamback*[1] Ring, which I knew was accounted a valuable Rarity in the *East*. This Tambac is a kind of Metal, whose scarcity renders it more valuable than Gold; as the *Corinthian* Brass had its Price augmented by its Rarity. 'Tis thought to be a kind of natural Compound of Gold, Silver, and Brass, and in some places the mixture is very Rich, as at *Borneo*, and the *Moneiloes*, in others more allay'd, as at *Siam*. But it is much more remarkable for its Virtues against all noxious Blasts, from the unhappy effects of which it effectually preserves him that wears it. This is commonly ascrib'd to it in *India*, and thus far receiv'd a Confirmation, that very lately some Persons walking abroad there, were Blasted on a suddain, among whom, those that wore those Rings were saved, and the rest killed. And to preserve me from such Misfortunes, the Gentleman was pleas'd to afford me one of them. Our

*The Value and Virtue of Tambac.*

[Manilla.]

[1] An alloy of copper and zinc, coming from Java and Siam, and greatly valued. Malay *tanbaga* from Skt. *tamra*, copper.

President at *Suratt* was presented while I was there with a Knife Haft of this Metal, which was thought a noble Gift.

At the same time a *German* Physitian, who had Travell'd for ten Years in the *East*, brought with him from *China* the Root *Nisan*, a pound of which sells there for two hundred and seventy Dollars. It is frequently used in Sickness, especially Deliquiums of the Spirit, which recommends it mightily to the King and his Nobility. He was afraid of its decay before he could arrive in *Holland*, and left it therefore to try its Fortune at the *Cape*, as an additional Ornament to that spacious and pleasant Garden. Yet 'tis affirm'd, that this Soil was no Stranger to this Root, before that this was Planted here.

*The Root Nisan.*

We Sail'd from the *Cape* on the 2*d* of *June*, 1693. in the Company of ten *Dutch East-India* Ships bound for *Europe*, and on the 4*th* of *July* made *Ascention*.

# THE ISLAND ASCENTION[1]

TO the *Westward* of St. *Helena*, appear the Isles of *Sancta Maria*, and of the *Trinity*, uninhabited, and serve for Signs unto the Mariners. To the *N. West* of this Island, towards the Coast of *Brasil*, is the Isle of *Ascention*, so denominated by *Tristan Acunna* its first Discoverer, who in his Return from the *Indies*, in the Year 1508, espyed it upon *Ascention* Day. It lies towards the Coast of *South America*; is extended in length about four Leagues, in breadth one, and distant from *America* about 100. *The Reason of the Name* Ascention. *Its discovery and Situation.*

This is made generally a place of Refreshment to the *East-India* Ships, homeward bound, lying in about 8 Degrees of *South* Latitude, directly in their way for *England*. The Land is Mountainous, as most other Lands are that are situate remotely from the Continent. And excepting some very few places, it is all steril and Desart, and the Surface Cinereous, cover'd with a kind of Sinders or Ashes, which gives occasion to some, of thinking it formerly to have been a *Fogo* or Burning Island: Yet in some parts the Soil seems fit for Culture and Fructification. But because it is wholly destitute of Springs and fresh Water, this prevents all Designs of any Inhabitants fixing there, tho' the Native Turf were never so promising and fruitful. However it affords some Accommodation and Refreshment for Ships tending towards *Europe*, to which also it gives a very safe and convenient Harbour. *The barrenness of this Island.*

The most inviting stay for Ships here, are the store of Turtle with which the Island abounds, some of which are *Store of Turtle.*

[1] Ascension Island, a solitary volcanic island in the Atlantic Ocean, 7° 56′ S., 14° 24′ W., and about 45 square miles in area, was discovered by Juan de Nova on Ascension Day, 1501. It was garrisoned during the incarceration of Napoleon. It was a favourite port of call of the old travellers, who all speak of the turtles which supplied fresh meat as an antidote for scurvy. The 'sea post-office' was also a familiar feature of the island. Fryer, ed. Crooke, iii. 182 ff.

grown to four or five hundred weight, but others are of less Dimensions; on these the hungry Marriners feed deliciously, for the space of ten or 15 Days sometimes together. They esteem it no less nourishing and healthful, than delightful, nor need they incur the danger of any Surfeit by the plenty of this dainty Food; but Chronical Distempers, and inveterate Diseases, have by this sort of Dyet been often abated; and those unwelcome Guests, by a constant use of the Food, have been forc'd to withdraw from their old accustomed Habitations. The Purgative quality in which it ends, carries away the Disease with it, and repairs the Body to its former strength and Constitution.

*The Birds very tame here.*

Besides these, here are Birds in great quantity, but very unpalatable, and so distastful to the Sailers, that they rarely touch them; by which usage they are kept in a gentle tameness and familiarity, and never stir from their Nests for fear, of any Passengers approach, but sit billing and pecking at such as pass by. Among these the Boobies are most numerous, a Fowl so stupidly tame, that it freely endures to be toucht and handled, without any timorousness or fear.

*Goats only live here.*

Some few Goats are also left here, a Creature of such a thriving Nature, that it finds Nourishment many times from what no other of the Animal Generations can subsist on; and therefore in *India* sustain themselves by grazing on the Milk-bush, the ordinary Hedge of that Country, the Juyces of which are so Malignant and Corrosive, that the tender parts of Man's Body are highly offended by the very touch.[1] The Goats grow not much in flesh upon this Island, because the leanness of the Ground, and want of Moisture, allow them no more than a bare subsistence, which yet secure their Lives from the violence of Famin and of the Mariners.

*A Discourse concerning the Turtle.*

The method made use of in taking the Turtle, is carefully to observe those particular times they come on Shoar, to lay or hatch their Eggs, at which times they turn them by surprizal upon their Backs, which is a Posture they are utterly unable to recover from, and are thereby frustrated of all

[1] The milk-bush, *Euphorbia tirucalli*, has an acrid juice.

Defence or Escape, and are a ready Prey to any that resolves to seize them. When the sensible Creatures find themselves in this desperate Posture, by which they know themselves in a lost and hopeless state, they then begin to lament their Condition in many heavy sighs, and mournful Groans, and shed abundance of water from their Eyes, in hopes, if possible, to secure their Safety by their Tears, and Mollifie the cruel Assaults upon their Lives. They are of celebrated strength, much beyond the Proportion of their Bulk, so much that I have seen one of a small size, not above eight Inches Broad, able to sustain the weight of a Man. And the inward strength of their Animal Spirits is equal to that of their outward Contexture, which is not easily abated or dissolved. For after the Neck of one of these had been quite cut off, except only a small piece of Skin by which it hung to the Body; and after its Bowels were ripp'd up, and its Heart was taken out, and plac'd upon the Deck of the Ship, it both open'd its Mouth, and the Heart for a long time after had a motion; which some of the Spectators affirm'd would continue for the space of two or three Hours; and some of them have been known to live twelve Hours after their Heads have been cut off. The parts of Reptiles continue, I think, animated for some considerable time after they are dissected from one another, because of the viscous Quality of their Animal Spirits, but for the Heart of so large an Animal as this, to move for some Hours after it was torn from the Body, seems a little more strange and surprizing. However, I made this Experiment my self upon a Cock-Roach, which is a sort of large unwieldy Flie, whose Spirits may be presum'd to be most volatile, the Head of which I sever'd from the Body, and kept it apart in a small Box for twenty four Hours, after which time looking on it, I saw it perfectly move some parts, but with a very faint slowness. As we see the Flesh of a Viper, after it is beheaded and imboweled, will move for the space of 24 Hours.

*Three sorts of Turtles.*

Of the Turtle or Marine Tortoise, there are three sorts, the Hawk-Bill, the Logerhead, and the Green Turtle, which swim in the Water, and creep upon Land. 'Tis of such an

Amphibious Nature, that you may fancy it Beast, or Bird, or Fish, as you please; for it lives in the Ocean like a Fish; it feeds upon Grass on Shoar, as an Ox; and lays Eggs, as a Bird, sometimes the quantity of a Bushel. The two Fins of it placed before, are in the shape of Wings; those two behind are broad and long like Feet, and its Head and Eyes, which it opens and shuts, resemble those of a Hawk; so that both in its shape and other qualities, the Body of it is divided among those Creatures whose proper Elements are Land, Water, and Air. The flesh of it is White, and Eats beyond any Veal, and admirably contributes to the Cure of the Scurvey, and as it's commonly affirmed, the Impure Disease. But the *Dutch*, notwithstanding the delicacy, will not touch it; and the Barbarity of the *French*, after they have been satiated with their Plenty, exposes them to starve and stink above Ground, by leaving many of them turn'd upon their Backs, upon their departure from the Island. The *English* treat none cruelly, but turn only such as are necessary for their Refreshment, being loath to express a severity to the very Beasts, especially such whose Deaths contribute so considerably to the Health, and support of their own Lives. Great plenty of these Shel-Fish are found in the *West Indies*, the Genitals of which dried, and drunk in Wine, are prescribed as singular Dissolvers of the Stone. The store of them upon this Island, where so little Herbage grows, seems to supply the Necessity of green Herbs for Curing the Scorbutick Humours in the Mariners, to which nothing does contribute more; as we happily experimented in the Voyage. For three or four *French* Vineroons[1] designed for St. *Helena*, were so lamentably over-run with the Scurvey, after we had spent two or three Months at Sea, that they were unable either to walk or stand upright; and yet three days eating of Purslain and other Herbs, after we were landed in *Africa*, rectifyed the ill Humours in the Blood, restor'd their Limbs, and recover'd their Stomachs and lost Health again. And were those made more frequently the Diet of these that live on

*The Scurvey Cur'd by Eating green herbs.*

[1] Fr. *vigneron*, vine-dresser.

Land, as they are sometimes of those at Sea, I doubt not but the Scorbutick Humours, and all that Train of Diseases that follows them, would be less numerous and prevailing than they are.

*The* Post Office.

Upon this Island is a certain place nam'd the ***Post-Office***, from the Letters left there by the last Commander that came thither, giving an Account of the time he came there, when he departed from the Island, and what other News of moment he thinks convenient. The Letter is commonly thrust into a Bottle corked close, which the succeeding Commander breaks in pieces to come to it, and leaves another in its stead. But I will leave this Barren Island, and proceed on the Voyage.

*A day set apart for the invoking a Blessing upon the Voyage.*

About the middle of our Passage from the *Cape* to *Europe*, the Captain Commandant of the Fleet called a Council of all the Commanders, and then enjoyn'd a particular Day to be set apart by every Ship, as a publick Thanksgiving for our past safety, and for imploring the Favour and Benediction of Heaven upon the Fleet for the rest of the Voyage; and desir'd from me a Form of Prayer, which was translated into *Dutch* for that purpose. This was a pitch of Piety, which well became his Care and Station, but was far beyond the common strain of a Sailer's Devotion. I doubt not but it was very Instrumental in our avoiding those threatning Dangers that incompassed us in our Voyage, and from which we had a very Fortunate Deliverance to *Europe*. For besides the Storm which increas'd to such a Rage, and on a sudden grew so insupportable and Fierce, that it separated the whole Fleet, and every Ship was forc'd to make the best of her way for her own safety; the *Benjamin*, besides this, had another Deliverance as happy, which was in her Escape from two *French* Privateers, the one a Head, the other a Stern, by the Commander, Captain *Leonard Brown*'s prudent Management of himself in that juncture. For having formerly shorten'd Sail, in hopes that one of them might be our Friend, as soon as ever he discern'd they were the Enemy, he order'd all Hands aloft, and commanded the Sails to be spread in a trice,

*A great Storm.*

*The Stratagem our Captain used to make his Escape from two* French *Privateers.*

by which he made them suppose, that our Ship was very well Man'd, and that we must therefore needs be a Man of War. This stratagem had its desired effect, for upon it they both left us; tho' the next Day following, they took a stout Fourth Rate, the *Diamond Frigat*.

*Our Arrival in* Ireland.

*The Officers and Sailers Charity, after the Voyage.*

On *September* the 18*th* 1693, we came into *Kingsale* in *Ireland*, where, as a Testimony of our Gratitude to our great Deliverer in the Voyage, the Captain, Officers, and Sailers, contributed amongst them, betwixt twenty and thirty Pounds, part of which, about four Pounds, was design'd as a small Oblation to the Minister, and the rest was given to the Poor of the place. Which was to be Recorded by a publick Inscription in the Church, as an Encouragement to others to imitate the Precedent that was given them.

*The kindness and civility of the* English *in* Ireland.

The *English* welcom'd us on Shoar with many generous Civilities, and shew'd to us the Ancient Temper of the *English* Nation, in their frank Hospitality, and the Spirit of liberal Entertainments. Tho' they lately smarted with intestine Broils, yet now they were at Peace, were unanimously Loyal, and universally Kind; not sowr'd with Faction, nor grown sordid by Covetousness, but here we found that Love and Allegiance which seem'd indeed to be the Genius of all the Protestants of that Kingdom. After we had stay'd here five Weeks, for want of a Convoy, we at last set Sail, and on the 5*th* of *December* arriv'd safe at *Gravesend*.

*FINIS*

# FORT *ST. GEORGE* JANUARY 1*ST*, ANNO $16^{79}_{80}$.

*A Collection of* Coyns *now Currant in the Kingdoms of* Indostan, Persia, Gulcondah, Vizapore, Japan, Syam, Pegu, Atchein, Quedda, Arabia, *&c. With their several Weights, Fineness and Values here at this present*, &c.

| No. | Ps. | | *oz.* | *dw.* | *gr.* | | *Matts* | *Pa* | *fa* | *ca:* | *Pa* | *fa* | *ca:* | *Pa* | *fa* | *ca:* |
|---|---|---|---|---|---|---|---|---|---|---|---|---|---|---|---|---|
| | | | | | | *Indostan.* | | | | | | | | | | |
| 1 | 1 | The Gold Mohurpo. | – | 7 | 2 | ——fine.—— | 9 $\frac{7}{8}$ | – | – | – | 3 | 22 | 3 | | | |
| 2 | 1 | The Silver Rupee. . . . . | – | 6 | 19 | — | 9 $\frac{1}{2}$ | – | – | – | – | 10 | 3 | | | |
| | 1 | The Copper Pice. . . . . | | | | | | | | | – | – | – | 3 | 33 | – |
| | | The Cowree Shell. . . . | | | | | | | | | | | | | | |
| | | | – | – | – | *Persia.* | | | | | | | | | | |
| 3 | 1 | The Silver Abass 5 sh. . . | – | 5 | 20 | — | 9 – | – | – | – | – | 8 | – | | | |
| 4 | 1 | Ditto of 4 Shahees.. . . . | – | 4 | 16 | — | 8 $\frac{1}{2}$ | – | – | – | – | 6 | 3 | | | |
| 5 | 2 | The Silver Mamoode. . . . | – | 2 | 8 | — | 7 $\frac{3}{4}$ | – | 2 | 4 | – | 4 | 8 | | | |
| | | | – | – | – | *Golcondah.* | | | | | – | – | – | – | 19 | 5 |
| 6 | 1 | The Silver Rupee. . . . . . | – | 7 | 2 | — | 9 $\frac{1}{2}$ | – | – | – | – | 11 | | | | |
| 7 | | Ditto Half. . . . . . . . | – | 3 | 13 | — | – – | – | – | – | – | 5 | 3 | | | |
| 8 | 4 | Quarter. . . . . . . . | – | 1 | 18$\frac{1}{2}$ | — | – – | – | 2 | 5 | – | 11 | – | | | |
| 9 | 4 | Eighths. . . . . . . . | – | – | 21$\frac{1}{4}$ | — | – – | – | 1 | 2$\frac{1}{2}$ | – | 5 | 3 | | | |
| 10 | 8 | Sixteenths. . . . . . . . | – | – | 10$\frac{5}{8}$ | — | – – | – | | 4$\frac{1}{4}$ | – | 5 | 3 | | | |
| | | | – | – | – | | | | | | – | – | – | 1 | 2 | 3 |
| 11 | 1 | The Pagoda of Madrass. . . | – | 2 | 5 | — | 8 $\frac{5}{8}$ | – | – | – | 1 | – | – | | | |
| 12 | 1 | Polliacatt. . . . . . . . | – | 2 | 5 | — | 8 $\frac{5}{8}$ | – | – | – | 1 | – | 3 | | | |
| 13 | 1 | Gulcondah. . . . . . . . | – | 2 | 4$\frac{1}{2}$ | — | 8 $\frac{1}{2}$ | – | – | – | – | 35 | 3 | | | |
| 14 | 1 | Ditto half Pa. . . . . . . | – | 1 | 2$\frac{1}{2}$ | — | 8 $\frac{5}{8}$ | – | – | – | – | 18 | 1 | | | |
| 15 | 1 | Cavere Pack. . . . . . . | – | 2 | 5 | — | 8 $\frac{1}{2}$ | – | – | – | – | 35 | 4 | | | |
| 16 | 1 | St. Thoma. . . . . . . . | – | 2 | 5 | — | 8 $\frac{1}{4}$ | – | – | – | – | 34 | – | – | | |
| | | | – | – | – | | | | | | – | – | – | – | | |
| | | | – | – | – | | | | | | – | – | – | 5 | 15 | 5 |

| No. | Ps. | | oz. | dw. | gr. | | Matts | | Pa | fa | ca: | Pa | fa | ca: | Pa | fa | ca: |
|---|---|---|---|---|---|---|---|---|---|---|---|---|---|---|---|---|---|
| 17 | 2 | The Gold Fannam of Madrass. | – | – | $2\frac{3}{4}$ | — | 4 | $\frac{3}{8}$ | – | 1 | – | – | 2 | – | | | |
| 18 | 1 | Polliacatt. . . . . . . . | – | – | 6 | — | 2 | $\frac{7}{8}$ | – | 1 | 2 | – | 2 | 4 | | | |
| 19 | 2 | Trevelore. . . . . . . . | – | – | 6 | — | 4 | $\frac{9}{16}$ | – | 2 | $\frac{1}{3}$ | – | 4 | $1\frac{1}{2}$ | | | |
| 20 | 1 | Carullepollam. . . . . . . | – | – | 6 | — | 4 | $\frac{9}{16}$ | – | 2 | $\frac{1}{8}$ | – | 2 | 1 | | | |
| 21 | 1 | Trippote. . . . . . . | – | – | 6 | — | 3 | – | – | – | – | – | 1 | 3 | | | |
| 22 | 1 | Madrepack.. . . . . . . | – | – | 6 | — | 3 | $\frac{1}{4}$ | – | – | – | – | 1 | 3 | | | |
| 23 | 1 | Apperingee. . . . . . . | – | – | 3 | — | 10 | – | – | – | – | – | 2 | – | | | |
| | | | – | – | – | — | | | | | | – | – | – | – | 16 | – |
| | 1 | The Copper Cash of Golcondah. | | | | | | | | | | | | | | | |
| | 2 | Madrass. . . . . . . . | | | | | | | | | | | | | | | |
| | 1 | Polliacatt. . . . . . . . | | | | | | | | | | | | | | | |
| | 1 | Metchlepatam. . . . . . | – | – | – | *Vizapore.* | | | | | | | | | | | |
| | | The Silver Coyns the same with Gulcondah, except the $\frac{1}{4}$ Rupee | | | | | | | | | | | | | | | |
| 24 | 1 | of Seere Cawn. . . . . . . | – | 1 | $18\frac{1}{2}$ | — | 9 | $\frac{1}{2}$ | — | – | – | – | 2 | 4 | | | |
| | | | – | | – | | | | | | | – | – | – | – | 2 | 4 |
| | | The Gold Pagoda of Sanagree.. | | | | | | | | | | | | | | | |
| 25 | 1 | | – | 2 | 4 | — | 8 | $\frac{1}{4}$ | – | – | – | – | 34 | 3 | | | |
| 26 | 1 | Chengie. . . . . . . . | – | 2 | $4\frac{1}{2}$ | — | 8 | $\frac{1}{4}$ | – | – | – | – | 34 | – | | | |
| 27 | 1 | Porto Novo. . . . . . . | – | 1 | 16 | — | 8 | $\frac{1}{2}$ | – | – | – | – | 27 | – | | | |
| 28 | 1 | Jellice $\frac{2}{3}$ Pa. . . . . . . | – | 1 | 2 | — | 8 | $\frac{1}{4}$ | – | – | – | – | 17 | – | | | |
| | | | – | – | – | | | | | | | – | – | – | 3 | 4 | 3 |
| 29 | 1 | The Gold Fannam of Candera.. | – | – | 6 | — | 5 | $\frac{3}{4}$ | va | – | – | – | 3 | – | | | |
| 30 | 2 | Arrellure. . . . . . . . | – | – | 6 | — | 3 | $\frac{1}{4}$ | – | – | – | – | 3 | – | | | |
| 31 | 1 | Neggapatam. . . . . . . | – | – | 6 | — | 3 | $\frac{1}{4}$ | – | 1 | – | – | 1 | 3 | | | |
| 32 | 1 | Madre Naigue. . . . . . . | – | – | $5\frac{3}{4}$ | — | 3 | – | – | – | – | – | 1 | 5 | | | |
| 33 | 2 | Jelcuroo. . . . . . . . | – | – | 6 | — | 3 | $\frac{1}{2}$ | – | 2 | 3 | – | 5 | – | | | |
| | | | | – | – | | | | | | | – | | – | – | 14 | 2 |
| | | | | | | *Atchein.* | | | | | | – | 10 | $1\frac{1}{2}$ | – | 10 | $1\frac{1}{2}$ |
| 34 | 2 | The Gold Mace. – . . . . | – | – | $9\frac{1}{2}$ | — | 7 | – | – | 5 | $\frac{1}{8}$ | | | | | | |
| | | | – | – | | *Quedda.* | | | | | | | | | | | |
| | | | | | | — | | | | | | | – | – | – | | |

| | | | | | | | | | | | | | | | | | |
|---|---|---|---|---|---|---|---|---|---|---|---|---|---|---|---|---|---|
| | | | | | | *Quedda.* | | | | | | | | | | | |
| 35 | 2 | The Gold Copan or Mace. . | – | – | 10 | — | 8 | – | – | 6 | – | – | 12 | – | | 12 | |
| | | | | | | | | | | | | – | – | | | | – |
| | | | | | | *Goa.* | | | | | | | | | | | |
| 36 | 1 | The Gold St. Thoma. . . . | – | 2 | 5½ | — | 7 | ¾ | – | – | – | – | 32 | 2 | | | |
| 37 | – | The Silv. Sherephene . . . | – | 7 | 4 | — | 7 | | – | – | 7 | – | 7 | – | | | |
| | | | | – | – | *Japan.* | | | | | | | – | – | 1 | 3 | 2 |
| | | | | | | — | | | | | | | | | | | |
| | | | | | | — | | | | | | | | | | | |
| 38 | | The Gold Copan. . . . . | – | 11 | 10 | | 8 | ½ | – | – | – | 5 | 6 | – | | | |
| | 1 | Ditto Quarters. . . . . | – | – | – | | | | | | | | | | | | |
| | | | | | | *Syam.* | | | | | | | | | | | |
| | | The Silver Tecull. . . . . | – | 7 | 4 | | 9 | ½ | – | 12 | – | – | – | – | | | |
| | | Ditto Halves. . . . . . | | | | — | | | | | | | | | | | |
| | | Quarters, . . . . . . | | | | | | | | | | | | | | | |
| 42 | | Eighths. . . . . . . | | | | | | | | | | | | | | | |
| | | | – | – | – | — | – | – | – | – | – | – | 1 | 3 | | | |
| | | Gold Matts 23——— . . . | | | | | N° | *Matts* | N° 12 th. | | *Ma.* | | – | – | – | – | – |
| | | *Ps.* their fineness, as p N° *viz.* p | | | | | | | | | | | | | | | |
| | | m° . . . . . . . . . | | | | | | | | | | | | | | | |

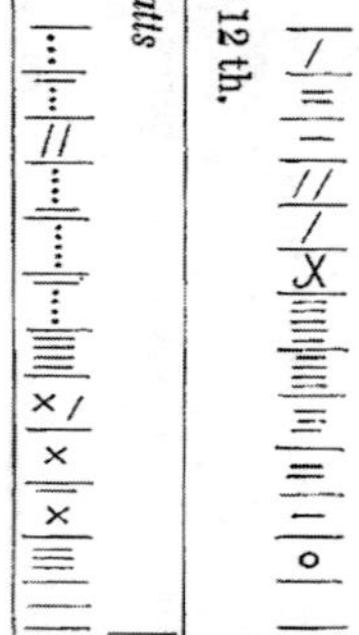

# APPENDIX

Mafoucko, p. 43, l. 20; p. 49, l. 1. Ovington speaks of this officer as a General. Apparently, however, this is wrong. Proyart, *History of Loango* (*apud* Pinkerton, vol. xvi, p. 572), says that the *m-fouka* is Minister of Commerce. 'He makes frequent voyages on the sea coasts where are the warehouses and factories of the Europeans.' No doubt he visited the *Benjamin* on a similar errand. Ovington is mixing him up with the *ma-kaka*, who is described by Proyart as the 'Minister of War and even Generalissimo of the Armies'. The prefix *ma*, Proyart tells us, is placed before the names of kings, princes, governors or chiefs of villages (*ibid.*, p. 592).

Zammampoango, p. 52, l. 32. Here again Ovington differs from Proyart (p. 594), who says the Supreme Being is called Zambi. 'They take his name in testimony of the truth: they even pretend that a species of malady called *Zambi-an-pongou* is the punishment for it.' Ovington seems to have confused the god and the malady! Zambi-an-bi, says Proyart, is the 'God of wickedness'.

Viecquam, p. 187, l. 35. Cf. Richards's *History of Tonquin*, in Pinkerton, ix. 271: 'Every Tonquinese not exempt is subject to the Viecquan or service of the monarch, that is to say, they are obliged, either by themselves or those they hire, to labour at the public works. . . . Artizans of all professions must employ six months in the year at the Viecquan.'

# INDEX-GLOSSARY

Ar. Arabic, Guj. Gujarāthi, Hind. Hindustani, Mar. Marāthi, Pers. Persian, Port. Portuguese.


Abāssi, Persian coin, 265.
Abasseens, Abyssinians, 268.
Abdul Ghafur, 239–40.
Abraham, 218, 278.
Āchār (Hind.), pickle, 179, 231.
Acheen, Achīn, 71; ivory from, 117.
Aden, 265 ff.
Agadir, 26.
*Ahimsā*, Jain doctrine, 196.
Akbar, Prince (Cha Egber), 108, 119.
Albatross, almitross, 279.
Albicore, species of fish, 33.
Albors, *see* Elburz.
Alexander the Great, 277.
Allajars, piece goods, 131.
Aloes, 268, 272.
Ambergris, 142, 182.
Amuck, amok, running, 141–2.
Anamat Khān, 110.
Annobon, 37 ff.
Apes, 210.
Apollonius, 45; of Tyana, 168.
Arabia Felix, 245 ff.
Arabian Sea, 260.
Aramra, 257.
Areca, arequier, araguer, 143, 202.
Arrack (Ar. *'arak*, sweat, sap, hence distilled spirit), 55, 117, 142, 230, 292.
Asafoetida, silphium, Hind. *hing*, 183, 231.
Ascension Island, 297 ff.
'Ashmen', name for Hindu ascetics, 211.
Asinus Pollio, 55.
Astrology, Indian, 194, 206.
Atlas, a species of satin, 125, 131, 167, 234.
Aungier, Gerald, xi, 89, 90, 206, 216.
Ayrack, Iraq, 219.
Azores, Islands, 30 ff.
Babbs (Ar. *Bāb*, a door), 267.
Bab el Mandeb, 267.
Babylon, 17.
Bacchus, 102.
Bahar, a weight, 269.
Bait al Fakih (Beetlefuckee), Arabian coffee mart, 271.
Balsera, Bulsār, town in Gujarāt, 204.
Bamboo, 149.
Bananas, bonanoes, 14, 29.
Bandar Abbās, *see* Gombroon.
Bang, Indian hemp, intoxicant, 216.
Banyan, Bunya (Guj. *Vāni*), Hindu trading class, 81, 130, 139, 163, 179, 184–8; brokers, 233–4; caste, 168; ceremonies, 197–200; 'Banyan Fight', battle of words, 163; Banyan day', *jour maigre*, 183.
Barbiers, prob. a form of beri-beri, 72, *note*, 205.
Bassein, 124.
Beetlefuckee, *see* Bait al Fakih.
Beetlenut, 75.
Begum Sāheb (Princess Jahanāra), 106.
Benimbe, W. African devil, 52–3.
*Benjamin*, the, x ff.; outward voyage of, 100 ff.; return, 279 ff.
Beri-beri, *see* Barbiers.
Bezoar Stone, 155.
Bijāpur (Viziapore), 120.
Bing, variety of China tea, 182.
Bisk, Bisque, kind of soup or pottage, 178.
Bohea, variety of China tea, 182.
Bombay, derivation, 79; cathedral, 90; castle, *ditto*; fort, 89; siege, 91–4; unhealthiness of, 85–7.

Bonito, Bonetto, species of fish, 33.
Bontius, Dutch naturalist, 157.
Boobies, 298.
Borneo, 295.
Boterus (Giovanni Botero), 113.
Brahma, Bramon, 147.
Brahmin, caste, 147; customs, 195–6; predictions by, 206–7.
Brest, 9.
Brokers, 233.
Brown, Captain, 301.
Burhānpur, 130.
But Kada, *see* Pagoda.

Caba (Pers. *kabā*), long coat, 185.
Cabcnda, *see* Kabinda.
Cabob (Hind. *kabāb*), roast meat, 231.
Caddy, tea, 181 *note*.
Caffries, coffries (Ar. *kafīr*, infidel), 243.
Cajan (Mal. *kajan*, thatch), plaited palm leaves, 130.
Calebash, 48.
Calico, 167.
Calicut, 235.
Cape of Good Hope (Cabo Tormentoso, Bone Esperanza), 31, 65, 103, 244, 279 ff.; Colony, 280 ff.
Casseen (Kishīn), 262–4.
Catoual, *see* Kotwāl.
Cattary (Hind. *Katār*, dagger), 141.
Cenotaph, 202.
Cerne Atlantica, 26.
Cha Egbcr, *see* Akbar, Prince.
Chamlet, piece goods, 134.
Chandra Gupta, 102.
Chaplain, at Surat Factory, 228, 235.
Charak Puja, *see* Hook-swinging.
Chaubuk (Hind. *Chābuk*, shambok, whip), 130.
Coco de Mer, Maldive Coconut, 157, *note*.
Coffee, 180, 271–2.
Cogy, *see* Kāzi.
Congo Bandar, 253.
Congo River, 40.
Congy (Hind. *kanji*), rice gruel, 206.
Cook, Mr., 58, 86.
Cooke, Humphrey, 96.
Coories, Cowries, 44.
Coromandel, 83.
Cosset, Cossid (Ar. *kāsid*), a courier, 242.
Council, at Surat Factory, 227.
Covit, covado, cubit, 269.
Cow, sacred, 138–9, 168, 183, 186, 219.
Cow-killing, 177–8.
Crampfish, 34.
Crasis (κρᾶσις), 15.
Cric (Mal. *krīs*), 106.
Crore, Couron, Hind. *kror*, one hundred lakhs, 116.
Culgar, piece goods, 131.
Customs House, at Surat, 208.
Cuttanee, piece goods, 131.

Daracha, Dārā Shāh, Dārā Shikoh, 106.
Darius, 197.
Daroo (Dāru), Parsi priest, 219.
Democritus, 179.
Dervish, 263–4.
'Dharna', sitting, Guj. custom, 195.
Dias, Bartholomew, 281.
Diu (Dieu), 268.
Dogs, English, in India, 160; employed at Parsi funeral, 220.
Dol (dāl), pulse, 183.
Dolphin, 32–3.
Dorset, Earl of, 4.
Dragon's Blood (Cinnabar), 262.
Dually (Dīvāli, Hindu festival), 233.
Dubois, Abbé, 215.
Ducat, 245, 270.
Dumpoked (Pers. *dampukht*, baked), 231.

Dungevorah (Danji Vora), 241.
Dutch, 180, 290.
Dutra (datūra), 141.
Dye (dahi), curds, 183.

Earthquake, at Surat, 203.
Edict of Nantes, 58, 280, *note*.
Ekādashi, Hindu holy day, 172.
Elaeus, river, 126.
Elburz, mountains, 219.
Elephanta, caves, 97 ff.
Elephants, 118.
Emmanuel, King of Portugal, 281.
Emmaupaxda (Humāyuñ Pādshāh), 103.
Empedocles, 179.
Eunuchs, 127.
Ezion Geber, 277.

Factory, English, at Surat, 225 ff.
Fakirs, faquirs, fuckeas, 123, 210, 269.
Fauzdār, fojdar, 139.
Fetish, 44.
Fevers, 204.
Fidalgo, 28.
Fireworshippers, Parsi, 217.
Fogo Island, 30.
Frasella, 269.
French, at the Cape, 290.
Fresco (freshness), 82.
Fryer, Dr., xiii, xvii, 2.
Funeral ceremonies, 198–200; Parsi, 220.

Galivat, jollyboat, 262.
'Gallinas dell Mer', 254.
Gargled, feigned, 128.
Gaures, Guebres, a name applied to Parsis, 218–19.
Gebel Farun, 277.
Gcmal (Jamāl), 154.
Gentoo, *i.e.* gentile or heathen, Port. name for Hindus, 139, 147, 202.
Gezon, Jizān, 273.
Ghārpuri, 97.
Ghee, 190.
Gilder, 292.
Goa Stone, 156.
Golconda, 121.
Gombroon (Bandar Abbās), 58, 119, 225, 253, 265.
Gorgades, gorgons, 28.
Grab (gurāb), 158, 262, 268.
Gravesend, x, 9, 302.
Gregory, African devil, 77.
Gregory Nazianzen, 219.
Grograms, piece goods, 134.
Gymnosophists, 211.

Hackery, bullock cart, 151.
Hajji, hoggee, one who has performed the *Haj*, 275.
Halālchors, scavengers, 221–4.
Hamilton, Capt. A., author of *A New Account of the East Indies*, xvi, xvii, 4, 89, 90, 99, 182, 253, 262, 277, 280.
Hammām, hummum, Turkish bath, 227, 276–7.
Hanno, 26, 28.
Hanuman, 210.
Harbad, Parsi priest, 220.
Harcarrah, harkara, messenger, 137.
Hasti, Hasta, lunar mansion, 83.
Hatman, *see* Topiwālā.
Hay Island, 29.
Henry the Navigator, 10.
Herbert, Sir Thos., 26.
Hermaphrodites, 288.
Hepatica, *see* Aloes.
Herodotus, 199.
Hierack Ajami (Irāq Ajami), 219.
Hindustan, 147.
Hodeida, 272.
Hook swinging, 215.
Hon, *see* Pagoda.
Hottentots, 284.
Hunting, in India, 160–2.
Hoy, a sloop, 131.

Iago, Saint, *see* Saint Jaques.
Ignatius Loyola, 21.
Impalement, 53.
*In Principio*, *see* Last Gospel.
Infanta of Portugal, 79.
Isa Cooly (Quli), 201.

Jaggary rack (arrack), 'a kind of Aqua Vitae', 117, 142.
Jahanāra, Princess, *see* Begum Sāheb.
Japan, 159, 167.
Jaques, Saint, Iago, Jago, Thiago, Island of, 20, 26, 28, 30, 39.
Jason, 134.
Jesuits, the, 20–1, 96.
Jiddah, 4.
Jizia, tax, 92.
Johanna (the Comoro Islands), 67.
John of Salisbury, 45.
'Jollyboat', *see* Galivat.
Josephus, 277.
Juan de Nova, 62.
Jugglers, Indian, 153–4.
*Jus primae noctis* in Malabar, 51.

Kabā, *see* Caba.
Kabinda, 40, 46.
Kaemfer, Dr. Engelbrecht, 34, 150.
*Kalamdān* (Hind.), inkstand, 148.
Kanchani, *see* Quencheni.
Kankies, maize flour cakes, 47.
*Karamat* (Pers.), wonder, 118.
Karun river, 126.
Karwar, Carwar, English Factory at, 160, 235.
*Kāsid*, *see* Cosset.
Kazi, Cazi, judge, 187.
Keda, Keddah, elephant kraal, 18.
Keil, ruddle, 50.
Kerenhappuk, 111.
Keziah, 111.
Khalifa, Caliph, 248.
*Khichri*, cooked *dāl*, 183.
*Khilāt* (Pers.), robe of honour, 243.
Kimchi, David, Rabbi, 261.
Kotwal, cutwal, police officer, 137.
Kouza (Pers. *Kuza*), a pot, 174.

Lac, *Lākh* (one hundred thousand), 109, 115, 116, 239.
Lac, lacquer, 167.
Laval, Pyrard de, x, 26.
Leeuenhoek, 286.
Limpo, Lingpao, 181.
Lizards, 17.
Loango, 46.
Lopus, Lopez, 46.
Lord, Rev. Henry, 2, 16.
Loupgarou, were-wolf, 164.
Lucretius, quoted, 85.
Lycurgus, 18.
Lysimachus, 202.

McCrindle, 102.
Macira, Masera, 251.
Madeira (Latin *Materia*, wood), 9–13.
Mafouko, W. African general, 43, 44, 48, Appendix.
Magic, sympathetic, 45.
— Indian, 153–4, 206.
— Black, *see* Necromancy.
Mahmudi, Indian coin, 265.
Malabar coast, 83, 128.
— pepper, 226, 235, 268.
Malacca, 135.
Maldive Islands, 83.
— coconut, 157.
Malemba, Molamba, 40.
Malphigi, 286.
Mandarin, 110, 181.
Manga Voluchoes, 'velvet sleeves', a sea bird, 279.
Mango, 179; Mango trick, 153–4.
Manichaeans, 175.
Marriage customs, Indian, 189, 194.
Maund (*mān*), 133, 269.
Mayo Island, 28.
Mayotta, 67.
Medecine, Indian, 205–6.
Megasthenes, 102.
Melizigiris, 79.
Milkbush, 298.
Mīr Bakshi, 242.
Mocha, 239, 260 ff.
Monilla, Mohilla, 67, 73, 74.
Moneilloes, Manilla, 294, 295.

Moor, a Mahommedan, 136, 146, 173–4, 185, 203 *et passim*.
— (Pers. *Mohur*), a gold coin, 114, 132.
Moradash (Morār Dās), 170.
Mordechine, cholera, 204.
Muazzam, Prince, 119.
Muktiyar Khān, 110.
Mulla, 145.
Murād Baksh, 106, 107.
Murchāl (morchāl), a peacock-feather fan, 82.
Muscat, 35, 58, 245 ff.
Musset, Masjid, mosque, 145.
Mussoun, monsoon, xii, 64, 79, 80, 90–1, 99, 130, 183, 203, 264.
Muzaffar Khān, 110.

Nabob, nabāb, nawab, 110, 115.
Nair, Nairo, 51, 169, 192.
Naubat, drum, 137.
Navapur, 179.
Necromancy, 77.
Nego, Nebo, Babylonian god, 219.
Nil, 100,000 million, 116.
Nutmeg, 135.

Okhāmandal, pirate haunt in Kāthiāwār, 99.
Olibanum, 263.
Omens, 194.
Omrah (Ar. plur. of *Amīr*), 106, 110, 118, 120, 126, 147, 226.
Osiris, 199.
Ottoman, 147.
Ovington, John, Introduction, *passim*.
Ovington family, ix.
Oxenden, Sir George, 236.

Padan (Skt. *padma*), 10,000 million, 116.
Padre, Port. 'father', 25, 96.
Pagod, a gold coin, 121. A Hindu temple (prob. Pers. *but kada*, idol house), 91, 97–8, 173.
Palamedes, 168.
Palanquin, 152.
Palladium, 46.
Pamarin, a cloth (Mar. *pāmāri*), 193, 207.
Parsis, 139, 216, 241.
Patagonians, 285.
Pātaliputra (Patna), 102.
Patimar, courier, 149.
Patta, 72, 158.
Pawn (Hind. *pān*, leaf), 75; a piece at chess, cf. *peon*, 228 *note*.
Peon (Port. *peão*, a footman), 82, 154, 180, 184, 228, 232.
Pepys, Mr., quoted, 182.
Phasis, river, 133.
Philostratus, 168.
Phoenicians, 172.
Picos Fragosas, 282.
Pigdan (Hind. *Pīkdān*), spittoon, 75.
Pilau, 140, 151, 231.
Pillaber, pillowcase, 185. 210.
Pillar dollar, 269.
Pilot fish, 32.
Pindar, pinda, 50.
Pinjrapol, animal hospital, 178.
Pirates, European, 64; Indian, 99, 254 ff.
Pishcash (Pers. *peshkash*), a present, 242.
Pismire, ant, 178.
Piso, Dutch naturalist, 157.
Pistachio, 232.
Plague, at Surat, 203; at Busra, 204.
Pliny, 28.
Polonia, 133.
Polygamy, 191–2.
'Poor Jack', 30.
Pork, forbidden to Mohammedans, 143–4.
Porpoise, 33.
Portuguese, reasons for their decline in India, 125.
Praya, 28.
Prayers, at Surat Factory, 238.
Prescot, Mr., 167.
President of Surat Factory, 227.

Propertius, quoted, 202.
Ptolemy, 79, 130.
Puggary (Hind. *pagri*, a turban), 185.
Pulparrock (Pulpāra), 210.
Punch, 55, 230. 'Punch-houses', xii.
'Purser Marine', at Surat Factory, 227.
Purslain, 61.
Pydoni, 79.
Pythagoras, 171.

Quail, quill, term for a prostitute, 128.
Quenchcni (Kanchani), a dancing girl, 153.

Rack, *see* Arrack, Jaggery Rack.
Rājputs, Resbouts, 108.
Rāma, 200, 210.
Rāmāyana, 210.
Ramazān, 144.
Ras el Hadd, 246.
Ras Musandin (Moccandun), 245.
Red Sea, 260.
Reede, Baron von, his tomb at Surat, 236.
Relics, 295.
Rhinocerus horn, its medicinal properties, 158–9.
Ristonius, Julianus, 45.
River Arabs, 251.
Roe, Sir Thos., 113.
Roshanāra Begum (Rauchenara Begum), 105 *note*, 106.
Rubies, Indian, 122.
Rudolf, Emperor, 157–8.
Rumphius, Dutch naturalist, 157.
Rupee, 109.
Ruttera, village in Travancore, 235.

Sab, Sāheb, 192.
Saint Augustine's Bay, 64.
Saint Helena, 57 ff.
Saint Lawrencc (Madagascar), 66.
Salābat Khān, 242.
Salem (*salaam*), 112.
Samarkhand, 104.
Sanganians, Indian pirates, 99, 254 ff.
Sanskrit, 148.
Santa, Santone (Guj.), saint, ascetic, 210, 256.
Saurāshtra, 130.
Say, Captain, his adventures with Sanganian pirates, 251 ff.
*Scandalum Magnatum*, 44.
Scrivan, a writer, clerk, 170.
Scrutore, writing-desk, 131, 167.
Sea post office, at Ascension Island, 297.
Seer, Indian measure, 133.
Seleukos Nikator, 102.
Semiramis, 102.
Sequin, Venetian coin, 243.
Shāh Abbās, 104.
Shāh Jahān (Cha Jehan), Emperor, 106, 112.
Shaikh Jammu, 242.
Sharks, 31–2; hammerheaded (*zygaena*), 43.
She King, Chinese book of Odes, 173.
Sherbert (Ar. *sherbet*), 249.
Sidi, the Moghal Admiral, attacks Bombay, 91, 93 ff.
Sinai, 276.
Singlo, variety of China tea, 182.
Sivāji, Marātha leader, 92, 114.
Snakes, tame, 154.
Snakestone, its supposed properties, 155–6.
Socotra, 260, 262.
Soofey, species of piece goods, 131.
Soosie (Hind. *sūsi*), Indian silk, 167.
Soy, a pickle, 231.
Spado (Ital. a sword), 16.
Spices, 135, 140.
'Spicy breezes', 38.
Standish, inkstand, 148.
Stock fish, 30.
Sucket, 13.

Sucking fish, 32.
Suez, 275, 277.
Surat, city, 130 ff.; English Factory at, 225 ff.; plundered by the Marāthas, 114. *Suratt, a Voyage to*, xiv ff.
Sureating, 151.
Surgeon, at Surat factory, 234.
Suttee (*sati*, the true wife), 190, 201.
Swally Road (*Suvāli*), at mouth of Tapti River, 92, 100.
Swan Societies, 150.

Tamasp, Shāh, 103.
Tambac, alloy of copper and zinc, 295.
Tamerlane, Tamberlaine, 103.
Tapty, Tindi (Hind. *Tāpi*, hot), river, 130, 152–3, 160, 210.
Taslim, tailim (Pers.), a deep salaam, 112.
Tate, Nahum, xvii, 7.
Tea, 180–3; *Essay upon the Nature and Qualities of Tea*, xv, 180 *note*.
Teonge, Rev. Henry, x.
Terry, Rev. Edward, 27, 32, 33, 254.
Thévenot, Sieur de, 130, 236.
Thiago, *see* Iago.
Toddy, tari (Hind. *tādi*), the juice of various palm trees, cf. arrack.
Tola, Indian weight, 133.
Tombs of the Surat Factors, 236 ff.
Tonson, Jacob, xviii.
Topiwālā, 'hatman', name for Europeans who wear the *sola topi* or pith helmet, 239.
Torpedo fish, 34.
Toss (Per. *tās*, a cup), 231.
Totanbeg, pewter, 183.
Towers of Silence (*dakmā*), 220 ff.
Trade wind, 31.
Trāga, Hindu custom, cf. Dharna, 195.
Trinity, Hindu (*Trimurti*), 99.
Triptolemus, 175.
Tunchal, Funchal, capital of Madeira, 19, 20, 25.
Tunny, 33.
Tunquin, Tonquin, 76, 133 168, 184, 187.
Turnado, Tornado, 27.
Turtles, their habits, 298 ff.

Urdu, 147.

Vacnavish (Pers. *vākia'h navīs*), a newswriter, registrar, 137, 241–2.
Vanderstel, Mynheer, Dutch Governor of Cape Colony, 292.
Vasco da Gama, 281.
Venvam, Chinese Emperor, 105.
Verde, Cape, 26.
Viecquam, form of slavery in Tonquin, 187, Appendix.
Vineroon (vigneron), 300.
Virgil, medieval legends about, 45.
Viziapur, *see* Bijāpur.

Warner family, xvii.
Waterclock, 167.
Watersnakes, 79, 80.
Waterspout, 41.
Wedding ceremonies, Indian, 193.
Weldon, Mr. George, 95.
Werewolf, *see* Loupgarou.
Widows, Hindu, 191.
Wine, Cape, 291 ff.; Madeira, 12; Shiraz, 230.

Yams, 61.
Yanbo, 275.
Yemen, 245, 266.
Yogi, 211.

Zaire, Congo River, 46.
Zammanpoango, W. African name for the Deity, 52, Appendix.
Zaphnath Paaneeah, 111.
Zarbaft, brocade, 131, 152.
Zoroaster, Zarathustra, Zardust, 217.

# CHINESE
## SELF-TAUGHT

BY THE NATURAL METHOD

WITH

PHONETIC PRONUNCIATION
(THIMM'S SYSTEM)

JOHN DARROCH

SECOND EDITION

GYAN

*Published by*

GYAN

Gyan Publishing House
5, Ansari Road
Daryaganj, New Delhi-110002
Phone: 011-47034999, 9811692060
E-mail: books@gyanbooks.com

*Distribution Network*
gyanbooks.com
India, USA, Canada, UK, Australia, France



ISBN : 978-81-212-4261-5 (PB)
First Published, Colombo, 1899

2nd Impression 2020

*Printed at:* Gyan Press, Delhi.



**Chinese Self-Taught**
Author: John Darroch